Civil Society

Also by John A. Hall

CIVIL SOCIETY: THEORY, HISTORY, COMPARISON (*editor*)

POWERS AND LIBERTIES

IS AMERICA BREAKING APART? (*with Charles Lindholm*)

Also by Frank Trentmann

PARADOXES OF CIVIL SOCIETY (*editor*)

MARKETS IN HISTORICAL CONTEXTS: IDEAS AND POLITICS IN THE MODERN
WORLD (*co-editor with Mark Bevir*)

Civil Society

A Reader in History, Theory and Global Politics

Edited by

John A. Hall
Department of Sociology,
McGill University, Montreal, Canada

and

Frank Trentmann
School of History,
Classics and Archaeology Birkbeck College,
University of London

palgrave
macmillan

First published 2005 by
PALGRAVE MACMILLAN
Houndmills, Basingstoke, Hampshire RG21 6XS and
175 Fifth Avenue, New York, N.Y. 10010
Companies and representatives throughout the world

PALGRAVE MACMILLAN is the global academic imprint of the Palgrave Macmillan division of St. Martin's Press, LLC and of Palgrave Macmillan Ltd. Macmillan® is a registered trademark in the United States, United Kingdom and other countries. Palgrave is a registered trademark in the European Union and other countries.

ISBN 1–4039–1542–3 hardback
ISBN 1–4039–1543–1 paperback

This book is printed on paper suitable for recycling and made from fully managed and sustained forest sources.

A catalogue record for this book is available from the British Library.

Library of Congress Cataloging-in-Publication Data
Civil society : a reader in history, theory and global politics / edited by John A. Hall and Frank Trentmann.
      p.   cm.
   Includes bibliographical references and index.
   ISBN 1–4039–1542–3 — ISBN 1–4039–1543–1 (pbk.)
   1. Civil society.   I. Hall, John A., 1949–   II. Trentmann, Frank.

JC337.C549 2004
300—dc22
                                                    2004056071

Printed and bound in Great Britain by
Antony Rowe Ltd, Chippenham and Eastbourne

Contents

Preface

This volume brings together the perspectives and concerns of a historian and sociologist. Greater awareness of the rich past and present traditions of civil society, we believe, is of mutual advantage to foster a dialogue between those interested in promoting and debating civil society today and those interested in understanding its historical evolution. This reader is a select pathway through central debates, adding some forgotten avenues, but also shortening some more conventional ones easily accessible elsewhere. It is an invitation to broaden, discuss and refine the terms of the debate in European and non-European contexts, not to present an essentialist vision. To make the volume attractive to readers from different social and public bodies as well as different academic disciplines, we have simplified the academic apparatus carried by many texts. We have chosen to preserve the footnotes of select passages only where they add substantially to an understanding of the main argument. Full details of the selected texts, however, are given and allow readers to check any particular reference for themselves. In addition to contemporary authors represented here, a select guide to further specialist reading can be found at the end of the volume. Inevitably, the selection of texts has been influenced not only by the editors' interests but also by considerations of size and by the willingness of different publishers to support this project. We should especially like to thank all those authors, colleagues, and publishers who have granted us permission at a modest or no fee. We also wish to make clear that we have always sought to gain copyright permission where possible, but have in a few instances been faced with the return of letters and the apparent disappearance of publishing houses. Where we were unable to reach an existing copyright holder, we would seek to remedy this matter at the earliest opportunity.

Yesim Bayar provided a very great deal of research and administrative assistance, and we are most grateful for her courtesy and efficiency. Additional thanks to Vanessa Taylor, Stefanie Nixon and Mary McDaid. We are grateful to Deborah Bennett for copy-editing and to Laura Bevir for providing the index. Over the last few years, we have learnt a lot about civil society from our students, and it it is to them that we dedicate the work.

John A. Hall, Montreal
Frank Trentmann, London

1
Contests over Civil Society: Introductory Perspectives

John A. Hall and Frank Trentmann

The last years of the second millennium saw the remarkable triumph of 'civil society'. Politicians repositioned themselves as friends of civil society; non-governmental organizations presented themselves as champions of a historic idea. The media disseminated its omnipresence. Such was the success of civil society, that its incorporation in academic grant proposals became an (almost) irresistible temptation. It became so 'universally talked about in tones that suggest it is a Great Good', *The Economist* observed in 2001, but 'for some people it presents a problem: what on earth is it? Unless you know, how can you tell if you would want to join it?'[1] Others started to complain of this cultural inflation and found it difficult to see 'how uncritical adoption and use of this term advances peoples' struggles for basic rights, for self-determination, liberation and decolonisation'.[2] What, then, to make of civil society: rediscovered thinking tool, emancipatory panacea, or new imperialism? A fundamental concept of civic education for pupils, scholars and politicians alike, or a confusion altogether, a mere multitude of competing tongues best kept out of 'serious' social theory and public policy?

This volume is a critical introduction to arguments about the nature of civil society – past and present. Significantly, the revival of interest in civil society has tended to reproduce rival and competing traditions, rather than to promote an open, critical engagement between different moments and traditions across time and space. Instead of avoiding disagreement or privileging one essential meaning of truth, this volume seeks to turn to good advantage the series of debates employing and contesting civil society in order to think about the attractions and limitations of this concept. These contemporary contests are, however, only the last in a series of historical debates over civil society. Rather than offering one tradition or the other, this reader is the first to offer a selection of central debates about the concept from sixteenth and seventeenth-century Europe to contemporary debates across the world. Instead of a 'Whiggish' triumphalist account of the contemporary resurrection of a particular essence of the idea, this essay and this volume, then, offer a pathway to enter and re-evaluate civil society through its competing

1

strands, strands that always combined anxieties as well as remedies for problems in human relations in the modern period.

This critical approach is complemented by a decision to broaden the frame of analysis in three directions. It looks beyond Britain, France and Germany to include imperial, post-colonial and transnational dimensions.[3] In decisive places it moves beyond the received canonical texts to illustrate the contested nature of civil society at certain historical moments. And it places some select documents of the diverse practices within civil society alongside intellectual sources. Such a critical and comparative approach, we hope, will make for productive reading – and re-reading – for those advocates and commentators on civil society who come to the debating table with little, selective or dogmatic knowledge of the competing traditions and practices of civil society as well for those scholars whose interest in the history of the subject rarely engages with the shifting political terrain of its use today.

As in the late twentieth century, civil society moved to the centre of discourse in late seventeenth and eighteenth century Europe as a useful concept to think about problems of society and politics as well as to describe social formations. Its historical fortunes have risen and ebbed, seeing a social and global expansion in the eighteenth and early nineteenth centuries, followed by challenges and crises resulting in its almost complete annihilation during the era of totalitarianism and cold war. These cycles structure this reader. What began in the sixteenth and seventeenth centuries as an argument about civil society *as* political society (pp. 26–30 Hooker, pp. 30–3 Locke), developed in the course of the eighteenth and nineteenth centuries into a series of competing ideas and practices about civil society as an independent universe, *distinct from* state and market. Civil society continued to be associated with the activities of government in some traditions,[4] but was now complemented by an expanding sense of the relatively autonomous universe of civil society. How did civil society work, what produced it, what and who should be part of it? What are and should be its relationship to state and market? Did the European concept have universal characteristics and, if so, what were the obligations and policies for advanced societies to export civil society to colonial peoples?

These questions produced different answers from different thinkers and social movements in the eighteenth and nineteenth centuries. This enriched normative and political debate was accompanied and fed by the unprecedented historic social expansion of civil society. As with the idea, the world of practice expanded at different speeds and rhythms in different countries but there can be little doubt about the massive proliferation of clubs, associations, reading societies, freemasonry and informal spaces of civil society in the modern period, stretching from Britain to Imperial Russia, and from American cities to German provincial towns.[5] In the English town of Norwich in 1750, for example, every fifth male was a member of an association. Some clubs were open to women. Freemasonry produced an international network, stretching from France with 40,000 members in 1789, including artisans and small traders, to administrative towns in Russia, where about 3,000 masons spread a new culture of philanthropy. This associational culture continued to expand in the late nineteenth and early twentieth centuries, but by now the idea of civil society was beginning to lose its attraction and was placed under siege by more totalizing modern ideologies. The remarkable revival of civil society from the late 1970s onwards took place against the backdrop of totalitarian experience in Europe, dictatorship in Latin America and communism in Asia.

This volume is structured around the ebb and flow of the concept, giving due attention to the competing meanings in different settings, past and present. At the same time, it is also an invitation to think about the European and global expansion of civil society. Much of the literature in the field has tended to observe civil society within a particular society or to explore a particular dimension at one moment in time. This has benefits of depth, but for the advocate as well as student of civil society it risks a loss of perspective on the changing overall contours of the civil society debate. Recent comparative studies and the debate over 'global civil society' prompt a more kaleidoscopic approach. Our purpose in this introduction is to map the characteristic tensions within a field of discourse, showing their presence and salience across time and space. The contests over civil society can be fruitfully viewed in terms of anxieties about difference, strains of commercial society, fears of totality and dependence, and the tensions between theory and praxis.

Anxieties about difference

The new mobilization of civil society in seventeenth and early eighteenth-century Europe, beyond the inherited classical framework of *societas civilis sive res publica*, occurred at a moment of anxiety, not confidence. The religious conflicts and tensions culminating in the reformation and counter-reformation in sixteenth-century Europe led to a more thematic exploration of the nature and claims of civil society as public government vis-à-vis rival theocratic claims of sovereignty by some protestant sects and Papacy – a question at the centre of Hooker's writings (pp. 26–30). The experience of war and civil wars across seventeenth-century Europe produced an even greater and more wide-ranging debate and conflict about how to cope with difference – difference between sects, ideas, and social groups. The eighteenth century is famously known as the age of enlightenment, but it is equally important to notice that, although diminishing, fears of conflict and of emotions and extremism running wild – beyond the scope of social or self-discipline – never altogether disappeared. Indeed, much of the growing emphasis on civility, on polite manners and the self-disciplining effects of living in civil society, can be understood as a way of coping with anxieties.[6] The pursuit of civility and the growing purchase of civil society as a way of viewing society here fed into each other. Civil society provided a language and a code of moral behaviour. Conversely, historical actors' pursuit of civility raised the standards, criteria and prominence of civil society as a model of integrating social relations peacefully. Open physical violence or confrontation became less acceptable as middling groups raised the norms of civility and the state acquired a monopoly of violence.

Much of this dynamic revolved around shifting attitudes to the possibility and limits of religious toleration. Yet the relative success of toleration in some European societies should not be viewed entirely as a culturally pre-determined transformation or some sudden act of enlightenment on behalf of rulers and ruled. Arguably, one factor in the more tolerant atmosphere was the unintended consequence of great power politics. Perhaps the most fundamental consideration to be taken into account in this regard was the inability of any side in the great European wars of religion to triumph absolutely over its rival. The political and social import of stalemate is beginning to be recognized by social and political theorists.[7] Bluntly, when one cannot triumph over a rival, the alternative of putting up with each other begins to suggest itself. This consideration should not distract attention from more specific mechanisms. In Britain after the revolution of 1688, for example, William III needed the political and fiscal support of dissenters and Catholics.[8] Still, at the most general level, domestic toleration was the beneficiary of international violence between states, especially the imperial conflict between Britain and France in Europe and North America.

This is not of course to say that commentators and actors were without vital and interesting ideas about mechanisms concerning violence and fanaticism internal to society. Dominique Colas's important *Civil Society and Fanaticism* traces some of these debates back to Luther, and then to Leibniz and Spinoza. Particular attention in our volume focuses on the high-powered difference of opinion between Hume and Smith, close friends and intellectual allies, uncharacteristically at odds on this occasion – albeit about means rather than ends. Both Hume and Smith loathed fanaticism. Hume was all too familiar with the power of the Presbyterian establishment that had blighted his chances for employment. Hume's argument is characteristically brilliant, and of very great interest since it sees him wobbling at a crucial juncture (pp. 37–43). At first sight his hope is for a diminution of enthusiasm within the established church – that is, the slow creation of a respectable pillar of society in which parsons, bishops and presbyters cease, as in the novels of Jane Austen, to be overly concerned with matters of belief. But Hume then argues against himself. The retention of an established church was not in itself desirable, for its adherents would never be friends to civil liberty. True friends to liberty were those who had experienced sectarian fanaticism, and progressed beyond it. Smith's position is wholly different.

Sectarian fanaticism could be controlled by the market principle. Let sects compete with each other, for in so doing they would block dangerous enthusiasm in general.[9]

If Smith had these fears, it is as important to note that he had hopes as well. Civil society within his work is best seen as a medium for forging new bonds of solidarity or for teaching new forms of discipline – especially if the social psychology described in *The Theory of Moral Sentiments* is read pre-scriptively rather than descriptively. The fact that we hate to be disturbed, especially by the pain of others, makes us wish not to disturb others – for we learn to judge our actions as if they were seen by a 'universal spectator'. Self-command and other-direction accordingly rule the day. Civility, orderliness and manners matter in this world, and most certainly militate against any unbridled assertion of the romantic self.

The social and cultural realities of eighteenth-century polite society reflected the advancing emphasis on civil behaviour and the growing preoccupation, indeed obsession, with fostering virtuous behaviour and sensibility, but also fears of passions and sociability spinning out of control. Already Hooker had emphasized sociability as a key characteristic of civil society (pp. 29–30). The prescriptive advice circulated in new journals like the *Spectator* and the *Tatler* in the early eighteenth century offered the middling classes a blue-print to try out new recipes of self-command, sensibility and sympathy (pp. 53–5). The Victorian discourse of the two spheres has clouded a sense to which this earlier eighteenth-century culture of sociability had also opened new social spheres for women.[10] As Millar's influential writings show, civil society could be seen to advance in tandem with a greater regard for women and their social and intellectual contribution to social life (pp. 55–60). Not all commentators, however, embraced the new world of clubs, associations and coffee houses with equal optimism. Many an eighteenth-century commentator made fun of the cult of clubs, an attitude well captured in the account of the 'Farting Club' (pp. 69–70). The *Female Tatler*, moreover, worried that coffee houses and the culture of sociability made men effeminate and undermined the virility of the British nation. In France, men mixed with women in conversation, giving them a knowledge of the world; in Britain, ladies were sent off to talk amongst themselves about domestic decorative goods (pp. 60–1).

The concern with fanaticism underlying the eighteenth-century debate about sects and toleration is as present in current debates. The classic statement here is Gellner's account of the ability of Islam to resist secularisation (pp. 268–71). Gellner's argument was stated well before the emergence of fundamentalist Islam,[11] but it gained widespread prominence as the result of the politics of Ayatollah Khomeini and of Islamic fundamentalism more generally. But his view has been subject to widespread criticism. Norton's selection in this volume is representative of thinkers who believe that those wishing to change the character of Islam, from a public religion of Godly rule to one of private consolation, will eventually win out.[12] A rather different and highly original critique is that of Varshney, quick to note the presence of a traditional and much criticized binary opposition between 'tradition' and 'modernity' within Gellner's account (pp. 271–5). Varshney's central contention is that there is far more civility within 'traditional' societies than is often realized. Whilst this carries weight, one wonders nonetheless whether a distinction ought to be drawn between tolerance before and tolerance after the entry of the people onto the political stage. It may be that the full meaning of the civil society is in the end best reserved for the latter.[13]

In current debates about the prospect of civil society it has been tempting to contrast such religious dimensions of social life in the East with a more secular history of civil society in the West. Such a contrast is debatable and disguises the ideological filtering of civil society in many liberal traditions. Canonical figures like Hume or Smith cannot be read on their own but need to be placed in the context of a rich on-going debate with competing versions of civil society. One such tradition, and perhaps the most widely disseminated and institutionally strongest version in eighteenth-century England, was an Anglican vision of an organic unity between civil society, established Christianity (Anglicanism) and monarchy. Here civil society was an essential arena of social trust and political stability, but always premised on the virtues provided by established religion. Next to Edmund Burke (pp. 96–9), the Rev. Thomas B. Clarke's sermon is a typical example of this tradition which made up the majority of titles concerned with civil society in the eighteenth and early nineteenth centuries. Social trust and reciprocity required a belief in the Supreme Being, for, as Clarke argued, 'surely he who despises his sacred duties towards the divinity, will not regard his social ones towards man.' (p. 50) Lack of faith promised '[w]ars perpetual, dissentions eternal, robbery universal.' (p. 49) Religion, not nature, produced a belief in social justice, these Anglican proponents of civil society argued.[14]

Even for Locke, the argument for civil society had a significant religious basis and offered a bounded sphere of toleration. Practical reason and Christian belief were inseparable. Atheism, Locke feared, would dissolve the functioning of practical reason, a reason that included fear of the avenging God and human obedience to His Law that was the Law of Nature.[15] Nor did the secular component necessarily gain in the Western evolution of civil society. In the nineteenth century, associational life was instilled, even inspired, by evangelicalism and pietism, and expanded into a transnational imperial network through missionary societies (pp. 119–28). Far from being marginal, abnormal or pathological, then, religion played an integral role in the historical evolution and exportation of European civil society. The spiritual influence in civil society movements in Central and Eastern Europe in the last few decades is not a novel development but part of this longer pattern.

Strains of commercial society

The great transformation causing these anxieties was the accelerating expansion and new dominance of commercial society in the seventeenth and eighteenth centuries. The Christian tradition of political theory in the West had of course produced a culture of distrust for money-making as a distraction from the care of one's soul. But the new world of commerce posed an unprecedented challenge to the received tradition of republicanism, which stressed the virtue and virility of civic-minded propertied citizens as vital sources for the maintenance and defence of public life and community. Did commerce threaten to sap the sources of this virtuous civic culture, or might it produce new sources of social solidarity as well as political strength?

In one subtle political argument civil society emerged in favourable alliance with this new world of commerce. Montesquieu (1689–1755) offers a way to follow this tightening connection. *The Persian Letters* makes much of the personal freedoms – especially for women – of the fashionable world of Paris, whilst *Considerations on the Greatness of the Romans* shows virtue to be both militaristic and so strenuous as to be hard to maintain. The 'douceur' of commerce, its moral and civilizing effect on social and international relations, is the theme of *The Spirit of the Laws* (1748; pp. 71–5 below). Commerce advanced civil society by breaking through 'the barbarism of Europe'. Commerce here appears 'a cure for the most destructive prejudices', both creating 'agreeable manners' within communities and fostering peace between them. Trade created conditions of mutual dependence and facilitated an interest in and curiosity about different cultures. Or as popular radical supporters of Free Trade in the nineteenth century would put it more bluntly: a shopkeeper does not keep a handgun under the counter to shoot his customers. With the evangelical revival, the secular argument for the douceur of commerce now began to mobilize Christian thought. Had not God created a world of different climates and resources so as to encourage humans to engage in peaceful exchange?

Yet, Montesquieu's new endorsement of commerce came with strong qualifications. Commerce could strengthen or weaken public life depending on the nature of government. Montesquieu made an important observation that has been all too easily forgotten in de-politicized liberal and neo-liberal approaches to this question: the spirit of commerce united nations and individuals in different ways. Where people were moved only by the spirit of commerce, it left behind societies where 'all the moral virtues' ended up for sale. In monarchies, the connection between merchants and public affairs left behind a culture of distrust. It was only in 'free states', that is republican governments which had a vibrant culture of civic virtue, that commerce provided 'safety'. Writing against the background of international wars and rivalry, there is a sense here that nations had a choice: they might preserve their independence in the form of territorial autocratic monarchies but it could also be generated by a more open and commercial nation. Montesquieu turned to England to find a society that had taken 'advantage of each of these great things at the same time: religion, commerce, and liberty.'[16]

The dominant critic of this appreciation of commerce's civilizing potential was Jean Jacques Rousseau, perhaps the greatest of all modern representatives of the tradition of civic virtue. What mattered for Rousseau was less the lack of social solidarity brought by civil society than the psychic misery and social dependence that it inevitably entailed. Rousseau took to task writers who had told of a linear, triumphant progression from a barbaric and vicious state of nature to civil society. Far from being a site of oppression and human misery where people were unfree and 'continually cutting one another's throats to indulge their brutality' (p. 75 below), the state of nature was marked by equality amongst people unpolluted by luxury or notions of power and servitude.[17] It was civil society, with the introduction of private property and an increasingly competitive pursuit of commercial gain, that introduced base motifs of domination and imitation. Before civil society, people could be happy with themselves; in civil society, they became slaves to the conventions of social tastes and habits and their happiness depended on the testimony of others: 'the savage lives within himself, while social man lives constantly outside himself, and only knows how to live in the opinion of others.' (p. 79 below) The vision of freedom in civil society, in other words, was far from free but embedded in power and involving the loss of independent consciousness.

Commerce was an important conduit of this social pathology. Commercial society promoted unprecedented social differentiation – the proliferation of specialized tasks and skills and the transgression of inherited social orders. For most social thinkers what mattered here was a general feeling that atomization would undermine social order. This argument lies at the back of Hegel and Marx. It is equally present in the mind of Smith. In a beautiful and profound passage in *The Theory of Moral Sentiments*, mixing social observation with social theory, (pp. 79–84 below), Smith accepts part of Rousseau's position, which he knew well, but in such manner as to go beyond Montesquieu's already diffident acceptance of the world of commerce. Smith had little doubt about the new culture of consumption unleashed by commerce on social groups, high and low. People had become obsessed with acquiring a seemingly infinite number of 'trinkets', 'frivolous objects' and a 'multitude of baubles'. The new commercial cultures of consumption made completely new people, changing their habits, appearance, their identity and interactions.[18] 'All their pockets are stuffed with little inconveniences', Smith observed. They even 'contrive new pockets, unknown in the clothes of other people, in order to carry a greater number.' (p. 80 below) The poor aspire to the comforts of the rich. Civil society is like a hamster-wheel where individuals are in an endless race for higher status and distinction. Only at the end, 'in the last dregs of life', does the disappointed individual find that 'wealth and greatness are mere trinkets of frivolous utility, no more adapted for procuring ease of body or tranquillity of mind than the tweezer-cases of the lover of toys.' (p. 81 below). Some eighteenth-century observers, like 'Mrs. Crackenthorpe', warned of the dangerous consequences of this civil society in action, with its new public spaces and its obsession with ever more refined 'tea-cups, sugar-tongues, salt-shovels' (p. 61 below) and the like: British society was losing its strength as men were becoming effeminate in coffee houses and women were being packed off to tea parties. Smith's view was more subtle and highlighted the paradoxical workings of civil society. Individuals might have become locked into a status-seeking game paying more regard to what 'the spectator' thought than their own free will. Yet, from the perspective of civil society as a whole, this 'deception' also had virtuous consequences. For it was 'this deception which rouses and keeps in continual motion the industry of mankind' (p. 83), leading to new technologies, better and more food, and communication between peoples. Competitive status-seeking and the pursuit of greater wealth also, Smith argued, carried a built-in mechanism for social harmony: being able to fantasize becoming rich made the poor person accept a culture of social inequality, rather than opting for violence or anarchy. Commerce and consumption, in short, created and stabilized a civil society.

The debate about the relative costs and benefits of commerce for civil society was not resolved by the irreversible transformation created by industrialization. Far from it, attention to industrial society created new anxieties about pauperism and the loss of community and self in a society structured around profit, markets and a division of labour. Hegel projected the social consequences from a market society into the future and turned to corporations as a way of reinstating ethical life (pp. 129–35). This projection, again, should be read as documenting fears of depersonalization rather than as evidence of material social transformation. But it was Marx who took this debate one step further, building, as is well known, on Hegel, but also drawing on Ferguson's emphasis on the social and civic costs arising from the division of labour. Modern society, for Marx, had not only fragmented a civic community by destroying an (admittedly idealized) organic unity of civic virtue and economic interest (pp. 135–8). It produced a split identity of the self. The economic creation of the bourgeoisie had been complemented by the political creation of the citizen in the French Revolution. In civil society, the rights of man, proclaimed by Tom Paine and revolutionaries in France and elsewhere (pp. 99–102), did not go beyond egoistic man. The French revolution dissolved the old society, but the freedom it granted was limited: man received the freedom of property and the freedom of trade, but was not freed from property or materialism as such. The self had become divided: abstract universal citizen in politics and materialistic individual in civil society. Full human emancipation, Marx argued, required the overcoming of this division and the recognition of personal forces as social forces.

There is of course a huge difference between Marx and western Marxism; that is, between a great theorist expecting a revolution for broadly materialist reasons and those descendants who explained the failure of a revolution to occur by stressing, not altogether in the spirit of the master, that cultural co-option of one sort or another had, so to speak, unmanned the working class. If the earliest of such thinkers was Lukacs and the most extreme Marcuse, the most important for our purposes was Gramsci.[19] Social life was structured quite as much by belief as by hard realities for Gramsci, with revolutionary fervour being undermined by the 'hegemony' of ruling ideas that existed within civil society (pp. 186–90). Still, the difference between Marx (and then Soviet Marxists) and western Marxism does not in the most crucial sense really matter. For both schools wished to end atomization and to restore the unity of mankind. Perhaps the greatest of all critiques of what it meant to live under regimes that sought to remove the differentiation of civil society so as to re-create a simple and unified solidarity was that penned by Leszek Kolakowski, the great historian of Marxism who lived for many years in communist Poland before being forced into exile in the West. In conditions of social complexity inherent in any industrial society, simplicity can only be achieved through brute force – a brute fact which promises that any such programme is self-defeating (pp. 206–9).

Late twentieth-century discussions show the on-going ambivalence about the pairing of commerce and civil society. Should commerce and markets be viewed as integral to civil society, or as a sphere of profits and materialism that distracts from a purer, more deliberative and higher ethical plane of civil society? Where today's commentators stand with regard to this question has as much to do with the intellectual and cultural traditions they bring to the rediscovery of civil society as with the material realities of the economy in their respective societies. Thus the normative model of deliberative politics developed by Jürgen Habermas remains sceptical of the commercial world of consumption long criticized by his Frankfurt School teachers (pp. 222–6). From a more communitarian perspective, American commentators like Robert Putnam have viewed media culture as a key source of a weakening civic life in the United States (pp. 227–31). For Michael Sandel, media and consumer markets are potential forces of disintegration, stretching people's more manageable sense of belonging to distinct communities (pp. 196–9). Similarly, Havel's plea for 'living in the truth' was directed not only at a post-totalitarian socialist regime but also written from within a deep suspicion of the ethical consequences of mass consumption. These intellectual traditions, then, drew on an older critique of consumer society where consumers were pictured as passive, unfree servants of corporate firms and culture industry – an approach that ignored the many ways in which consumers have at times been 'active' and emancipatory agents in civil society, fashioning new identities for themselves and others in the process.[20]

It is easier to be critical of markets when one has the benefit of living with a market system of provision, and one reason for the sometimes passionate and idealistic embrace of markets by many civil society champions in Eastern Europe was precisely that markets held out an attractive counter-weight to the power of the state. Critical voices pointed out that such appeals were often inflated and down-played the sources of social solidarity under socialism (pp. 203–6, Hann). Yet, in market-based societies too, past and present commentators have highlighted the frequent (though far from automatic) synergies between commercial development and civil society. Conscious and organized consumers have often been at the forefront of social activism and civic engagement, from cooperatives, British Free Traders, and consumer leagues in America and Europe in the generations before the First World War, to more recent transnational consumer activism.[21] Far from being some pure autonomous sphere, John Keane argues, global civil society was in part fuelled by the transnational energies of turbo-capitalism (pp. 287–92).

The current debate about the nature and future of 'global civil society' is an opportune moment to recall the earlier international dimension of this problematic relationship between commerce and civil society. After Montesquieu's 'douceur of commerce', a cosmopolitan strand of ethics emerged from within the lodges of freemasons and texts by writers like Kant that searched for ethical transnational bonds beyond the bonds provided by commercial exchange. For Kant, civil society became an attractive frame for administering *universal* justice (pp. 93–5). It is not necessary, however, to imagine a stark contrast between cosmopolitan unity in civil society and social separation in traditional society. As Lessing makes clear in his Masonic dialogues, freemasonry always divided as well as united different people (pp. 43–8). Civil society offered people a way of thinking beyond states, communities and ranks, but this did not mean that commentators were blind to the fact that division was an integral component of civil society: 'It cannot unite men without parting them.' (p. 45) Freemasonry was diversified just as civil society was.

It would be a mistake to project onto civil society a linear view of a growing awareness of cosmopolitan ethics and peace. Rather, the debate about ethical bonds uniting people in different states developed alongside a debate about the implications of commercial civil society for the military demands of states. Civil society might be nice, but how would political communities be able to survive and exert their will in an increasingly commercial world? The selections from Ferguson and Gibbon amount to an exchange about the necessities for military defence. No thinker is more ambivalent about the new world than Ferguson in his great *Essay on the History of Civil Society* (pp. 83–8). His approval of a world of polish and refinement in which virtue is no longer, as it was for the Spartans, the business of the state breaks down when confronting questions of defence and service to the community. Commerce, polish and refinement will make us soft, and so unable to defeat nomads and tribesmen, trained by the adverse conditions of peripheries to be fit and blessed with military skills. His worries are all too easy to understand: Highlanders had, after all, marched through Edinburgh in 1745. Nonetheless, Gibbon countered this view, despite his admiration for Roman virtue (pp. 88–92). The world had changed. Riches now allowed us to buy weapons of such effectiveness that nomadic conquerors would never again be able to destroy the centres of civilization. That is by and large the view held by our own generation. Or is it? Did not the assault on the Twin Towers of New York on September 11th demonstrate the military effectiveness of outsiders? If history has not yet seen fit to answer that question, one can at least say that the outsiders in question believed commercial society to be soft and weak.

Paradoxes of totality

The revival of interest in the notion of civil society in the twentieth century has a particular flavour, somewhat removed from the fears of atomization and social decay noted in earlier historical moments. What has come to the fore now is a reaction to ideologies of all sorts that seek to make the world whole. Jean-Paul Sartre's account of Marxism made much of its totalizing ambition, and it is precisely this quality that is in question here. What is at issue takes us back to Rousseau, that is, the desire to re-create – or perhaps to create – unitary selves in a world in which self and society merge seamlessly into each other. Indeed, a similar position can be traced to a heated and bloody confrontation in Reformation Europe in the 1530s–50s when Luther, Melanchton and Calvin rallied to the defence of civil society against those millenarians who believed they could overcome the gulf between civil society and the City of God.[22] It was modern totalizing ideologies in the nineteenth and twentieth centuries that sought to erase differences on this earth. In contrast to Sartre's emphasis, Marxism was not the only totalizing philosophy of the modern world. Equal attention should be given to the ideas and practices of at least two other forces: nationalism and liberalism. There is no want of literature on nationalism and liberalism but, interestingly, these subjects have rarely received the recognition they deserved in relation to the changing dynamics and spaces of civil society.

Instead of positioning civil society straightaway opposite fascism and socialism, it may be helpful to broaden the question, to ask about the more general pressure put on civil society – as a concept and practice – by the rise of new modern ideologies. This has the additional advantage of proceeding with a more appropriate temporal perspective on the transvaluation and declining significance of civil society, for it makes us look beyond the era of the two world wars. Clearly, the tremendous suffering caused by the social and ethnic projects of fascism and socialism was the backdrop for the more optimistic retrieval of civil society in the 1980s–90s, but this does not tell us much about the history of the crisis of civil society leading up to the inter-war years. Fascism and socialism combined in an attempt to finish off civil society. Leninist policies and Lenin's rejection of the rights of man were a brutal version of Marx's earlier critique of the split of man into citizen and bourgeois (pp. 135–8, pp. 180–2). Neither was very squeamish about the use of violence to overcome this perceived duality and restore totality. Yet totalizing programmes confronted a concept of civil society that had already become a weak player, softened by the changing use and potential in modern ideologies and increasingly losing its earlier more autonomous strength. Guild socialism and pluralism gave civil society a new flowering at the turn of the twentieth century (pp. 155–73), but this was a short-lived spring in a generally much harsher climate which saw the overall decline of civil society as a moral and intellectual project in the second half of the nineteenth century. Liberal imperialism and nationalism left their imprint on civil society.

If liberalism provided an arena to explore representational aspects of democracy for civil society, especially at the level of local self-government, it also worked as an expansionist framework in which civility and imperial mission operated in tandem. James Mill reveals the tensions at work. Here was a liberal utilitarian whose long-term hopes for Indian society were informed by a stark opposition between the advanced moral, physical and institutional culture of British civil society and the barbarous, rude and litigious habits of the Hindu. Civil society here required trust and reciprocity, which required modern law. As a liberal mission for exportation, civil society therefore required legal and institutional transformation as well as cultural uplifting. Communities, and the natural environment in which they lived, needed acts of social reconstruction to become the realm of civil society, through the exercise of power as well as persuasion.[23] It would be wrong, however, to see this process only in a one-directional manner. Imperial administrators also returned from India to Britain with new knowledge and questions that could make them challenge a civilizing equation between property-rights and a society based on contract.[24] At the same time, there can be little doubt that colonizers and colonized had uneven positions of power in this relationship. Liberal Christian imperialism was less pluralistic than many earlier forms of European power and conversion, such as that of the Jesuits. Missionaries' optimistic visions of building a new society of brotherhood in the early nineteenth century gave way to a bleaker more racialized view of biologically inferior subjects in the second half of the nineteenth century.[25]

These imperial sources are usefully read alongside more recent post-colonial writings. For they show that civil society cannot be located exlusively within European nation-states. Civil society contained an expansionist imperial strand which placed metropole and colony as interactive and dependent settings within the same framework. For the current debate about which societies have the historical qualifications for becoming a member of the civil society club, this means that it is problematic to invoke some exclusive European advantage. The imperial nature of many European states meant that civil society left its impact on non-European societies whether they wanted it or not. For the more recent debate about civil society in former colonies, this has had conflicting repercussions. The imperial flavour of earlier confrontations, made for a good deal of scepticism, even suspicion, leading some post-colonial writers to look to community rather than civil society. Anti-colonial nationalism refused to accept membership in a 'civil society of subjects' and opted instead for its own narrative of community, as suggested in Chatterjee's work (p. 284). Emphasizing the contradictions of Western civil society and arguing against a holistic dichotomy between metropole and colony, the Comaroffs have argued that attempts to retrieve the idea of civil society for Africa need to locate the uncivil dimension of colonization against the specificities of local histories (pp. 279–83).[26]

Nationalism was a second ideological and social project that changed the trajectory of civil society. As a concept cherishing difference, civil society can be seen as the opposite of nationalism and, as we have already noted, new ideas of cosmopolitanism and new transnational networks were one strand in the modern history of civil society. Yet we should not ignore that in some contexts nationalist ideas also presented themselves as the natural and appropriate expression of civil society. The selection from Sieyès already reveals the desire for a common, unitary social will (pp. 102–5). Nineteenth and early twentieth-century European history generalized this desire. The use of civil society for the preservation of difference now moved into new terrain. Instead of a pluralist embrace of different ethical or normative positions, difference could now mean protecting different social classes and nations against a drift of flattening uniformity. Civil society was endorsed as the natural setting of social hierarchy and separation of distinct national cultures. 'Civil society in a rich nation is always an aristocracy, even under a democratic constitution,' (p. 139) emphasized Heinrich von Treitschke, the liberal nationalist historian and advocate of a Prussian-led united Germany. Civil society here stood in opposition to social liberal and social-democratic ideas of full civic participation, social mobility, and deliberative politics. Social democracy represented 'unpatriotic cosmopolitanism.' Civil society preserved national consciousness and power. Its pillars were property, piety and patriotism. Much had been made by earlier writers on civil society about property as a starting point in the history of civil society – Locke importantly included property of life and person in his definition. For Treitschke, property now functions not only as a defensive position against social redistribution, but as a resource of national identity, pride and cultural diversity against a homeless, globalizing homogeneity: 'out of love to the inherited domestic four posts arises the noble pride of love for the fatherland and the certainty that the multi-faceted richness of national civilization shall never be replaced by the same old dull routine of a cosmopolitan bourgeoisie [Weltbürgertum].' (p. 139) Treitschke looked backwards to Aristotle to legitimize civil society as a frame stabilizing social relations and state power alike by keeping 'the masses' in their place, preventing class antagonism, and fostering respect for the nation-state.

There was already a good deal of suspicion of popular democracy in this national-liberal appropriation of civil society – the 'masses' were not fit for government.[27] The next two generations saw a more profound, decisive assault on the participatory and deliberative traits of civil society. The attempt to exclude the people from the political arena came to an end. But the mobilization of the masses was not managed on liberal democratic lines; on the contrary, dislike of liberalism pervaded the intellectual and social atmosphere of the time. Parties were attacked as vehicles of sectional interest, not instruments of deliberate reasoning bringing out a higher rationale of civil society. Both Lenin and Schmitt had little trust in different groups being able to reach peaceful agreement through plurality and reasoning (pp. 180–2; 182–5). Accordingly, both bolshevism and fascism offered versions of the truth to which the people should be led – the key implication being that those who would not accept the truth were nothing less than traitors. The cult of leader appealed to this non-deliberative, organic imagery of the popular will, as evident in bolshevism as in fascism.

If reactions to the French revolution had begun a move toward national awakening, geopolitical competition then suggested to many state elites that a more homogeneous citizen body would increase the functional capacities of their states. This was certainly true of late Tsarist Russia, hopeful that Ukrainians could be turned into Russians proper so that a multinational empire could become a classical nation-state. The fact that states fought over their peoples, that conflicts between homelands and minorities structured politics, did much to create those fears of disloyalty that made ethnic cleansing such a popular force in Europe's dark twentieth century. This is the world in which, as Perez-Diaz put it, the state became a moral project (pp. 193–6). If social and national unity were state tasks, so too was the need for economic development – the final social force in question. The intermingling of such forces took various forms. If Hitler and Stalin between them did much to homogenize the populations of Eastern Europe in the midst of war, both were so deeply attractive to their supporters because their great moralities promised to give unity and meaning to life. Furthermore, both led to imitative strategies elsewhere. Communism is perhaps best seen as a late development strategy in general, but authoritarian nationalism equally laid claim, especially in Latin America, to be a successful late development strategy.

Life within authoritarian states armed with a moral project became in time unbearable. Kolakowski's writings in the mid-1970s are a particularly eloquent and high-powered account of why this is so (pp. 206–9). In conditions of social complexity, attempts to create unity between self and society must involve coercion – and, one can add, of nations quite as much as of classes. The world of civil society is accordingly one of diminished ambition, a world which seeks softness rather than absolute truth. This is nicely emphasized here by Walzer, who has approached civil society as a project of projects (pp. 209–12). Civil society here becomes a determination to live with differences. It is a common agreement, a consensual matter, that difference cannot be avoided.

Certain implications follow from this. To begin with, the post-communist prism of anti-totality helps to sharpen our view of earlier anxieties about state power. The Elizabethan theologian Richard Hooker had been among the first systematically to explore civil society as political society and its relationship to the independent claims of religious groups like Calvinists and Papists. Here civil society was a social and political response by individuals, fearful of violence, delegating the protection of their interest to a 'civil regiment' or governing institutions (pp. 26–9). By the time of John Locke, a century later, the argument for civil society had broadened into a consideration of a government abusing its powers and into an argument for the right of resistance. Civil society was now mobilized against totalizing regimes like absolute monarchy. For Locke, civil society was still a political society, but not all political societies (such as absolute governments) were civil societies (pp. 30–3). Here was the paradigmatic birth of the modern anti-totalizing uses of the civil society argument.

The tremendous expansion and ideological legitimation of state power in the late nineteenth century saw a fresh emphasis on the social spaces and social character of citizens. 'What we actually see in the world', J.N. Figgis observed on the eve of the First World War, 'is not on the one hand the State, and on the other a mass of unrelated individuals; but a vast complex of gathered unions, in which alone we find individuals, families, clubs, trades unions, colleges , professions, and so forth', all groups that exercised functions 'which are of the nature of government.' (p. 161) Debates about collectivism, socialism and 'mass society' produced a variety of attempts to protect civil society against centralizing state tendencies or collectivism. The answers advanced by different European thinkers and social reformers reflected the ways in which different national traditions viewed state, liberalism and commercial society. In France, Durkheim argued that the state was simply too far away from the modern individual for any connection leading to moral integration to be established; equally, the family had become too small a unit to allow general integration within a society for a modern society with division of labour. Balance in society dependent upon the creation of a mid-level within society that, for Durkheim, prevented the atomization of society by market forces. Professional organizations, that is, a modernized guild system, would be able at once to incorporate the individual whilst being of sufficient size to speak to and to be taken seriously by the state (pp. 173–9). In Germany, Gierke was more critical of guilds as compulsory associations and favoured a more organic image of community (pp. 155–60). Tönnies used the concepts of *Gemeinschaft* und *Gesellschaft* to draw attention to the different modes of ideas and practice between exclusive social systems and more open, inclusive and market-oriented civil societies (pp. 152–5). But this distinction, though real, should not be overdone; for Tönnies the two systems were not sequential, one replacing the other, but co-existed.[28] Cattaneo's focus of concern was slightly different. Nation-state formation could create such homogeneity as to squeeze out minorities. Accordingly, he sought to find a better balance within society by championing federal arrangements (pp. 163–8). Differently put, political arrangements could be created which would further democracy in the fullest sense, by creating a frame within which national differences could be respected – and not extirpated by the false democracy wherein a simple majority could establish its own tyranny. The enemy for the guild socialists was rather different, namely the bureaucratization of the world envisioned by the Webbs.[29] Socialism has indeed always been somewhat schizophrenic, being drawn alternately to the poles of liberty or efficiency. Cole represented a move towards the libertarian end of the spectrum (pp. 168–73). Any full consideration of his work must note, however, his ultimate inability to create a truly plausible constitutional arrangement for the society he so much wished to bring into being.

Furthermore, there is a world of difference between a liberal tradition stressing difference and civility and a republican tradition of civic virtue always hankering after a degree of unity – or, indeed, Anglican, conservative and national uses of civil society equally concerned to create unity between church and state or between classes and nation. For consensus, albeit limited in scope, lies at the heart of liberalism. There is a boundedness to the liberal project precisely because not everything is allowed. This insight should not be left at the purely theoretical level. There is a paradox about the history of civil society. The insistence on a measure of consensus, on types of behaviour necessary to civil conduct within society, could be decidedly illiberal, as the imperial and post-colonial texts make clear, as do the nationalist selections where civil society becomes a bulwark against mass democracy. Civil society could be mobilized quite as much for expansionist projects that sought to minimize, overcome or erase cultural differences. Just as civil society was not always opposite or outside political society, so it was not always a 'soft' opposite to totalizing ideologies, but sometimes harnessed to modern ideologies themselves. Advocates in today's world do well not to erase these illiberal workings of civil society from their collective memory.

Praxis and theory

Praxis and theory flow in and out of each other in the approach to civil society outlined above. Civil society here is always a construct of ideas and a social praxis that disseminates norms of civility, structures social and political behaviour, and informs knowledge of self and others. This reciprocal relationship needs emphasis, since most studies or policies of civil society have tended to proceed from either a purely theoretical, discursive position or from an analysis of social action and associational practice. The selection of some sources detailing social practices alongside more philosophical texts here is therefore not merely to approach civil society from below as well as from above. In addition, it is an argument for a more dynamic cultural and political understanding of civil society that views social actors and concepts as interacting in the same framework. We can distinguish between two levels of praxis. First, there is the use of civil society as a working tool informing actors' habits and views of themselves and of others, already discussed. Second, there is the reverse flow, that is how practices of civil society shape new norms and habits of political action and reasoning.

This second level of practice concerns the benefits of social self-organization. The classic statement of this position is of course that of Tocqueville, the great exponent of the view that a taste for liberty results from the practice of self-government (pp. 106–16). Tocqueville's argument is more subtle than is often realized. In particular, he makes much of various spill-over effects. Political activity has the capacity to create a lively citizen body able to organize all sorts of spheres of social life. Equally, the lively citizens of a commercial world will tend to participate in political life. There is at least the possibility of a beneficent cycle here. Still, Tocqueville remains aware that commerce might yet lead to passivity and so to despotism. It is this latter strain that has been developed by Robert Putnam, especially when lamenting the effects of television viewing (pp. 227–31).

This modern appropriation of Tocqueville is, however, not entirely appropriate. On the one hand, Tocqueville is well aware that social self-organization by itself may in fact undermine a civil society. French politics had after all seen the clandestine activity of secret societies, keen to undermine the social order. The brilliant argument about the social and political conditions that ensure that groups add to civil life makes this clear (pp. 116–18). On the other hand, the extent to which Tocqueville changed his mind in his later work is not generally appreciated. His insistence on the potentially corrupting influence of commerce, that is, his loyalty to the tradition of civic virtue in general and his love of Rousseau in particular, always made him suspicious of popular activity. Only in his work on the French revolution did he come to argue that distrust, the incapacity to join together in liberty in the democratic age, resulted from the legacy of the old regime – which had so separated the classes, through a policy of divide and rule, as to make it impossible for them to co-operate together (pp. 118–19). There is an interesting resonance here with Skocpol's assault on Putnam. She too refuses to blame the people. Particular background social conditions are required in order for participation and co-operation to flourish (pp. 234–7).

The contemporary debate about changing associational habits should be treated as an invitation to a more complex and contingent view of associational life in relationship to social and political identities and processes, past and present. The impact of associations on social and political procedures and mentalities does not follow along a universal equation, but is determined by the political traditions and cultural resources that actors bring with them to the clubhouse. The then unprecedented high levels of associational membership in Weimar Germany did not diminish the degree of violence – far from it.[30] High levels of associational membership in today's Federal Republic of Germany, by contrast, coincide with peaceful, democratic culture. Surely, there is a world of difference between groups of men and women joining a voluntary automobile veterans' club and young men joining the stormtroopers. Philanthropy, a crucial sphere of associational culture from the seventeenth century to the present, often involved projects of paternalism and social discipline that were a far cry from the often rosy picture of pluralism painted today (pp. 143–6). Rather than being a natural home for deliberative reasoning associational life reflected the changing emotional household of society and culture. Evangelicalism and pietism injected an unprecedented emotional energy into clubs and societies, of which missionary and domestic reform associations made up a growing bulk in nineteenth-century Europe.

In addition to different purposes and motivation, the political traditions and cultural values and resources that precirculate in society also influence the practices of associational life in and outside the associational meeting. A popular radical tradition of emancipation, for example, can provide disadvantaged members of society, like Ms. Layton of the Women's Cooperative Guild, with a script of personal empowerment (pp. 146–9). By contrast, in a less vibrant democratic culture, associations can become havens of retreat from the complex and frightening demands of modern social and political life, as for the men of the turn of the twentieth-century Schlaraffia in Hamburg who developed an elaborate cultural world of nostalgia and romanticism away from mass society (pp. 149–51). Associational life can make for myopia and political passivity as well as for liberation and civic connectedness, a point well known to satirists and social observers since the eighteenth century (pp. 69–70; pp. 185–6).

These limitations, ambivalences, or deficits in the high age of civil society in Europe are important because they suggest the need for a more open consideration of associational practices in other cultures today. Against the background of these complex, ambivalent histories, it is problematic to invoke a European ideal-type. Much of the debate about the prospects of civil society in non-European settings has been conducted on an uneven debating field, comparing their social historical potential (the number of associations in the past, the relative openness of professional and urban groups, their relationship to state power, etc.) with models of the public sphere in eighteenth-century Europe developed by Habermas in the 1960s that have since been viewed more as an ideal type than as a meaningful representation of the more conflictuous and hierarchical and less deliberative processes of the multiple forms of publics at work in modern Europe.[31] Associations in China, informal neighbourhood networks in the Middle East, and religious groupings in India, may look less like unfamiliar potential members of the civil society club if viewed against European civil societies that recognize their social complexities, tensions, and limits.

Conclusions

The great revival of interest in the concept of civil society began in the 1970s and perhaps reached something of a peak two decades later. At the level of global civil society, the numerical expansion of international non-governmental organizations in the 1990s is remarkable: transnational social movements (like missionary or anti-slavery movements) can be traced back to the early nineteenth century, but over one quarter of the 11,693 INGOs in existence in 2000 (and more than a third of their members) emerged after 1990.[32] These were years in which there was so visceral a reaction against totalizing politics that the introduction of market forces to balance state power seemed an unadulterated good. Recent years have seen some questioning of the salience and usefulness of the concept of civil society. One worry that came to the fore concerned the nature of social groups themselves. Merely to strengthen group life was not to guarantee civility or decency in social life. 'Compelled associations', Nancy Rosenblum correctly argues, can be repulsive in so far as they resemble cages from which human beings cannot then escape (pp. 244–9). Perhaps more important was the revival of a generalized disquiet about commerce. For one thing, there was ever greater awareness of the brutal consequences that had followed on privatization, especially in the former Socialist Bloc. More generally, the increasing intensity and speed of economic connections around the world threatened to so disrupt nations and states as to rule out of court the base of social solidarity upon which civil society depends.

A change in mood should not for a moment be taken as an injunction to take the concept of civil society less seriously. Perhaps the most obvious point to be made in conclusion is that historical awareness forces us to see that the debates about civil society have waxed and waned, again and again. It is very likely that this will continue. However, before ending with a final note as to why that is so, it is useful to review three particular new insights that follow from putting together the varied texts in this reader.

We can note, to begin with, that civil society is very distinctly not the same, conceptually or in terms of reality, as democracy. Civil society in the late nineteenth and early twentieth centuries was not particularly well equipped to handle the demands or questions derived from popular politics. Accordingly, civil society did not lose its central position in social theory for no reason; indeed, on the contrary, one can argue that many thinkers in the tradition of civil society assembled here did not concern themselves centrally with democratic politics. All in all, it might not be wise to overburden the concept of civil society with contemporary projects of democratic renewal. This is not, however, to say that the concept has nothing to offer democratic theorists. Bluntly, it always behoves us to remember that democracy is not necessarily 'nice', as de Tocqueville so clearly realized. Fascism was a popular moral project, at least for a period, whilst ethnic cleansing has not been, as recent years have demonstrated, without its popular supporters. In the last analysis, democracy is only really attractive when it takes unto itself some of the characteristics associated with civil society.

This particular set of readings makes us realize that non-European or global debates about civil society are not simply a new episode. Very much to the contrary: they continue to engage with many of the problems and debates European societies had as well – the relationship between inclusiveness and exclusiveness, between plurality and order, between shared religious and cultural values and toleration, between self-governing associations and their relative dependence on states and markets. Liberal and conservative versions of civil society co-existed with nationalist readings. It is unwise to view the concept of civil society through some sort of Whiggish or evolutionary narrative of democratic perfection that advances with time. Most civil society ideas were developed as arguments about political society, and as such involved the state, be it as secular governing authority or as Christian state with a religious establishment. Civil society could be utilized by thinkers and social movements to reinforce ideas of nation-state and imperial mission just as much as an emancipatory idea checking the abuse of state power. Either way, the idea of civil society developed in tandem with, not in isolation from, political society broadly defined.

Let us conclude finally by offering an explanation as to why the fortunes of civil society have risen and fallen over time, and why this is likely to remain so. The concept is, to use Bryce Gallie's useful term, 'essentially contested'.[33] The idea of difference which lies at the heart of civil society has enormous moral attraction. Do we know everything? Are we certain that a particular set of standards is always correct? The fact that the answer must be negative suggests a degree of relativism. But we know that any full-blooded relativism must be repulsive, and very dangerous. So a civil society will always wobble between allowing difference, and insisting that such difference be bounded. Hence civil society must be at once an agreement, a consensus, and a recognition of difference. There can be no final balance here, for historical forces have shifted and will continue to shift boundaries. We would not accept the Anglican view that all must believe in God, but have long accepted a great deal from the Enlightenment – the condemnation of slavery and the rights of man (and woman). It seems that questions of human rights are now altering the balance again. Civil society is not and will not somehow become closed and final, either theoretically or practically.

Notes

1 John Grimond, 'Civil Society,' in *The World in 2002* (London: Economist Newspaper Ltd, 2001), p.18.
2 Aziz Choudry, *GATT Watch*, 5 January 2002. Select further reading from the vast and growing literature on civil society can be found on p. 301 of this volume, below.
3 This historical–geographical broadening could, of course, be continued in other fruitful directions as well, for example the attraction of civil society ideas to Chinese intellectuals in the generation before the 1911 Revolution, such as Liang Qichao; see Don C. Price , 'From Civil Society to Party Government', in Joshua A. Fogel and Peter G. Zarrow (eds), *Imagining the People: Chinese Intellectuals and the Concept of Citizenship, 1890–1920* (Armonk, New York: M.E. Sharpe, 1997), pp. 142–64.
4 This is also true for modern Britain, which has often wrongly been seen as an anti-statist tradition in contrast to continental ideas. See now Jose Harris, 'From Richard Hooker to Harold Laski: Changing Perceptions of Civil Society in British Political Thought, Late Sixteenth to Early Twentieth Centuries', in Jose Harris (ed.), *Civil Society in British History: Ideas, Identities, Institutions* (Oxford: Oxford University Press, 2004), pp. 13–37.
5 See R.J. Morris, 'Clubs, Societies, Associations', in F.M.L. Thompson (ed.), *The Cambridge Social History of Britain 1750–1950, Vol. III: Social Agencies and Institutions* (Cambridge: Cambridge University Press, 1990); Peter Clark, *British Clubs and Societies, 1580–1800: The Origins of an Associational World* (Oxford: Clarendon Press, 2000); Leonore Davidoff and Catherine Hall, *Family Fortunes: Men and Women of the English Middle Class 1780–1850* (London: Routledge, 1991); Thomas Nipperdey, 'Verein als soziale Struktur in Deutschland im späten 18. und frühen 19. Jahrhundert', in Thomas Nipperdey, *Gesellschaft, Kultur, Theorie* (Göttingen: Vandenhoeck & Ruprecht, 1976); Frank Trentmann (ed.), *Paradoxes of Civil Society: New Perspectives on Modern German and British History* (Oxford and New York: Berghahn Books, 2nd edn 2003); Nancy Bermeo and Philip Nord (eds), *Civil Society Before Democracy: Lessons from Nineteenth-Century Europe* (Lanham, Md: Rowman & Littlefield, 2000); Stefan-Ludwig Hoffman, *Die Politik der Geselligkeit* (Göttingen: Vandenhoeck & Ruprecht, 2003); M.C. Jacob, *Living the Enlightenment: Freemasonry and Politics in Eighteenth-Century Europe* (Oxford: Oxford University Press, 1991); Daniel Roche, *Le Siècle des Lumières en Province: Académies et Académiciens Provinciaux, 1680–1789* (Paris: Mouton, 1978); R.D. Brown, 'The Emergence of Urban Society in Rural Massachusetts, 1760–1820', in *Journal of American History*, 61 (1974), pp. 29–51; J. Bradley, 'Subjects into Citizens: Societies, Civil Society, and Autocracy in Tsarist Russia', in *American Historical Review*, 107 (2002), pp. 1094–123.
6 For different approaches, see Norbert Elias, *Über den Prozess der Zivilisation (1939)*, Eng. trans. by Edmund Jephcott, *The Civilizing Process*, 2 vols (Oxford: Blackwell,

1978–82); Jorge Arditi, *A Genealogy of Manners: Transformations of Social Relations in France and England from the Fourteenth to the Eighteenth Century* (Chicago and London: University of Chicago Press, 1998). For violence and toleration, see Dominique Colas, *Civil Society and Fanaticism: Conjoined Histories*, trans. by Amy Jacobs (Stanford, Calif.: Stanford University Press, 1997); John A. Hall, 'Reflections on the Making of Civility in Society', in Trentmann (ed.), *Paradoxes of Civil Society*; and also now Sven Reichardt, 'Gewalt' in Dieter Gosewinkel, Dieter Rucht, Wolfgang van den Daele, and Jürgen Kocka (eds), *Zivilgesellschaft – national und transnational* (WZB-Jahrbuch 2003: edition sigma, 2003), pp. 61–81.

7 Ernest Gellner, *Conditions of Liberty: Civil Society and its Rivals* (London, Hamish Hamilton, 1994); Guillermo O'Donnell and Philippe Schmitter, *Transitions from Authoritarian Rule: Tentative Conclusions about Uncertain Democracies* (Baltimore and London: Johns Hopkins University Press, 1986).

8 TBC in Ole Peter Grell, Jonathan I. Israel and Nicholas Tyacke (eds), *From Persecution to Toleration: The Glorious Revolution and Religion in England* (Oxford: Clarendon Press, 1991).

9 This view is that of the US constitution, and more generally of Madison regarding political parties in Federalist no. 10.

10 See Mary Catherine Moran, ' "The Commerce of the Sexes": Gender and the Social Sphere in Scottish Enlightenment Accounts of Civil Society', in Trentmann (ed.), *Paradoxes of Civil Society*, pp. 61–84.

11 John Hall, *Ernest Gellner*, ch. 5, forthcoming.

12 See also S. Zubaida, 'Is There a Muslim Society? Ernest Gellner's Sociology of Islam', in *Economy and Society*, 24 (1995); Robert Hefner, *Civil Islam: Muslims and Democratization in Indonesia* (Princeton, NJ and Oxford: Princeton University Press, 2000).

13 See also Shalini Randeria, 'Kastensolidarität als Modus zivilgesellschaftlicher Bindungen?', in Gosewinkel, *Zivilgesellschaft*, pp. 223–43.

14 For this Anglican tradition, see also the notes in Frank Trentmann, 'The Problem with Civil Society: Or Putting Modern European History Back into Contemporary Debate', in Marlies Glasius, Mary Kaldor, David Lewis and Hakan Seckinelgin (eds), *Exploring Civil Society: Political and Cultural Contexts* (London: Routledge, 2004).

15 John Dunn, 'The contemporary political significance of John Locke's conception of civil society', in Sudipta Kaviraj and Sunil Kilnani (eds), *Civil Society: History and Possibilities* (Cambridge: Cambridge University Press, 2001), pp. 39–57.

16 Charles de Secondat Montesquieu, *The Spirit of the Laws*, trans. and ed. by Anne M. Cohler, Basia Carolyn Miller, Harold Samuel Stone (Cambridge: Cambridge University Press, 1989), Part Four, ch. 7, p. 343. For the changing assessment of Britain as a model of commercial development and political power, see now Gareth Stedman Jones, 'National bankruptcy and social revolution: European observers on Britain, 1813–1844', in Patrick O'Brien and Donald Winch (eds), *The Political Economy of British Historical Experience, 1688–1914* (Oxford, Oxford University Press, 2002), pp. 61–92, and Richard Whatmore, 'The Politics of Political Economy in France from Rousseau to Constant', in Mark Bevir and Frank Trentmann (eds), *Markets in Historical Contexts: Ideas and Politics in the Modern World* (Cambridge: Cambridge University Press, 2004), pp. 46–69.

17 For the luxury debates, see Christopher J. Berry, *The Idea of Luxury: A Conceptual and Historical Investigation* (Cambridge: Cambridge University Press, 1994).

18 Whether we should think about this in terms of a 'consumer revolution' or the birth of global consumerism is subject to debate: Neil McKendrick, John Brewer and J.H. Plumb, *The Birth of a Consumer Society: The Commercialization of Eighteenth-Century England* (London: Europa, 1982); John Brewer and Roy Porter (eds), *Consumption and the World of Goods* (London: Routledge, 1992); Arjun Appadurai (ed.), *The Social Life of Things: Commodities in Cultural Perspective* (Cambridge: Cambridge University Press, 1986); Peter Stearns, *Consumerism in World History* (2002); Frank Trentmann, 'Beyond Consumerism: New Historical Perspectives on Consumption', in *Journal of Contemporary History*, vol. 39, 3 (2004) pp. 373–401; John Brewer and Frank Trentmann (eds), *Consuming Cultures, Global Perspectives* (London and New York: Berg, forthcoming).

19 Jose G. Merquior, *Western Marxism* (London: Paladin, 1986).

20 Daniel Miller (ed.), *Acknowledging Consumption: A Review of New Studies* (London: Routledge, 1995). Erika Diane Rappaport, *Shopping for Pleasure: Women in the Making of London's West End*: (Princeton, NJ: Princeton University Press, 2000); John Fiske, *Reading the Popular* (London: Unwin Hyman, 1989); Frank Trentmann, 'Civil Society, Commerce, and the "Citizen-Consumer": Popular Meanings of Free Trade in Modern Britain', in Trentmann (ed.), *Paradoxes of Civil Society*, pp. 306–31.

21 Frank Trentmann and Patricia Maclachlan, 'Civilising Markets: Traditions of Consumer Politics in Twentieth-Century Britain, Japan, and the United States', in Bevir and Trentmann (eds), *Markets in Historical Contexts*; Ellen Furlough and Carl Strikwerda (eds), *Consumers Against Capitalism?: Consumer Cooperation in Europe, North America, and Japan* (Lanham, Md and Oxford: Rowman & Littlefield, 1999); Dietlind Stolle, Marc Hooghe and Michele Micheletti, 'Zwischen Markt und Zivilgesellschaft: politischer Konsum als bürgerliches Engagement', in Gosewinkel, *Zivilgesellschaft*, pp. 151–71.

22 Colas, *Civil Society and Fanaticism*, Ch. 3.

23 The way in which the project of civil society has involved acts of the transformation of the natural environment, and the way in which civil society was naturalized in turn, is a subject that deserves more attention; suggestive is Michael Redclift, *The Frontier Environment and Social Order: The Letters of Francis Codd from Upper Canada* (Cheltenham: Edward Elgar, 2000).

24 See Sandra den Otter, 'Freedom of Contract, the Market and Imperial Law-making', in Mark Bevir and Frank Trentmann (eds), *Critiques of Capital in Modern Britain and America* (Houndmills and New York: Palgrave Macmillan, 2002), pp. 49–72.

25 See Catherine Hall, *Civilising Subjects: Metropole and Colony in the English Imagination, 1830–1867* (Cambridge: Polity, 2002).

26 See also Jack Goody, 'Civil society in Extra-European Perspective', in Kaviraj and Kilnani (eds), *Civil Society: History and Possibilities*, pp. 149–64.

27 For Italy, see Adrian Lyttelton, 'Liberalism and Civil Society in Italy: From Hegemony to Mediation', in Bermeo and Nord (eds), *Civil Society Before Democracy*, pp. 61–81.

28 See Jose Harris, 'Tönnies on 'community and 'civil society', in Bevir and Trentmann, *Markets in Historical Contexts*, pp. 129–44.

29 See Paul Hirst, *The Pluralist Theory of the State* (London: Routledge, 1989).

30 See most recently, Sven Reichardt, *Faschistische Kampfbünde: Gewalt und Gemeinschaft im italienischem Squadrismus und in der deutschen SA* (Cologne: Böhlau, 2002).

31   Craig Calhoun (ed.), *Habermas and the Public Sphere* (Cambridge, Mass.: MIT Press, 1992).
32   Helmut Anheier, Marlies Glasius and Mary Kaldor (eds), *Global Civil Society 2001* (Oxford: Oxford University Press, 2001), Table R 19; see now also the revised data for NGOs in Marlies Glasius, Mary Kaldor and Helmut Anheier (eds), *Global Civil Society 2002* (Oxford: Oxford University Press, 2002).
33   Bryce Gallie, *Philosophy and the Historical Understanding* (London: Chatto & Windus, 1964).

2
Emergent Properties of Civil Society

Civil society as political society

Richard Hooker (1554–1600), the influential Elizabethan divine, studied and taught at Oxford. As Master of the Temple he was chief pastor of the centre of legal studies in London. In the last ten years of his life he gave up this position to focus on writing his famous Of the Laws of Ecclesiastical Polity. *In this selection, he offers an early thematic discussion of civil society as a form of public government and the role of human sociability. Hooker's text was an influential source for later discussions of civil society, well into the modern period.**

Nature itself teacheth laws and statutes to live by. The laws which have been hitherto mentioned do bind men absolutely, even as they are men, although they have never any settled fellowship, never any solemn agreement amongst themselves what to do or not to do. But forasmuch as we are not by ourselves sufficient to furnish ourselves with competent store of things needful for such a life as our nature doth desire, a life fit for the dignity of man, therefore to supply those defects and imperfections which are in us living single and solely by ourselves, we are naturally induced to seek communion and fellowship with others. This was the cause of men's uniting themselves at the first in political societies, which societies could not be without government, nor government without a distinct kind of law from that which hath been already declared. Two foundations there are which bear up public societies – the one, a natural inclination, whereby all men desire sociable life and fellowship; the other, an order expressly or secretly agreed upon, touching the manner of their union in living together. The latter is that which we call the law of a common weal, the very soul of a politic body, the parts whereof are by law animated, held together, and set on work in such actions as the common good requireth. Laws politic, ordained for external order and regiment amongst men, are never framed as they should be, unless presuming the will of man to be inwardly obstinate, rebellious, and averse from all obedience unto the sacred laws of his nature;

26

in a word, unless presuming man to be in regard of his depraved mind, little better than a wild beast, they do accordingly provide notwithstanding so to frame his outward actions, that they be no hindrance unto the common good for which societies are instituted; unless they do this, they are not perfect. It resteth therefore that we consider how Nature findeth out such laws of government, as serve to direct even nature depraved to a right end. All men desire to lead in this world an happy life. The life is led most happily wherein all virtue is exercised without impediment or let. The Apostle, in exhorting men to contentment, although they have in this world no more than very bare food and raiment, giveth us thereby to understand, that those are even the lowest of things necessary, that if we should be stripped of all those things without which we might possibly be, yet these must be left; that destitution in these is such an impediment, as, till it be removed, suffereth not the mind of man to admit any other care. For this cause first God assigned Adam maintenance of life, and then appointed him a law to observe. For this cause, after men began to grow to a number, the first thing we read they gave themselves unto, was the tilling of the earth, and the feeding of cattle. Having by this means whereon to live, the principle actions of their life afterward are noted by the exercise of their religion. True it is, that the Kingdom of God must be the first thing in our purposes and desires; but, inasmuch as righteous life presupposeth life, inasmuch as to live virtuously it is impossible except to live; therefore the first impediment, which naturally we endeavour to remove, is penury and want of things without which we cannot live.

Unto life many implements are necessary; more, if we seek (as all men naturally do) such a life as hath in it joy, comfort, delight, and pleasure. To this end we see how quickly sundry arts mechanically were found out in the very prime of the world. As things of greatest necessity are always first provided for, so things of greatest dignity are most accounted of by all such as judge rightly. Although, therefore, riches be a thing which every man wisheth, yet no man of judgment can esteem it better to be rich, than wise, virtuous, and religious. If we be both, or either of these, it is not because we are so born. For into the world we come as empty of the one as of the other, as naked in mind as we are in body. Both which necessities of man had at the first no other helps and supplies, than only domestically; such as that which the Prophet implieth, saying 'Can a mother forget her child?'. Such as that which the Apostle mentioneth, saying, 'He that careth not for his own is worse than an infidel'; such as that concerning Abraham, 'Abraham will command his sons and his household after him, that they keep the way of the Lord'. But, neither that which we learn of ourselves, nor that which others teach us can prevail, where wickedness and malice have taken deep root. If, therefore, when there was but as yet one only family in the world, no means of instruction, human or Divine, could prevent effusion of blood; how could it be chosen but that when families were multiplied and increased upon earth, after separation, each providing for itself, envy, strife, contention, and violence must grow amongst them? For hath not Nature furnished man with wit and valour, and as it were with armour, which may be used as well unto extreme evil as good? Yea, were they not used by the rest of the world unto evil; unto the contrary only by Seth, Enoch, and those few the rest in that line? We all make complaint of the iniquity of our times; not unjustly, for the days are evil. But compare them with those times wherein there were no civil societies, with those times wherein there was as yet no manner of public regiment established, with those times wherein there were not above eight righteous persons living upon the face of the earth; and we have surely good cause to think that God hath blessed us exceedingly, and hath made us behold most happy days.

To take away all such mutual grievances, injuries, and wrongs, there was no way but only by growing unto composition and agreement amongst themselves; by ordaining some kind of government public, and by yielding themselves subject thereunto; that unto whom they granted authority to rule and govern, by them the peace, tranquility, and happy estate of the rest might be procured. Men always knew that when force and injury was offered, they might be defenders of themselves; they knew that howsoever men may seek their own commodity, yet if this were done with injury unto others, it was not to be suffered, but by all men and by all good means to be withstood; finally, they knew that no man might in reason take upon him to determine his own right, and according to his own determination proceed in maintenance thereof, inasmuch as every man is towards himself, and them whom he greatly affecteth, partial; and therefore that strifes and troubles would be endless, except they gave their common consent all to be ordered by some whom they should agree upon: without which consent, there were no reason that one man should take upon him to be lord or judge over another; because although there be according to the opinion of some very great and judicious men, a kind of natural right in the noble, wise, and virtuous, to govern them which are of servile disposition; nevertheless for manifestation of this their right, and men's more peacable contentment on both sides, the assent of them who are to be governed seemeth necessary.

To fathers within their private families Nature hath given a supreme power; for which cause we see throughout the world, even from the first foundation thereof, all men have ever been taken as lords and lawful kings in their own houses. Howbeit over a whole grand multitude having no such dependency upon any one, and consisting of so many families as every politic society in the world doth, impossible it is that any should have complete lawful power, but by consent of men, or immediate appointment of God; because not having the natural superiority of fathers, their power must needs be either usurped, and then unlawful; or if lawful, then either granted or consented unto by them over whom they exercise the same, or else given extraordinarily from God, unto whom all the world is subject. It is no improbable opinion therefore which the arch-philosopher was of, that as the chiefest person in every household was always as it were a king, so when numbers of households joined themselves in civil societies together, where kings were the first kind of governors amongst them. Which is also as it seemeth the reason, why the name of father continued still in them, who of fathers were made rulers: as also the ancient custom of governors to do as Melchisedec, and being kings, to exercise the office of priests, which fathers did at the first, grew perhaps by the same occasion. Howbeit not this the only kind of regiment that hath been received in the world. The inconveniences of one kind have caused sundry other to be devised. So that in a word all public regiment, of what kind soever, seemeth evidently to have risen from deliberate advice, consultation, and composition between men, judging it convenient and behoveful; there being no impossibility in Nature considered by itself, but that men might have lived without any public regiment. Howbeit the corruption of our nature being presupposed, we may not deny but that the law of Nature doth now acquire of necessity some kind of regiment; so that to bring things unto the first course they were in, and utterly to take away all kind of public government in the world, were apparently to overturn the whole world. The case of man's nature standing therefore as it doth, some kind of regiment the law of Nature doth require, yet the kinds thereof being many, Nature tieth not to any one, but leaveth the choice as a thing arbitrary.

...

Civil society doth more content the nature of man than any private kind of solitary living, because, in society, this good of mutual participation is so much larger than otherwise. Herewith notwithstanding we are not satisfied, but we covet (if it might be) to have a kind of society and fellowship even with all mankind. Which thing Socrates intending to signify, professes himself a citizen, not of this or that commonwealth, but of the world. And an effect of that very natural desire in us (a manifest token that we wish after a sort an universal fellowship with all men), appeareth by the wonderful delight men have, some to visit foreign countries, some to discover nations not heard of in former ages; we all to know the affairs and dealings of other people, yea, to be in league of amity with them: and this, not only for traffic's sake or to the end that when many are confederated each may make other the more strong, but for such cause also as moved the Queen of Sheba to visit Solomon, and, in a word, because Nature doth presume that how many men there are in the world, so many gods, as it were, there are, or at leastwise such they should be towards men. Touching laws which are to serve men in this behalf, even as those laws of reason, which (man retaining his original integrity) had been sufficient to direct each particular person in all his affairs and duties, are not sufficient but require the access of other laws, now that man and his offspring are grown thus corrupt and sinful; again, as those laws of polity and regiment which would have served men living in public society, together with that harmless disposition which then they should have had, are not able now to serve when men's iniquity is so hardly restrained within any tolerable bounds: in like manner the national laws of natural commerce between societies of that former and better quality might have been other than now, when nations are so prone to offer violence, injury, and wrong. Hereupon hath grown in every of these three kinds, that distinction between primary and secondary laws, the one grounded upon sincere, the other built upon depraved, nature.

* From Richard Hooker, *The Laws of Ecclesiastical Polity* (London: George Routledge and Sons, 1888 [1593–97]), 91–5; 100–101.

John Locke (1632–1704), English philosopher and critic of Thomas Hobbes. Locke, often seen as the founding father of liberal constitutional government, had himself experienced the power of the state: he was living in exile in Holland for several years until the Glorious Revolution of 1688 brought the reign of James II to an end. In this section from the Two Treatises on Civil Government, *he sets out the distinction between a state of nature – which included absolute monarchy – and civil society/political society formed by social contract.**

God, having made man such a creature that in his own judgment it was not good for him to be alone, put him under strong obligations of necessity, convenience, and inclination to drive him into society, as well as fitted him with understanding and language to continue and enjoy it. The first society was between man and wife, which gave beginning to that between parents and children; to which, in time, that between master and servant came to be added; and though all these might, and commonly did meet together, and make up but one family, wherein the master or mistress of it had some sort of rule proper to a family; each of these, or all together, came short of political society, as we shall see, if we consider the different ends, ties, and bounds of each of these.

. . .

But there is another sort of servants, which by a peculiar name we call slaves, who, being captives taken in a just war, are by the right of nature, subjected to the absolute dominion and arbitrary power of their masters. These men having, as I say, forfeited their lives, and with them their liberties, and lost their estates – and being in the state of slavery, not capable of any property – cannot in that state be considered as any part of civil society, the chief end whereof is the preservation of property.

. . .

Man being born, as has been proved, with a title to perfect freedom, and an uncontrolled enjoyment of all the rights and privileges of the law of nature equally with any other man or number of men in the world, hath by nature a power not only to preserve his property – that is, his life, liberty, and estate – against the injuries and attempts of other men, but to judge of and punish the breaches of that law in others as he is persuaded the offence deserves, even with death itself, in crimes where the heinousness of the fact in his opinion requires it. But because no political society can be nor subsist without having in itself the power to preserve the property, and in order thereunto, punish the offences of all those of that society, there, and there only, is political society, where everyone of the members hath quitted this natural power, resigned it up into the hands of the community in all cases that exclude him not from appealing for protection to the law established by it; and thus all private judgment of every particular member being excluded, the community comes to be umpire; and by understanding indifferent rules and men authorised by the community for their execution, decides all the differences that may happen between any members of that society concerning any matter of right, and punishes those offences which any member hath committed against the society with such penalties as the law has established; whereby it is easy to discern who are and are not in political society together. Those who are united into one body, and have a common established law and judicature to appeal to, with authority to decide controversies between them and punish offenders, are in civil society one with another; but those who have no such common appeal – I mean on earth – are still in the state of nature, each being, where there is no other, judge for himself and executioner, which is, as I have before shown it, the perfect state of nature.

And thus the commonwealth comes by a power to set down what punishment shall belong to the several transgressions they think worthy of it committed amongst the members of that society, which is the power of making laws, as well as it has the power to punish any injury done unto any of its members by anyone that is not of it, which is the power of war and peace; and all this for the preservation of the property of all the members of that society as far as is possible. But though every man who has entered into civil society, and is become a member of any commonwealth, has thereby quitted his power to punish offences against the law of nature in prosecution of his own private judgment, yet with the judgment of offences which he has given up to the magistrate, he has given a right to the commonwealth to employ his force for the execution of the judgments of the commonwealth whenever he shall be called to it; which, indeed, are his own judgments, they being made by himself or his representative. And herein we have the original of the legislative and executive power of civil society, which is to judge by standing laws how far offences are to be punished when committed within the commonwealth, and also to determine by occasional judgments founded on the present circumstances of the fact, how far injuries from without are to be vindicated; and in both these to employ all the force of all the members when there shall be need.

Wherever, therefore, any number of men so unite into one society, as to quit everyone his executive power of the law of nature, and to resign it to the public, there, and there only is a political, or civil society. And this is done wherever any number of men, in the state of nature, enter into society to make one people, one body politic, under one supreme government, or else when any one joins himself to, and incorporates with, any government already made. For hereby he authorises the society, or which is all one, the legislative thereof, to make laws for him, as the public good of the society shall require, to the execution whereof his own assistance (as to his own decrees) is due. And this puts men out of a state of nature into that of a commonwealth, by setting up a judge on earth with authority to determine all the controversies and redress the injuries that may happen to any member of the commonwealth; which judge is the legislative or magistrates appointed by it. And wherever there are any number of men, however associated, that have no such decisive power to appeal to, there they are still in the state of nature.

Hence it is evident that absolute monarchy, which by some men is counted for the only government in the world, is indeed inconsistent with civil society, and so can be no form of civil government at all. For the end of civil society being to avoid and remedy those inconveniencies of the state of nature which necessarily follow from every man's being judge in his own case, by setting up a known authority to which every one of that society may appeal upon any injury received, or controversy that may arise, and which every one of the society ought to obey; wherever any persons are who have not such an authority to appeal to and decide any difference between them there, those persons are still in the state of nature. And so is every absolute prince in respect of those who are under his dominion.

. . .

But, whatever flatterers may talk to amuse people's understandings, it never hinders men from feeling; and when they perceive that any man, in what station soever, is out of the bounds of the civil society they are of, and that they have no appeal on earth against any harm they may receive from him, they are apt to think themselves in the state of nature, in respect of him whom they find to be so; and to take care, as soon as they can, to have that safety and security in civil society for which it was first instituted, and for which only they entered into it. And therefore, though perhaps at first . . . some one good and excellent man having got a pre-eminence amongst the rest, had this deference paid to his goodness and virtue, as to a kind of natural authority, that the chief rule, with arbitration of their differences, by a tacit consent devolved into his hands, without any other caution but the assurance they had of his uprightness and wisdom; yet when time, giving authority, and (as some men would persuade us) sacredness to customs which the negligent and unforeseeing innocence of the first ages began, had brought in successors of another stamp, the people finding their properties not secure under the government as then it was (whereas government has no other end but the preservation of property), could never be safe, nor at rest, nor think themselves in civil society, till the legislature was so placed in collective bodies of men, call them Senate, Parliament, or what you please. By which means every single person became subject, equally with other the meanest men, to those laws, which he himself, as part of the legislative, had established; nor could any one, by his own authority, avoid the force of the law when once made, nor by any pretence of superiority plead exemption, thereby to license his own, or the miscarriages of any of his dependents. No man in civil society can be exempted from the laws of it. For if any man may do what he thinks fit, and there be no appeal on earth for redress or security against any harm he shall do, I ask whether he be not perfectly still in the state of nature, and so can be no part or member of that civil society; unless any one will say the state of nature and civil society are one and the same thing, which I have never yet found any one so great a patron of anarchy as to affirm.

* John Locke, *The Second Treatise of Civil Government, and a Letter Concerning Toleration*, J.W. Gough, ed. (Oxford: Basil Blackwell, 1946), 39; 42–5; 47–8. Locke most likely wrote the Second Treatise in 1679.

*Gottfried Wilhelm Leibniz (1646–1716), after a life in the service of German princes as diplomatic advisor, librarian and historian, he became the first president of the scientific academy in Berlin. He is especially known for his work on metaphysics and logic. Here he places civil society within a classification of natural society that follows Aristotle.**

Justice is a social duty [*Tugend*], or a duty which preserves society.

A society [*Gemeinschaft*] is a union of different men for a common purpose.

A natural society is one which is demanded by nature [*so die Natur haben will*]. The signs by which one can conclude that nature demands something, are that nature has given us a desire and the powers or force to fulfill it: for nature does nothing in vain.

Above all, when the matter involves a necessity or a permanent [*beständigen*] utility: for nature everywhere achieves the best.

The most perfect society is that whose purpose is the general and supreme happiness [*Glückseligkeit*].

Natural law is that which preserves or promotes natural societies.

The first natural society is between man and wife, for it is necessary to preserve the human race.

The second [is] between parents and children; it arises at once out of the former; for when children are once created, or freely adopted, they must be reared, that is, governed and nourished. In return they owe their parents obedience and help after they are raised. For [it] is in hope of such gratitude [that] such societies are preserved and promoted, though nature demands them primarily for the sake of children. For they may one day reach perfection. Parents, then, exist primarily for the sake of children, [and] the present, which does not last long, for the future.

The third natural society is between master and servant [*Herr und Knecht*], which is conformable to nature when a person lacks understanding but does not lack the strength to nourish himself. For such a person is a servant by nature who must work as another directs him, and [who] derives therefrom his livelihood; the rest is for the master. For everything that the servant is, he is on account of his master, since all other powers exist only for the sake of the understanding [*Verstand*]. In this case the understanding is in the master, but all other powers are in the servant. Since such a servant exists for the sake of the master, his master owes him only his maintenance, for his [the master's] sake, in order that he not ruin him.

...

[N]atural servitude takes place among unintelligent men, in so far as it is not restricted by the rules concerning the fear of God.

The fourth natural society is the household, which is composed of all the above-mentioned societies – some or all. Its purpose is [the satisfaction of] daily needs.

The fifth natural society is the civil [*bürgerliche*] society. If it is small, it is called a city; a province is a society of different cities, and a kingdom or a large dominion is a society of different provinces – all to attain happiness for to be secure in it – whose members sometimes live together in a city sometimes spread out over the land. Its purpose is temporal welfare.

The sixth natural society is the Church of God, which would probably have existed among men even without revelation [*Offenbarung*], and been preserved and spread by pious and holy men. Its purpose is eternal happiness. And it is no wonder that I call it a natural society, since there is a natural religion and a desire for immortality planted in us. This society of saints [*Heiligen*] is catholic or universal, and binds the whole human race together. If revelation is added, this bond is not torn, but strengthened.

Classification of societies or communities (*Divisio societatum*)

Every society is equal [*gleich*] or unequal. [It is] equal when one has as much power in it as another, unequal when one rules another.

Every society is either unlimited [*unbeschränkt*] or limited. An unlimited society concerns the whole life and the common good [*gemeine Beste*]. A limited society concerns certain subjects, for example trade and commerce, navigation, warfare and travel.

An unlimited equal society exists between true friends. And such [a society] exists particularly between man and wife, between parents and grown children, between masters and freedmen, and in general between all intelligent men who are adequately acquainted with each other.

An unlimited unequal society exists between rulers and subjects. Such rule happens for the sake either of improvement or of conservation. If it is for the sake of improvement, it really takes place between parents and children, and also between us and those whom we accept in place of children, or whom we raise so that they receive their welfare from us, and are under our sole rule. This has no place between teacher and student, since the latter is subject [to the former] only in a certain degree or way; here however, we are speaking of unlimited society which involves the whole of life and welfare. Stupid men are grown children. But if such rule [*Regierung*] is for the sake of conversation, it exists between master and servant and consists in this, that the master makes the servant's welfare secure, while the latter submits to the rule of the former.

All of these societies are simple or composite [*zusammengesetzt*], and also [exist] between a few or many men. Accordingly all unlimited or comprehensive societies [*Lebengesellschaften*] can be reduced to certain points, namely to education and instruction, rule and obedience, friendship or co-operation, *adjutorium*, etc.

Children, in so far as they have been reared, already owe obedience as far as their powers permit, [and] as they attain understanding, friendship and assistance to the master as well, although their education is not completed.

Man and wife are bound by nature to friendship and mutual assistance in a brotherly way. In the same way parents and children, and also relatives and members of a community must have an understanding of each other; for understanding belongs to friendship.

One can educate, who is himself being educated, and also rule, while he is being ruled. But there must be subordination in this case.

All unlimited societies do indeed aim at welfare, but they do not all attain it; hence more men have had to unite to create greater and stronger communities. Thus households, clans, villages, monasteries, orders, cities, provinces, and finally the whole human race, which also constitutes a community under the rule of God, [have united].

If everything in the world were arranged in the most perfect way, then, first of all, parents, children and relatives would be the best of friends, and whole families would have chosen an art of living, would have arranged everything that they have to this end, would abide in it and continue to perfect themselves in their art and direct their children to the same end, and would marry people of the same calling [*Beruf*] in order to be united through education from their parents. These clans would make up guilds or castes out of which cities would arise; these would enter into provinces and all countries, finally, would stand under the church of God.

* From Gottfried Wilhelm Leibniz, 'On Natural Law', in Patrick Riley, ed., *Leibniz: Political Writings* (Cambridge: Cambridge University Press, 1988, 2nd edn), 77–80. Reprinted with the permission of Cambridge University Press.

Toleration and its limits

David Hume (1711–76), a key member of the Scottish node of the European Enlightenment, was denied employment as an academic because of his atheism. 'Of Superstition and Enthusiasm' makes clear his general view that religion is opposed to the spirit of civility because it encourages fanaticism. But the argument is subtle: the enthusiasm of the sects may in the long run, by creating opposition, be less of a danger to society than the dull and unchallenged religion of the establishment.*

That *the corruption of the best of things produces the worst*, is grown into a maxim, and is commonly proved, among other instances, by the pernicious effects of *superstition* and *enthusiasm*, the corruptions of true religion.

. . .

My *first* reflection is, *that superstition is favourable to priestly power, and enthusiasm not less, or rather more contrary to it, than sound reason and philosophy*. As superstition is founded on fear, sorrow, and a depression of spirits, it represents the man to himself in such despicable colours, that he appears unworthy, in his own eyes, of approaching the Divine presence, and naturally has recourse to any other person, whose sanctity of life, or perhaps impudence and cunning, have made him be supposed more favoured by the Divinity. To him the superstitious intrust their devotions: to his care they recommend their prayers, petitions, and sacrifices: and by his means, they hope to render their addresses acceptable to their incensed Deity. Hence the origin of PRIESTS, who may justly be regarded as an invention of a timorous and abject superstition, which, ever diffident of itself, dares not offer up its own devotions, but ignorantly thinks to recommend itself to the Divinity, by the mediation of his supposed friends and servants. As superstition is a considerable ingredient in almost all religions, even the most fanatical; there being nothing but philosophy able entirely to conquer these unaccountable terrors; hence it proceeds, that in almost every sect of religion there are priests to be found: but the stronger mixture there is of superstition, the higher is the authority of the priesthood.

On the other hand, it may be observed, that all enthusiasts have been free from the yoke of ecclesiastics, and have expressed great independence in their devotion, with a contempt of forms, ceremonies and traditions. The *Quakers* are the most egregious, though, at the same time, the most innocent enthusiasts that have yet been known; and are perhaps the only sect that have never admitted priests among them. The *Independents*, of all the English sectaries, approach nearest to the *Quakers* in fanaticism, and in their freedom from priestly bondage. The *Presbyterians* follow after, at an equal distance, in both particulars. In short, this observation is founded in experience; and will also appear to be founded in reason, if we consider, that, as enthusiasm arises from a presumptuous pride and confidence, it thinks itself sufficiently qualified to approach the Divinity, without any human mediator. Its rapturous devotions are so fervent, that it even imagines itself *actually to approach* him by the way of contemplation and inward converse; which makes it neglect all those outward ceremonies and observances, to which the assistance of the priests appears so requisite in the eyes of their superstitious votaries. The fanatic consecrates himself, and bestows on his own person a sacred character, much superior to what forms and ceremonious institutions can confer on any other.

My *second* reflection with regard to these species of false religion is, *that religions which partake of enthusiasm, are, on their first rise, more furious and violent than those which partake of superstition; but in a little time become more gentle and moderate*. The violence of this species of religion, when excited by novelty, and animated by opposition, appears from numberless instances; of the *Anabaptists* in Germany, the *Camisars* in France, the *Levellers*, and other fanatics in England, and the *Covenanters* in Scotland. Enthusiasm being founded on strong spirits, and a presumptuous boldness of character, it naturally begets the most extreme resolutions; especially after it rises to that height as to inspire the deluded fanatic with the opinion of Divine illuminations, and with a contempt for the common rules of reason, morality, and prudence.

It is thus enthusiasm produces the most cruel disorders in human society; but its fury is like that of thunder and tempest, which exhaust themselves in a little time, and leave the air more calm and serene than before. When the first fire of enthusiasm is spent, men naturally, in all fanatical sects, sink into the greatest remissness and coolness in sacred matters; there being no body of men among them endowed with sufficient authority, whose interest is concerned to support the religious spirit; no rites, no ceremonies, no holy observances, which may enter into the common train of life, and preserve the sacred principles from oblivion. Superstition, on the contrary, steals in gradually and insensibly; renders men tame and submissive; is acceptable to the magistrate, and seems inoffensive to the people: till at last the priest, having firmly established his authority, becomes the tyrant and disturber of human society, by his endless contentions, persecutions, and religious wars. How smoothly did the Romish church advance in her acquisition of power! But into what dismal convulsions did she throw all Europe, in order to maintain it! On the other hand, our sectaries, who were formerly such dangerous bigots, are now become very free reasoners; and the *Quakers* seem to approach nearly the only regular body of *Deists* in the universe, the *literati*, or the disciples of Confucius in China.

My *third* observation on this head is, *that superstition is an enemy to civil liberty, and enthusiasm a friend to it*. As superstition groans under the dominion of priests, and enthusiasm is destructive of all ecclesiastical power, this sufficiently accounts for the present observation. Not to mention that enthusiasm, being the infirmity of bold and ambitious tempers, is naturally accompanied with a spirit of liberty; as superstition, on the contrary, renders men tame and abject, and fits them for slavery. We learn from English history, that, during the civil wars, the *Independents* and *Deists*, though the most opposite in their religious principles, yet were united in their political ones, and were alike passionate for a commonwealth. And since the origin of *Whig* and *Tory*, the leaders of the *Whigs* have either been *Deists* or professed *Latitudinarians* in their principles; that is, friends to toleration, and indifferent to any particular sect of *Christians*: while the sectaries, who have all a strong tincture of enthusiasm, have always, without exception, concurred with that party in defence of civil liberty. The resemblance in their superstitions long united the High-Church *Tories* and the *Roman Catholics*, in support of prerogative and kingly power; though experience of the tolerating spirit of the *Whigs* seems of late to have reconciled the *Catholics* to that party.

The *Molinists* and *Jansenists* in France have a thousand unintelligible disputes, which are not worthy the reflection of a man of sense: but what principally distinguishes these two sects, and alone merits attention, is the different spirit of their religion. The *Molinists*, conducted by the *Jesuits*, are great friends to superstition, rigid observer of external forms and ceremonies, and devoted to the authority of the priests, and to tradition. The *Jansenists* are enthusiasts, and zealous promoters of the passionate devotion, and of the inward life; little influenced by authority; and, in a word, but half Catholics. The consequences are exactly conformable to the foregoing reasoning. The *Jesuits* are the tyrants of the people, and the slaves of the court: and the *Jansenists* preserve alive the small sparks of the love of liberty which are to be found in the French nation.

* From David Hume, 'Of Superstition and Enthusiasm', in his *Essays, Moral, Political and Literary* (London: H. Frowde, 1904 [1741]), 75–80.

Adam Smith (1723–90), close friend of David Hume and equally important member of the Scottish Enlightenment, was at once moral philosopher, political theorist and economist – and variously employed as academic, tutor and tax collector. Here he disagrees with Hume as to the best way to contain the threat that religion poses to civil society, stressing particularly the way in which market competition between enthusiastic sects will ensure that none can dominate.

The interested and active zeal of religious teachers can be dangerous and troublesome only where there is either but one sect tolerated in the society, or where the whole of a large society is divided into two or three great sects; the teachers of each acting by concert, and under a regular discipline and subordination. But that zeal must be altogether innocent where the society is divided into two or three hundred, or perhaps into as many thousand small sects, of which no one could be considerable enough to disturb the public tranquility. The teachers of each sect, seeing themselves surrounded on all sides with more adversaries than friends, would be obliged to learn that candour and moderation which is so seldom to be found among the teachers of those great sects whose tenets, being supported by the civil magistrate, are held in veneration by almost all the inhabitants of extensive kingdoms and empires, and who therefore see nothing round them but followers, disciples, and humble admirers. The teachers of each little sect, finding themselves almost alone, would be obliged to respect those of almost every other sect, and the concessions which they would mutually find it both convenient and agreeable to make to one another, might in time probably reduce the doctrine of the greater part of them to that pure and rational religion, free from every mixture of absurdity, imposture, or fanaticism, such as wise men have in all ages of the world wished to see established; but such as positive law has perhaps never yet established, and probably never will establish, in any country: because, with regard to religion, positive law always has been, and probably always will be, more or less influenced by popular superstition and enthusiasm. This plan of ecclesiastical government, or more properly of no ecclesiastical government, was what the sect called Independents, a sect no doubt of very wild enthusiasts, proposed to establish in England towards the end of the civil war. If it had been established, though of a very unphilosophical origin, it would probably by this time have been productive of the most philosophical good temper and moderation with regard to every sort of religious principle. It has been established in Pennsylvania, where, though the Quakers happen to be the most numerous, the law in reality favours no one sect more than another, and it is there said to have been productive of this philosophical good temper and moderation.

But though this equality of treatment should not be productive of this good temper and moderation in all, or even in the greater part of the religious sects of a particular country, yet provided those sects were sufficiently numerous, and each of them consequently too small to disturb the public tranquility, the excessive zeal of each for its particular tenets could not well be productive of any very harmful effects, but, on the contrary, of several good ones: and if the government was perfectly decided both to let them all alone, and to oblige them all to let alone one another, there is little danger that they would not of their own accord subdivide themselves fast enough so as soon to become sufficiently numerous.

In every civilised society, in every society where the distinction of ranks has once been completely established, there have been always two different schemes or systems of morality current at the same time; of which the one may be called the strict or austere; the other the liberal, or, if you will, the loose system. The former is generally admired and revered by the common people: the latter is commonly more esteemed and adopted by what are called people of fashion. The degree of disapprobation with which we ought to mark the vices of levity, the vices which are apt to arise from great prosperity, and from the excess of gaiety and good humour, seems to constitute the principal distinction between those two opposite schemes or systems. In the liberal or loose system, luxury, wanton and even disorderly mirth, the pursuit of pleasure to some degree of intemperance, the breach of chastity, at least in one of the two sexes, etc., provided they are not accompanied with gross indecency, and do not lead to falsehood or injustice, are generally treated with a good deal of indulgence, and are easily either excused or pardoned altogether. In the austere system, on the contrary, those excesses are regarded with the utmost abhorrence, and detestation. The vices of levity are always ruinous to the common people, and a single week's thoughtlessness and dissipation is often sufficient to undo a poor workman for ever, and to drive him through despair upon committing the most enormous crimes. The wiser and better sort of the common people, therefore, have always the utmost abhorrence and detestation of such excesses, which their experience tells them are so immediately fatal to people of their condition. The disorder and extravagance of several years, on the contrary, will not always ruin a man of fashion, and people of that rank are very apt to consider the power of indulging in some degree of excess as one of the advantages of their fortune, and the liberty of doing so without censure or reproach as one of the privileges which belong to their station. In people of their own station, therefore, they regard such excesses with but a small degree of disapprobation, and censure them either very slightly or not at all.

Almost all religious sects have begun among the common people, from whom they have generally drawn their earliest as well as their most numerous proselytes. The austere system of morality has, accordingly, been adopted by these sects almost constantly, or with very few exceptions; for there have been some. It was the system by which they could best recommend themselves to that order of people to whom they first proposed their plan of reformation upon what had been before established. Many of them, perhaps the greater part of them, have even endeavoured to gain credit by refining upon this austere system, and by carrying it to some degree of folly and extravagance; and this excessive rigour has frequently recommended them more than anything else to the respect and veneration of the common people.

A man of rank and fortune is by his station the distinguished member of a great society, who attend to every part of his conduct, and who thereby oblige him to attend to every part of it himself. His authority and consideration depend very much upon the respect which this society bears to him. He dare not do anything which would disgrace or discredit him in it, and he is obliged to a very strict observation of that species of morals, whether liberal or austere, which the general consent of this society prescribes to persons of his rank and fortune. A man of low condition, on the contrary, is far from being a distinguished member of any great society. While he remains in a country village his conduct may be attended to, and he may be obliged to attend to it himself. In this situation, and in this situation only, he may have what is called a character to lose. But as soon as he comes into a great city he is sunk in obscurity and darkness. His conduct is observed and attended by nobody, and he is therefore very likely to neglect it himself, and to abandon himself to every sort of low profligacy and vice. He never emerges so effectually from this obscurity, his conduct never excites so much the attention of any respectable society, as by his becoming the member of a small religious sect. He from that moment acquires a degree of consideration which he never had before. All his brother sectaries are, for the credit of the sect, interested to observe his conduct, and if he gives occasion to any scandal, if he deviates very much from those austere morals which they almost always require of one another, to punish him by what is always a very severe punishment, even where no civil effects attend it, expulsion or excommunication from the sect. In little religious sects, accordingly, the morals of the common people have been almost always remarkably regular and orderly; generally much more so than in the established church. The morals of those little sects, indeed, have frequently been rather disagreeably rigorous and unsocial.

There are two very easy and effectual remedies, however, by whose joint operation the state might, without violence, correct whatever was unsocial or disagreeably rigorous in the morals of all the little sects into which the country was divided.

The first of those remedies is the study of science and philosophy, which the state might render almost universal among all people of middling or more than middling rank and fortune; not by giving salaries to teachers in order to make them negligent and idle, but by instituting some sort of probation, even in the higher and more difficult sciences, to be undergone by every person before he was permitted to exercise any liberal profession, or before he could be received as a candidate for any honourable office of trust or profit. If the state imposed upon this order of men the necessity of learning, it would have no occasion to give itself any trouble about providing them with proper teachers. They would soon find better teachers for themselves than any whom the state could provide for them. Science is the great antidote to the poison of enthusiasm and superstition; and where all the superior ranks of people were secured from it, the inferior ranks could not be much exposed to it.

The second of those remedies is the frequency and gaiety of public diversions. The state, by encouraging, that is by giving entire liberty to all those who for their own interest would attempt, without scandal or indecency, to amuse and divert the people by painting, poetry, music, dancing; by all sorts of dramatic representations and exhibitions, would easily dissipate, in the greater part of them, that melancholy and gloomy humour which is almost always the nurse of popular superstition and enthusiasm. Public diversions have always been the objects of dread and hatred to all the fanatical promoters of those popular frenzies. The gaiety and good humour which those diversions inspire were altogether inconsistent with that temper of mind which was fittest for their purpose, or which they could best work upon. Dramatic representations, besides, frequently exposing their artifices to public ridicule, and sometimes even to public execration, were upon that account, more than all other diversions, the objects of their peculiar abhorrence.

In a country where the law favoured the teachers of no one religion more than those of another, it would not be necessary that any of them should have any particular or immediate dependency upon the sovereign or executive power; or that he should have anything to do either in appointing or in dismissing them from their offices. In such a situation he would have no occasion to give himself any concern about them, further than to keep the peace among them in the same manner as among the rest of his subjects; that is, to hinder them from persecuting, abusing, or oppressing one another. But it is quite otherwise in countries where there is an established or governing religion. The sovereign can in this case never be secure unless he has the means of influencing in a considerable degree the greater part of the teachers of that religion.

* From Adam Smith, 'Of the Expense of the Institutions for the Instruction of People of All Ages' in *An Inquiry Into the Nature and Causes of the Wealth of Nations*, in W. Benton, ed., *Encyclopedia Britannica: Great Books of the Western World*, Vol. 39 (Chicago: Chicago University Press, 1952 [1776]), 345–8.

*Gotthold Lessing (1729–81), German philosopher and writer, enlightenment thinker and freemason. Lessing here uses a dialogue to reveal the true nature of freemasonry as a way of creating a cosmopolitan humanity – and to criticize a cult of mysticism and rituals. Falk has joined a Masonic society and explains to his critical friend Ernst the meaning of freemasonry, and the place of states, as human products, next to a cosmopolitan network of humanity and tolerance.**

Ernst.   You have been initiated; you know all –

Falk.   Others have likewise been initiated and profess to know.

Ernst.   Is it, then, possible to be initiated without knowing what you know?

Falk.   Unfortunately!

Ernst.   How can that be?

Falk.   Because many who perform the ceremony of initiation, do not themselves know it. The few, however, who do know, cannot tell it.

Ernst.   And is it possible to know what you know, without being initiated?

Falk. Why not? Freemasonry is nothing arbitrary, nothing superfluous. Rather is it something necessary, which is grounded in the nature of man and of civil society [*bürgerliche Gesellschaft*]. Consequently one must also be able to chance to think of it just as well through his own meditation as be guided to it by instruction.

Ernst. Freemasonry is nothing arbitrary? Has it not words and signs and rites which could be taken for something different; and therefore they are arbitrary?

Falk. It has these things; but these words and signs and rites are not Freemasonry.

Ernst. Freemasonry is nothing superfluous? How, then, did people manage before Freemasonry came into existence?

Falk. Freemasonry existed always.

. . .

Falk. We assume, accordingly, the ideal political constitution [*Staatsverfassung*] to have been devised; we assume that all people in the world are living under this ideal constitution; would all people in the world form, on that account, only one State?

Ernst. Hardly. So immense a State would be incapable of administration. It would therefore have to be split up into several small States, all of which would be subject to the same laws.

Falk. That is to say: people would even then be still Germans and Frenchmen, Dutchmen and Spaniards, Russians or Swedes, or whatever else they were called.

Ernst. Most certainly.

Falk. Then we have already got one defect. For is it not true that each of these small States would have its own interests, and each of its members the interests of his particular State?

Ernst. How could it be otherwise?

Falk. These different interests would frequently come into conflict, as at present; and two members from two different States would be able to meet one another with just as little impartial feeling as a German meets a Frenchman or a Frenchman an Englishman, at the present time.

Ernst. Very probably.

Falk. That is to say, if a German meets a Frenchman at present, or a Frenchman an Englishman, or *vice versa*, then it is no longer a mere man meeting a mere man [*Mensch*], who by virtue of their identical nature will be attracted one to the other; but a particular kind of man who are conscious of their different tendency, which makes them cold, reserved, suspicious of each other, even before they have the slightest dealings with one another for their individual selves.

Ernst.   That is unhappily true.

Falk.   Then it must likewise be true that the means which unify people, for the purpose of ensuring their happiness through this unification, at the same time divide people.

Ernst.   If you understand it so.

Falk.   Go a step farther. Many of the small States would have an altogether different climate; consequently altogether different needs and enjoyments; consequently altogether different customs and manners; consequently altogether different ethics; consequently altogether different religions. Do you not agree?

Ernst.   That is a tremendous step.

Falk.   People would likewise still be Jews and Christians and Mohammedans, and so on.

Ernst.   I dare not deny it.

Falk.   If they were so, they would also . . . conduct themselves towards one another in no different way from that in which our Christians and Jews and Mohammedans have at all times conducted themselves – not as mere men towards mere men, but as particular men towards particular men who contend with one another, about a certain spiritual superiority, and establish rights thereupon which could by no means occur to the natural man.

Ernst.   That is very sad, but still, unfortunately, very probable.

Falk.   Only probable?

Ernst.   At any rate, I should imagine, as you have assumed all States to have a uniform constitution, that they all could possibly have a uniform religion. Yes, I cannot conceive how a uniform political constitution is at all possible without a uniform religion.

Falk.   And I just as little. I only made that assumption to cut off your road of retreat. One is certainly just as impossible as the other. One State, several States. Several States, several political constitutions. Several political constitutions, several religions.

Ernst.   Yes, yes. It appears to be so.

Falk.   It is so. Now consider the second evil which the civil society [*bürgerliche Gesellschaft*] creates, quite contrary to its purpose. It cannot unite men without parting them; it cannot part them without establishing gulfs among them, without drawing partition-walls through them.

Ernst.   And how terrible those gulfs! How insurmountable these partition-walls often are!

Falk.   Let me also add a third point. It is not enough that civil society [*bürgerliche Gesellschaft*] divides and separates men into different peoples and religions. This division into a few large sections, each of which becomes a whole for itself, would always still be better than no whole at all. No, civil society [*bürgerliche Gesellschaft*] continues its division even in each of these sections almost to infinity.

Ernst.   How is that?

Falk.   Or is it your opinion that a State can be thought of without difference of ranks [*Ständen*]? It may be good or bad; it may approach perfection more or less; but it is impossible for all its members to have the same relation to each other. Even if all have a share in the legislature, yet they cannot all have the same share – at least, not the same direct share. There will consequently be members of superior and inferior rank. Even if, to start with, all the possessions of the State have been equally divided between them, this equal division cannot last for two generations. One will know how to use his property to better advantage than another. One will have to divide his worse-used property in the same way as the other among a larger lumber of successors. There will, as a consequence, be richer and poorer members.

Ernst.   Obviously.

Falk.   Reflect, now, how much evil there may be in the world which has not its origin in this variety of ranks [*Ständen*].

. . .

Falk.   Very much to be wished that there may be in every State men whom social eminence does not dazzle nor social insignificance disgust, in whose society the eminent man is readily condescending and the insignificant person boldly asserts himself.

Ernst.   Very much to be wished!

Falk.   And should this wish be realized?

Ernst.   Realized? There will certainly be such men here and there, now and then.

Falk.   Not merely here and there; not merely now and then.

Ernst.   At certain times, in certain countries, there would also be several.

Falk.   What if there were men of this sort everywhere, and must further be for all time?

Ernst.   God will it!

Falk.   And what if these men lived, not in an ineffective separateness, not always in an invisible Church?

Ernst.   A beautiful dream!

Falk.   To come to the point. And what if these men were the Freemasons?

Ernst. What do you say?

Falk. How, if it were the Freemasons who have made it part of their business to draw together as narrow as possible those divisions through which men become so strange to each other?

...

Ernst. That equality which you declared to me to be a fundamental law of the Order; that equality which filled my whole soul with such unexpected hope – to be able to breathe it at last in a society of people [*Gesellschaft von Menschen*] who understand how to think beyond all civic modifications, without sinning against anyone to the disadvantage of a third.

Falk. Well?

Ernst. It should still exist, if it ever did exist! Let an enlightened Jew come and announce himself! 'Yes,' it will be said, 'a Jew? The Freemason must at least be a Christian.' It does not matter very much what sort of a Christian. Without distinction of religion only means without distinction of the three religions, openly tolerated in the Holy Roman Empire. Are you of the same opinion?

Falk. Certainly not.

Ernst. Let an honest cobbler, who has enough leisure at his last to have many good thoughts [be it even a Jacob Boehme or Hans Sachs] – let him come and announce himself! 'Yes,' it will be said, 'A cobbler! indeed, a cobbler!' Let a faithful, experienced, tried domestic servant come and announce himself! 'Yes,' it will be said, 'such people indeed, who do not choose the colour of their coat for themselves. We are such good society among ourselves!'

...

Falk. ...From the point of its nature, Freemasonry is as old as civil society [*bürgerliche Gesellschaft*]. Neither could originate apart from each other. If civil society be not indeed merely an offshoot of Freemasonry. For the flame in the focus is also an efflux of the sun.

Ernst. I also have a notion of that.

Falk. It may be mother and daughter, or sister and sister; their mutual fate has always worked reciprocally one upon the other. Whatever was the condition of the civic community, so also was Freemasonry in all places, and *vice versa*. It was always the surest indication of a healthy, vigorous political constitution [*Staatsverfassung*] if it allowed Freemasonry to flourish by its side; just as it is still the infallible characteristic of a weak, timorous State if it will not openly tolerate what it must tolerate in secret, whether it will or no.

Ernst. You mean: Freemasonry!

Falk.   Surely! For it rests fundamentally not upon external bonds which deteriorate so easily into civic regulations, but upon the common feeling of sympathetic spirits.

Ernst.   And who is bold enough to rule it?

Falk.   Yet indeed, Freemasonry has always and everywhere been obliged to adapt itself and bend in accord with civil society, since the latter was always the stronger. Diversified as civil society was, Freemasonry also could not avoid adopting as many varied forms, and each new form had naturally its new name. How can you believe that the name Freemasonry can be older than that ruling way of thinking of the State, according to which it had been exactly modelled?

* Based on *Lessing's Masonic Dialgoues* (Ernst and Falk), translated and edited by A. Cohen (London: Baskerville Press, 1927 [1776–78]), 26–7; 45–9; 52–3; 77–8; 97–8, with some changes by the present editors to better reflect the German original.

The Rev. Thomas B. Clarke came to England about 1784, then pursued statistical and diplomatic studies in Göttingen (Germany), before returning to England to become a fervent critic of the French Revolution. The rev. doctor was secretary to the library of the Prince of Wales and he also planned the Naval Asylum for the orphans and children of seamen and marines, which he served as auditor – an office that cost him dearly for it led to him being deprived of sizeable other income: benefices worth £1,200 per year, because of non-residence. Clarke's sermon selected here was a typical voice in the official repudiation of revolutionary principles, stressing the centrality of organized, established religion to British society, and principles of social trust and obedience.*

A Sermon
XXVII Psalm, 36 37 verses.

> 'I MYSELF HAVE SEEN THE UNGODLY IN GREAT
> POWER AND FLOURISHING LIKE A GREEN BAY-TREE
> I WENT BY, AND LO HE WAS GONE, I SOUGHT HIM
> BUT HIS PLACE COULD NO WHERE BE FOUND.'

How lively! But how awful is this representation, which pleads to us with all the energy of example. It is the portrait of man fallen through impiety. We look farther, and behold, it is the picture of Nations, we discover the decline of religion followed by the dissolution of States. Yet what avails this sacred record of truth to day? who hearkens to this warning voice, though confirmed by what profane history proclaims from the Creation to this moment – that the civil and, religious existence of Nations is inseparable, that, the stroke which shocks the one pervades the other: sap Religion and you sap the State.

In this age and country, it may perhaps be said, immorality grows up with *civilized* luxury at home, or is introduced by polished depravity from abroad. Be it admitted. Nay, be it further admitted, that were this or any other Nation, even more dreaded, and as much endangered by immoral grossness, as it is by corrupt refinement: there is, however, a rampart to check, and a power to repel the incursions of vice. There is, thank God, a system that gives new force to old virtues; it is the pure and simple precepts of Christianity.

But if the disciples of philosophy in those Empires, that have fallen, far surpassed the professors of Christianity, in those which exist, we have indeed reason to be alarmed: it is high time to rise up, to watch and pray to the Great Ruler of events against a similitude of fate. Neither will the God of mercy be deaf to our prayers, nor dull to our exertions. Let us be ardent, be instant, for the stake is momentous. It is our *civil* and *religious* welfare; our temporal and eternal interests; it is our happiness here and hereafter.

Menaced as these are, let us adopt in pursuit of moral remedies, the sound practice in physical complaints; let us follow the disorders to their source, and there combat for the cure . . .

Let them [the philosophers], but for one moment, consider incredulity in the Supreme Being as universal. Let them consider but a single State, where there was neither Sovereign Power nor Ruler, and what must be its condition? In full impunity every man would be master to undertake for his interests whatever he preferred. But as the interests of one person rarely accord with the interests of another, what must ensue from hence? Wars perpetual, dissentions eternal, robbery universal. Every man must have his arms always in his hands for the defence of his property and his life: private quarrels would be revenged by murder, confusion must become general, and the overthrow total. I draw the picture – but of a single State, whereas this impious man would extend it, and furnish the Universe as the original when he combats the existence of a God. Are not these effects sufficient then to rouse us against the cause? the [sic] sham Philosophy of the day. Should they not attach us with tenfold force to the system of christianity? If once the altar be undermined, the Throne and the Nation must be swallowed in the abyss: 'and their place be no where found.' Who is there then that feels a spark of love for God and his country, that will not reject with horror this dangerous and pretended Philosophy. But we shall convince you further, while we shew as our SECOND point, that the very relation between the old and this new Philosophy exists in corruption.

The professors of both agree in the necessity of having some Gods. But then they are Gods of their own fashion. The Romans of old, through insupportable pride, instead of submitting themselves to their Gods, erected themselves into their judges and censors. They deliberated, in full senate, if they should admit such a God into their Capitol or not. Were it agreeable to the judges, he passed to the number of the Gods, but if the juridical approbation failed, he was rejected. So that if these pretended Gods did not please those men, those men decided that they were no longer Gods. What then must be the case with these men professing the impious principles of the new Philosophy? will [sic] they decide for the God of Christianity or those Gods of the Pagans?

The God of Christianity they have alas rejected! Therefore man has every thing to fear from them; for the God formed by their caprice, is one whom they need not either love or dread: and surely he who despises his sacred duties towards the divinity, will not regard his social ones towards man. Such too was the principle of ancient Paganism. Its disciples disarmed all severity by forming their divinity into the God of passions and of crimes: whose commission therefore, instead of shame secured honor. Infamy, incest, and every shameful disorder was authorised by divine example. But the God of Christianity is holy and pure by the necessity of his being, and is incapable, through all the artifice and torture of speculation, to be accommodated with the sensuality of passion or inclinations of crime.

Hence it is that the Libertine knowing him to be such, and despairing of being able to change him, disavows him for his God. And if he does not give into the idolatrous errors of Paganism, he abandons himself to irreligion, erasing from his mind every idea of the divinity, under the pretence, forsooth, of Philosophy. But whether he be Atheist, or whether he be idolatrous, he is indeed to be lamented; – and that he is to be *feared* also, I shall further prove, which leads me to my THIRD point.

When we consider the effects of Christianity and Philosophy upon States, the superiority of Christianity beams forth like the Sun in pure and transcendent lustre above a dusky cloud. This pre-eminence is visible in two indisputable remarks upon these different systems. The first is, that those philosophers were unable to support either themselves, or the states which protected them. Nor can this seem surprising from the picture, which we have placed before you. The next is, that the Christian Religion, on the contrary, by its purity and force triumphed over persecution, prospered without protection, and raised States and Society to an elevation unknown before. To substantiate those truths, it is not necessary to have recourse for proofs to the dark and distant ages: they are furnished by the unequivocal testimony of more modern times. Greece perished, when its Philosophy was at the highest. Rome fell when its doctrines and its schools were most flourishing. And France, that prospered beneath Christianity, decayed as its Philosophy gained ground.

If we examine the elevation of States, of individuals, or if we consider their downfal [sic], we shall find that there is no foundation so sure for the one, no precaution so sure against the other, as the simple principle of virtue. That system therefore, which teaches this principle most fully, must be the best. In respect to man individually this argument cannot be denied, socially too it must be admitted: for if no Government be bad, when well administered, and no Government be good if ill administered, and if no Government can be well administered where immorality prevails, – consequently – secure the moral [sic] and you secure the civil happiness of Nations. But then what system is the best to secure the moral happiness of men? It is that which teaches the simple principle of virtue most purely and most fully. And that system is proved by its effects, to be Christianity: which as far transcends philosophy as Heaven doth Earth. Where can civil Legislation derive principles more sublime? Or whence can religion draw precepts more pure? These States, and those religions, that have not known, or that have deviated from this basis of Divine wisdom, have all tottered into annihilation. Whatever is human is perishable, that which is divine is immortal, philosophy is the morality of man, Christianity is the religion of God.

But as to the mock philosophy of modern men what is it? Speculative corruption and daring immorality! It is a traiterous sanction for vice, which seeks the introduction of licentious principles under the dignified cloak of an high founding name. Lamentable indeed is the case of those, who ought to have been the conductors and instructors of mankind! but fearing the immoral authors of those doctrines men of letters and libertinism, and who, hoping to conciliate or avert their penetration upon other points, did not dare to oppose, but protected their opinions. What a lesson for us! Hence Christianity fell. Hence the Septre has been shaken from the hands of Royalty: hence powers and possessions have been dissipated: hence the crimes of the Nation are written in the blood of thousands, and upon the tombs of Royal victims. Alas! and are we to have a repetition of those crimes? Are we to set at nought the blessings and the curses of Heaven? Are we to diffuse those doctrines over earth in the blood of millions of fellow creatures, friends, parents, brothers and children? Oh! the foul startles at the thought, and rising with all the energy of virtue, rouses every faculty of man to duty. It prompts the wise and the good to oppose with the power of reason, and all the purity of religion, the vicious precepts of a corrupt philosophy: it warns the superior classes of society, in particular, to instruct the people by the influence of example. The mode to correct them is to correct themselves. The voice of religion calls upon us, the salvation of the State cries aloud, love your God and you love yourselves. Search the records of history from the formation of the first to the downfal of the last State, and what do all the volumes of their united wisdom unfold? Hear it in the affecting lamentations of past ages, see it in the unparralled horrors of the living time, oh feel it, feel it for yourselves and your surrounding little ones, it is that, *relaxation in the morals of a Nation, how polished soever by refinement, or aggravated by grossness, must, if not checked, terminate in civil ruin*: 'though flourishing to day, lo! To morrow, and it shall be gone'. Would you then, exemplify this? Ah! never may it be viewed in Britain! consider what are all these sublime monuments of

Grecian splendor, there piles of Roman grandeur, now mouldering into dust.: what are those feats of French magnificence and power, all overturned: they are the melancholy ruins of National depravity, the pictures of fallen manners, [sic]

We, thank God! are not however abandoned wholly to despair: if we pass from those melancholy scenes of corruption abroad and turn our view toward home, there is something consolatory for the mind, some prop for hope to rest upon: there is perhaps, if it pleases the great and All-merciful creator, some security for us, that HE, whom providence was graciously pleased to save of late for his manfold virtues, may tend to save us by the influence of his good example.

* Rev. Dr. Thomas B. Clarke, *The Benefits of Christianity Contrasted with the Pernicious Influence of Modern Philosophy upon Civil Society, Being a Sermon on a Day of Thanksgiving for the Providential Escape of His Majesty from the Late Atrocious Outrage upon His Sacred Person* (London, 1796), pp. 5f., 14–20.

Civility, sociability, associational life

Joseph Addison (1672–1719), English poet and statesman. In Parliament from 1708 until his death, Addison also contributed to the Tatler *and the* Spectator, *a new genre of journals in which essayists explored the regime of taste and civility and sought to engage readers' habits and steer them towards greater politeness, moderation, and harmony. Here he discusses the qualities of 'good-nature'.**

> Sic vita erat: facile omnes perferre ac pati:
> Cum quibus erat cunque una, his sese dedere,
> Eorum obsequi studiis: advorsus nemini;
> Nunquam praeponens se aliis: Ita facillime
> Sine invidia invenias laudem. — Ter. And.
> Ter. Andr. Act i, Sc. I.

His manner of life was this: to bear with everybody's humours: to comply with the inclinations and pursuits of those he convers'd with; to contradict nobody; never to assume authority over others. This is the ready way to gain applause without exciting envy.

Man is subject to innumerable Pains and Sorrows by the very Condition of Humanity, and yet, as if Nature had not sown Evils enough in Life, we are continually adding Grief to Grief, and aggravating the common Calamity by our cruel Treatment of one another. Every Man's natural Weight of Afflictions is still made more heavy by the Envy, Malice, Treachery, or Injustice of his Neighbour. At the same time that the Storm beats upon the whole Species, we are falling foul upon one another.

Half the Misery of Human Life might be extinguished, would Men alleviate the general Curse they lie under, by mutual Offices of Compassion, Benevolence, and Humanity. There is nothing therefore, which we ought more to encourage in our selves and others, than that Disposition of Mind which in our Language goes under the Title of Good-nature, and which I shall chuse for the Subject of this Day's Speculation.

Good-nature is more agreeable in Conversation than Wit, and gives a certain Air to the Countenance which is more amiable than Beauty. It shows Virtue in the fairest Light, takes off in some measure from the Deformity of Vice, and makes even Folly and Impertinence supportable.

There is no Society or Conversation to be kept up in the World without Good-nature, or something which must bear its Appearance, and supply its Place. For this Reason Mankind have been forced to invent a kind of Artificial Humanity, which is what we express by the Word *Good-Breeding*. For if we examine thoroughly the Idea of what we call so, we shall find it to be nothing else but an Imitation and Mimickry of Good-nature, or in other Terms, Affability, Complaisance and Easiness of Temper reduced into an Art.

These exterior Shows and Appearances of Humanity render a Man wonderfully popular and beloved when they are founded upon a real Good-nature; but without it are like Hypocrisy in Religion, or a bare Form of Holiness, which, when it is discovered, makes a Man more detestable than professed Impiety.

Good-nature is generally born with us: Health, Prosperity and kind Treatment from the World are great Cherishers of it where they find it; but nothing is capable of forcing it up, where it does not grow of it self. It is one of the Blessings of a happy Constitution, which Education may improve but not produce.

Xenophon in the Life of his Imaginary Prince, whom he describes as a Pattern for Real ones, is always celebrating the *Philanthropy* or Good-nature of his Hero, which he tells us he brought into the World with him, and gives many remarkable Instances of it in his Childhood, as well as in all the several Parts of his Life. Nay, on his Death-bed, he describes him as being pleased, that while his Soul returned to him made it, his Body should incorporate with the great Mother of all things, and by that means become beneficial to Mankind. For which Reason, he gives his Sons a positive Order not to enshrine it in Gold or Silver, but to lay it in the Earth as soon as the Life was gone out of it.

An Instance of such an Overflowing of Humanity, such an exuberant Love to Mankind, could not have entered into the Imagination of a Writer, who had not a Soul filled with great Ideas, and a general Benevolence to Mankind.

In that celebrated Passage of *Salust*, where *Caesar* and *Cato* are placed in such beautiful, but opposite Lights; *Caesar's* Character is chiefly made up of Good-nature, as it shewed it self in all its Forms towards his Friends or his Enemies, his Servants or Dependants, the Guilty or the Distressed. As for *Cato's* Character, it is rather awful than amiable. Justice seems most agreeable to the Nature of God, and Mercy to that of Man. A Being who has nothing to Pardon in himself, may reward every Man according to his Works; but he whose very best Actions must be seen with Grains of Allowance, cannot be too mild, moderate, and forgiving. For this reason, among all the monstrous Characters in Human Nature, there is none so odious, nor indeed so exquisitely Ridiculous, as that of a rigid severe Temper in a Worthless Man.

This Part of Good-nature, however, which consists in the pardoning and overlooking of Faults, is to be exercised only in doing our selves Justice, and that too in the ordinary Commerce and Occurrences of Life; for in the publick Administrations of Justice, Mercy to one may be Cruelty to others.

It is grown almost into a Maxim, that Good-natured Men are not always Men of the most Wit. This Observation, in my Opinion, has no Foundation in Nature. The greatest Wits have conversed with are Men eminent for their Humanity. I take therefore this Remark to have been occasioned by two Reasons. First, Because Ill-nature among ordinary Observers passes for Wit.

A spiteful Saying gratifies so many little Passions in those who hear it, that it generally meets with a good Reception. The Laugh rises upon it, and the Man who utters it is looked Upon as a shrewd Satyrist. This may be one Reason, why a great many pleasant Companions appear so surprisingly dull, when they have endeavoured to be Merry in Print; the Publick being more just than Private Clubs or Assemblies, in distinguishing between what is Wit and what is Ill-nature.

Another Reason why the Good-natured Man may sometimes bring his Wit in Question, is, perhaps, because he is apt to be moved with Compassion for those Misfortunes or Infirmities, which another would turn into Ridicule, and by that means gain the Reputation of a Wit. The Ill-natured Man, though but of equal Parts, gives himself a larger Field to expatiate in; he exposes those Failings in Human Nature which the other would cast a Veil over, laughs at Vices which the other either excuses or conceals, gives utterance to Reflections which the other stifles, falls indifferently upon Friends or Enemies, exposes the Person [who] has obliged him, and, in short, sticks at nothing that may establish his Character of a Wit. It is no Wonder therefore he succeeds in it better than the Man of Humanity, as a Person who makes use of indirect Methods, is more likely to grow Rich than the Fair Trader.

*Joseph Addison, in the *Spectator*, No. 169 (13 September 1711).

John Millar (1735–1801), chief disciple of Adam Smith, at Glasgow, where he taught civil law. Millar was a key contributor to conjectural histories of progress. Here he explores the changing gender relations as societies advance towards civil society.

But though the wife is not apt to incur the settled displeasure of her husband [in a rude society], which might lead him to banish her from the family, she may often experience the sudden and fatal effects of his anger and resentment. When unlimited power is committed to the hands of a savage, it cannot fail, upon many occasions, to be grossly abused. He looks upon her in the same light with his other domestic servants, and expects from her the same implicit obedience to his will. The least opposition kindles his resentment; and, from the natural ferocity of his temper, he is frequently excited to behave with a degree of brutality which, in some cases, may prove the unhappy occasion of her death.

Among the ancient inhabitants of Gaul, the husband exercised the power of life and death over his wives, and treated them with all the severity of an absolute tyrannical master. In that country, whenever a person of distinction was thought to have died a violent death, his wives lay under the same suspicion of guilt with his other domestic servants; and in order to discover who had committed the crime, they were all subjected to the torture.

But of all the different branches of power which in a rude age the husband is usually invested, we meet with the fullest and most complete illustration in the ancient law of the Romans. By that law a wife was originally considered as, in every respect, the slave of her husband. She might be sold by him, or she might be put to death by an arbitrary exertion of authority. From the ceremonies which were used in the more solemn and regular celebration of marriage, it seems probable that, in early times, the wife was purchased with a real price from her relations. She was held incapable of having any estate of her own, and whatever she possessed at the time of her marriage, became the absolute property of her husband.

It will be thought, perhaps, a mortifying picture that is here presented to us, when we contemplate the barbarous treatment of the female sex in early times, and the rude state of those passions which may be considered as the origin of society. But this rudeness and barbarism, so universally discovered in the early inhabitants of the world, is not unsuitable to the mean condition in which they are placed, and to the numberless hardships and difficulties which they are obliged to encounter. When men are in danger of perishing for hunger; when they are exerting their utmost efforts to procure the bare necessaries of life; when they are unable to shelter themselves from beasts of prey, or from enemies of their own kind, no less ferocious; their constitution would surely be ill adapted to their circumstances, were they endowed with a refined taste of pleasure, and capable of feeling the delicate distresses and enjoyments of love, accompanied with all those elegant sentiments, which, in a civilized and enlightened age, are naturally derived from that passion. Dispositions of this nature would be altogether misplaced in the breast of a savage: They would even be exceedingly hurtful, by turning his attention from real wants to the pursuit of imaginary, and what, in his situation, must be accounted fantastical gratifications. Neither will it escape observation, that this refinement would be totally inconsistent with the other parts of his character. Nations who have so little regard to property as to live in the continual exercise of theft and rapine; who are so destitute of humanity, as, in cold blood, to put their captives to death with the most excruciating tortures; who have the shocking barbarity to feed upon their fellow-creatures, a practice rarely to be found among the fiercest and most rapacious of the brute animals; such nations, it is evident, would entirely depart from their ordinary habits and principles of action, were they to display much tenderness or benevolence, in consequence of that blind appetite which unites the sexes. It ought, at the same time to be remembered, that, how poor and wretched soever the aspect of human nature in this early state, it contains the seeds of improvement which, by long care and culture, are capable of being brought to maturity. ...

...

[In the era of chivalry of medieval Europe, knightly] dispositions and manners of thinking became fashionable, and were gradually diffused by the force of education and example. To be in love was looked upon as one of the necessary qualifications of a knight; and he was no less ambitious of showing his constancy and fidelity to his mistress, than of displaying his military virtues. He assumed the title of her slave, or servant. By this he distinguished himself in every combat; and his success was supposed to redound [sic] to her honour. If she had bestowed upon him a present to be worn in the field of battle in token of her regard, it was considered as a pledge of victory, and as laying upon him the strongest obligation to render himself worthy of the favour.

The sincere and faithful passion, which commonly occupied the heart of every warrior, and which he professed upon all occasions, was naturally productive of the utmost purity of manners, and of great respect and veneration for the female sex. The delicacy of sentiment which prevailed, had a tendency to divert the attention from sensual pleasure, and created a general abhorrence of debauchery. Persons who felt a strong propensity to magnify and exalt the object of their own wishes, were easily led to make allowance for the same disposition in their neighbours; and such individuals as made a point of defending the reputation and dignity of that particular lady to whom they were devoted, became extremely cautious, lest by any insinuation or impropriety of behaviour, they should hurt the character of another, and be exposed to the just resentment of those by whom she was protected. A woman who deviated so far from the established maxims of the age as to violate the laws of chastity, was indeed deserted by every body, and was universally contemned and insulted. But those who adhered to the strict rules of virtue, and maintained an unblemished reputation, were treated like beings of a superior order. The love of God and of the ladies was one of the first lessons inculcated upon every young person who was initiated into the military profession. He was instructed with care in all those forms of behaviour which, according to the received notions of gallantry and politeness, were settled with the most frivolous exactness. He was frequently put under the tuition of some matron of rank and distinction, who in this particular directed his education, and to whom he was under a necessity of revealing all his sentiments, thoughts, and actions. An oath was imposed upon him, by which he became bound to vindicate the honour of the ladies, as well as to defend them from every species of injustice and the uncourteous knight who behaved to them with rudeness, or who ventured to injure and insult them, became the object of general indignation and vengeance, and was treated as the common enemy of all those who were actuated by the true and genuine principles of chivalry.

The sentiments of military honour, and the love and gallantry so universally diffused among those nations, which were displayed in all the amusements and diversions of the people, had necessarily a remarkable influence upon the genius and taste of their literary compositions. Men were pleased with a recital of what they admired in real life; and the first poetical historians endeavoured to embellish those events which had struck their imagination, and appeared the most worthy of being preserved.

Such was the employment of the bards, who about the eleventh century are said, along with their minstrels, to have attended the festivals and entertainments of princes, and to have sung, with the accompaniment of musical instruments, a variety of small poetical pieces of their own composition, describing the heroic sentiments, as well as the love and gallantry of the times.

They were succeeded by the writers of romance, who related a longer and more connected series of adventures, in which were exhibited the most extravagant instances of valour and generosity, of patience and fortitude, of respect to the ladies, of disinterested love, and inviolable fidelity; subjects the most capable of warming the imagination, and of producing the most sublime and refined descriptions; but which were often disgraced by the unskilfulness of the author, and by that excessive propensity to exaggeration, and turn for the marvelous, which prevailed in those ages of darkness and superstition. These performances, however, with all their faults, may be regarded as striking monuments of the Gothic taste and genius, to which there is nothing similar in the writings of antiquity, and at the same time as useful records, that contain some of the outlines of the history, together with a faithful picture of the manners and customs of those remarkable periods.

. . .

These improvements [brought by industry and commerce] are the source of very important changes in the state of society, and particularly in relation to the women. The advancement of a people in manufactures and commerce has a natural tendency to remove those circumstances which prevented the free intercourse of the sexes, and contributed to heighten and inflame their passions. From the cultivation of the arts of peace, the different members of society are more and more united, and have occasion to enter into a greater variety of transactions for their mutual benefit. As they become more civilized, they perceive the advantages of establishing a regular government; and different tribes who lived in a state of independence, are restrained from injuring one another, and reduced under subjection to the laws. Their former animosities, the cause of so much disturbance, are no longer cherished by fresh provocation, and at length are buried in oblivion. Being no longer withheld by mutual fear and jealousy, they are led by degrees to contract an acquaintance, and to carry on a more intimate correspondence. The men and women of different families are permitted to converse with more ease and freedom, and meet with less opposition to the indulgence of their inclinations.

But while the fair sex become less frequently the objects of those romantic and extravagant passions, which in some measure arise from the disorders of society, they are more universally regarded upon account of their useful or agreeable talents.

When men begin to disuse their ancient barbarous practices, when their attention is not wholly engrossed by the pursuit of military reputation, when they have made some progress in arts, and have attained to a proportional degree of refinement, they are necessarily led to set a value upon those female accomplishments and virtues which have so much influence upon every species of improvement, and which contribute in so many different ways to multiply the comforts of life. In this situation, the women become, neither the slaves, nor the idols of the other sex, but the friends and companions. The wife obtains that rank and station which appears most agreeable to reason, being suited to her character and talents. Loaded by nature with the first and most immediate concern in rearing and maintaining the children, she is endowed with such dispositions as fit her for the discharge of this important duty, and is at the same time particularly qualified for all such employments as require skill and dexterity more than strength, which are so necessary in the interior management of the family. Possessed of peculiar delicacy, and sensibility, whether derived from original constitution, or from her way of life, she is capable of securing the esteem and affection of her husband, by dividing his cares, by sharing his joys, and by soothing his misfortunes.

. . .

The progressive improvements of a country are still attended with farther variations in the sentiments and manners of the inhabitants [as mankind advances from the acquisition of the mere necessaries of life to a state of luxury and refinement]. In such a state, the pleasures which nature has grafted upon the love between the sexes, become the source of an elegant correspondence, and are likely to have a general influence upon the commerce of society. Women of condition come to be more universally admired and courted upon account of the agreeable qualities which they possess, and upon account of the amusement which their conversation affords. They are encouraged to quit that retirement which was formerly esteemed so suitable to their character, to enlarge the sphere of their acquaintance, and to appear in mixed company, and in public meetings of pleasure. They lay aside the spindle and the distaff, and engage in other employments more agreeable to the fashion. As they are introduced more into public life, they are led to cultivate those talents which are adapted to the intercourse of the world, and to distinguish themselves by polite accomplishments that tend to heighten their personal attractions, and to excite those peculiar sentiments. and passions of which they are the natural objects.

These improvements, in the state and accomplishments of the women, might be illustrated from a view of the manners in the different nations of Europe. They have been carried to the greatest height in France, and in some parts of Italy, where the fine arts have received the highest cultivation, and where a taste for refined and elegant amusement has been generally diffused. The same improvements have made their way into England and Germany; though attention of the people to the more necessary and useful arts, and their slow advancement in those which are subservient to entertainment, has, in these countries, prevented the intercourse of the sexes from being equally extended. Even in Spain, where, from the defects of administration, or from whatever causes, the arts have for along time been almost entirely neglected, the same effects of refinement are at length beginning to appear, by the admission of the women to that freedom which they have in the other countries of Europe.

Thus we may observe, that in refined and polished nations there is the same free communication between the sexes as in the ages of rudeness and barbarism. In the latter, women enjoy the most unbounded liberty, because it is thought of no consequence what use they shall make of it. In the former, they are entitled to the same freedom, upon account of those agreeable qualities which they possess, and the rank and dignity which they hold as members of society.

It should seem, however, that there are certain limits beyond which it is impossible to push the real improvements arising from wealth and opulence. In a simple age, the free intercourse of the sexes is attended with no bad consequences; but in opulent and luxurious nations, it gives rise to licentious and dissolute manners, inconsistent with good order, and with the general interest of society.

* From John Millar, *The Origin of the Distinction of Ranks, or, An Inquiry into the Circumstances Which Give Rise to Influence and Authority in the Different Members of Society* (London: Longman, Hurst, Rees, & Orme, 1806 [1778]), pp. 42–6, 78–82, 88–90, 100–2.

Mrs. Crackenthorpe was the pseudonym of Dalrivier Manley, a playwright, novelist, and satiric writer. The Female Tatler, *which she started in 1709, was one of the growing number of papers and broadsides on sale in London – many in the new public spaces of the coffee houses, which have often been seen as new models of the public sphere and deliberative reason, but are satirized here for the negative impact on masculine national virility, while at the same time making a pitch for the equal ability and intelligence of women.**

The *French* Nation have so Complaisant a Regard for the *Fair Sex*, that they always mix with 'em in Conversation, entertain 'em with Discourses on every Topic, which gives them a short Knowledge of the World, what other Nations are agitating as well as their own; and if a Lady has the Misfortune to lose a Husband, or Brother in the Field of Battle, it must in very great measure abate her Grief, to know he dy'd Honourably in the Service of his Country: But *English Ladies*, the Moment they rise from Table, are pack'd off to their *Tea-Tables*, where they spend half their Lives time in talking of *Fans* and *Tea-Cups*, *Sugar-Tongues*, *Salt-Shovels*, and *Gloves* made up in *Wall-nut-shells*.

Therefore as I would avoid reprimanding any body in my *Own Apartment*, I take this Opportunity, to intreat Absence of all *Effeminate Fops*, that drink *Milk and Water*, wear *Cherry colour'd Stockings* and *Stich'd Waistcoats*, and in a Counter-tenor Voice, complain of *Vapours* and the *Spleen*; impudent *Beau-Jews*, that talk obscenely in modest Womens Company, then stare'em in the Face, and burst out a laughing, who, so far from being admitted into Civil Society, ought to be expell'd the Nation [sic]; all *Comic Gentlemen*, that act in Tragedies for their Diversion, *Designing Persons*, that make Assignations at public *Drawing-Rooms*; and *Foreign Beaus*, that assume the Title of *Counts*, that just make an outside Show, to engage some great Fortune, and when they have receiv'd her Money, fly away with it into their own Country.

* From Mrs. Crackenthorpe, 'A Lady that knows every thing' *The Female Tatler*, July 11–13, No. 3 (1709).

*The Friends United were one of the growing number of friendly societies, which in the late eighteenth century still remained open to many women. The selections from the rules, orders and regulations reproduced here give an insight into the characteristics of self-help and participation but also into modes of internal regulation, discipline, and exclusion that were practised in these new voluntary associations.**

Article I.

That this Society shall consist of seventy-one Members, who shall be under the age of Forty Years, and above the age of twenty Years, at the time of their entrance, who shall meet at the aforesaid House to pay their Contribution and other Monies on every third Tuesday in the Month, from six o'Clock in the Evening till eight, in the Winter half year, (that is to say) from the first Meeting Night in October till the Meeting Night in March, and from seven o'Clock till nine in the Summer half year.

II.

That the Landlord of the House where the Society is kept shall keep the Room in good order, with all necessaries for the use of the Society; and on every Meeting Night, from Michaelmas to Lady Day, the Landlord shall provide a good Fire, with Candles, lighted by Six o'Clock in the Evening, or forfeit One Shilling for each neglect.

III.

That there shall be provided by this Society a Box with three different locks and keys, and the Stewardesses for the time being shall each have one key, and the Landlord of the House the other, and that the Landlord, with some other person, who shall be approved of by the Society, shall enter into such security for the produce of the Box and Cash, and all other things belonging to this Society, as the Members of this Society shall think necessary, whenever the same shall be demanded.

IV.

That the Landlord giving such security as may be required of him for the purpose aforesaid.

V.

That every Member shall at their entrance pay two Shillings and Six-pence; that is to say, One Shilling and Eight-Pence to the Box, three-pence to the Clerk, three-pence to be spent, and Four-pence for a Copy of these Articles: and One Shilling and Four-pence per Month on every third Tuesday throughout the year, as Contribution-Money; and every time a Member neglects to pay her Contribution Money, One Penny shall be allowed the Landlord, and the remaining two-pence to be put into the Box. Be it known, that every Member must pay to the Box twelve Calendar Months from the date of their entrance before they shall receive any benefit from the same, but if a Member should die before she shall be free, this Society doth agree to return to her Friends the Money she may have paid into the Box, together with Six-pence from each Member towards her funeral.

VI.

That no person of a hazardous or pernicious trade or Calling, or having any bodily infirmity, no Papist, Irish-woman, Barrow-woman, Basket-woman, Fish-woman, or any one that gets her living in the streets, shall be admitted a Member of this Society, and none but of a fair honest Character.

...

IX.

That if any Member after her admission, shall follow a new trade or Calling, and should be afflicted by the alteration of her trade, she shall not be allowed any benefit from the Box during her illness, and should her illness terminate in death, she shall be allowed the same for her funeral as any other Member. – N.B. A Physician shall determine the cause of her said illness.

...

XVII.

That every free Member when sick, lame, blind, or any ways disabled, and declares on this Society, shall be allowed Eight Shillings per Week, but shall pay at the same time to the Society, the same as another Member.

XVIII.

That on the death of every free Member's husband the sum of ten Pounds shall be allowed for the same, and Five Pounds for the death of every free Member's Nominee.

...

XXI.

That no Member shall be visited above three Miles from the Club-House; and if any Member while on the Box, is suspected of defrauding this Society by working at her trade or Calling, or doing any business whatever, mending, making, cleaning, or any household work in her family, or shall be seen disguised in liquor, gaming, or keeping a score for any game, or shall act any ways prejudicial to her recovery or health, on proof of any of the aforesaid matters, such Members so acting shall be excluded.

...

XXIII.

That if any Member while on the Box should go out to take the air, she shall leave word where she is gone to, and if she neglects so to do she shall forfeit One Shilling; and if any Member's illness comes by Fighting, or occasioned by the Venereal Disease, Drunkenness, or by any other irregular practices brought upon herself, or by the ill treatment of a husband or companion, shall receive no benefit from the Box.

. . .

XXVIII.

That no Member shall be allowed more than fifty-two Weeks as full pay, at the rate of Eight Shillings per Week, while on the Box, after which time such Member shall be reduced to half-pay for Twelve Months more, if such Member's illness continue so long, and if she is still incurable, she shall have Two Shillings per Week during her life; but when any Member becomes a Pensioner, she shall have but Three Pounds allowed for her funeral; and if any Member shall obtain a public or private place of Charity for her support, (except an Hospital) for the cure of any Disorder, such Member shall withdraw herself from such Charity before she shall receive the benefit of the Box; likewise Servants shall withdraw themselves from their place of service whenever they shall demand any benefit of this Society. And if a Member be so reduced as to go to her Parish House, such Member shall be allowed two shillings per Week during life, as before-mentioned; and when any Member becomes a Pensioner she shall never receive full Pay any more.

. . .

XXXV.

That there shall be chosen, by rotation as they stand on the list, two Stewardesses and four Assistants, and if any be absent, or refuse to stand for the same when called-on, she shall pay a fine of One Shilling and Six-pence each time for so refusing, and One Shilling fine for refusing to stand Assistant. The list to be called punctually at seven o'Clock the Winter half year, and eight o'Clock the Summer half year.

XXXVI.

That the Stewardesses and Clerk shall attend every Meeting Night at the time-appointed, or be fined One Shilling, unless prevented by illness.

. . .

XLI.

That if at any time it shall seem necessary to summon the Members, the Stewardesses shall give the Clerk orders so to do; and if any Member neglects to attend the same she shall be fined One shilling, but the Members shall not be summoned, nor the list called over, if there is an Article full and sufficient to determine the business in dispute. No Member shall leave the Room before the business is finished, on penalty of the above fine.

XLII.

That if any Member speaks by way of reflection on a sister Member's having received more benefit from this Society, on proof thereof, the said Member shall pay a fine of Two Shillings and Six-pence, or be excluded.

. . .

L.

That if any member or members come disguised in liquor during meeting hours and shall cause any disturbance during the same, or shall curse, swear, or use any scurrilous, indecent, or provoking language one towards another, she shall for each offence pay One shilling. And every member shall keep their feats, and behave in a quiet and decent manner during Club hours. And if any member is called to order by the Stewardesses and does not obey the same, she shall pay a fine of One shilling, and if she disobeys the second call, she shall pay a fine of Two shillings more, and for not obeying the third call she shall be fined Five shillings, and leave the Room. And if any member or members do cause any dispute or disturbance in any part of the house during Club hours, on any matter relating to the society, such member or members so offending, shall pay a fine of Two shillings and six-pence each, on the next meeting night following, or be excluded.

LI.

That if any member or members, shall publicly or privately promote or encourage the breaking up or dividing this society, she or they so offending shall be expelled from this society, and never more admitted; and this society shall not be broken nor the Cash divided so long as three members continue to pay the same.

. . .

LIV.

That no member shall bring a stranger into the Club room without first asking leave of the Stewardesses, under the fine of sixpence; such stranger shall spend fourpence and behave in a decent manner, or shall be fined two shillings and sixpence, which shall be paid by the member that introduced such stranger, and no man shall be allowed to sit down or stay in the room except it be a deceased member's husband, an Undertaker upon business, or the Landlord and Clerk.

. . .

LVI.

That if any Member belongs to another Society of this kind, she shall upon proof, be expelled immediately.

. . .

LIX.

[T]hat all matters in dispute that cannot be settled by these Rules and Orders shall be determined by a majority of the society.

PHILLIS THOMPSON,   *Stewardesses*
ELIZABETH CRANWELL.

WILLIAM HAWES, Clerk, *Hoxton*

* From *Rules, Orders and Regulations of the Friendly Society Called the Friends United* (1792), 3–5; 7–10; 12–14; 16–19.

Adam Smith (1723–90), made his reputation as an analyst of human psychology many years before concentrating his attention on the workings of the economy. These selections from The Theory of Moral Sentiments *(1759) argue that an other-directed sense of propriety is both necessary for and happily available to modern commercial society.**

How selfish soever man may be supposed, there are evidently some principles in his nature, which interest him in the fortune of others, and render their happiness necessary to him, though he derives nothing from it except the pleasure of seeing it. Of this kind is pity or compassion, the emotion which we feel for the misery of others, when we either see it, or are made to conceive it in a very lively manner. That we often derive sorrow from the sorrow of others, is a matter of fact too obvious to require any instances to prove it; for this sentiment, like all the other original passions of human nature, is by no means confined to the virtuous and humane, though they perhaps may feel it with the most exquisite sensibility. The greatest ruffian, the most hardened violator of the laws of society, is not altogether without it.

As we have no immediate experience of what other men feel, we can form no idea of the manner in which they are affected, but by conceiving what we ourselves should feel in the like situation. Though our brother is upon the rack, as long as we ourselves are at our ease, our senses will never inform us what he suffers. They never did, and never can, carry us beyond our own person, and it is by the imagination only that we can form any conception of what are his sensations. Neither can the faculty help us to this any other way, than by representing to us what would be our own, if we were in his case. It is the impressions of our own senses only, not those of his, which our imaginations copy. By the imagination we place ourselves in his situation, we conceive ourselves enduring all the same torments, we enter as it were into his body, and become in some measure the same person with him, and thence form some idea of his sensations, and even feel something which, though weaker in degree is not altogether unlike them. His agonies, when they are thus brought home to ourselves, when we have thus adopted and made them our own, begin at last to affect us, and we then tremble and shudder at the thought of what he feels.

. . .

Sympathy, therefore, does not arise so much from the view of the passion, as from that of the situation which excites it. We sometimes feel for another, a passion of which he himself seems to be altogether incapable; because, when we put ourselves in his case, that passion arises in our breast from the imagination, though it does not in his from the reality. We blush for the impudence and rudeness of another, though he himself appears to have no sense of the impropriety of his own behaviour; because we cannot help feeling with what confusion we ourselves should be covered, had we behaved in so absurd a manner.

Of all the calamities to which the condition of mortality exposes mankind, the loss of reason appears, to those who have the least spark of humanity, by far the most dreadful, and they behold that last stage of human wretchedness with deeper commiseration than any other. But the poor wretch, who is in it, laughs and sings perhaps, and is altogether insensible of his own misery. The anguish which humanity feels, therefore, at the sight of such an object, cannot be the reflection of any sentiment of the sufferer. The compassion of the spectator must arise altogether from the consideration of what he himself would feel if he was reduced to the same unhappy situation, and, what perhaps is impossible, was at the same time able to regard it with his present reason and judgment.

. . .

To act according to the dictates of prudence, of justice, and proper beneficence, seems to have no great merit where there is no temptation to do otherwise. But to act with cool deliberation in the midst of the greatest dangers and difficulties; to observe religiously the sacred rules of justice in spite both of the greatest interests which might tempt, and the greatest injuries which might provoke us to violate them; never to suffer the benevolence of our temper to be damped or discouraged by the malignity and ingratitude of the individuals towards whom it may have been exercised; is the character of the most exalted wisdom and virtue. Self-command is not only itself a great virtue, but from it all the other virtues seem to derive their principal lustre.

. . .

[T]he degree of any passion which the impartial spectator approves of, is differently situated in different passions. In some passions the excess is less disagreeable than the defect; and in such passions the point of propriety seems to stand high, or nearer to the excess than to the defect. In other passions, the defect is less disagreeable than the excess; and in such passions the point of propriety seems to stand low, or nearer to the defect than to the excess. The former are the passions which the spectator is most, the latter, those which he is least disposed to sympathize with. The former, too, are the passions of which the immediate feeling or sensation is agreeable to the person principally concerned; the latter, those of which it is disagreeable. It may be laid down as a general rule, that the passions which the spectator is most disposed to sympathize with, and in which, upon that account, the point of propriety may be said to stand high, are those of which the immediate feeling or sensation is more or less agreeable to the person principally concerned; and that, on the contrary, the passions which the spectator is least disposed to sympathize with, and in which, upon that account, the point of propriety may be said to stand low, are those of which the immediate feeling or sensation is more or less disagreeable, or even painful, to the person principally concerned. This general rule, so far as I have been able to observe, admits not of a single exception. A few examples will at once, both sufficiently explain it and demonstrate the truth of it.

The disposition to the affections which tend to unite men in society, to humanity, kindness, natural affection, friendship, esteem, may sometimes be excessive. Even the excess of this disposition, however, renders a man interesting to every body. Though we blame it, we still regard it with compassion, and even with kindness and never with dislike. We are more sorry for it than angry at it. To the person himself, the indulgence even of such excessive affections is, upon many occasions, not only agreeable, but delicious. Upon some occasions, indeed, especially when directed, as is too often the case, towards unworthy objects, it exposes him to much real and heartfelt distress. Even upon such occasions, however, a well-disposed mind regards him with the most exquisite pity, and feels the highest indignation against those who affect to despise him for his weakness and imprudence. The defect of this disposition, on the contrary, what is called hardness of heart, while it renders other people equally insensible to his; and, by excluding him from the friendship of all the world, excludes him from the best and most comfortable of all social enjoyments.

The disposition to the affections which drive men from one another, and which tend, as it were, to break the bands of human society; the disposition to anger, hatred, envy, malice, revenge; is, on the contrary, much more apt to offend by its excess than by its defect. The excess renders a man wretched and miserable in his own mind, and the object of hatred, and sometimes even of horror, to other people. The defect is very seldom complained of. It may, however, be defective. The want of proper indignation is a most essential defect in the manly character, and, upon many occasions, renders a man incapable of protecting either himself or his friends from insult and injustice ...

*From Adam Smith, *The Theory of Moral Sentiments*, 2 Vols (Edinburgh: s.n., 1808 [1759]), I, 1–3; 9–10; II, 123, 127–30.

'Of the Farting Club' is from a satirical account of the craze for clubs in early eighteenth-century Britain, also including accounts of 'The No-Nose Club' and the 'Man-Killing Club'. Its many editions marketed it as a 'work of great use and curiosity'.

Of all the fantastical Clubs that ever took Pains to make themselves stink in the Nostrils of the Public, sure no ridiculous Community ever came up to this windy Society, which was certainly establish'd by a Parcel of empty Sparks, about Thirty Years since, at a Public House in *Cripplegate* Parish, where they used to meet once a Week to poison the neighbouring Air with their unsavory *Crepitations*, and were so vain in their Ambition to out Fart one another, that they used to diet themselves against their Club-Nights with Cabbage, Onions, and Pease-Porridge, that every one's Bumfiddle might be the better qualify'd to found forth its Emulation. The Stewards, who were chosen once a Quarter, being the *Auricular* Judges of all Fundamental Disputes that should arise between the Buttocks of the odoriferous Assembly. The Liquors that they drank, in order to tune their Arses, were new Ale and Juniper Water, till every one was swell'd like a blown Bag Pipe, and then they began to Thunder out whole Vollies, like a Regiment of Trainbands in a vigorous Attack upon *BunhillFields* Dunghill, till the Room they sat in stunk ten Times stronger than a Tom-Turd's Lay-stall: Yet, in their windy Eruptions, they had so nice a Regard to Lapet-Cleanliness, that an old Alms-Woman had a better Pension from the Club, than she had from the Parish, to give her constant Attendance in the next Room, and if any Member was suspected of a Brewers Miscarriage, he was presently sent in to be examined by the Matron, who, after searching his Breeches, and narrowly inspecting the hind Lappet of his Shirt, thro' her crack'd Spectacles, made her Report accordingly; if unsoil'd, then a Spank on the Bum was given to the Looby, as a Token of his Cleanliness; but if the nasty Bird had befoul'd his Nest, then, *Beshit upon Honour*, was her return to the Board, and the laxative Offender was amerc'd for his Default. When ever any Health was begun in the Society, it was always honour'd with the windy Compliment of a Gun from the Stern, and drank with as much Formality, as Commmanders push about the Royal Health, on board their wooden Citadels, every Member's Affection to the Person nam'd, being measured by the Strength and Loudness of the stinking Report with which he crown'd his Bumper, Thus whoever wanted a Fart for a Great Man's Health, was enjoy'd the Pennance of a Brimmer extraordinary; also look'd upon by the whole Company as an unmannerly Fellow. They were all profitable Customers to the Grey-Pea-Woman, who used to double her Quantity upon the Club Night, for the Benefit of the Society, and attend them as constantly as the Dame with her Firmity does the Hospital Gate every *Smithfield* Market, each charging his Guts with the Fartative Pills, by shoveling down whole Handfuls, that what went in like Bullets, might come out like Gunpowder. Tho' their Weekly Meeting was held in Honour to the Rump, yet every Club Night they drank the King's Health, and then there was such Trumping about to signalize their Loyalty, that the Victualler was forced to burn Rosemary in his Kitchen, for fear the Expansion of the nauseous Fumes should poison his other Customers: So that though the Society was begun and carried on for some Time with abundance of Secrecy, yet they were soon smelt out, insomuch that the Sound of their Bumfiddles reach'd the Ears of the Neighbourhood.

* From 'Of the Farting Club', in *A Compleat and Humorous Account of all the Remarkable Clubs and Societies in the Cities of London and Westminster* (London, 1756, 7th edn), 31–3.

Paradoxes of commercial life

Charles Louis de Secondat, Baron Montesquieu (1689–1755), novelist, political theorist and wine producer, provided a good deal of the sociological categories upon which the European Enlightenment depended. This selection from The Spirit of the Laws *(1748) argues that commerce can produce a softer but still stable system of social order for modernity.**

The following subjects deserve to be treated in a more extensive manner than the nature of this work will permit. Fain would I glide down a gentle river, but I am carried away by a torrent.

Commerce is a cure for the most destructive prejudices; for it is almost a general rule, that wherever we find agreeable manners, there commerce flourishes; and that wherever there is commerce, there we meet with agreeable manners.

Let us not be astonished, then, if our manners are now less savage than formerly. Commerce has everywhere diffused a knowledge of the manners of all nations: these are compared one with another, and from this comparison arise the greatest advantages.

Commercial laws, it may be said, improve manners for the same reason that they destroy them. They corrupt the purest morals. This was the subject of Plato's complaints; and we every day see that they polish and refine the most barbarous.

Of the Spirit of Commerce

Peace is the natural effect of trade. Two nations who traffic with each other become reciprocally dependent; for if one has an interest in buying, the other has an interest in selling; and thus their union is founded on their mutual necessities.

But if the spirit of commerce unites nations, it does not in the same manner unite individuals. We see that in countries where the people move only by the spirit of commerce, they make a traffic of all the humane, all the moral virtues; the most trifling things, those which humanity would demand, are there done, or there given, only for money.

The spirit of trade produces in the mind of a man a certain sense of exact justice, opposite, on the one hand, to robbery, and on the other to those moral virtues which forbid our always adhering rigidly to the rules of private interest, and suffer us to neglect this for the advantage of others.

The total privation of trade, on the contrary, produces robbery, which Aristotle ranks in the number of means of acquiring; yet it is not at all inconsistent with certain moral virtues. Hospitality, for instance, is most rare in trading countries, while it is found in the most admirable perfection among nations of vagabonds.

It is a sacrilege, says Tacitus, for a German to shut his door against any man whomsoever, whether known or unknown. He who has behaved with hospitality to a stranger goes to show him another house where this hospitality is also practised; and he is there received with the same humanity. But when the Germans had founded kingdoms, hospitality had become burdensome. This appears by two laws of the code of the Burgundians; one of which inflicted a penalty on every barbarian who presumed to show a stranger the house of a Roman; and the other decreed, that whoever received a stranger should be indemnified by the inhabitants, everyone being obliged to pay his proper proportion.

Of the Poverty of the People

There are two sorts of poor; those who are rendered such by the severity of government: these are, indeed, incapable of performing almost any great action, because their indigence is a consequence of their slavery. Others are poor, only because they either despise or know not the conveniences of life; and these are capable of accomplishing great things, because their poverty constitutes a part of their liberty.

Commerce in different Governments

Trade has some relation to forms of government. In a monarchy, it is generally founded on luxury; and though it be also founded on real wants, yet the principal view with which it is carried on is to procure everything that can contribute to the pride, the pleasure, and the capricious whims of the nation. In republics, it is commonly founded on economy. Their merchants, having an eye to all the nations of the earth, bring from one what is wanted by another. It is thus that the republics of Tyre, Carthage, Athens, Marseilles, Florence, Venice, and Holland engaged in commerce.

This kind of traffic has a natural relation to a republican government: to monarchies it is only occasional. For as it is founded on the practice of gaining little, and even less than other nations, and of remedying this by gaining incessantly, it can hardly be carried on by a people swallowed up in luxury, who spend much, and see nothing but objects of grandeur.

Cicero was of this opinion, when he so justly said, 'that he did not like that the same people should be at once both the lords and factors of the whole earth.' For this would, indeed, be to suppose that every individual in the state, and the whole state collectively, had their heads constantly filled with grand views, and at the same time with small ones; which is a contradiction.

Not but that the most noble enterprises are completed also in those states which subsist by economical commerce: they have even an intrepidity not to be found in monarchies. And the reason is this:

One branch of commerce leads to another, the small to the moderate, the moderate to the great; thus he who has gratified his desire of gaining a little raises himself to a situation in which he is not less desirous of gaining a great deal.

Besides, the grand enterprises of merchants are always necessarily connected with the affairs of the public. But, in monarchies, these public affairs give as much distrust to the merchants as in free states they appear to give safety. Great enterprises, therefore, in commerce are not for monarchical, but for republican, governments.

In short, an opinion of greater certainty, as to the possession of property in these states, makes them undertake everything. They flatter themselves with the hopes of receiving great advantages from the smiles of fortune; and thinking themselves sure of what they have already acquired, they boldly expose it in order to acquire more; risking nothing, but as the means of obtaining.

I do not pretend to say that any monarchy is entirely excluded from an economical commerce; but of its own nature it has less tendency towards it: neither do I mean that the republics with which we are acquainted are absolutely deprived of the commerce of luxury; but it is less connected with their constitution.

With regard to a despotic state, there is no occasion to mention it. A general rule: A nation in slavery labors more to preserve than to acquire; a free nation, more to acquire than to preserve.

. . .

How Commerce broke through the Barbarism of Europe

Aristotle's philosophy being carried to the west, pleased the subtle geniuses who were the *virtuosi* of those times of ignorance. The schoolmen were infatuated with it, and borrowed from the philosopher a great many notions on lending upon interest, whereas its source might have been easily traced in the gospel; in short, they condemned it absolutely and in all cases. Hence commerce, which was the profession only of mean persons, became that of knaves; for whenever a thing is forbidden, which nature permits or necessity requires, those who do it are looked upon as dishonest.

Commerce was transferred to a nation covered with infamy, and soon ranked with the most shameful usury, with monopolies, with the levying of subsidies, and with all the dishonest means of acquiring wealth.

The Jews, enriched by their exactions, were pillaged by the tyranny of princes; which pleased indeed, but did not ease, the people.

What passed in England may serve to give us an idea of what was done in other countries. King John having imprisoned the Jews, in order to obtain their wealth, there were few who had not at least one of their eyes plucked out. Thus did that king administer justice. A certain Jew, who had a tooth pulled out every day for seven days successively, gave ten thousand marks of silver for the eighth. Henry III extorted from Aaron, a Jew at York, fourteen thousand marks of silver, and ten thousand for the queen. In those times they did by violence what is now done in Poland with some semblance of moderation. As princes could not dive into the purses of their subjects because of their privileges, they put the Jews to the torture, who were not considered as citizens.

At last a custom was introduced of confiscating the effects of those Jews who embraced Christianity. This ridiculous custom is known only by the law which suppressed it. The most vain and trifling reasons were given in justification of that proceeding; it was alleged that it was proper to try them, in order to be certain that they had entirely shaken off the slavery of the devil. But it is evident that this confiscation was a species of the right of amortization, to recompense the prince, or the lords, for the taxes levied on the Jews, which ceased on their embracing Christianity. In those times, men, like lands, were regarded as property. I cannot help remarking, by the way, how this nation has been sported with from one age to another: at one time, their effects were confiscated when they were willing to become Christians; and at another, if they refused to turn Christians, they were ordered to be burned.

In the meantime, commerce was seen to arise from the bosom of vexation and despair. The Jews, proscribed by turns from every country, found out the way of saving their effects. Thus they rendered their retreats forever fixed; for though princes might have been willing to get rid of their persons, yet they did not choose to get rid of their money.

The Jews invented letters of exchange; commerce, by this method, became capable of eluding violence, and of maintaining everywhere its ground; the richest merchant having none but invisible effects, which he could convey imperceptibly wherever he pleased.

The Theologians were obliged to limit their principles; and commerce, which they had before connected by main force with knavery, re-entered, if I may so express myself, the bosom of probity.

Thus we owe to the speculations of the schoolmen all the misfortunes which accompanied the destruction of commerce; and to the avarice of princes, the establishment of a practice which puts it in some measure out of their power.

From this time it became necessary that princes should govern with more prudence than they themselves could ever have imagined; for great exertions of authority were, in the event, found to be impolitic; and from experience it is manifest that nothing but the goodness and lenity of a government can make it flourish.

We begin to be cured of Machiavelism, and recover from it every day. More moderation has become necessary in the councils of princes. What would formerly have been called a master-stroke in politics would be now, independent of the horror it might occasion, the greatest imprudence.

Happy is it for men that they are in a situation in which, though their passions prompt them to be wicked, it is, nevertheless, to their interest to be humane and virtuous.

ι

*Montesquieu, *The Spirit of the Laws*, translated by Thomas Nugent (New York: Hafner, 1949 [1748]), 316–19; 364–6.

Jean Jacques Rousseau (1712–78), philosopher, novelist, musician and political theorist, broke with his early friends from Enlightenment circles by attacking their belief in human progress. At the core of 'The Discourse on the Origins of Inequality' lies the insistence that modernity will make us unhappy by so opening avenues for difference that we will cease to be happy with ourselves, imagining that the grass is greener elsewhere.

Men in a state of nature being confined merely to what is physical in love, and fortunate enough to be ignorant of those excellences, which whet the appetite while they increase the difficulty of gratifying it, must be subject to fewer and less violent fits of passion, and consequently fall into fewer and less violent disputes. The imagination, which causes such ravages among us, never speaks to the heart of savages, who quietly await the impulses of nature, yield to them involuntarily, with more pleasure than ardour, and, their wants once satisfied, lose the desire. It is therefore incontestable that love, as well as all other passions, must have acquired in society that glowing impetuosity, which makes it so often fatal to mankind. And it is more absurd to represent savages as continually cutting one another's throats to indulge their brutality, because this opinion is directly contrary to experience; the Caribbeans, who have as yet least of all deviated from the state of nature, being in fact the most peaceable of people in their amours, and the least subject to jealousy, though they live in a hot climate which seems always to inflame the passions.

. . .

It is in fact easy to see that many of the differences which distinguish men are merely the effect of habit and the different methods of life men adopted in society. Thus a robust or delicate constitution, and the strength or weakness attaching to it, are more frequently the effects of a hardy or effeminate method of education than of the original endowment of the body. It is the same with the powers of the mind; for education not only makes a difference between such as are cultured and such as are not, but even increases the differences which exist among the former, in proportion to their respective degrees of culture: as the distance between a giant and a dwarf on the same road increases with every step they take. If we compare the prodigious diversity, which obtains in the education and manner of life of the various orders of men in the state of society, with the uniformity and simplicity of animal and savage life, in which every one lives on the same kind of food and in exactly the same manner, and does exactly the same things, it is easy to conceive how much less the difference between man and man must be in a state of nature than in a state of society, and how greatly the natural inequality of mankind must be increased by the inequalities of social institutions.

But even if the nature really affected, in the distribution of her gifts, that partiality which is imputed to her, what advantage would the greatest of her favourites derive from it, to the detriment of others, in a state that admits of hardly any kind of relation between them? Where there is no love, of what advantage is beauty? Of what use is wit to those who do not converse, or cunning to those who have no business with others? I hear it constantly repeated that, in such a state, the strong would oppress the weak; but what is here meant by oppression? Some, it is said, would violently domineer over others, who would groan under a servile submission to their caprices. This indeed is exactly what I observe to be the case among us; but I do not see how it can be inferred of men in a state of nature, who could not easily be brought to conceive what we mean by dominion and servitude. One man, it is true, might seize the fruits which another had gathered, the game he had killed, or the cave he had chosen for shelter; but how would he ever be able to exact obedience, and what ties of dependence could there be among men without possessions? If, for instance, I am driven from one tree, I can go to the next; if I am disturbed in one place, what hinders me from going to another? Again, should I happen to meet with a man so much stronger than myself, and at the same time so depraved, so indolent, and so barbarous, as to compel me to provide for his sustenance while he himself remains idle; he must take care not to have his eyes off me for a single moment; he must bind me fast before he goes to sleep, or I shall certainly either knock him on the head or make my escape. That is to say, he must in such a case voluntarily expose himself to much greater trouble than he seeks to avoid, or can give me. After all this, let him be off his guard ever so little; let him but turn his head aside at any sudden noise, and I shall be instantly twenty paces off, lost in the forest, and, my fetters burst asunder, he would never see me again.

Without my expatiating thus uselessly on these details, every one must see that as the bonds of servitude are formed merely by the mutual dependence of men on one another and the reciprocal needs that unite them, it is impossible to make any man a slave, unless he be first reduced to a situation in which he cannot do without the help of others; and, since such a situation does not exist in a state of nature, every one is there his own master, and the law of the strongest is of no effect.

Having proved that the inequality of mankind is hardly felt, and that its influence is next to nothing in a state of nature, I must next show its origin and trace its progress in the successive developments of the human mind. Having shown that human *perfectibility*, the social virtues, and the other faculties which natural man potentially possessed, could never develop of themselves, but must require the fortuitous concurrence of many foreign causes that might never arise, and without which he would have remained for ever in his primitive condition, I must now collect and consider the different accidents which may have improved the human understanding while depraving the species, and made man wicked while making him sociable; so as to bring him and the world from that distant period to the point at which we now behold them.

...

The first man who, having enclosed a piece of ground, bethought of himself of saying *This is mine*, and found people simple enough to believe him, was the real founder of civil society. From how many crimes, wars and murders, from how many horrors and misfortunes might not any one have saved mankind, by pulling up the stakes, or filling up the ditch, and crying to his fellows, 'Beware of listening to this impostor; you are undone if you once forget that the fruits of the earth belong to us all, and the earth itself to nobody.' But there is great probability that things had then already come to such a pitch, that they could no longer continue as they were; for the idea of property depends on many prior ideas, which could only be acquired successively, and cannot have been formed all at once in the human mind. Mankind must have made very considerable progress, and acquired considerable knowledge and industry which they must also have transmitted and increased from age to age, before they arrived at this last point of the state of nature. Let us then go farther back, and endeavour to unify under a single point of view that slow succession of events and discoveries in the most natural order.

...

So long as men remained content with their rustic huts, so long as they were satisfied with clothes made of the skins of animals and sewn together with thorns and fish-bones, adorned themselves only with feathers and shells, and continued to paint their bodies different colours, to improve and beautify their bows and arrows and to make with sharp-edged stones fishing boats or clumsy musical instruments; in a word, so long as they undertook only what a single person could accomplish, and confined themselves to such arts as did not require joint labour of several hands, they lived free, healthy, honest and happy lives, so long as their nature allowed, and as they continued to enjoy the pleasures of mutual and independent intercourse. But from the moment one man began to stand in need of the help of another; from the moment it appeared advantageous to any one man to have enough provisions for two, equality disappeared, property was introduced, work became indispensable, and vast forests became smiling fields, which man had to water with the sweat of his brow, and where slavery and misery were soon seen to germinate and grow up with the crops.

...

If the reader thus discovers and retraces the lost and forgotten road, by which man have passed from the state of nature to the state of society; if he carefully restores, along with the intermediate situations which I have just described, those which want of time has compelled me to suppress, or my imagination has failed to suggest, he cannot fail to be struck by the vast distance which separates the two states. It is in tracing this slow succession that he will find the solution of a number of problems of politics and morals, which philosophers cannot settle. He will feel that, men being different in different ages, the reason why Diogenes could not find a man was that he sought among his contemporaries a man of an earlier period. He will see that Cato died with Rome and liberty, because he did not fit the age in which he lived; the greatest of men served only to astonish a world which he would certainly have ruled, had he lived five hundred years sooner. In a word, he will explain how the soul and the passions of men insensibly change their very nature; why our wants and pleasures in the end seek new objects; and why, the original man having vanished by degrees, society offers to us only an assembly of artificial men and factitious passions, which are the work of all these new relations, and without any real foundation in nature. We are taught nothing on this subject, by reflection, that is not entirely confirmed by observation. The savage and the civilised man differ so much in the bottom of their hearts and in their inclinations, that what constitutes supreme happiness of one would reduce the other to despair. The former breathes only peace and liberty; he desires only to live and be free from labour; even the *ataraxia* of the Stoic falls far short of his profound indifference to every other object. Civilised man, on the other hand, is always moving, sweating, toiling and racking his brains to find still more laborious occupations: he goes on in drudgery to his last moment, and even seeks death to put himself in a position to live, or renounced life to acquire immortality. He pays his court to men in power, whom he hates, and to the wealthy, whom he despises; he stops at nothing to have the honour of serving them; he is not ashamed to value himself on his own meanness and their protection; and, proud of his slavery, he speaks with disdain of those, who have not the honour of sharing it. What a sight would the perplexing and envied labours of a European minister of State present to the eyes of a Caribbean! How many cruel deaths would not this indolent savage prefer to the horrors of such a life, which is seldom even sweetened by the pleasure of doing good! But, for him to see into the motives of all this solicitude, the words *power* and *reputation*, would have to bear some meaning in his mind; he would have to know that there are men who set a value on the opinion of the rest of the world; who can be made happy and satisfied with themselves rather on the testimony of other people than on their own. In reality, the source of all these differences is, that the savage lives within himself, while social man lives constantly outside himself, and only knows how to live in the opinion of others, so that he seems to receive the consciousness of his own existence merely from the judgment of others concerning him. It is not to my present purpose to insist on the indifference to good and evil which arises from this disposition, in spite of our many fine works on morality, or to show how, everything being reduced to appearances, there is but art and mummery in even honour, friendship, virtue, and often vice itself, of which we at length learn the secret of boasting; to show, in short, how, always asking others what we are, and never daring to ask ourselves, in the midst of so much philosophy, humanity and civilisation, and of such sublime codes of morality, we have nothing to show for ourselves but a frivolous and deceitful appearance, honour without virtue, reason without wisdom, and pleasure without happiness. It is sufficient that I have proved that this is not by any means the original state of man, but that it is merely the spirit of society, and the inequality which society produces, that thus transform and alter all our natural inclinations.

* From Jean Jacques Rousseau, 'On the Origin of Inequality', translated by G.D.H. Cole, *Encyclopedia Britannica: Great Books of the Western World* (Chicago: University of Chicago Press, 1952 [1754]), 346–8; 352; 362.

Adam Smith (1723–90), does not, as is often believed, offer a naïve endorsement of economic life. In this selection from The Theory of Moral Sentiments *(1759) he takes issue with the principle of utility, associated in his mind with Hume, according to which an increase in goods will make people happy, and so ensure social stability. He argues a very different case: goods will not make us happy, but the naïve belief that they will, based on a desire to distinguish oneself from others, will happily so deceive human beings as to allow for a softer and more prosperous social order.**

The cause too, why utility pleases, has of late been assigned by an ingenious and agreeable philosopher, who joins the greatest depth of thought to the greatest elegance of expression, and possesses the singular and happy talent of treating the abstrusest subjects not only with the most perfect perspicuity, but with the most lively eloquence. The utility of any object, according to him, pleases the master by perpetually suggesting to him the pleasure or conveniency which it is fitted to promote. Every time he looks at it, he is put in mind of this pleasure; and the object in this manner becomes a source of perpetual satisfaction and enjoyment. The spectator enters by sympathy into the sentiments of the master, and necessarily views the object under the same agreeable aspect. When we visit the palaces of the great, we cannot help conceiving the satisfaction we should enjoy if we ourselves were the masters, and were possessed of so much artful and ingeniously contrived accommodation. A similar account is given why the appearance of inconveniency should render any object disagreeable both to the owner and to the spectator.

But that this fitness, this happy contrivance of any production of art, should often be more valued, than the very end for which it was intended; and that the exact adjustment of the means for attaining any conveniency or pleasure, should frequently be more regarded, than that very conveniency or pleasure, in the attainment of which their whole merit would seem to consist has not, so far as I know, been yet taken notice of by any body. That this however is very frequently the case, may be observed in a thousand instances, both in the frivolous and in the most important concerns of human life.

...

How many people ruin themselves by laying out money on trinkets of frivolous utility? What pleases these lovers of toys is not so much the utility, as the aptness of the machines which are fitted to promote it. All their pockets are stuffed with little inconveniencies. They contrive new pockets, unknown in the clothes of other people, in order to carry a greater number. They walk about loaded with a multitude of baubles, in weight and sometimes in value not inferior to an ordinary Jew's-box, some of which may sometimes be of some little use, but all of which might at all times be very well spared, and of which the whole utility is certainly not worth the fatigue of bearing the burden.

Nor is it only with regard to such frivolous objects that our conduct is influenced by this principle; it is often the secret motive of the most serious and important pursuits of both private and public life.

The poor man's son, whom heaven in its anger has visited with ambition, when he begins to look around him, admires the condition of the rich. He finds the cottage of his father too small for his accommodation, and fancies he should be lodged more at his ease in a palace. He is displeased with being obliged to walk a-foot, or to endure the fatigue of riding on horseback. He sees his superiors carried about in machines, and imagines that in one of these he could travel with less inconveniency. He feels himself naturally indolent, and willing to serve himself with his own hands as little as possible; and judges, that a numerous retinue of servants would save him from a great deal of trouble. He thinks if he had attained all these, he would sit still contentedly, and be quiet, enjoying himself in the thought of the happiness and tranquillity of his situation. He is enchanted with the distant idea of this felicity. It appears in his fancy like the life of some superior rank of beings, and, in order to arrive at it, he devotes himself for ever to the pursuit of wealth and greatness. To obtain the conveniences which these afford, he submits in the first year, nay in the first month of his application, to more fatigue of body and more uneasiness of mind than he could have suffered through the whole of his life from the want of them. He studies to distinguish himself in some laborious profession. With the most unrelenting industry he labours night and day to acquire talents superior to all his competitors. He endeavours next to bring those talents into public view, and with equal assiduity solicits every opportunity of employment. For this purpose he makes his court to all mankind; he serves those whom he hates, and is obsequious to those whom he despises. Through the whole of his life he pursues the idea of a certain artificial and elegant repose which he may never arrive at, for which he sacrifices a real tranquillity that is at all times in his power, and which, if in the extremity of old age he should at last attain to it, he will find to be in no respect preferable to that humble security and contentment which he had abandoned for it. It is then, in the last dregs of life, his body wasted with toil and diseases, his mind galled and ruffled by the memory of a thousand injuries and disappointments which he imagines he has met with from the injustice of his enemies, or from the perfidy and ingratitude of his friends, that he begins at last to find that wealth and greatness are mere trinkets of frivolous utility, no more adapted for procuring ease of body or tranquillity of mind than the tweezer-cases of the lover of toys; and like them too, more troublesome to the person who carries them about with him than all the advantages they can afford him are commodious. There is no other real difference between them, except that the conveniences of the one are somewhat more observable than those of the other. The palaces, the gardens, the equipage, the retinue of the great, are objects of which the obvious conveniency strikes every body. They do not require that their masters should point out to us wherein consists their utility. Of our own accord we readily enter into it, and by sympathy enjoy, and thereby applaud the satisfaction which they are fitted to afford him. But the curiosity of a toothpick, of an earpicker, of a machine for cutting the nails, or of any other trinket of the same kind, is not so obvious. Their conveniency may perhaps be equally great, but it is not so striking, and we do not so readily enter into the satisfaction of the man who possesses them. They are therefore less reasonable subjects of vanity than the magnificence of wealth and greatness; and in this consists the sole advantage of these last. They more effectually gratify that love of distinction so natural to man. To one who was to live alone in a desolate island it might be a matter of doubt, perhaps, whether a palace, or a collection of such small conveniencies as are commonly contained in a tweezer-case, would contribute most to his happiness and enjoyment. If he is to live in society, indeed, there can be no comparison, because in this, as in all other cases, we constantly pay more regard to the sentiments of, the spectator, than to those of the person principally concerned, and consider rather how his situation will appear to other people, than how it will appear to himself. If we examine, however, why the spectator distinguishes with such admiration the condition of the rich and the great, we shall find that it is not so much upon account of the superior ease or pleasure which they are supposed to enjoy, as of the numberless artificial and elegant contrivances for promoting this ease or pleasure. He does not even imagine that they are really happier than other people: but he imagines that they possess more means of happiness. And it is the ingenious and artful adjustment of those means to the end for which they were intended, that is the principal source of his admiration. But in the languor of disease and the weariness of old age, the pleasures of the vain and empty distinctions of greatness disappear. To one, in this situation, they are no longer capable of recommending those toilsome pursuits in which they had formerly engaged him. In his heart he curses ambition, and vainly regrets the ease and the indolence of youth, pleasures which are fled for ever, and which he has foolishly sacrificed for what, when he has got it, can afford him no real satisfaction. In this miserable aspect does greatness appear to every man when reduced either by spleen or disease to observe with attention his own situation, and to consider what it is that is really wanting to his happiness. Power, and riches appear then to be, what they are, enormous and operose machines contrived to produce a few trifling conveniencies of the body, consisting of springs the most nice and delicate, which must be kept in order with the most anxious attention, and which, in spite of all our care, are ready every moment to burst into pieces, and to crush in their ruins their unfortunate possessor. They are immense fabrics, which it requires the labour of a life to raise, which threaten every moment to overwhelm the person that dwells in them, and, which while they stand, though they may save him from some smaller inconveniencies, can protect him from none of the severer inclemencies of the season. They keep off the summer shower, not the winter storm, but leave him always as much, and sometimes more exposed than before, to anxiety, to fear, and to sorrow; to diseases, to danger, and to death.

But though this splenetic philosophy, which in time of sickness or low spirits is familiar to every man, thus entirely depreciates those great objects of human desire, when in better health and in better humour, we never fail to regard them under a more agreeable aspect. Our imagination, which in pain and sorrow seems to be confined and cooped up within our own persons, in times of ease and prosperity expands itself to every thing around us. We are then charmed with the beauty of that accommodation which reigns in the palaces and economy of the great; and admire how every thing is adapted to promote their ease, to prevent their wants, to gratify their wishes, and to amuse and entertain their most frivolous desires. If we consider the real satisfaction which all these things are capable of affording, by itself and separated from the beauty of that arrangement which is fitted to promote it, it will always appear in the highest degree contemptible and trifling. But we rarely view it in this abstract and philosophical light. We naturally confound it in our imagination with the order, the regular and harmonious movement of the system, the machine or economy by means of which it is produced. The pleasures of wealth and greatness, when considered in this complex view, strike the imagination as something grand, and beautiful, and noble, of which the attainment is well worth all the toil and anxiety which we are so apt to bestow upon it.

And it is well that nature imposes upon us in this manner. It is this deception which rouses and keeps in continual motion the industry of mankind. It is this which first prompted them to cultivate the ground, to build houses, to found cities and commonwealths, and to invent and improve all the sciences and arts, which ennoble and embellish human life; which have entirely changed the whole face of the globe, have turned the rude forests of nature into agreeable and fertile plains, and made the trackless and barren ocean a new fund of subsistence, and the great high road of communication to the different nations of the earth. The earth, by these labours of mankind, has been obliged to redouble her natural fertility, and to maintain a greater multitude of inhabitants. It is to no purpose, that the proud and unfeeling landlord views his extensive fields, and without a thought for the wants of his brethren, in imagination consumes himself the whole harvest that grows upon them. The homely and vulgar proverb, that the eye is larger than the belly, never was more fully verified than with regard to him. The capacity of his stomach bears no proportion to the immensity of his desires, and will receive no more than that of the meanest peasant. The rest he is obliged to distribute among those who prepare, in the nicest manner, that little which he himself makes use of, among those who fit up the palace in which this little is to be consumed, among those who provide and keep in order all the different baubles and trinkets, which are employed in the economy of greatness; all of whom thus derive from his luxury and caprice, that share of the necessaries of life, which they would in vain have expected from his humanity or his justice. The produce of the soil maintains at all times nearly that number of inhabitants which it is capable of maintaining. The rich only select from the heap what is most precious, and agreeable. They consume little more than the poor, and in spite of their natural selfishness and rapacity, though they mean only their own conveniency, though the sole end which they propose from the labours of all the thousands whom they employ, be the gratification of their own vain and insatiable desires, they divide with the poor the produce of all their improvements.

They are led by an invisible hand to make nearly the same distribution of the necessaries of life, which would have been made, had the earth been divided into equal portions among all its inhabitants; and thus, without intending it; without knowing it, advance the interest of the society, and afford means to the multiplication of the species. When providence divided the earth among a few lordly masters, it neither forgot nor abandoned those who seemed to have been left out in the partition. These last too enjoy their share of all that it produces. In what constitutes the real happiness of human life, they are in no respect inferior to those who would seem so much above them. In ease of body and peace of mind, all the different ranks of life are nearly upon a level, and the beggar, who suns himself by the side of the highway, possesses that security which kings are fighting for.

*From Adam Smith, *The Theory of Moral Sentiments*, 2 Vols. (Edinburgh: s.n., 1808 [1759]), 430–1; 433–44.

Civil society, war, and cosmopolitan peace

Adam Ferguson (1723–1816), soldier, cleric and academic, was familiar with the two social worlds of eighteenth century Scotland – the tribal Highlands and the commercial Lowlands. An Essay on the History of Civil Society *(1773) replicates this division: whilst acknowledging the polish of the new world, it insists that stability, and its maintenance, can only be assured by continuing to take military virtues seriously.* *

Without the rivalship of nations, and the practice of war, civil society itself could scarcely have found an object, or a form. Mankind might have traded without any formal convention, but they cannot be safe without a national concert. The necessity of a public defence, has given rise to many departments of state, and the intellectual talents of men have found their busiest scene in wielding their national forces. To overawe, or intimidate, or, when we cannot persuade with reason, to resist with fortitude, are the occupations which give its most animating exercise, and its greatest triumphs, to a vigorous mind; and he who has never struggled with his fellow-creatures, is a stranger to half the sentiments of mankind.

The quarrels of individuals, indeed, are frequently the operations of unhappy and detestable passions; malice, hatred and rage. If such passions alone possess the breast, the scene of dissension becomes an object of horror; but a common opposition maintained by numbers, is always allayed by passions of another sort. Sentiments of affection and friendship mix with animosity; the active and strenuous become the guardians of their society; and violence itself is, in their case, an exertion of generosity as well as of courage.

. . .

[I]t is vain to expect that we can give to the multitude of a people a sense of union among themselves, without admitting hostility to those who oppose them. Could we at once, in the case of any nation, extinguish the emulation which is excited from abroad, we should probably break or weaken the bands of society at home, and close the busiest scenes of national occupations and virtues.

. . .

By the separation of arts and professions, the sources of wealth are laid open; every species of material is wrought up to the greatest perfection, and every commodity is produced in the greatest abundance. The state may estimate its profits and its revenues by the number of its people. It may procure, by its treasure, that national consideration and power, which the savage maintains at the expence of his blood.

The advantage gained in the inferior branches of manufacture by the separation of their parts, seem to be equalled by those which arise from a similar device in the higher departments of policy and war. The soldier is relieved from every care but that of his service; statesmen divide the business of civil government into shares; and the servants of the public, in every office, without being skilful in the affairs of state, may succeed, by observing forms which are already established on the experience of others. They are made, like the parts of an engine, to concur to a purpose, without any concert of their own: and, equally blind with the trader to any general combination, they unite with him, in furnishing to the state its resources, its conduct, and its force.

. . .

The subdivision of arts and professions, in certain examples, tends to improve the practice of them, and to promote their ends. By having separated the arts of the clothier and the tanner, we are better supplied with shoes and with cloth. But to separate the arts which form the citizen and the statesman, the arts of policy and war, is an attempt to dismember the human character, and to destroy those very arts we mean to improve. By this separation, we in effect deprive a free people of what is necessary to their safety; or we prepare a defence against invasions from abroad, which gives a prospect of usurpation, and threatens the establishment of military government at home.

. . .

If this be the end of political struggles, the design, when executed, in securing to the individual his estate, and the means of subsistence, may put an end to the exercise of those very virtues that were required in conducting its execution. A man who, in concert with his fellow-subjects, contends with usurpation in defence of his estate or his person, may find an exertion of great generosity, and of a vigorous spirit; but he who, under political establishments, supposed to be fully confirmed, betakes him, because he is safe, to the mere enjoyment of fortune, has in fact turned to a source of corruption the very advantages which the virtues of the other procured. Individuals, in certain ages, derive their protection chiefly from the strength of the party to which they adhere; but in times of corruption, they flatter themselves, that they may continue to derive from the public that safety which, in former ages, they must have owed to their own vigilance and spirit, to the warm attachment of their friends, and to the exercise of every talent which could render them respected, feared, or beloved. In one period, therefore, mere circumstances serve to excite the spirit, and to preserve the manners of men; in another, great wisdom and zeal for the good of mankind on the part of their leaders, are required for the same purposes.

Rome, it may be thought, did not die of a lethargy, nor perish by the remission of her political ardours at home. Her distemper appeared of a nature more violent and acute. Yet if the virtues of Cato and of Brutus found an exercise in the dying hour of the republic, the neutrality, and the cautious retirement of Atticus, found its security in the same tempestuous season; and the great body of the people lay undisturbed, below the current of a storm, by which the superior ranks of men were destroyed. In the minds of the people, the sense of a public was defaced; and even the animosity of faction had subsided: they only could share in the commotion, who were the soldiers of a legion, or the partisans of a leader. But this state fell not into obscurity for want of eminent men. If at the time of which we speak, we look only for a few names distinguished in the history of mankind, there is no period at which the list was more numerous. But those names became distinguished in the contest for dominion, not in the exercise of equal rights: the people was corrupted; the empire of the known world stood in need of a master.

Republican governments, in general, are in hazard of ruin from the ascendant of particular factions, and from the mutinous spirit of a populace, who being corrupted, are no longer fit to share in the administration of state. But under other establishments, where liberty may be more successfully attained if men are corrupted, the national vigour declines from the abuse of that very security which is procured by the supposed perfection of public order.

. . .

Nations are most exposed to corruption from this quarter, when the mechanical arts, being greatly advanced, furnish numberless articles, to be applied in ornament to the person, in furniture, entertainment, or equipage; when such articles as the rich alone can procure are admired; and when consideration, precedence, and rank, are accordingly made to depend on fortune.

. . .

It appears, therefore, that although the mere use of materials which constitute luxury, may be distinguished from actual vice; yet nations under a high state of the commercial arts, are exposed to corruption, by their admitting wealth, unsupported by personal elevation and virtue, as the great foundation of distinction, and by having their attention turned on the side of interest, as the road to consideration and honour.

With this effect, luxury may serve to corrupt democratical states, by introducing a species of monarchical subordination, without that sense of high birth and hereditary honours which render the boundaries of rank fixed and determinate, and which teach men to act in their stations with force and propriety. It may prove the occasion of political corruption, even in monarchical governments, by drawing respect towards mere wealth; by casting a shade on the luster of personal qualities, or family-distinctions; and by infecting all orders of men, with equal venality, servility, and cowardice.

...

If the ordinary arts of policy, or rather, if a growing indifference to objects of a public nature, should prevail, and, under any free constitution, put an end to those disputes of party, and silence that noise of dissension, which generally accompany the exercise of freedom, we may venture to prognosticate corruption to the national manners, as well as remissness to the national spirit. The period is come, when, no engagement remaining on the part of the public, private interest, and animal pleasure, become the sovereign objects of care. When men, being relieved from the pressure of great occasions, bestow their attention on trifles; and having carried what they are pleased to call *sensibility* and *delicacy*, on the subject of ease or molestation, as far as real weakness or folly can go, have recourse to affectation, in order to enhance the pretended demands, and accumulate the anxieties, of a sickly fancy, and enfeebled mind.

In this condition, mankind generally flatter their own imbecility under the name of *politeness*. They are persuaded, that the celebrated ardour, generosity, and fortitude, of former ages, bordered on frenzy, or were the mere effects of necessity, on men who had not the means of enjoying their ease, or their pleasure. They congratulate themselves on having escaped the storm which required the exercise of such arduous virtues; and with that vanity which accompanies the human race in their meanest condition, they boast of a scene of affectation, of languor, of folly, as the standard of human felicity, and as furnishing the properest exercise of a rational nature.

* From Adam Ferguson, *An Essay on the History of Civil Society* (London, 1809 [1773]), 39–41; 303–4; 370–2; 384; 420; 425–6; 428–9.

Edward Gibbon (1737–94), soldier and historian of Rome, here takes issue with Ferguson's view as to the necessity for a core of military virtue within modern society. The riches brought by commerce are so great as to counteract the military virtues of tribesmen living in the peripheries of modern civilization.

If the decline of the Roman empire was hastened by the conversion of Constantine, his victorious religion broke the violence of the fall, and mollified the ferocious temper of the conquerors.

This awful revolution may be usefully applied to the instruction of the present age. It is the duty of a patriot to prefer and promote the exclusive interest and glory of his native country; but a philosopher may be permitted to enlarge his views, and to consider Europe as one great republic, whose various inhabitants have attained almost the same level of politeness and cultivation. The balance of power will continue to fluctuate, and the prosperity of our own or the neighbouring kingdoms may be alternately exalted or depressed, but these partial events cannot essentially injure our general state of happiness, the system of arts, and laws, and manners, which so advantageously distinguish, above the rest of mankind, the Europeans and their colonies. The savage nations of the globe are the common enemies of civilized society; and we may inquire with anxious curiosity, whether Europe is still threatened with a repetition of those calamities which formerly oppressed the arms and institutions of Rome. Perhaps the same reflections will illustrate the fall of that mighty empire, and explain the probable causes of our actual security.

I. The Romans were ignorant of the extent of their danger, and the number of their enemies. Beyond the Rhine and Danube, the northern countries of Europe and Asia were filled with innumerable tribes of hunters and shepherds, poor, voracious, and turbulent; bold in arms, and impatient to ravish the fruits of industry. The Barbarian world was agitated by the rapid impulse of war; and the peace of Gaul or Italy was shaken by the distant revolutions of China. The Huns, who fled before a victorious enemy, directed their march towards the West; and the torrent was swelled by the gradual accession of captives and allies. The flying tribes who yielded to the Huns assumed in *their* turn the spirit of conquest; the endless column of Barbarians pressed on the Roman empire with accumulated weight; and, if the foremost were destroyed, the vacant space was instantly replenished by new assailants. Such formidable emigrations can no longer issue from the North; and the long repose, which has been imputed to the decrease of population, is the happy consequence of the progress of arts and agriculture. Instead of some rude villages, thinly scattered among its woods and morasses, Germany now produces a list of two thousand three hundred walled towns; the Christian kingdoms of Denmark, Sweden, and Poland, have been successively established; and the Hanse merchants, with the Teutonic knights, have extended their colonies along the coast of the Baltic, as far as the Gulf of Finland. From the Gulf of Finland to the Eastern Ocean, Russia now assumes the form of a powerful and civilized empire. The plough, the loom, and the forge, are introduced on the banks of the Volga, the Oby, and the Lena; and the fiercest of the Tartar hordes have been taught to tremble and obey. The reign of independent Barbarism is now contracted to a narrow span; and the remnant of Calmucks or Uzbecks, whose forces may be almost numbered, cannot seriously excite the apprehensions of the great republic of Europe. Yet this apparent security should not tempt us to forget that new enemies, and unknown dangers, may *possibly* arise from some obscure people, scarcely visible in the map of the world. The Arabs or Saracens, who spread their conquests from India to Spain, had languished in poverty and contempt, till Mahomet breathed into those savage bodies the soul of enthusiasm.

II. The empire of Rome was firmly established by the singular and perfect coalition of its members. The subject nations, resigning the hope, and even the wish, of independence, embraced the character of Roman citizens; and the provinces of the West were reluctantly torn by the Barbarians from the bosom of their mother-country. But this union was purchased by the loss of national freedom and military spirit; and the servile provinces, destitute of life and motion, expected their safety from the mercenary troops and governors, who were directed by the orders of a distant court. The happiness of an hundred millions depended on the personal merit of one or two men, perhaps children, whose minds were corrupted by education, luxury, and despotic power. The deepest wounds were inflicted on the empire during the minorities of the sons and grandsons of Theodosius; and, after those incapable princes seemed to attain the age of manhood, they abandoned the church to the bishops, the state to the eunuchs, and the provinces to the Barbarians. Europe is now divided into twelve powerful, though unequal, kingdoms, three respectable commonwealths, and a variety of smaller, though independent, states; the chances of royal and ministerial talents are multiplied, at least with the number of its rulers; and a Julian, or Semiramis, may reign in the North, while Arcadius and Honorius again slumber on the thrones of the South. The abuses of tyranny are restrained by the mutual influence of fear and shame; republics have acquired order and stability; monarchies have imbibed the principles of freedom, or, at least, of moderation; and some sense of honour and justice is introduced into the most defective constitutions by the general manners of the times. In peace, the progress of knowledge and industry is accelerated by the emulation of so many active rivals: in war, the European forces are exercised by temperate and undecisive contests. If a savage conqueror should issue from the deserts of Tartary, he must repeatedly vanquish the robust peasants of Russia, the numerous armies of Germany, the gallant nobles of France, and the intrepid freemen of Britain; who, perhaps, might confederate for their common defence. Should the victorious Barbarians carry slavery and desolation as far as the Atlantic Ocean, ten thousand vessels would transport beyond their pursuit the remains of civilized society; and Europe would revive and flourish in the American world, which is already filled with her colonies and institutions.[1]

III. Cold, poverty, and a life of danger and fatigue, fortify the strength and courage of Barbarians. In every age they have oppressed the polite and peaceful nations of China, India, and Persia, who neglected, and still neglect, to counterbalance these natural powers by the resources of military art. The warlike states of antiquity, Greece, Macedonia, and Rome, educated a race of soldiers; exercised their bodies, disciplined their courage, multiplied their forces by regular evolutions, and converted the iron which they possessed, into strong and serviceable weapons. But this superiority insensibly declined with their laws and manners; and the feeble policy of Constantine and his successors armed and instructed, for the ruin of the empire, the rude valour of the Barbarian mercenaries. The military art has been changed by the invention of gunpowder; which enables man to command the two most powerful agents of nature, air and fire. Mathematics, chemistry, mechanics, architecture, have been applied to the service of war; and the adverse parties oppose to each other the most elaborate modes of attack and of defence. Historians may indignantly observe that the preparations of a siege would found and maintain a flourishing colony; yet we cannot be displeased that the subversion of a city should be a work of cost and difficulty, or that an industrious people should be protected by those arts, which survive and supply the decay of military virtue. Cannon and fortifications now form an impregnable barrier against the Tartar horse; and Europe is secure from any future irruption of Barbarians; since, before they can conquer, they must cease to be barbarous. Their gradual advances in the science of war would always be accompanied, as we may learn from the example of Russia, with a proportionable improvement in the arts of peace and civil policy; and they themselves must deserve a place among the polished nations whom they subdue.

Should these speculations be found doubtful or fallacious, there still remains a more humble source of comfort and hope. The discoveries of ancient and modern navigators, and the domestic history, or tradition, of the most enlightened nations, represent the *human savage*, naked both in mind and body, and destitute of laws, of arts, of ideas, and almost of language. From this abject condition, perhaps the primitive and universal, state of man, he has gradually arisen to command the animals, to fertilise the earth, to traverse the ocean, and to measure the heavens. His progress in the improvement and exercise of his mental and corporeal faculties has been irregular and various, infinitely slow in the beginning, and increasing by degrees with redoubled velocity; ages of laborious ascent have been followed by a moment of rapid downfall; and the several climates of the globe have felt the vicissitudes of light and darkness. Yet the experience of four thousand years should enlarge our hopes, and diminish our apprehensions; we cannot determine to what height the human species may aspire in their advances towards perfection; but it may safely be presumed that no people, unless the face of nature is changed, will relapse into their original barbarism. The improvements of society may be viewed under a threefold aspect. 1. The poet or philosopher illustrates his age and country by the efforts of a *single* mind; but these superior powers of reason or fancy are rare and spontaneous productions, and the genius of Homer, or Cicero, or Newton, would excite less admiration, if they could be created by the will of a prince or the lessons of a preceptor. 2. The benefits of law and policy, of trade and manufactures, of arts and sciences, are more solid and permanent; and *many* individuals may be qualified, by education and discipline, to promote, in their respective stations, the interest of the community. But this general order is the effect of skill and labour; and the complex machinery may be decayed by time or injured by violence. 3. Fortunately for mankind, the more useful, or, at least, more necessary arts can be performed without superior talents or national subordination; without the powers of *one* or the union of *many*. Each village, each family, each individual, must always possess both ability and inclination to perpetuate the use of fire and of metals; the propagation and service of domestic animals; the methods of hunting and fishing; the rudiments of navigation; the imperfect cultivation of corn or other nutritive grain; and the simple practice of the mechanic trades. Private genius and public industry may be extirpated; but these hardy plants survive the tempest, and strike an everlasting root into the most unfavourable soil. The splendid days of Augustus and Trajan were eclipsed by a cloud of ignorance; and the Barbarians subverted the laws and palaces of Rome. But the scythe, the invention or emblem of Saturn, still continued annually to mow the harvests of Italy: and the human feasts of the Laestrygons have never been renewed on the coast of Campania.

Since the first discovery of the arts, war, commerce, and religious zeal have diffused, among the savages of the Old and New World, those inestimable gifts: they have been successively propagated; they can never be lost. We may therefore acquiesce in the pleasing conclusion that every age of the world has increased, and still increases, the real wealth, the happiness, the knowledge, and perhaps the virtue, of the human race.[2]

* From Edward Gibbon, *The Decline and Fall of the Roman Empire*, Vol. 4 (London: Methuen & Co., 1901 [1776–78]), 163–9.

[1] America now contains about six millions of European blood and descent; and their numbers, at least in the North, are continually increasing. Whatever may be the changes of their political situation, they must preserve the manners of Europe; and we may reflect with some pleasure that the English language will probably be diffused over an immense and populous continent.

[2] The merit of discovery has too often been stained with avarice, cruelty, and fanaticism; and the intercourse of nations has produced the communication of disease and prejudice. A singular exception is due to the virtue of our own times and country. The five great voyages successively undertaken by the command of his present Majesty were inspired by the pure and generous love of science and of mankind. The same price adapting his benefactions to the different stages of society has founded a school of painting in his capital, and has introduced into the islands of the South Sea the vegetables and animals most useful to human life.

Civil society, nation, cosmopolitanism

Immanuel Kant (1724–1804), German philosopher. Kant was less the cold reasoning intellect that he is often portrayed as: he also indulged in merry entertainment and drink in his youth. Here he situates the discussion of civil society within external relations and looks forward to civil society as a cosmopolitan sphere of law and justice.*

Fifth Proposition

The greatest problem for the human race, to the solution of which it is compelled by Nature, is the establishment of a Civil Society, which can universally administer justice.

It is only in a society which possesses the greatest freedom, and which consequently involves a thorough Antagonism of its members – with, however, the most exact determination and guarantee of the limits of this freedom in order that it may coexist with the freedom of others – that the highest purpose of nature, which is the development of all her capacities, can be attained in the case of mankind. Now Nature also wills that the human race shall attain through itself to this, as to all the other ends for which it was destined. Hence a society in which freedom *under external laws* may be found combined in the greatest possible degree with irresistible Power, or a perfectly *just* civil constitution, is the highest natural problem prescribed to the human species. And this is so, because Nature can only by means of the solution and fulfilment of this problem, realise her other purposes with our race. A certain necessity compels man, who is otherwise so greatly prepossessed in favour of unlimited freedom, to enter into this state of coercion and restraint. And indeed, it is the greatest necessity of all that does this; for it is created by men themselves whose inclinations make it impossible for them to exist long beside each other in wild lawless freedom. But in such a complete growth as the civil union, these very inclinations afterwards produce the best effects. It is with them as with the trees in a forest; for just because everyone strives to deprive the other of air and sun, they compel each other to seek them both above, and thus they grow beautiful and straight, whereas those that in freedom and apart from one another shoot out their branches at will, grow stunted and crooked and awry. All the culture and art that adorn humanity, and the finest social order, are fruits of that unsociableness which is necessitated of itself to discipline itself and which thus constrains man, by compulsive art, to develop completely the germs of his nature.

. . .

Seventh Proposition

The problem of the establishment of a perfect civil constitution is subordinate to the problem of the regulation of the external relations between states governed by law; and without the solution of this latter problem it cannot be solved. *

What avails it to labour at the arrangement of a commonwealth as a civil constitution regulated by law among individual men? The same unsociableness which forced men to it, becomes again the cause of each commonwealth assuming the attitude of uncontrolled freedom in its external relations, that is, as one state in relation to other states; and consequently, any one state must expect from any other the same sort of evils as oppressed individual men and compelled them to enter into a civil union regulated by law. Nature has accordingly again used the unsociableness of men, and even of great societies and political bodies, her creatures of this kind, as a means to work out through their mutual antagonism a condition of rest and security. It works through wars, through the strain of never relaxed preparation for them, and through the necessity which every state is at last compelled to feel within itself, even in the midst of peace, to begin some imperfect efforts to carry out her purpose. And, at last, after many devastations, overthrows, and even complete internal exhaustion of their powers, the nations are driven forward to the goal which reason might have well impressed upon them, even without so much sad experience. This is none other than the advance out of the lawless state of savages and the entering into a federation of peoples. It is thus brought about that every state, including even the smallest, may rely for its safety and its rights, not on its own power or its own judgement of right, but only on this great international federation (*Foedus Amphictionum*), on its combined power, and on the decision of the common will according to laws.

. . .

We have glanced at what has been done by the seemingly purposeless state of savages; how it checked for a time all the natural capacities of our species but at last by the very evils in which it involved mankind, it compelled them to pass from this state, and to enter into a civil constitution, in which all the germs of humanity could be unfolded. And, in like manner, the barbarian freedom of states when once they were founded, proceeded in the same way of progress. By the expenditure of all the resources of the commonwealth in military preparations against each other, by the devastations occasioned by war, and still more by the necessity of holding themselves continually in readiness for it, the full development of the capacities of mankind are undoubtedly retarded in their progress; but, on the other hand, the very evils which thus arise, compel men to find out means against them. A law of equilibrium is thus discovered for the regulation of the really wholesome antagonism of contiguous states as it springs up out of their freedom; and a united power, giving emphasis to this law, is constituted, whereby there is introduced a cosmopolitan system of public security. And so that the powers of mankind may not fall asleep, this condition is not entirely free from *danger*; but it is at the same time not without a principle which operates, so as to *equalise* the mutual action and reaction of these powers, that they may not destroy each other. Before the last step of bringing in a universal union of the states is taken – and accordingly when human nature is only half way in its progress – it has to endure the hardest evils of all, under the deceptive semblance of outward prosperity; and Rousseau was not so far wrong when he preferred the state of the savages, if the last stage which our race has yet to surmount be left out of view. We are *cultivated* in a high degree by Science and Art. We are *civilised*, even to excess, in the way of all sorts of social forms of politeness and elegance. But there is still much to be done before we can be regarded as *moralised*. The idea of morality certainly belongs to culture; but an application of this idea which extends no farther than the likeness of morality in the sense of honour and external propriety, merely constitutes civilisation. So long, however, as states lavish all their resources upon vain and violent schemes of aggrandisement, so long as they continually impede the slow movements of the endeavour to cultivate the newer habits of thought and character on the part of the citizens, and even withdraw from them all the means of furthering it, nothing in the way of moral progress can be expected. A long internal process of improvement is thus required in every commonwealth as a condition for the higher culture of its citizens. But all apparent good that is not grafted upon a morally good disposition, is nothing but mere illusion and littering misery. In this condition the human race will remain until it shall have worked itself, in the way that has been indicated, out of the existing chaos of its political relations.

* Based on the translation in W. Hastie, ed., *Kant's Principles of Politics* (Edinburgh: T & T Clark, 1891 [1784]), 12–17; 19–21, with a few changes by the editors better to reflect the German original.

3
Civil Society in the Midst of Modern Ideologies

Radicalism vs. conservatism

Edmund Burke (1729–97), born in Ireland, British statesman and writer. Burke rose to fame through his membership of the Whig party of Rockingham, his patron. Emphasizing the responsibilities of empire and also supporting many liberal reforms, his historical legacy has been mainly informed by his defence of organic institutions against the principles of the French Revolution. Here he argues for the central role of established religion in civil society.*

We know, and what is better, we feel inwardly; that religion is the basis of civil society and the source of all good and of all comfort. ... In England we are so convinced of this, that there is no rust of superstition with which the accumulated absurdity of the human mind might have crusted it over in the course of ages, that ninety-nine in a hundred of the people of England would not prefer to impiety. We shall never be such fools as to call in an enemy to the substance of any system to remove its corruptions, to supply its defects, or to perfect its construction. If our religious tenets should ever want a further elucidation, we shall not call on atheism to explain them. We shall not light up our temple from that unhallowed fire. It will be illuminated with other lights. It will be perfumed with other incense than the infectious stuff which is imported by the smugglers of adulerated metaphysics. If our ecclesiastical establishment should want a revision, it is not avarice or rapacity, public or private, that we shall employ for the audit, or receipt, or application of its consecrated revenue. Violently condemning neither the Greek nor the Armenian, nor, since heats are subsided, the Roman system of religion, we prefer the Protestant, not because we think it has less of the Christian religion in it, but because, in our judgment, it has more. We are Protestants, not from indifference, but from zeal.

We know, and it is our pride to know, that man is by his constitution a religious animal; that atheism is against, not only our reason, but our instincts; and that it cannot prevail long. But if, in the moment of riot and

96

in a drunken delirium from the hot spirit drawn out of the alembic of hell, which in France is now so furiously boiling, we should uncover our nakedness by throwing off that Christian religion which has hitherto been our boast and comfort, and one great source of civilization amongst us and amongst many other nations, we are apprehensive (being well aware that the mind will not endure a void) that some uncouth, pernicious, and degrading superstition might take place of it.

...

Society is indeed a contract. Subordinate contracts for objects of mere occasional interest may be dissolved at pleasure – but the state ought not to be considered as nothing better than a partnership agreement in a trade of pepper and coffee, calico, or tobacco, or some other such low concern, to be taken up for a little temporary interest, and to be dissolved by the fancy of the parties. It is to be looked on with other reverence, because it is not a partnership in things subservient only to the gross animal existence of a temporary and perishable nature. It is a partnership in all science; a partnership in all art; a partnership in every virtue and in all perfection. As the ends of such a partnership cannot be obtained in many generations, it becomes a partnership not only between those who are living, but between those who are living, those who are dead, and those who are to be born. Each contract of each particular state is but a clause in the great primeval contract of eternal society, linking the lower with the higher natures, connecting the visible and invisible world, according to a fixed compact sanctioned by the inviolable oath which holds all physical and all moral natures, each in their appointed place. This law is not subject to the will of those who by an obligation above them, and infinitely superior, are bound to submit their will to that law. The municipal corporations of that universal kingdom are not morally at liberty at their pleasure, and on their speculations of a contingent improvement, wholly to separate and tear asunder the bands of their subordinate community and to dissolve it into an unsocial, uncivil, unconnected chaos of elementary principles. It is the first and supreme necessity only; a necessity that is not chosen but chooses, a necessity paramount to deliberation, that admits no discussion and demands no evidence, which alone can justify a resort to anarchy. This necessity is no exception to the rule, because this necessity itself is a part, too, of that moral and physical disposition of things to which man must be obedient by consent or force; but if that which is only submission to necessity should be made the object of choice, the law is broken, nature is disobeyed, and the rebellious are outlawed, cast forth, and exiled from this world of reason, and order, and peace, and virtue, and fruitful penitence, into the antagonist world of madness, discord, vice, confusion, and unavailing sorrow.

...

Persuaded that all things ought to be done with reference, and referring all to the point of reference to which all should be directed, they think themselves bound, not only as individuals in the sanctuary of the heart or as congregated in that personal capacity, to renew the memory of their high origin and cast, but also in their corporate character to perform their national homage to the institutor and author and protector of civil society; without which civil society man could not by any possibility arrive at the perfection of which his nature is capable, nor even make a remote and faint approach to it. They conceive that He who gave our nature to be perfected by our virtue willed also the necessary means of its perfection. He willed therefore the state – He willed its connection with the source and original archetype of all perfection. They who are convinced of this His will, which is the law of laws and the sovereign of sovereigns, cannot think it reprehensible that this our corporate fealty and homage, that this our recognition of a seigniory paramount, I had almost said this oblation of the state itself as a worthy offering on the high altar of universal praise, should be performed as all public, solemn acts are performed, in buildings, in music, in decoration, in speech, in the dignity of persons, according to the customs of mankind taught by their nature; that is, with modest splendor and unassuming state, with mild majesty and sober pomp. For those purposes they think some part of the wealth of the country is as usefully employed as it can be in fomenting the luxury of individuals. It is the public ornament. It is the public consolation. It nourishes the public hope. The poorest man finds his own importance and dignity in it, whilst the wealth and pride of individuals at every moment makes the man of humble rank and fortune sensible of his inferiority and degrades and vilifies his condition. It is for the man in humble life, and to raise his nature and to put him in mind of a state in which the privileges of opulence will cease, when he will be equal by nature and may be more than equal by virtue, that this portion of the general wealth of his country is employed and sanctified.

I assure you I do not aim at singularity. I give you opinions which have been accepted amongst us, from very early times to this moment, with a continued and general approbation, and which indeed are worked into my mind that I am unable to distinguish what I have learned from others from the results of my own meditation.

It is on some such principles that the majority of the people of England, far from thinking a religious national establishment unlawful, hardly think it lawful to be without one. In France you are wholly mistaken if you do not believe us above all other things attached to it, and beyond all other nations; and when this people has acted unwisely and unjustifiably in its favor (as in some instances they have done most certainly), in their very errors you will at least discover their zeal.

This principle runs through the whole system of their polity. They do not consider their church establishment as convenient, but as essential to their state, not as a thing heterogeneous and separable, something added for accommodation, what they may either keep or lay aside according to their temporary ideas of convenience. They consider it as the foundation of their whole constitution, with which, and with every part of which, it holds an indissoluble union. Church and state are ideas inseparable in their minds, and scarcely is the one ever mentioned without mentioning the other.

*From Edmund Burke, *Reflections on the Revolution in France* (London: Dent; New York: E.P. Dutton, 1910 [1790]), 87–8; 93–4; 95–6.

*Thomas Paine (1737–1809), transatlantic radical. Paine began his radical career when as a tax officer he agitated for higher salaries. After being dismissed, he emigrated to America in 1774 where he became a champion for the independence of the American colonies from the British Empire. After his return to Britain he defended the French Revolution against Burke – his critique of English institutions led to his prosecution and flight to Paris. Here he argues for the limited role of government as an association acting on behalf of society.**

Great part of that order which reigns among mankind is not the effect of Government. It has its origin in the principles of society and the natural constitution of man. It existed prior to Government, and would exist if the formality of Government was abolished. The mutual dependence and reciprocal interest which man has upon man, and all the parts of a civilised community upon each other, create that great chain of connection which holds it together. The landholder, the farmer, the manufacturer, the merchant, the tradesman, and every occupation, prospers by the aid which each receives from the other, and from the whole. Common interest regulates their concerns, and forms their law; and the laws which common usage ordains, have a greater influence than the laws of Government. In fine, society performs for itself almost everything which is ascribed to Government.

To understand the nature and quantity of Government proper for man, it is necessary to attend to his character. As nature created him for social life, she fitted him for the station she intended. In all cases she made his natural wants greater than his individual powers. No one man is capable, without the aid of society, of supplying his own wants; and those wants, acting upon every individual, impel the whole of them into society, as naturally as gravitation acts to a centre.

But she has gone further. She has not only forced man into society by a diversity of wants which the reciprocal aid of each other can supply, but she has implanted in him a system of social affections, which, though not necessary to his existence, are essential to his happiness. There is no period in life when this love for society ceases to act. It begins and ends with our being.

If we examine with attention the composition and constitution of man, the diversity of his wants and talents in different men for reciprocally accommodating the wants of each other, his propensity to society, and consequently to preserve the advantages resulting from it, we shall easily discover that a great part of what is called Government is mere imposition.

Government is no farther necessary than to supply the few cases to which society and civilisation are not conveniently competent; and instances are not wanting to show, that everything which Government can usefully add thereto, has been performed by the common consent of society, without Government.

For upwards of two years from the commencement of the American War [of Independence] and to a longer period in several of the American States, there were no established forms of Government. The old Governments had been abolished, and the country was too much occupied in defence to employ its attention in establishing new Governments; yet during this interval order and harmony were preserved as inviolate as in any country in Europe. There is a natural aptness in man, and more so in society, because it embraces a greater variety of abilities and resources, to accommodate itself to whatever situation it is in. The instant formal Government is abolished, society begins to act: a general association takes place, and common interest produces common security.

So far is it from being true, as has been pretended, that the abolition of any formal Government is the dissolution of society, that it acts by a contrary impulse, and brings the latter the closer together. All that part of its organization which it had committed to its Government, devolves again upon itself, and acts through its medium. When men, as well from natural instinct as from reciprocal benefits, have habituated themselves to social and civilised life, there is always enough of its principles in practice to carry them through any changes they may find necessary or convenient to make in their Government. In short, man is so naturally a creature of society that it is almost impossible to put him out of it.

Formal Government makes but a small part of civilised life; and when even the best that human wisdom can devise is established, it is a thing more in name and idea than in fact. It is to the great and fundamental principles of society and civilisation – to the common usage universally consented to, and mutually and reciprocally maintained – to the unceasing circulation of interest, which, passing through its million channels, invigorates the whole mass of civilised man – it is to these things, infinitely more than to anything which even the best instituted Government can perform, that the safety and prosperity of the individual and of the whole depends.

The more perfect civilisation is, the less occasion has it for Government, because the more it does regulate its own affairs, and govern itself; but so contrary is the practice of old Governments to the reason of the case, that the expences of them increase in the proportion they ought to diminish. It is but few general laws that civilised life requires, and those of such common usefulness, that whether they are enforced by the forms of government or not, the effect will be nearly the same. If we consider what the principles are that first condense men into society, and what the motives that regulate their mutual intercourse afterwards, we shall find, by the time we arrive at what is called Government, that nearly the whole of the business is performed by the natural operation of the parts upon each other.

Man, with respect to all those matters, is more a creature of consistency than he is aware, or that Governments would wish him to believe. All the great laws of society are laws of nature. Those of trade and commerce, whether with respect to the intercourse of individuals or of nations, are laws of mutual and reciprocal interests. They are followed and obeyed, because it is the interest of the parties so to do, and not on account of any formal laws their Governments may impose or interpose.

But how often is the natural propensity to society disturbed or destroyed by the operations of Government! When the latter, instead of being ingrafted on the principles of the former, assumes to exist for itself, and acts by partialities of favour and oppression, it becomes the cause of the mischiefs it ought to prevent.

If we look back to the riots and tumults which at various times have happened in England, we shall find that they did not proceed from the want of a Government, but that Government was itself the generating cause: instead of consolidating society it divided it; it deprived it of its natural cohesion, and engendered discontents and disorders which otherwise would not have existed. In those associations, which men promiscuously form for the purpose of trade, or of any concern in which Government is totally out of the question, we see how naturally the various parties unite; and this shows, by comparison, that Governments, so far from being always the cause or means of order, are often the destruction of it.

. . .

One of the great advantages of the American Revolution has been, that it led to a discovery of the principles, and laid open the imposition of Governments. All these Revolutions till then had been worked within the small sphere of a Court, and never on the great floor of a Nation. The parties were always of the class of courtiers; and whatever was their rage for reformation, they carefully preserved the fraud of the profession.

In all cases they took care to represent Government as a thing made up of mysteries, which only themselves understood; and they hid from the understanding of the Nation the only thing that was beneficial to know, namely, *that Government is nothing more than a national association acting on the principles of society.*

* From Thomas Paine, *Rights of Man* (London: J.M. Dent & Sons Ltd, 1944 [1792]), 157–60; 162.

Emmanuel-Joseph Sieyès (1748–1836), clergyman and constitutional theorist, gained great fame as the result of the publication in January 1789 of What is the Third Estate? *This pamphlet identified the underprivileged Third Estate with the French nation, and asserted that it had the right to draft the constitution. In this selection, one sees the demand for a unitary social will, a demand likely to be at odds with the notion of difference so central to civil society.**

In the first period we assume a fairly considerable number of isolated individuals who wish to unite; by this fact alone, they already constitute a nation: they enjoy all the rights of a nation and it only remains for them to exercise them. This first period is characterised by the activity of the *individual* wills. The association is their work; they are the origin of all power.

The second period is characterised by the action of the *common* will. The associates give consistency to their union; they want to fulfil its aim. They therefore discuss and agree amongst themselves on public needs and on ways of satisfying them. We see that power, then, belongs to the community. Individual wills still constitute its origin and form its essential components; but, taken separately, they would be powerless. Power exists only in the aggregate. The community needs a common will; without *singleness* of will it could not succeed in being a willing and acting body. It is certain, also, that this body has no rights other than such as derive from the common will.

But let us leap the lapse of time. The associates are now too numerous and occupy too large an area to exercise their common will easily by themselves. What do they do? They separate out whatever is necessary to attend to and satisfy public requirements; and they put a few of their number in charge of exercising this portion of the national will, that is to say this portion of power. We have now reached the third period, the period of *government by proxy*. Let us point out a few facts: 1) The community does not cast aside its right to will: this is inalienable; it can only delegate the exercise of that right. This principle is elaborated elsewhere. 2) Nor can it delegate the full exercise of it. It delegates only that portion of its total power which is needed to maintain order. In this matter, no more is surrendered than necessary. 3) Therefore, it does not rest with the body of delegates to alter the limits of the power that has been entrusted to them. Obviously such a competence would be self-contradictory.

I distinguish the third period from the second in that it is no longer the *real* common will which is in operation, but *representative* common will.

...

The power exercised by the government has substance only in so far as it is constitutional; it is legal only in so far as it is based on the prescribed laws. The national will, on the contrary, never needs anything but its own existence to be legal. It is the source of all legality.

Not only is the nation not subject to a constitution, but it *cannot* be and it *must not* be; which is tantamount to saying that it is not.

It *cannot* be. From whom indeed could it have received positive form? Is there a prior authority which could have told a multitude of individuals: 'I put you together under such and such laws; you will form a nation on the conditions I prescribe.' We are not speaking here of brigandage or domination, but of a legitimate, that is to say voluntary and free, association.

Can it be said that a nation, by a primary act of will which is completely untrammelled by any procedure, can bind itself to express its will thereafter only in certain determined ways? In the first place a nation can neither alienate nor waive its right to will; and whatever its decisions, it cannot lose the right to alter them as soon as its interest requires. Secondly, with whom would this nation have entered into such a contract? I see how it can *bind* its members, its mandatories, and all those who belong to it; but can it in any sense impose on itself duties towards itself? What is a contract with oneself? Since both parties are the same will, they are obviously always able to free themselves from the purported engagement.

Even if it could, a nation *must* not subject itself to the shackles of a defined procedure. That would put it in danger of losing its liberty for ever, for tyranny, under the pretext of giving the People a constitution, would only need a momentary success to bind it so closely by procedural rules that it would lose the ability to express its own will, and, consequently, to shake off the yoke of despotism. We must conceive the nations of the world as being like men living outside society or 'in a state of nature', as it is called. The exercise of their will is free and independent of any civil form. Existing only within the natural order, their will can take full effect provided it bears the *natural* characteristics of a will. The manner in which a nation exercises its will does not matter; the point is that it does exercise it; any procedure is adequate, and its will is always the supreme law. To imagine a legitimate society, we assumed that the purely natural individual will had enough moral power to form the association; how then can we refuse to recognise a similar power in the equally natural *common* will? A nation is always in a state of nature and, amidst so many dangers, it can never have too many possible methods of expressing its will. Let us not be afraid of repeating it: a nation is independent of any procedures; and no matter how it exercises its will, the mere fact of its doing so puts an end to positive law, because it is the source and the supreme master of positive law.

But there is even stronger proof that our principles are correct, though further arguments are really superfluous.

A nation must not and cannot identify itself with constitutional forms, for as soon as a conflict arises between different parts of that constitution, what will become of a nation organised by the very constitution that is in dispute? Mark how important it is, socially, that citizens shall be able to look to some department of the executive to provide an authoritative solution for their private litigation. In the same way, the various branches of the executive must be at liberty, in a free nation, to appeal to the legislative body for a decision whenever they meet unforeseen difficulties. But if the legislative body itself – the very basis of the constitution – is in a state of disruption, who then will be the supreme judge? For without one, order must give way to anarchy.

How can one believe that a constituted body may itself decide on its own constitution? One or more component parts of a corporate body are of no consequence individually. Power belongs only to the whole. As soon as a part protests, the whole ceases to exist; if non-existent, then how can it pass judgement? From this it follows that the constitution of a country would cease to exist at the slightest difficulty arising between its component parts, if it were not that the nation existed independently of any rule and any constitutional form.

In the light of these explanations, we can answer the question we asked ourselves. The component parts of what you believe to be the French constitution are quite obviously at loggerheads. Whose task is it to decide? It is the nation's, independent as it necessarily is of any positive forms. Even if the nation enjoyed regular States-General, this constituted body would be incompetent to decide on a dispute concerning its own constitution. It would be a *petitio principii*, a vicious circle.

The *ordinary* representatives of a nation are charged with the exercise, under the constitution, of that portion of the common will which is necessary to maintain a good social administration. Their power is confined to governmental affairs.

Extraordinary representatives will have whatever new powers the nation chooses to give them. Since a large nation cannot physically assemble when extraordinary circumstances make this necessary, it must entrust extraordinary representatives with the necessary powers on such occasions. If it could meet and express its will before your eyes, would you dare to dispute it on the ground that it did so by one procedure rather than another? Here reality is everything, the form is nothing.

A body of extraordinary representatives takes the place of the assembly of the nation. It does not, of course, need to be in charge of the *whole* of the national will; it needs only special powers, and those only in rare cases; but it is in the same position as the nation itself in respect of *independence* from any constitutional forms.

...

It is a certain that among the national representatives, whether ordinary or extraordinary, influence must be proportionate to the number of citizens who have the *right* to be represented. If it is to accomplish its task, the representative body must always be the substitute for the nation itself. It must partake of the same *nature*, the same *proportions* and the same *rules*.

To conclude: these principles are all self-consistent and prove: a) only an extraordinary representative body can establish or amend the constitution; b) this constituent representative body must be set up without regard to the distinction between orders.

* From Emmanuel-Joseph Sieyès, *What is the Third Estate?*, S.E. Finer, ed., translated by M. Blondel (Essex: The Pall Mall Press, 1963 [1789]), 121–2; 126–31; 137.

Liberalism and empire

Alexis de Tocqueville (1805–59), politician and liberal theorist, began his career believing that the entry of the people onto the political stage was likely to militate against the very possibility of political liberty. However, Democracy in America *(1835 and 1840) gives a very positive account of the ability to combine equal social conditions with political liberty in the United States. Central to de Tocqueville's position was his admiration for associational life, capable in his view of creating a taste for liberty because of the very practice of liberty. The selection that follows praises associational life, explains why it has a different character in the United States against France, and notes the spillover effects from associations to political and economic endeavours.**

Political Associations in the United States

Different ways in which the right of association is understood in Europe and in the United States – Different use which is made of it.

The most natural privilege of man, next to the right of acting for himself, is that of combining his exertions with those of his fellow-creatures, and of acting in common with them. I am therefore led to conclude that the right of association is almost as inalienable as the right of personal liberty. No legislator can attack it without impairing the very foundations of society. Nevertheless, if the liberty of association is a fruitful source of advantages and prosperity to some nations, it may be perverted or carried to excess by others, and the element of life may be changed into an element of destruction. A comparison of the different methods which associations pursue in those countries in which they are managed with discretion, as well as in those where liberty degenerates into license, may perhaps be thought useful both to governments and to parties.

The greater part of Europeans look upon an association as a weapon which is to be hastily fashioned, and immediately tried in the conflict. A society is formed for discussion, but the idea of impending action prevails in the minds of those who constitute it: it is, in fact, an army; and the time given to parley serves to reckon up the strength and to animate the courage of the host, after which they direct their march against the enemy. Resources which lie within the bounds of the law may suggest themselves to the persons who compose it as means, but never as the only means, of success.

Such, however, is not the manner in which the right of association is understood in the United States. In America the citizens who form the minority associate, in order, in the first place, to show their numerical strength, and so to diminish the moral authority of the majority; and, in the second place, to stimulate competition, and to discover those arguments which are most fitted to act upon the majority; for they always entertain hopes of drawing over their opponents to their own side, and of afterwards disposing of the supreme power in their name. Political associations in the United States are therefore peaceable in their intentions, and strictly legal in the means which they employ; and they assert with perfect truth that they only aim at success by lawful expedients.

The difference which exists between the Americans and ourselves depends on several causes. In Europe there are numerous parties so diametrically opposed to the majority that they can never hope to acquire its support, and at the same time they think that they are sufficiently strong in themselves to struggle and to defend their cause. When a party of this kind forms an association, its object is, not to conquer, but to fight. In America the individuals who hold opinions very much opposed to those of the majority are no sort of impediment to its power, and all other parties hope to win it over to their own principles in the end. The exercise of the right of association becomes dangerous in proportion to the impossibility which excludes great parties from acquiring the majority. In a country like the United States, in which the differences of opinion are mere differences of hue, the right of association may remain unrestrained without evil consequences. The inexperience of many of the European nations in the enjoyment of liberty leads them only to look upon the liberty of association as a right of attacking the Government. The first notion which presents itself to a party, as well as to an individual, when it has acquired a consciousness of its own strength, is that of violence: the notion of persuasion arises at a later period and is only derived from experience. The English, who are divided into parties which differ most essentially from each other, rarely abuse the right of association, because they have long been accustomed to exercise it. In France the passion for war is so intense that there is no undertaking so mad or so injurious to the welfare of the State, that a man does not consider himself honoured in defending it, at the risk of his life.

But perhaps the most powerful of the causes which tend to mitigate the excesses of political association in the United States is Universal Suffrage. In countries in which universal suffrage exists the majority is never doubtful, because neither party can pretend to represent that portion of the community which has not voted. The associations which are formed are aware, as well as the nation at large, that they do not represent the majority: this is, indeed, a condition inseparable from their existence; for if they did represent the preponderating power, they would change the law instead of soliciting its reform. The consequence of this is that the moral influence of the Government which they attack is very much increased, and their own power is very much enfeebled.

In Europe there are few associations which do not affect to represent the majority, or which do not believe that they represent it. This conviction or this pretension tends to augment their force amazingly, and contributes no less to legalize their measures. Violence may seem to be excusable in defence of the cause of oppressed right. Thus it is, in the vast labyrinth of human laws, that extreme liberty sometimes corrects the abuses of license, and that extreme democracy obviates the dangers of democratic government. In Europe, associations consider themselves, in some degree, as the legislative and executive councils of the people, which is unable to speak for itself. In America, where they only represent a minority of the nation, they argue and they petition.

The means which the associations of Europe employ are in accordance with the end which they propose to obtain. As the principal aim of these bodies is to act, and not to debate, to fight rather than to persuade, they are naturally led to adopt a form of organization which differs from the ordinary customs of civil bodies, and which assumes the habits and the maxims of military life. They centralize the direction of their resources as much as possible, and they entrust the power of the whole party to a very small number of leaders.

The members of these associations respond to a watchword, like soldiers on duty; they profess the doctrine of passive obedience; say rather, that in uniting together they at once abjure the exercise of their own judgment and free will; and the tyrannical control which these societies exercise is often far more insupportable than the authority possessed over society by the Government which they attack. Their moral force is much diminished by these excesses, and they lose the powerful interest which is always excited by a struggle between oppressors and the oppressed. The man who in given cases consent to obey his fellows with servility, and who submits his activity and even his opinions to their control, can have no claim to rank as a free citizen.

The Americans have also established certain forms of government which are applied to their associations, but these are invariably borrowed from the forms of the civil administration. The independence of each individual is formally recognised; the tendency of the members of the association points, as it does in the body of the community, towards the same end, but they are not obliged to follow the same track. No one abjures the exercise of his reason and his free will; but everyone exerts that reason and that will for the benefit of a common undertaking.

. . .

The political associations which exist in the United States are only a single feature in the midst of the immense assemblage of associations in that country. Americans of all ages, all conditions, and all dispositions, constantly form associations. They have not only commercial and manufacturing companies, in which all take part, but associations of a thousand other kinds – religious, moral, serious, futile, extensive or restricted, enormous or diminutive. The Americans make associations to give entertainments, to found establishments for education, to build inns, to construct churches, to diffuse books, to send missionaries to the antipodes; and in this manner they found hospitals, prisons, and schools. If it be proposed to advance some truth, or to foster some feeling by the encouragement of a great example, they form a society. Wherever, at the head of some new undertaking, you see the Government in France, or a man of rank in England, in the United States you will be sure to find an association. I met with several kinds of associations in America, of which I confess I had no previous notion; and I have often admired the extreme skill with which the inhabitants of the United States succeed in proposing a common object to the exertions of a great many men, and in getting them voluntarily to pursue it. I have since travelled over England, whence the Americans have taken some of their laws and many of their customs; and it seemed to me that the principle of association was by no means so constantly or so adroitly used in that country. The English often perform great things singly; whereas the Americans form associations for the smallest undertakings. It is evident that the former people consider association as a powerful means of action, but the latter seem to regard it as the only means they have of acting.

Thus the most democratic country on the face of the earth is that in which men have in our time carried to the highest perfection the art of pursuing in common the object of their common desires, and have applied this new science to the greatest number of purposes. Is this the result of accident? or is there in reality any necessary connection between the principle of association and that of equality? Aristocratic communities always contain, amongst a multitude of persons who by themselves are powerless, a small number of powerful and wealthy citizens, each of whom can achieve great undertakings single-handed. In aristocratic societies men do not need to combine in order to act, because they are strongly held together. Every wealthy and powerful citizen constitutes the head of a permanent and compulsory association, composed of all those who are dependent upon him, or whom he makes subservient to the execution of his designs. Amongst democratic nations, on the contrary, all the citizens are independent and feeble; they can do hardly anything by themselves, and none of them can oblige his fellow-men to lend him their assistance. They all, therefore, fall into a state of incapacity, if they do not learn voluntarily to help each other. If men living in democratic countries had no right and no inclination to associate for political purposes, their independence would be in great jeopardy; but they might long preserve their wealth and their cultivation: whereas if they never acquired the habit of forming associations in ordinary life, civilization itself would be endangered. A people amongst which individuals should lose the power of achieving great things single-handed, without acquiring the means of producing them by united exertions, would soon relapse into barbarism.

Unhappily, the same social condition which renders associations so necessary to democratic nations, renders their formation more difficult amongst those nations than amongst all others. When several members of an aristocracy agree to combine, they easily succeed in doing so; as each of them brings great strength to the partnership, the number of its members may be very limited; and when the members of an association are limited in number, they may easily become mutually acquainted, understand each other, and establish fixed regulations. The same opportunities do not occur amongst democratic nations, where the associated members must always be very numerous for their association to have any power.

I am aware that many of my countrymen are not in the least embarrassed by this difficulty. They contend that the more enfeebled and incompetent the citizens become, the more able and active the Government ought to be rendered, in order that society at large may execute what individuals can no longer accomplish. They believe this answers the whole difficulty, but I think they are mistaken. A Government might perform the part of some of the largest American companies; and several States, members of the Union, have already attempted it; but what political power could ever carry on the vast multitude of lesser undertakings which the American citizens perform every day, with the assistance of the principle of association? It is easy to foresee that the time is drawing near when man will be less and less able to produce, of himself alone, the commonest necessaries of life. The task of the governing power will therefore perpetually increase, and its very efforts will extend it every day. The more it stands in the place of associations, the more will individuals, losing the notion of combining together, require its assistance: these are causes and effects which unceasingly engender each other. Will the administration of the country ultimately assume the management of all the manufactures, which no single citizen is able to carry on? And if a time at length arrives, when, in consequence of the extreme subdivision of landed property, the soil is split into an infinite number of parcels, so that it can only be cultivated by companies of husbandmen, will it be necessary that the head of the government should leave the helm of state to follow the plough? The morals and the intelligence of a democratic people would be as much endangered as its business and manufactures, if the government ever wholly usurped the place of private companies.

Feelings and opinions are recruited, the heart is enlarged, and the human mind is developed by no other means than by the reciprocal influence of men upon each other. I have shown that these influences are almost null in democratic countries; they must therefore be artificially created, and this can only be accomplished by associations.

When the members of an aristocratic community adopt a new opinion, or conceive a new sentiment, they give it a station, as it were, beside themselves, upon the lofty platform where they stand; and opinions or sentiments so conspicuous to the eyes of the multitude are easily introduced into the minds or hearts of all around. In democratic countries the governing power alone is naturally in a condition to act in this manner; but it is easy to see that its action is always inadequate, and often dangerous. A government can no more be competent to keep alive and to renew the circulation of opinions and feelings amongst a great people, than to manage all the speculations of productive industry. No sooner does a government attempt to go beyond its political sphere and to enter upon this new track, than it exercises, even unintentionally, an insupportable tyranny; for a government can only dictate strict rules, the opinions which it favours are rigidly enforced, and it is never easy to discriminate between its advice and its commands. Worse still will be the case if the government really believes itself interested in preventing all circulation of ideas; it will then stand motionless, and oppressed by the heaviness of voluntary torpor. Governments therefore should not be the only active powers: associations ought, in democratic nations, to stand in lieu of those powerful private individuals whom the equality of conditions has swept away.

As soon as several of the inhabitants of the United States have taken up an opinion or a feeling which they wish to promote in the world, they look out for mutual assistance; and as soon as they have found each other out, they combine. From that moment they are no longer isolated men, but a power seen from afar, whose actions serve for an example, and whose language is listened to. The first time I heard in the United States that a hundred thousand men had bound themselves publicly to abstain from spirituous liquors, it appeared to me more like a joke than a serious engagement; and I did not at once perceive why these temperate citizens could not content themselves with drinking water by their own firesides. I at last understood that three hundred thousand Americans, alarmed by the progress of drunkenness around them, had made up their minds to patronise temperance. They acted just in the same way as a man of high rank who should dress very plainly, in order to inspire the humbler orders with a contempt of luxury. It is probable that if these hundred thousand men had lived in France, each of them would singly have memorialised the government to watch the public-houses all over the kingdom.

Nothing, in my opinion is more deserving of our attention than the intellectual and moral associations of America. The political and industrial associations of that country strike us forcibly; but the others elude our observation, or if we discover them, we understand them imperfectly, because we have hardly ever seen anything of the kind. It must, however, be acknowledged that they are as necessary to the American people as the former, and perhaps more so. In democratic countries the science of association is the mother of science; the progress of all the rest depends upon the progress it has made. Amongst the laws which rule human societies there is one which seems to be more precise and dear than all others. If man are to remain civilised, or to become so, the art of associating together must grow and improve in the same ratio in which the equality of conditions is increased.

...

There is only one country on the face of the earth where the citizens enjoy unlimited freedom of association for political purposes. This same country is the only one in the world where the continual exercise of the right of association has been introduced into civil life, and where all the advantages which civilisation can confer are procured by means of it. In all the countries where political associations are prohibited, civil associations are rare. It is hardly probable that this is the result of accident; but the inference should rather be, that there is a natural, and perhaps a necessary, connection between these two kinds of associations. Certain men happen to have a common interest in some concern – either a commercial undertaking is to be managed, or some speculation in manufactures to be tried; they meet, they combine, and thus by degrees they become familiar with the principle of association. The greater is the multiplicity of small affairs, the more do men, even without knowing it, acquire facility in prosecuting great undertakings in common. Civil associations, therefore, facilitate political association: but, on the other hand, political association singularly strengthens and improves associations for civil purposes. In civil life every man may, strictly speaking, fancy that he can provide for his own wants; in politics, he can fancy no such thing. When a people, then, have any knowledge of public life, the notion of association, and the wish to coalesce, present themselves every day to the minds of the whole community: whatever natural repugnance may restrain men from acting in concert, they will always be ready to combine for the sake of a party. Thus political life makes the love and practice of association more general; it imparts a desire of union, and teaches the means of combination to numbers of men who would have always lived apart.

Politics not only give birth to numerous associations, but to associations of great extent. In civil life it seldom happens that any one interest draws a very large number of men to act in concert; much skill is required to bring such an interest into existence: but in politics opportunities present themselves every day. Now it is solely in great associations that the general value of the principle of association is displayed. Citizens who are individually powerless, do not very clearly anticipate the strength which they may acquire by uniting together; it must be shown to them in order to be understood. Hence it is often easier to collect a multitude for a public purpose than a few persons; a thousand citizens do not see what interest they have in combining together – ten thousand will be perfectly aware of it. In politics men combine for great undertakings; and the use they make of the principle of association in important affairs practically teaches them that it is their interest to help each other in those of less moment. A political association draws a number of individuals at the same time out of their own circle: however they may be naturally kept asunder by age, mind, and fortune, it places them nearer together and brings them into contact. Once met, they can always meet again.

Men can embark in few civil partnerships without risking a portion of their possessions; this is the case with all manufacturing and trading companies. When men are as yet but little versed in the art of association, and are unacquainted with its principal rules, they are afraid, when first they combine in this manner, of buying their experience dear. They therefore prefer depriving themselves of a powerful instrument of success to running the risks which attend the use of it. They are, however, less reluctant to join political associations, which appear to them to be without danger, because they adventure no money in them. But they cannot belong to these associations for any length of time without finding out how order is maintained amongst a large number of men, and by what contrivance they are made to advance, harmoniously and methodically, to the same object. Thus they learn to surrender their own will to that of all the rest, and to make their own exertions subordinate to the common impulse – things which it is not less necessary to know in civil than in political associations. Political associations may therefore be considered as large free schools, where all the members of the community go to learn the general theory of association.

But even if political association did not directly contribute to the progress of civil association, to destroy the former would be to impair the latter. When citizens can only meet in public for certain purposes, they regard such meetings as a strange proceeding of rare occurrence, and they rarely think at all about it. When they are allowed to meet freely for all purpose, they ultimately look upon public association as the universal, or in a manner the sole means, which men can employ to accomplish the different purposes they may have in view. Every new want instantly revives the notion. The art of association then becomes, as I have said before, the mother of action, studied and applied by all.

When some kinds of associations are prohibited and others allowed, it is difficult to distinguish the former from the latter beforehand. In this state of doubt men abstain from them altogether, and a sort of public opinion passes current, which tends to cause any association whatsoever to be regarded as a bold and almost an illicit enterprise.[1]

It is therefore chimerical to suppose that the spirit of association, when it is repressed on some one point, will nevertheless display the same vigour on all others; and that if men be allowed to prosecute certain undertakings in common, that is quite enough for them eagerly to set about them. When the members of a community are allowed and accustomed to combine for all purposes, they will combine as readily for the lesser as for the more important ones; but if they are only allowed to combine for small affairs, they will be neither inclined nor able to effect it. It is in vain that you will leave them entirely free to prosecute their business on joint-stock account: they will hardly care to avail themselves of the rights you have granted to them; and, after having exhausted your strength in vain efforts to put down prohibited associations, you will be surprised that you cannot persuade men to form the associations you encourage.

I do not say that there can be no civil associations in a country where political association is prohibited; for men can never live in society without embarking in some common undertakings: but I maintain that in such a country civil associations will always be few in number, feebly planned, unskillfully managed, that they will never form any vast designs, or that they will fail in the execution of them.

This naturally leads me to think that freedom of association in political matters is not so dangerous to public tranquillity as is supposed; and that possibly, after having agitated society for some time, it may strengthen the State in the end. In democratic countries political associations are, so to speak, the only powerful persons who aspire to rule the State. Accordingly, the governments of our time look upon associations of this kind just as sovereigns in the Middle Ages regarded the great vassals of the crown: they entertain a sort of instinctive abhorrence of them, and they combat them on all occasions. They bear, on the contrary, a natural goodwill to civil associations, because they readily discover that, instead of directing the minds of the community to public affairs, these institutions serve to divert them from such reflections; and that, by engaging them more and more in the pursuit of objects which cannot be attained without public tranquillity, they deter them from revolutions. But these governments do not attend to the fact that political associations tend amazingly to multiply and facilitate those of a civil character, and that in avoiding a dangerous evil they deprive themselves of an efficacious remedy.

When you see the Americans freely and constantly forming associations for the purpose of promoting some political principle, of raising one man to the head of affairs, or of wresting power from another, you have some difficulty in understanding that men so independent do not constantly fall into the abuse of freedom. If, on the other hand, you survey the infinite number of trading companies which are in operation in the United States, and perceive that the Americans are on every side unceasingly engaged in the execution of important and difficult plans, which the slightest revolution would throw into confusion, you will readily comprehend why people so well employed are by no means tempted to perturb the State, nor to destroy that public tranquillity by which they all profit.

Is it enough to observe these things separately, or should we not discover the hidden tie which connects them? In their political associations, the Americans of all conditions, minds, and ages, daily acquire a general taste for association, and grow accustomed to the use of it. There they meet together in large numbers, they converse, they listen to each other, and they are mutually stimulated to all sorts of undertakings. They afterwards transfer to civil life the notions they have thus acquired, and make them subservient to a thousand purposes. Thus it is by the enjoyment of a dangerous freedom that the Americans learn the art of rendering the dangers of freedom less formidable.

If a certain moment in the existence of a nation be selected, it is easy to prove that political associations perturb the State, and paralyse productive industry; but take the whole life of a people, and it may perhaps be easy to demonstrate that freedom of association in political matters is favourable to the prosperity and even to the tranquillity of the community.

I said in the former part of this work, 'The unrestrained liberty of political association cannot be entirely assimilated to the liberty of the press. The one is at the same time less necessary and more dangerous than the other. A nation may confine it within certain limits without ceasing to be mistress of itself; and it may sometimes be obliged to do so in order to maintain its own authority.' And further on I added: 'It cannot be denied that the unrestrained liberty of association for political purposes is the last degree of liberty which a people is fit for. If it does not throw them into anarchy, it perpetually brings them, as it were, to the verge of it.' Thus I do not think that a nation is always at liberty to invest its citizens with an absolute right of association for political purposes; and I doubt whether, in any country or in any age, it be wise to set no limits to freedom of association. A certain nation, it is said, could not maintain tranquillity in the community, cause the laws to be respected, or establish a lasting government, if the right of association were not confined within narrow limits. These blessings are doubtless invaluable, and I can imagine that, to acquire or to preserve them, a nation may impose upon itself severe temporary restrictions: but still it is well that the nation should know at what price these blessings are purchased. I can understand that it may be advisable to cut off a man's arm in order to save his life; but it would be ridiculous to assert that he will be as dexterous as he was before he lost it.

---

* From Alexis de Tocqueville, *Democracy in America*, 2 Vols, translated by Henry Reeve (London: Longmans, Green, and Co., 1899 [1835–1840]), Vol. 1, 194–7; Vol. 2, 97–102; 105–10, 194–7.

[1] This is more especially true when the executive government has a discretionary power of allowing or prohibiting associations. When certain associations are simply prohibited by law, and the courts of justice have to punish infringements of that law, the evil is far less considerable. Then every citizen knows beforehand pretty nearly what he has to expect. He judges himself before he is judged by the law, and, abstaining from prohibited associations, he embarks in those which are legally sanctioned. It is by these restrictions that all free nations have always admitted that the right of association might be limited. But if the legislature should invest a man with a power of ascertaining beforehand which associations are dangerous and which are useful, and

should authorise him to destroy all associations in the bud or allow them to be formed, as nobody would be able to foresee in what cases associations might be established and in what cases they would be put down, the spirit of association would be entirely paralysed. The former of these laws would only assail certain associations; the latter would apply to society itself, and inflict an injury upon it. I can conceive that a regular government may have recourse to the former, but I do not concede that any government has the right of enacting the latter.

Alexis de Tocqueville (1805–59), had considerable fears for the future of political liberty in the United States, even though Democracy in America *(1835 and 1840) presents a generally positive account of that society. In this selection he expresses one of his greatest fears: that passivity will lead to the emergence of authoritarianism.**

There is, indeed, a most dangerous passage in the history of a democratic people. When the taste for physical gratifications amongst such a people has grown more rapidly than their education and their experience of free institutions, the time will come when men are carried away, and lose all self-restraint, at the sight of the new possessions they are about to lay hold upon. In their intense and exclusive anxiety to make a fortune, they lose sight of the close connection which exists between the private fortune of each of them and the prosperity of all. It is not necessary to do violence to such a people in order to strip them of the rights they enjoy; they themselves willingly loosen their hold. The discharge of political duties appears to them to be a troublesome annoyance, which diverts them from their occupations and business. If they be required to elect representatives, to support the Government by personal service, to meet on public business, they have no time – they cannot waste their precious time in useless engagements: such idle amusements are unsuited to serious men who are engaged with the more important interests of life. These people think they are following the principle of self-interest, but the idea they entertain of that principle is a very rude one; and the better to look after what they call their business, they neglect their chief business, which is to remain their own masters.

As the citizens who work do not care to attend to public business, and as the class which might devote its leisure to these duties has ceased to exist, the place of the Government is, as it were, unfilled. If at that critical moment some able and ambitious man grasps the supreme power, he will find the road to every kind of usurpation open before him. If he does but attend for some time to the material prosperity of the country, no more will be demanded of him. Above all he must ensure public tranquillity: men who are possessed by the passion of physical gratification generally find out that the turmoil of freedom disturbs their welfare, before they discover how freedom itself serves to promote it. If the slightest rumour of public commotion intrudes into the petty pleasures of private life, they are aroused and alarmed by it. The fear of anarchy perpetually haunts them, and they are always ready to fling away their freedom at the first disturbance.

...

I readily admit that public tranquillity is a great good; but at the same time I cannot forget that all nations have been enslaved by being kept in good order. Certainly it is not to be inferred that nations ought to despise public tranquillity; but that state ought not to content them. A nation which asks nothing of its government but the maintenance of order is already a slave at heart – the slave of its own well-being, awaiting but the hand that will bind it. By such a nation the despotism of faction is not less to be dreaded than the despotism of an individual. When the bulk of the community is engrossed by private concerns, the smallest parties need not despair of getting the upper hand in public affairs. At such times it is not rare to see upon the great stage of the world, as we see at our theatres, a multitude represented by a few players, who alone speak in the name of an absent or inattentive crowd: they alone are in action whilst all are stationary; they regulate everything by their own caprice; they change the laws, and tyrannise at will over the manners of the country; and then men wonder to see into how small a number of weak and worthless hands a great people may fall.

Hitherto the Americans have fortunately escaped all the perils which I have just pointed out; and in this respect they are really deserving of admiration. Perhaps there is no country in the world where fewer idle men are to be met with than in America, or where all who work are more eager to promote their own welfare. But if the passion of the Americans for physical gratifications is vehement, at least it is not indiscriminating; and reason, though unable to restrain it, still directs its course. An American attends to his private concerns as if he were alone in the world, and the next minute he gives himself up to the common weal as if he had forgotten them. At one time he seems animated by the most selfish cupidity, at another by the most lively patriotism. The human heart cannot be thus divided. The inhabitants of the United States alternately display so strong and so similar a passion for their own welfare and for their freedom, that it may be supposed that these passions are united and mingled in some part of their character. And indeed the Americans believe their freedom to be the best instrument and surest safeguard of their welfare: they are attached to the one by the other. They by no means think that they are not called upon to take a part in the public weal; they believe, on the contrary, that their chief business is to secure for themselves a government which will allow them to acquire the things they covet, and which will not debar them from the peaceful enjoyment of those possessions which they have acquired.

* From Alexis de Tocqueville, *Democracy in America*, Vol. 2 (London: Longmans, Green, and Co., 1889 [1835–40]), 126–8.

Alexis de Tocqueville (1805–59), turned in his last years to a rigorous analysis of his own society, and in particular of its seeming inability to combine political liberty with equal social conditions. This selection from L'Ancien Régime et la Revolution *sees a fundamental shift in his intellectual position as a whole. He no longer considers popular politics per se to blame for the creation of the distrust that undermines liberty. Rather, the people have been taught by the divide and rule politics of the old regime to distrust each other. Popular political culture is thus seen as a reaction to an elite, rather than an independent cause of political development.**

If the English had, from the period of the Middle Ages, altogether lost, like the French, political freedom and all those local franchises which cannot long exist without it, it is highly probable that each of the different classes of which the English aristocracy is composed would have seceded from the rest, as was the case in France and more or less all over the continent, and that all those classes together would have separated themselves from the people. But freedom compelled them always to remain within reach of each other, so as to combine their strength in time of need.

It is curious to observe how the British aristocracy, urged even by its own ambition, has contrived, whenever it seemed necessary, to mix familiarly with its inferiors, and to feign to consider them as its equals.

. . .

Lastly, it was this desire of preventing the nation, when asked for its money, from asking back its freedom, which gave rise to an incessant watchfulness in separating the classes of society, so that they should never come together, or combine in a common resistance, and that the Government should never have on its hands at once more than a very small number of men separated from the rest of the nation. In the whole course of this long history, in which have figured so many princes remarkable for their ability, sometimes remarkable for their genius, almost always remarkable for their courage, not one of them ever made an effort to bring together the different classes of his people, or to unite them otherwise than by subjecting them to a common yoke. One exception there is, indeed, to this remark: one king of France there was who not only desired this end, but applied himself with his whole heart to attain it; that prince – for such are the inscrutable judgments of Providence – was Louis XVI.

The separation of classes was the crime of the old French monarchy, but it became its excuse; for when all those who constitute the rich and enlightened portion of a nation can no longer agree and co-operate in the work of government, a country can by no possibility administer itself, and a master *must* intervene.

'The nation,' said Turgot, with an air of melancholy, in a secret report addressed to the King, 'is a community, consisting of different orders ill compacted together, and of a people whose members have very few ties among themselves, so that every man is exclusively engrossed by his personal interest. Nowhere is any common interest discernible. The villages, the towns, have not any stronger mutual relations than the districts to which they belong. They cannot even agree among themselves to carry on the public works which they require. Amidst this perpetual conflict of pretensions and of undertakings your Majesty is compelled to decide everything in person or by your agents. Your special injunctions are expected before men will contribute to the public advantage, or respect the rights of others, or even sometimes before they will exercise their own.'

It is no slight enterprise to bring more closely together fellow-citizens who have thus been living for centuries as strangers as enemies to each other, and to teach them how to carry on their affairs in common.

To divide them was a far easier task than it then becomes to reunite them. Such has been the memorable example given by France to the world. When the different classes which divided the ancient social system of France came once more into contact sixty years ago, they encountered each other on those points on which they felt most poignantly, and they met in mutual hatred. Even in this our day their jealousies and their animosities have survived them.

* From Alexis de Tocqueville, *The State of Society in France Before the Revolution of 1789 and the Causes which Led to that Event*, translated by Henry Reeve (London: John Murray, 1888 [1856]), 84; 92–3.

James Mill (1773–1836), British philosopher and political economist. Mill left the clergy to become a professional writer. His History of British India, *from which this extract is taken, secured him a permanent job with the East India Company. It became the imperial bible on India. Here he looks at the system of law and punishment, and at the mix of dependence and passion in Hindu culture as an example of a community before civil society.*

The leading institutions of the Hindus bear evidence that they were devised at a very remote period, when society yet retained its rudest and simplest form. So long as men roam in the pastoral state, no division of classes or of labour is known. Every individual is a shepherd, and every family provides for itself the commodities with which it is supplied. As soon as the cultivation of land, which yields a more secure and plentiful subsistence, occupies a great share of the common attention, the inconvenience of this universal mixture of employments is speedily felt. The labours of the field are neglected, while the cultivator is engaged at the loom, or repelling the incursions of an enemy. His clothing and lodging are inadequately provided for, while the attention of himself and his family are engrossed by the plough. Men quit not easily, however, the practices to which they have been accustomed; and a great change in their manners and affairs does not readily suggest itself as a remedy for the evils which they endure. When the Hindus were lingering in this uneasy situation, it would appear that there arose among them one of those superior men, who are capable of accelerating the improvement of society. Perceiving the advantage which would accrue to his countrymen from a division of employments, he conceived the design of overcoming at once the obstacles by which this regulation was retarded; and, clothing himself with a Divine character, established as a positive law, under the sanction of Heaven, the classification of the people, and the distribution of occupations. Nor was it enough to introduce this vast improvement; it was right to secure that the original members of the different classes should be supplied with successors, and that the community should not revert to its former confusion. The human race are not destined to make many steps in improvement at once. Ignorant that professions, when once separated, were in no danger of being confounded, he established a law, which the circumstances of the time very naturally suggested, but which erected a barrier against further progress; that the children of those who were assigned to each of the classes, into which he distributed the people, should invariably follow the occupation of their father through all generations.

. . .

Two principles therefore universally characterize the penal code of a barbarous people: severity and retaliation. The early laws of the Greeks and the Romans were cruel; the laws of the twelve tables, says Mr. Gibbon, like the statutes of Draco, were written in characters of blood. By the laws of Moses, blasphemy, idolatry, profaning the sabbath, homicide, adultery, incest, rapes, crime against, nature, witchcraft, smiting or cursing father or mother, were punished with death, and with burning and stoning, the most cruel kinds of death. Of the sanguinary character imprinted on the laws of the Egyptians, the following instance may be adduced. They thrust little pieces of reeds, about a finger's length, into all parts of the bodies of parricides; and then, surrounding them with thorns, set them on fire. The barbarous punishments which prevail among the Chinese are too familiarly known to require illustration. Perhaps of all the rude nations of whom we have any account, our own Saxon and German ancestors were the most distinguished for the mildness of their punishments; a singularity, however, to be accounted for by the use of a very barbarous expedient, a compensation in money for almost every species of crime, Yet in various instances, particularly that of theft, their laws were not only severe, but inhuman.

Notwithstanding the mildness which has generally been attributed to the Hindu character, hardly any nation is distinguished for more sanguinary laws.

. . .

One of the strongest characteristics of a rude age, or of a corrupt government, is, to make laws which cannot, or ought not, to be executed; and then to give dispensations for them. 'In all cases of violence, of theft and adultery, of defamation and assault,' says the Hindu law, 'the judge must not examine too strictly the competence of witnesses.'

. . .

Of all the perverse proceedings of a superstitious mind, which the history of rude nations presents to us, few will be found more at variance with reason, than the establishment of the following law: 'The witness, who has given evidence, and to whom, within seven days after, a misfortune happens from disease, fire, or the death of a kinsman, shall be condemned to pay the debt and a fine.'

. . . .

The condition of the women is one of the most remarkable circumstances in the manners of nations. Among rude people, the women are generally degraded; among civilized people they are exalted.[1] In the barbarian, the passion of sex is a brutal impulse, which infuses no tenderness; and his undisciplined nature leads him to abuse his power over every creature that is weaker than himself. The history of uncultivated nations uniformly represents the women as in a state of abject slavery, from which they slowly emerge, as civilization advances. Among some of the negro tribes on the coast of Africa, the wife is never permitted to receive any thing from the hands of her husband, or even to appear in his presence, except on her knees. In the empire of Congo, where the people are sufficiently advanced to be united in a large community; and in most of the nations which inhabit the southern regions of Africa, the women are reckoned unworthy to eat with the men. In such a state of society property is an advantage which it may naturally be supposed that the degraded sex are by no means permitted to enjoy. Not only among the African and other savage tribes, and the Tartars of the present day, but among the ancient inhabitants of Chaldea and Arabia, and all the nations of Europe in their ancient unciv-ilized state, the women were excluded from the inheritance of the family. Being condemned to severe and perpetual labour, they are themselves regarded as useful property. Hence a father parts not with his daughter but for a valuable consideration; hence the general custom, among barbarous nations, as in Pegu, in Siberia, among the Tartars, among the negroes on the coast of Guinea, among the Arabs, and even among the Chinese, of purchasing the bride by a dower. It is only in that improved state of property and security, when the necessities of life have ceased to create perpetual solicitude, and when a large share of attention may be given to its pleasures; that the, women, from their influence on those pleasures, begin to be an object of regard. As society refines upon its enjoyments, and advances into that state of civilization, in which various corporeal qualities become equal or superior in value to corporeal strength, and in which the qualities of the mind are ranked above the qualities of the body, the condition of the weaker sex is gradually improved, till they associate on equal terms with the men, and occupy the place of voluntary and useful coadjutors [assistants].

A state of dependence more strict and humiliating than that which is ordained for the weaker sex among the Hindus cannot easily be conceived. 'Day and night,' says Menu, 'must women be held by their protectors in a state of dependence'. Who are meant by their protectors is immediately explained: 'Their fathers protect them in childhood; their husbands protect them in youth; their sons protect them in age: a woman,' it is added, 'is never fit for independence.'

. . .

It commonly happens that in a rude period of society, the virtue of hospitality, generously and cordially displayed, helps to cast into the shade the odious passions which adhere to man in his uncultivated state. The unhappy circumstances, religious and political, of the Hindu, have tended to eradicate even this, the virtue of a rude age, from his breast. After noticing, in various parts of his journey, the striking instances which he witnessed, of the want of hospitality, Dr. Buchanan says in one passage, 'I mention these difficulties, which are very frequently met with by travellers in all parts of India where Europeans have not long resided, to show the inhospitable nature of its inhabitants.' For one of his sepoys, who was seized with an acute disease, and left in agony by the side of the road, he could not, except by force, in a large village, obtain a cot, though he was assured there was one in every house.

. . .

The ancient literature of the Hindus affords many proofs that no inconsiderable degree of ferocity has at all times been mingled with the other ingredients of their character. The Yadavas, a sacred race, the kindred of Orishna, in a drunken fray, took arms and butchered one another, to the utter extinction of the race.

. . .

Notwithstanding the degree to which the furious passions enter into the character of the Hindu, all witnesses agree in representing him as a timid being. With more apparent capacity of supporting pain than any other race of men; and, on many occasions, a superiority to the fear of death, which cannot be surpassed, this people run from danger with more trepidation and eagerness than has been almost ever witnessed in any other part of the globe.

It is the mixture of this fearfulness with their antisocial passions, which has given existence to that litigiousness of character which almost all witnesses have ascribed to this ancient race. As often as courage fails them in seeking a more daring gratification to their hatred or revenge, their malignity finds a vent in the channel of litigation. 'That pusillanimity and sensibility of spirit,' says Mr. Orme, 'which renders the Gentoos incapable of supporting the contentions of danger, disposes them as much to prosecute litigious contests. No people are of more inveterate and steady resentments in civil disputes. The only instance in which they seem to have a contempt for money, is their profusion of it in procuring the redress and revenge of injuries at the bar of justice. Although they can, with great resignation, see themselves plundered to the utmost by their superiors, they become mad with impatience, when they think they are defrauded of part of their property by their equals. Nothing can be more adapted to the feminine spirit of a Gentoo, than the animosities of a law-suit.'[2]

A modification of the same passions gives rise to another, and seemingly a strong ingredient in the Hindu character, a propensity to the war of contentious tongues. The following picture, if not finely, is at least clearly drawn. 'The timidity of the Hindu may, in general, prevent his fighting, boxing, or shedding of blood; but it by no means restrains him from scolding and upbraiding his neighbours. In this respect they are the most litigious and quarrelsome of all men. Have two persons a misunderstanding? Let them meet in the street, and they will upbraid each other for an hour together, with every foul epithet of abuse which their imagination can suggest, or their language supply. A few natives engaged in one of these bickerings display a furious gesticulation: a volubility of words, and coarseness of expression, which leave the eloquence of Billingsgate far behind.'

* From James Mill, *The History of British India*, Vol. 1, Horace Hayman Wilson, ed. (London: James Madden, 1858 [1817]), 125–6; 176; 192; 309–10; 327–30.

[1] This important subject is amply and philosophically illustrated by Professor Millar, in his *Inquiry Into the Distinction of Ranks*, ch. i. (See also pp. 55–60 in this volume.)

[2] Orme, on the *Government and People of Indostan*, p. 443. In the committee of the House of Commons, 1781, on the petition of John Touchet, &c., Charles W. Boughton Rouse, Esq. testified that 'there cannot be a race of men upon the earth more litigious and clamorous than the inhabitants of Dacca.' Mr. Park takes notice of the passion of the negroes in Africa for law-suits, and adds: 'If I may judge from their harangues which I frequently attended, I believe that in the forensic qualifications of procrastination and cavil, and the arts of confounding and perplexing a cause, they are not always surpassed by the ablest pleaders in Europe.' Park's *Travels In Africa*. p. 20. Dr. Robertson was sadly mistaken, when he considered the litigious subtlety of the Hindus as a sign of high civilization. See Robertson's *Historic. Disq. concerning India*, p. 217. Travellers have remarked that no where is this subtlety carried higher than among the wildest of the Irish.

*The Church Missionary Society, founded in 1799, was the Anglican branch of a whole wave of missionary societies founded in Britain and Europe in the late eighteenth and early nineteenth century. By the late nineteenth century the CMS had distributed five million tracts and papers like this one. The extract here is from a dialogue reminding Victorians of the divine plan of the British Empire, and their duty to civilize and convert colonial peoples.**

Thomas Rogers. Neighbour, Smith, I did not see you at the Missionary Meeting some nights ago. Didn't you hear of it? Our Minister gave it out in Church last Sunday, and begged us all to go.

Edward Smith. I am sorry to say that I wasn't at Church last Sunday, for I was poorly, and therefore didn't hear Mr. Goodwin give it out; but if I had, I should not have gone to the Meeting, because I do not know anything of Missionaries.

Thomas. The sooner you learn about them, Ned, the better.

. . .

Edward. I see I have done wrong in neglecting to hear about the Heathen, and to pray, for them; but you said something about collecting money to help to send out Missionaries. How can I, or how can you, give money to help in this good business?

Thomas. One of the gentlemen who spoke, told us at the Meeting, that the Church Missionary Society collect about 90,000 pounds a-year. Now how much do you think comes from us poor people – from our pennies? Why, I'll tell you – or rather the speaker said, probably 20,000 pounds: in some places, he said, the yearly sums under 10 shillings came to more than was given in sums above 10 shillings. I remember he said that at Bristol, 732 pounds were collected in sums under 10 shillings a-year, and only 365 pounds in annual subscriptions of 10 shillings and upwards.

Edward. I could not have thought that our poor help in so great a work would have done so much; but I see that if to our prayers we added even a penny a-week which makes 4 shillings 4 pence a-year, this would be much, coming from each of the thousands and thousands that belong to the Church of England. My children often get a stray penny – aye, often more than a penny a-week – to spend on things that do them more harm than good, and I am too fond of a pipe myself; so that, by a very little self-denial, my wife and I can surely give one penny a-week; and I know that in such a business as this she will be more ready to help than I am, when she once understands it as you have explained it to me.

Thomas. I think, Edward, that if all the labouring people in our parish could see how much might be done by their help, in this great and good cause, they would be ready and glad to become regular subscribers. Only think, Ned, if 100 poor people, in each of the 12,000 congregations belonging to the Church of England, were to give a penny a-week, or 48 shillings 4 pence a-year, to the Church Missionary Society, it would come to 260,000 pounds – about three times as much as the Society now get from rich and poor together. So you see how little is done, after all, by our Church for the poor Heathen. It is not the sums given at collections or Meetings, and Sermons, that do so much for the Society, as the regular payments of sub-scribers. Let us therefore speak to all our friends, and ask them to give one penny a-week each to our kind collectors, who visit us so regularly. I often admire these excellent ladies, Mrs. Stokes, and Mrs. Smith and her two daughters, for giving so much of their time and labour for the Society. I hear that Squire Stokes gives nearly 100 pounds a-year to the Society.

. . .

Thomas. ...I hear that there are some black men in London, who sometimes speak at Meetings, who were once wild Heathen – now turned Christians, and under teaching to become Missionaries. I heard of one of these blacks the other day, from James Short, who had been in London to get a job.

Edward. And was James at a great Missionary meeting in London?

Thomas. No. Poor James, like many a man that goes to London, couldn't get work, so, rather than starve, he took to breaking stones on the road, at a place called Hampstead, near London; and while he was hammering away, one morning, a black man came up and asked his way to Hampstead Heath. So James, who is a good, civil fellow, rose up too show him, and asked the black man where he came from. He answered, 'From Sierra Leone, in Africa.' James said, 'I hope the London people are kind to you?' 'Yes,' said the African, 'they are indeed. I am taken great care of at the Church Missionary Institution, at Islington.' This, James was glad to hear – for the name of the Church Missionary is very dear to James – so he said to the African, 'I am thankful to hear what you say, for I have been a subscriber to the Church Missionary Society for twenty years.'

. . .

Thomas.   No one, Ned, can learn what this great Missionary Society is doing, by only going to one Missionary Meeting, nor by going to a dozen Meetings. It is like other things: one must take a little trouble to inquire. The subscribers to this Society have plenty of information, because they get the books that come out from the Church Missionary House in London every month, and by reading these we learn all that is doing in the Heathen lands afar off.

. . .

In every hundred person living upon the earth, there are only six or seven Protestants, *three times as many* professors of false Christianity, and *ten times as many* wandering in darkness and the shadow of death.

Or, suppose the case of a small village, with a population of nearly one hundred souls, in thirty families. Suppose that in only two of these families is the Bible found, or God worshipped according to His Word, while eight or nine families have put away their Bibles, and set up images, to bow down before them, contrary to the Second Commandment, and transgress the Word of God in many other particulars. Suppose, further, that all the other nineteen or twenty families know *nothing* of God; but have erected idol-temples and devil-houses, and oppress their women, and offer human sacrifices, and put children to death, and do such things as it would be a shame to speak of. What would you say of such a village? Would you not pity and weep over its sad condition?

. . .

Rev. J. Goodwin   Now, Edward Smith and Thomas Rogers I am ready to give you information upon any of the Missions about which you would like to ask me.
Thomas.   We have talked a little about New Zealand, and we should now like to hear something about India.

. . .

Is it not wonderful that God has seen fit to place this great country, and these vast bodies of people, under British rule and influence? Look at Britain!

how small in comparison with India, and with a population – in England, Scotland, and Ireland – of 26 millions only, or one-eighth of that of India; and with only about 50,000 of our countrymen in India; yet all the wealth and resources of that vast region are at the disposal, or under the influence, of a great Company of English Merchants, called the East-India Company, under the Queen and Government of Great Britain.

You see, now, that it would be quite impossible for Britain to maintain rule over these great kingdoms of which India is made up, if God had not put the power into our hands, and turned the hearts of these people to submit us.

...

I must now tell you, my good friends, that God has clearly chosen England to be the great Missionary nation, not only by putting India and other nations under our rule, but also by bestowing upon us unheard-of means and facilities for giving His pure Gospel to these nations. Our great Bible Society prints His blessed Word in 144 languages. Our kingdom is placed in the best spot in the world for sending out our ships to every nation. All the tribes throughout the world are waiting for and desiring intercourse with our merchants, which they monthly and daily receive: there is not a coast nor an island on the habitable globe which does not receive visits from our seamen. And just see how every thing around us comes from Heathen or foreign countries. Our coats are dyed with indigo bought from Bengal; our cotton articles of dress are of material grown in Tinnevelly, Bombay, or other parts of India; we have our tea from China; our coffee from Arabia or Ceylon; our wax from India; even our railway cars have palm-oil from Guinea for oiling the wheels; our medicines come from all parts of the globe; our spices from Travancore and the Eastern Isles of India; Bengal rice is in all our shops; and what would become of our Manchester manufacturers and Liverpool merchants without the cotton that comes from foreign countries? Thus we are bound, by close ties of common interest, to multitudes of nations who are ignorant of God and of His Christ.

...

It now rests, not with the Government, but with *us* to deliver this people – these *two hundred millions* – from the cruel bondage of Satan; and although I cannot in so short a time as in our meeting this evening tell you all about this bondage, I will just say that the idolatry of the Hindus is of the most cruel, silly, degrading, and sensual kind.

You must not think that these Hindus are wild, stupid savages: no, far from this, they are gentle and polite in their manners – a clever, searching people, having many good points of character; but their idolatry, their notions of God, are such as are pointed out in Romans: They have 'changed the glory of the uncorruptible God into an image made like to corruptible man, and to birds, and four-footed beasts, and creeping things.' This text of Scripture fully describes what you would see in every village and town in India: idols of every form and shape that the diseased imagination of corrupt sensual man can devise – from the little painted clay image in a poor man's house, up to the huge image of gold in one of their great pagodas or temples of worship, or to the image of a bull, twenty feet high, cut out of a rock. To describe these images would be impossible, and in many cases indecent.

. . .

We have not time to speak of all the abominations of this system of idolatry, nor of the horrid, cruel, filthy practices which spring from it. The soil of India covers the blood of thousands strangled by the Thugs, men who practise murder and plunder as a religious duty, and actually pray to their goddess to show by a sign the right moment for killing their victim. The fields of India are stained with the blood of boys and girls offered in sacrifice to devils, in order to make the ground yield a good harvest.

* From *Church Missionary Tracts – The Village Missionary Meeting, A Dialogue Between Thomas Rogers and Edward Smith*, No. 1 and 3 (London, 1852), No. 1, 3; 7–10; 15; and No. 3, 4; 7–9; 10–11; 13–14.

Bürgerliche Gesellschaft

Georg Wilhelm Friedrich Hegel (1770–1831), German philosopher. After working as private tutor, newspaper editor, and school director, he became a professor at Heidelberg and Berlin where he was famous for his lectures. Hegel developed his view of civil society, writing against the background of the Napoleonic triumph over the German states and fearful of the atomizing and pauperizing trends associated with industrial society. Civil society for Hegel was the modern world. Here he turns to corporations as a way of putting structure and ethics back into a civil society otherwise atomized into its particularist elements.*

182. The concrete person, who is himself the object of his particular aims, is, as a totality of wants and a mixture of caprice and physical necessity, one principle of civil society. But the particular person is essentially so related to other particular persons that each establishes himself and finds satisfaction by means of the others, and at the same time purely and simply by means of the form of universality, the second principle here.

183. In the course of the actual attainment of selfish ends – an attainment conditioned in this way by universality – there is formed a system of complete interdependence; wherein the livelihood, happiness, and legal status of one man is interwoven with the livelihood, happiness, and rights of all. On this system, individual happiness, &c., depend, and only in this connected system are they actualized and secured. This system may be prima facie regarded as the external state, the state based on need, the state as the understanding envisages it.

184. The Idea in this stage of division imparts to each of its moments characteristic embodiment; to particularity it gives the right to develop and launch forth in all directions; and to universality the right to prove itself not only the ground and necessary form of particularity, but also the authority standing over it and its final end. It is the system of the ethical order, split into its extremes and lost, which constitutes the Idea's abstract moment, its moment of reality. Here the Idea is present only as a relative totality and as the inner necessity behind this outward appearance.

185. Particularity by itself, given free rein in every direction to satisfy its needs, accidental caprices, and subjective desires, destroys itself and its substantive concept in this process of gratification. At the same time, the satisfaction of need, necessary and accidental alike, is accidental because it breeds new desires without end, is in thoroughgoing dependence on caprice and external accident, and is held in check by the power of universality. In these contrasts and their complexity, civil society affords a spectacle of

extravagance and want as well as of the physical and ethical degeneration common to them both.

The development of particularity to self-subsistence ... is the moment which appeared in the ancient world as an invasion of ethical corruption and as the ultimate cause of that world's downfall. Some of these ancient states were built on the patriarchal and religious principle, others on the principle of an ethical order which was more explicitly intellectual, though still comparatively simple; in either case they rested on primitive unsophisticated intuition. Hence they could not withstand the disruption of this state of mind when self-consciousness was infinitely reflected into itself; when this reflection began to emerge, they succumbed to it, first in spirit and then in substance, because the simple principle underlying them lacked the truly infinite power to be found only in that unity which allows, both sides of the antithesis of reason to develop themselves separately in all their strength and which has so overcome the antithesis – that it maintains itself in it and integrates it in itself.

In his *Republic*, Plato displays the substance of ethical life in its ideal beauty and truth; but he could only cope with the principle of self-subsistent particularity, which in his day had forced its way into Greek ethical life, by setting up in opposition to it his purely substantial state. He absolutely excluded it from his state, even in its very beginnings in private property ... and the family, as well as in its more mature form as the subjective will, the choice of a social position, and so forth. It is this defect which is responsible both for the misunderstanding of the deep and substantial truth of Plato's state and also for the usual view of it as a dream of abstract thinking, as what is often called a 'mere ideal.' The principle of the self-subsistent inherently infinite personality of the individual, the principle of subjective freedom, is denied its right in the purely substantial form which Plato gave to mind in its actuality. This principle dawned in an inward form in the Christian religion is and in an external form (and therefore in one linked with abstract universality) in the Roman world. It is historically subsequent to the Greek world, and the philosophic reflection which descends to its depth is likewise subsequent to the substantial Idea of Greek philosophy.

186. But in developing itself independently to totality, the principle of particularity passes over into universality, and only there does it attain its truth and the right to which its positive actuality is entitled. This unity is not the identity which the ethical order requires, because at this level, that of division ... both principles are self-subsistent. It follows that this unity is present here not as freedom but as necessity, since it is by compulsion that the particular rises to the form of universality and seeks and gains its stability in that form.

. . .

229. In civil society, the Idea is lost in particularity and has fallen asunder with the separation of inward and outward. In the administration of justice, however, civil society returns to its concept, to the unity of the implicit universal with the subjective particular, although here the latter is only that present in single cases and the universality in question is that of *abstract* right. The actualization of this unity through its extension to the whole ambit of particularity is (i) the specific function of the Police, though the unification which it effects is only relative; (ii) it is the Corporation which actualizes the unity completely, though only in a whole which, while concrete, is restricted.

230. In the system of needs, the livelihood and welfare of every single person is a possibility whose actual attainment is just as much conditioned by his caprices and particular endowment as by the objective system of needs. Through the administration of justice, offences against property or personality are annulled. But the right actually present in the particular requires, first, that accidental hindrances to one aim or another be removed, and undisturbed safety of person and property be attained; and secondly, that the securing of every single person's livelihood and welfare be treated and actualized as a right, i.e. that particular welfare as such be so treated.

. . .

237. Now while the possibility of sharing in the general wealth is open to individuals and is assured to them by the public authority, still it is subject to contingencies on the subjective side (quite apart from the fact that this assurance must remain incomplete), and the more it presupposes skill, health, capital, and so forth as its conditions, the more is it so subject.

238. Originally the family is the substantive whole whose function it is to provide for the individual on his particular side by giving him either the means and the skill necessary to enable him to earn his living out of the resources of society, or else subsistence and maintenance in the event of his suffering a disability. But civil society tears the individual from his family ties, estranges the members of the family from one another, and recognizes them as self-subsistent persons. Further, for the paternal soil and the external inorganic resources of nature from which the individual formerly derived his livelihood, it substitutes its own soil and subjects the permanent existence of even the entire family to dependence on itself and to contingency. Thus the individual becomes a son of civil society which has as many claims upon him as he has rights against it.

239. In its character as a universal family, civil society has the right and duty of superintending and influencing education, inasmuch as education bears upon the child's capacity to become a member of society. Society's right here is paramount over the arbitrary and contingent preferences of parents, particularly in cases where education is to be completed not by the parents but by others. To the same end, society must provide public educational facilities so far as is practicable.

240. Similarly, society has the right and duty of acting as trustee to those whose extravagance destroys the security of their own subsistence or their families'. It must substitute for extravagance the pursuit of the ends of society and the individuals concerned.

241. Not only caprice, however, but also contingencies, physical conditions, and factors grounded in external circumstances ... may reduce men to poverty. The poor still have the needs common to civil society, and yet since society has withdrawn from them the natural means of acquisition ... and broken the bond of the family – in the wider sense of the clan ... – their poverty leaves them more or less deprived of all the advantages of society, of the opportunity of acquiring skill or education of any kind, as well as of the administration of justice, the public health services, and often even of the consolations of religion, and so forth. The public authority takes the place of the family where the poor are concerned in respect not only of their immediate want but also of laziness of disposition, malignity, and the other vices which arise out of their plight and their sense of wrong.

242. Poverty and, in general, the distress of every kind to which every individual is exposed from the start in the cycle of his natural life has a subjective side which demands similarly subjective aid, arising both from the special circumstances of a particular case and also from love and sympathy. This is the place where morality finds plenty to do despite all public organization. Subjective aid, however, both in itself and in its operation, is dependent on contingency and consequently society struggles to make it less necessary, by discovering the general causes of penury and general means of its relief, and by organizing relief accordingly.

Casual almsgiving and casual endowments, e.g. for the burning of lamps before holy images, &c., are supplemented by public alms-houses, hospitals, street-lighting and so forth. There is still quite enough left over and above these things for charity to do on its own account. A false view is implied both when charity insists on having this poor relief reserved solely to private sympathy and the accidental occurrence of knowledge and a charitable disposition, and also when it feels injured or mortified by universal regulations and ordinances which are *obligatory*. Public social conditions are on the contrary to be regarded as all the more perfect the less (in comparison with what is arranged publicly) is left for an individual to do by himself as his private inclination directs.

...

250. In virtue of the substantiality of its natural and family life, the agricultural class has directly within itself the concrete universal which it lives. The class of civil servants is universal in character and so has the universal explicitly as its ground and as the aim of its activity. The class between them, the business class, is essentially concentrated on the particular, and hence it is to it that Corporations are specially appropriate.

251. The labour organization of civil society is split, in accordance with the nature of its particulars, into different branches. The implicit likeness of such particulars to one another becomes really existent in an association, as something common to its members. Hence a selfish purpose, directed towards its particular self-interest, apprehends and evinces itself at the same time as universal; and a member of civil society is in virtue of his own particular skill a member of a Corporation, whose universal purpose is thus wholly concrete and no wider in scope than the purpose involved in business, its proper task and interest.

252. In accordance with this definition of its functions, a Corporation has the right, under the surveillance of the public authority, (a) to look after its own interests within its own sphere, (b) to co-opt members, qualified objectively by the requisite skill and rectitude, to a number fixed by the general structure of society, (c) to protect its members against particular contingencies, (d) to provide the education requisite to fit others to become members. In short, its right is to come on the scene like a second family for its members, while civil society can only be an indeterminate sort of family because it comprises everyone and so is farther removed from individuals and their special exigencies.

The Corporation member is to be distinguished from a day labourer or from a man who is prepared to undertake casual employment on a single occasion. The former who is, or will become, master of his craft, is a member of the association not for casual gain on single occasions but for the whole range, the universality, of his personal livelihood.

Privileges, in the sense of the rights of a branch of civil society organized into a Corporation, are distinct in meaning from privileges proper in the etymological sense. The latter are casual exceptions to universal rules; the former, however, are only the crystallization, as regulations, of characteristics inherent in an essential branch of society itself owing to its nature as particular.

253. In the Corporation, the family has its stable basis in the sense that its livelihood is assured there, conditionally upon capability, i.e. it has a stable capital. ... In addition, this nexus of capability and livelihood is a recognized fact, with the result that the Corporation member needs no external marks beyond his own membership as evidence of his skill and his regular income and subsistence, i.e. as evidence that he is a somebody. It is also recognized that he belongs to a whole which is itself an organ of the entire society, and that he is actively concerned in promoting the comparatively disinterested end of this whole. Thus he commands the respect due to one in his social position.

The institution of Corporation corresponds, on account of its assurance of capital, to the introduction of agriculture and private property in another sphere. ...

When complaints are made about the luxury of the business classes and their passion for extravagance – which have as their concomitant the creation of a rabble of paupers ... – we must not forget that besides its other causes (e.g. increasing mechanization of labour) this phenomenon has an ethical ground, as was indicated above. Unless he is a member of an authorized Corporation (and it is only by being authorized that an association becomes a Corporation), an individual without rank or dignity, his isolation reduced his business to mere self-seeking, and his livelihood and satisfaction become insecure. Consequently, he has to try to gain recognition for himself by giving external proofs of success in his business, and to these proofs no limits can be set. He cannot live in the manner of his class, for no class really exists for him, since in civil society it is only something common to particular persons which really exists, i.e. something legally constituted and recognized. Hence he cannot achieve for himself a way of life proper to his class and less idiosyncratic.

Within the Corporation the help which poverty receives loses its accidental character and the humiliation wrongfully associated with it. The wealthy perform their duties to their fellow associates and thus riches cease to inspire either pride or envy, pride in their owners, envy in others. In these conditions rectitude obtains its proper recognition and respect.

254. As the family was the first, so the Corporation is the second ethical root of the state, the one planted in civil society. The former contains the moments of subjective particularity and objective universality in a substantial unity. But these moments are sundered in civil society to begin with; on the one side there is the particularity of need and satisfaction, reflected into itself, and on the other side the universality of abstract rights. In the Corporation these moments are united in an inward fashion, so that in this union particular welfare is present as a right and is actualized.

The sanctity of marriage and the dignity of Corporation membership are the two fixed points around which the unorganized atoms of civil society revolve.

256. The end of the Corporation is restricted and finite, while the public authority was an external organization involving a separation and a merely relative identity of controller and controlled. The end of the former and the externality and relative identity of the latter find their truth in the absolutely universal end and its absolute actuality. Hence the sphere of civil society passes over into the state.

The town is the seat of the civil life of business. There reflection arises, turns upon itself, and pursues its atomizing task; each man maintains himself in and through his relation to others, who, like himself, are persons possessed of rights. The country, on the other hand, is the seat of an ethical life resting on nature and the family. Town and country thus constitute the two moments, still ideal moments, whose true ground is the state, although it is from them that the state springs.

The philosophic proof of the concept of the state is this development of ethical life from its immediate phase through civil society, the phase of division, to the state, which then reveals itself as the true ground of these phases. A proof in philosophic science can only be a development of this kind.

Since the state appears as a result in the advance of the philosophic concept through displaying itself as the true ground [of the earlier phases], that show of medication is now cancelled and the state has become directly present before us. Actually, therefore, the state as such is not so much the result as the beginning. It is within the state that the family is first developed into civil society, and it is the Idea of the state itself which disrupts itself into these two moments. Through the development of civil society, the substance of ethical life acquires its infinite form, which contains in itself these two moments: (1) infinite differentiation down to the inward experience of independent self-consciousness, and (2) the form of universality involved in education, the form of thought whereby mind is objective and actual to itself as an organic totality in laws and institutions which are its will in terms of thought.

* From Georg Wilhelm Friedrich Hegel, *The Philosophy of Right*, translated by T.M. Knox, in W. Benton, ed., *Encyclopaedia Britannica: Great Books of the Western World*, Vol. 46 (Chicago: University of Chicago Press, 1952 [1821]), 64; 75–80.

Karl Marx (1818–83), German theorist and founder of communism. As student, Marx advanced from the idealism of Hegel to materialism. Radical newspaper editor, he became a socialist in the course of the 1840s, writing with Friedrich Engels the Communist Manifesto *(1848). After the failed 1848 revolutions, he went into exile and lived in poverty in North London, where, with the assistance of Engels and the British Museum, he produced* Das Kapital. *The selection here is from the young Marx and focuses on his view of a historic split between citizen and bourgeois, pulling the political sphere apart from a material world of civil society. Without a transformation of self and society, religious emancipation would not lead to human emancipation.**

Security is the supreme social conception of civil society [*bürgerliche Gesellschaft*], the conception of the police, the idea that society as a whole only exists to guarantee to each of its members the maintenance of his person, his rights, and his property.

By the conception of security civil society does not raise itself above its egoism. Security is rather the confirmation of its egoism.

None of the so-called rights of man, therefore, goes beyond the egoistic individual, beyond the individual as a member of civil society, withdrawn into his private interests and separated from the community. Far from regarding the individual as a generic being, the generic life, Society itself, rather appears as an external frame for the individual, as a limitation of his original independence. The sole bond which connects him with his fellows is a natural necessity, material needs and private interest, the preservation of his property and his egoistic person.

. . .

The riddle admits of easy solution.

The political emancipation is at the same time the dissolution of the old society, upon which was based the civil society, or the rulership alienated from the people. The political revolution is the revolution of civil society. What was the character of the old society? It can be described in one word. Feudality. The old civic society had a directly political character, that is, the elements of civic life, as for example property or the family, or the mode and kind of labour, were raised to the level of elements of the community in the form of landlordism, status, and corporation. In this form they determined the relation of the individual to the community, that is his political relation, his relationship of separation and exclusion from the other constituent parts of society. For the latter organization of popular life did not raise property or labour to the level of social elements, but rather completed their separation from the political whole and constituted them as special societies within society. Thus the vital functions and vital conditions of society continued to be political, although political in the sense of feudality, which means that they excluded the individual from the political whole, and transformed the special relation of his corporation to the political whole into his own general relation to the popular life. As a consequence of this organization, the political unity necessarily appears as the consciousness, the will and the activity of the political unity, and likewise the general State power as the special concern of a ruler and his servants sundered from the people.

The political revolution, which overthrew this domination and raised political affairs to the rank of popular affairs, which constituted the political State as a general concern, that is as a real State, necessarily shattered all Estates, corporations, guilds, privileges, which were just so many expressions of the separation of the people from their community. The political revolution thereby abolished the political character of civil society.

It dissolved civil society into its elemental parts, on the one hand, into the individuals, on the other hand, into the material and spiritual elements, which formed the vital content, the civil situation of these individuals. It released the political spirit, which was imprisoned in fragments in the various blind alleys of the feudal society; it collected all these dispersed parts of it, liberated it from its entanglement with the civil life, and constituted it as the sphere of the community, of the general popular concerns in ideal independence from its particular elements of civil life. The specific life activity and the specific life situation settled into a merely general significance. They no longer formed the general relation of the individual to the political whole. The public business as such became rather the general business of every individual and the political function became his general function.

But the completion of the idealism of the State was at the same time the completion of the materialism of civil society.

The throwing off of the political yoke was at the same time the throwing off of the bond which had curbed the egoistic spirit of civil society. The political emancipation was at the same time the emancipation of civil society from politics, from even the semblance of a general content.

Feudal society was resolved into its basic elements, its individual members. But into the individuals who really formed its basis, that is, the egoistic individual.

This individual, the member of civil society, is now the basis, the assumption of the political State. He is recognized as such in the rights of man.

The liberty of the egoistic individual and the recognition of this liberty are, however, tantamount to the recognition of the unbridled movement of the intellectual and material elements which inform him.

The individual was therefore not liberated from religion; he received religious freedom. He was not freed from property; he received freedom of property. He was not freed from the egoism of industry; he received industrial freedom.

The constitution of the political State and the dissolution of civil society into independent individuals – whose relation is right, as the relation of the members of Estates and of guilds was privilege – is accomplished in one and the same act. But the individual as a member of civil society, the unpolitical individual, necessarily appears as the natural individual. The rights of man appear as natural rights, for the self-conscious activity concentrates itself upon the political act. The egoistic individual is the sediment of the dissolved society, the object of immediate certitude, and therefore a natural object. The political revolution dissolves the civil society into its constituent parts without revolutionizing and subjecting to criticism those parts themselves. It regards civil society, the world of needs, of labour, of private interests, as the foundation of its existence, as an assumption needing no proof, and therefore as its natural basis. Lastly, the individual as a member of civil society counts as the proper individual, as the man in contradistinction to the citizen, because he is man in his sensual, individual, closest existence, whereas political man is only the abstract, artificial individual, the individual as an allegorical, moral person. The real man is only recognized in the shape of the egoistic individual, the true man is only recognized in the shape of the abstract citizen.

The abstraction of the political man was very well described by Rousseau: *He who dares undertake to give instructions to a nation ought to feel himself capable as it were of changing human nature; of transforming every individual who in himself is a complete and independent whole into part of a greater whole, from which he receives in some manner his life and his being; of altering man's consti-tution, in order to strengthen it; of substituting a social and moral existence for the independent and physical existence which we have all received from nature. In a word, it is necessary to deprive man of his native powers, in order to endow him with some which are alien to him, and of which he cannot make use without the aid of other people.* All emancipation leads back to the human world, to relationships, to men themselves.

Political emancipation is the reduction of man, on the one side, to the member of civil society, to the egoistic, independent individual, on the other side, to the citizen, to the moral person.

Not until the real, individual man is identical with the citizen, and has become a generic being in his empirical life, in his individual work, in his individual relationships, not until man has recognized and organized his own capacities as social capacities, and consequently the social force is no longer divided by the political power, not until then will human emancipa-tion be achieved.

* From Karl Marx 'On the Jewish Question' [1843], in *Selected Essays*, translated by H.J. Stenning (London: Leonard Parsons, 1926), 75–6; 79–85, with a few changes by the editors better to reflect the German original.

Heinrich von Treitschke (1834–96), historian, politician and powerful advocate of a Prussian-led unified Germany. A liberal nationalist as a young man his *nationalist views become more conservative in mature age. A member of the Reichstag and Prussia's state historiographer, his historical and contemporary writings shaped much of imperial German culture and politics. Here he defends a view of civil society as naturally hierarchical and unequal against socialist and radical–democratic programmes.**

Civil society is the essence of a mutually dependent relationship, which is given thanks to the natural inequality of people, the distribution of property and education [*Bildung*], and which in infinite ways develops anew through everyday interactions. . . .

Without a sharp separation between ruling and serving ranks, it is impossible to either demonstrate or imagine the beginnings of civilization [*Kultur*]. From the laziness of the barbarians towards slavery, from there to feudal labour and finally to free labour: that, broadly speaking, is the story of the rise of society. . . . No one any longer believes in the war of all against all, with which Thomas Hobbes once scared the world. The individual is not fighting against the individual at the beginnings of history; rather one tribe is suspicious of another tribe and sees in the foreigner the enemy. The first contact between unfinished people is always hostile; only courageous tribes have potential, a future, while the cowardly ones will wither away without history. . . . History only steadies, once the winners have learnt not to drive away or destroy the losers, but instead to use them as serving members by integrating them into their own communal body. . . .

Man alone is a historical being and hence also the only truly sociable being. He absorbs the works of his fathers through language and culture, law and economy; these live with him and he contributes to them; he stands as a vital and, if he wants, as a conscious link in the chain of time. Every step he takes he feels the limits, which are placed on the will of history. He only lives by subordinating himself to the collective development of his nation [*Volk*]. . . .

Property, often equated with selfishness, in fact instills in society an ethic that is the very opposite of selfishness – piety, respect of existing things. Property envelops people with the blessing of custom; out of love to the inherited domestic four posts arises the noble pride of love for the fatherland and the certainty that the multi-faceted richness of national civilization shall never be replaced by the same old dull routine of a cosmopolitan bourgeoisie [*Weltbürgertum*]. Socialism's temptations that promise 'all goods of culture to all people' will inevitably fail at the powerful historic sentiment of humanity. The Icelandic man very well knows that his unproductive home can only offer him a small fraction of these goods. Nonetheless, he is strongly and loyally tied to this poor soil and thus proves through such pious self-discipline that proud Germanic blood is flowing through his veins.

Civil society in a rich nation [*Volk*] is always an aristocracy, even under a democratic constitution. Or if we are to say it directly in a hated but true phrase: class rule, or more precisely order by classes, follows as inevitably from the nature of society as the contrast between rulers and ruled follows from the nature of the state. Social Democracy admits by its very name that its aims are nonsense. ... Even a state of unlimited competition only means that individuals move up or down the ladder of society more quickly, but it does not eliminate the ladder altogether. ... Even in this age of social change the law remains valid: only a minority is destined to enjoy the ideal goods of culture completely; the vast majority's lot will be work. ... No social reform will ever be able to give the working classes a greater blessing than the simple reminder: pray and work! A person who only pursues material goods, who has ceased to be able to love and to believe in a just world order, is the most pitiful of all beings. ...

All of the above only illuminates afresh that the aristocratic order of society can only disappear with humanity itself. ... The masses [*Masse*] will remain the masses. That is to say: the big majority of people performs its part in the work of society by employing more or less consciously its physical force for the economic purposes of the community and by thus preserving the soul of nations [*Völker*]. This order is just, for no one is barred from the true happiness of life, peace of one's soul and pleasures of love. And it is necessary since the complete properties of humanity can only to be developed in this way. ... If people were to try and disrupt this order ... they would inevitably be swallowed up in the mental processes of socialism which is always consumed by the madness of believing evil could be extirpated from this earth. One would lose respect of the historical world.

Our state nowhere grants a political right for which there is not a corresponding duty; it demands of all those who wish to take part in any way in the direction of public life that they must first earn this power through property and education; it is ceaselessly active on behalf of a wider and deeper spiritual life; it mitigates even the most general of its civic duties, the duty of bearing arms, in favour of these spiritual forces. ... Universal suffrage goes clean against these basic ethical conceptions of the German state; it rewards ignorance and awakens pride in the stupid. Anyone who has taken the trouble to be born receives, after a few years and without limitations, in a state that gives unprecedented honour to culture, the highest political right of the citizen! It can be no surprise that the poor man who enjoys such a right comes to the conclusion that in society also birth is a valid passport to power without work for every man. There can be no doubt that universal suffrage has immeasurably encouraged the fantastic over-estimation of their own power and their own value among the masses. The irreconcilable contrast between the democratic equality of political suffrage and the necessary aristocratic structure of society proves to the dissatisfied little man with all possible clarity the social decadence of the present and makes him into a credulous victim of demagogues. In this state of noble culture universal suffrage means organized indiscipline, it amounts to a recognition of the revolt of sovereign ignorance, the revolt of the soldier against his officer, of the journeyman against his master, of the worker against his employer. But these destructive effects have already taken place excessively and are no longer to be eliminated; to abolish the right which has already been granted would only encourage all the more the arrogance of the uncivilised. All we can do, therefore, is at least to protect the foundations of our monarchical state, the administration of our localities and communities, from the invasion of republican principles and to protest against the assertion that the reward of ignorance is a result of enlightened social policy. . . .

Such a crudely materialist doctrine [as that propagated by Social Democracy] can know no fatherland, can know no respect for the personality of the national state. The idea of nationalism, the moving force of history in our century, remains inconceivable to socialism. Socialism is everywhere in league with unpatriotic cosmopolitanism and with a weakness of loyalty toward the state. . . .

The masses have not the capacity to fulfil the serious duties of government or to occupy the higher offices of self-government. Even the modest problems of jury service are often inadequately solved because the education of our lower middle class is not sufficient, and no thinking person will wish to make up jury lists by going even lower down in the social scale. . . . Almost all great mass movements of history have had their roots in economic necessity or in religious feeling. Purely political party questions seldom affect the little man; his enthusiasm can be kindled only for the highest political good, for the existence of the fatherland.

A correct assessment of this character of the masses leads to the sober Aristotelian advice which has been followed in all well-ordered states, namely: social peace is preserved best if the higher classes do not allow the masses to become too powerful and do not do them any injustice. . . . If that advice is not followed, if the masses succeed in taking power directly for themselves, then the world is turned upside down, state and society are dissolved, and rule by force sets in, which put an end to a thousand years of Greek civilisation. . . .

There is another and surer way of mitigating class antagonisms: to remove the barriers which prevent those who are born in poverty from rising into the group of the propertied and educated. The state and society can never do enough in this direction. . . . If it is impossible to allow the great majority of people to participate in all the pleasures of culture, nevertheless every enterprising person must be able to hope to leave this majority. The state should not merely enable people to work and to give the poor man the right to lift himself up out of his class, it should also by means of good elementary schools and an easily accessible higher education make it possible for the genuinely talented really to exercise these rights. This is the only way to infuse fresh blood into the upper classes constantly. This is the only way to come close to that equalizing of demand. . . . Free competition among all for the benefits of civilisation which can only ever be attained in full measure by a minority – this is what I regard as sensible equality. . . .

*From Heinrich von Treitschke, 'Der Sozialismus und seine Goenner,' in *Zehn Jahre Deutscher Kaempfe, 1865–1874* (Berlin: Georg Reimer, 1874), 466–519.

Associational practices: moral order, popular emancipation, and escapism

This is an excerpt from The Girls' Friendly Society, Special Report of the Branch Secretaries' Meeting, held June 25th, 1879. The Girls' Friendly Society, founded in 1875, was one of many Christian philanthropic associations in the business of social improvement. The extract here shows the combination between paternalism and a culture of Christian fellowship.*

At the request of the Vice-President, Mrs. Brooke-Houston next addressed the meeting to the following effect:

At our Branch Secretaries' meeting last year I tried to show how much good might be done amongst out-door business girls by the G.F.S. ... There are hundreds of young women of business in London and other large cities for whose well-being out of business hours no one seems to be responsible. Many employers of labour do not seem to feel themselves bound to look after the moral, social, or religious welfare of their employees. Except in high-class houses, young women have no separate sitting-rooms. They are thus compelled either to spend their evenings in the common sitting-room, which has been the breakfast, dining, and tea-room during the day, and in the society of young men who are frequently strangers to them, or seek amusement out-of-doors. True, their bedrooms remain; but they are frequently close, crowded, ill ventilated, and uncomfortable, and sometimes devoid of even the most ordinary means of security from intrusion. After business hours, then, it is not surprising that young girls go out-of-doors, and remain out either walking or in some place of public amusement, till the very last moment; and coming home late at night from a theatre or music-hall, they cannot fail to see and hear much that is very injurious, while the unhealthy existence is ill calculated to fit them physically or mentally for another day's work. And they work very hard, the great majority of them twelve or thirteen hours; standing on their feet, except during the interval of meals; not permitted, even when standing idle, to speak to each other; continually trying to please their customers, and dispose of their goods whether they are suitable or not. It is a wearing, wearying, dispiriting life, and one that needs a little cheering. Surely for those workers the G.F.S. can do much, and I would venture to suggest that the best, surest, most effectual way is by personal influence. If every Associate could make a *friend* of even one business girl, the result would soon be surprising. Those girls are solitary, often quite friendless in London, and it cannot fail to give them pleasure to find that some one takes an interest in them. I believe some girls get led into evil courses simply because they think no one will know or care. Many more do wrong, not from any disposition or taste for vice, but from sheer loneliness and recklessness. Many more simply drift along with whatever current for the time being runs by them, too weak and indifferent to mark out a clear and distinct course for themselves and follow it, but willing to be led hither and thither. For business girls I think we can and *should* do much. We should open clubs and recreation-rooms where they can spend their evenings when they leave business – bright, pleasant, cheery rooms, supplied with books, and, where it is possible, music-rooms even on a very small scale, capable of accommodating even a dozen or two girls. There will be no need to supply amusement – they have enough of that already; nor refreshment, except in exceptional cases – books, music, a pleasant room, and the presence of a pleasant friend who will take an interest in them, will be sufficient to change many a weary and often ill-spent evening into a pleasant, restful, and profitable one. And I would venture to hint to our Associates, that by endeavouring to become personally acquainted with our business girls, they may have the power to prevent them from drifting; as they so frequently do, away from the Church into which they were baptized and confirmed, and attending other places of worship, because, they say, 'The people notice and seem glad to see them at chapel, while no one ever knows or cares, whether they go to church or not.' The more I see and hear about them, the more convinced am I that our business girls, as a class, are sorely in need of help and sympathy.

. . .

One of our leading maxims is 'Purity made possible by extended help;' and it seems to me that we, as Associates, have not yet fully realised our responsibility to our Members in this particular.

The G.F.S. has discovered to us classes of girls of whose existence even we were not aware, and we do not yet know perhaps how awful is the moral condition of a large number of our English girls, and how wide-spread the evil we long to remedy. Many of us started with long lists of Members, ignorantly, and with more or less of utopian views as to their future; and then, through some painful disappointment or startling discovery, getting glimpses of sin of which we had never dreamed, we have been thrown back, frightened at the vista opening before us, and ready almost to despair of every girl; or else, realising for the first time *their* need of rescue, we have been tempted to work for *them* rather than for the Members to whom we are pledged. Yes, here is my point. When we become Working Associates of the G.F.S., we are pledged to our Members to love and help them every way we can. I know that I am speaking to-day to ladies of far greater experience in work than myself, but may I be forgiven if I sound a note of earnest warning? More than once during the last few weeks have I been grieved by hearing from our own Associates this remark, 'Oh, but the others are far more interesting' and girls are constantly heard to say, 'When a girl has been unfortunate, ladies take much more real interest in her' and I felt the climax was reached when our Matron told me that often – twice in one day lately – ladies seeking servants have actually expressed a preference for those who had fallen.

Fellow Associates, let us beware. We are banded together in this Society for one object – the working for such, and such only, as may come up to the standard of the third Central Rule. This stamp of character is the glory of our Society, and it should ever be our pride to maintain it in its beauty and simplicity. Members are watching us with very jealous eyes, and I am convinced that far better had there never been a G.F.S. than that we should ever by word or deed lower the standard, and lead our Members to suppose for a moment that anything *could be* more interesting to us than a pure and holy life.

Is not ours the only Society which makes purity a *sine qua non*? And have not hundreds of parents allowed their daughters to join it on that very ground? Aye, and thousands of girls themselves have been attracted by the same rule. Ever since the Society has been at work we have been called 'Pharisaical' 'hard' and what not, and constant requests have been made that the third rule might be altered or modified in some shape or form. But does it never strike these objectors that even *were such a thing possible* we should be breaking faith with some 22,000 Members? And oh! our Members do need help. They are sheep in the midst of wolves.

. . .

And again in a body or a body politic, there are always members weaker than other members; those that need more care, more guarding, more training and strengthening. And these, too, in every sound body, and in every well-ordered commonwealth, are watched and protected, and helped and confirmed. It does not do for the strong to neglect the weak. The weak may perish from the neglect, but the strong will suffer too. God has so knit us together, even in things natural, that we cannot (only on selfish principles) safely neglect the interests of our neighbour. The unchecked pestilence in the alley lays low the children of the palace; the water which is polluted in the farm brings fever into the streets of the city; the vice and ignorance of the hovel let loose on society the thief, and the house-breaker, and the assassin. It is the commonest of common places to say how this is true of neglected childhood and untrained youth; how the parent lets the weed-crop grow in his infant's heart, and finds too late that there is poison where there should have been fruit, and that the poison overflows into his own cup and embitters all his later years with sorrow and with shame.

. . .

Now, I think, brethren, that in our great body politic, the great body of Christ's Church, that kingdom of God in the midst of us, there are few members and subjects more needing the care and watchfulness and help of stronger members and more prosperous subjects, than the thousands of young girls from our country cottages, and our bye-lanes and alleys, and even from our workhouses, who are constantly growing up and going out to service in the homes of the upper and middle classes of men, or into our factories, or serving in our shops.

*From The Girls' Friendly Society, *Special Report of the Branch Secretaries' Meeting, held June 25th 1879, the Workhouse Associates' Meeting, held June 24th, 1879, and of the Service at St. Paul's Cathedral, held June 26th, 1879* (London: 1879), 24–7; 49.

*Mrs. Layton was born in Bethnal Green in the East End of London in 1855. The WCG was founded in 1883 and became the largest independent women's organization, campaigning for the vote and equal rights as well as for social reforms such as maternity benefits. Here Mrs Layton writes of her entry in the guild and her sense of empowerment through membership in associational life and the public responsibilities and opportunities that came with it.**

I was born in Bethnal Green, April 9th, 1855, a tiny scrap of humanity. I was my mother's seventh child, and seven more were born after me – fourteen in all – which made my mother a perfect slave.

. . .

When I was ten years old I began to earn my own living. I went to mind the baby of a person who kept a small general shop. My wages were 1/6 a week and my tea, and 2 pence a week for myself. I got to work at eight in the morning and left at eight at night, with the exception of two nights a week when I left at seven o'clock to attend a night school, one of a number started by Lord Shaftesbury, called Ragged Schools. I was very happy in my place and was very fond of the baby.

. . .

It was at a mission hall, where I went when I found the church too stiff and conservative, that I met my husband. We were both keenly interested in social problems. It was he who interested me in free education.

. . .

When my husband's wages reached the magnificent sum of £1 1 shilling a week, he joined the Railwaymen's Trade Union. At first I thought 5 pence a week a lot of money for what I considered very little benefit. I did not understand the principle of the Trade Union Movement, but I have since had cause to be thankful that my husband joined a Trade Union. For twenty-six years I paid all subscriptions, and willingly paid a levy of 1/-a year for political purposes, believing it to be one of the ways the workers could emancipate themselves, and I have done my best to get members into Parliament, not by speaking in public but by working in any way I could.

Soon after my husband joined his Trade Union, a Co-operative Store was formed at Child's Hill [in North West London]. I gave my husband the necessary 1/6 to join. There, I thought, was a chance of getting something back. I had been told about the wonderful dividend and the interest on share capital, but nothing about the principles that should govern the Co-operative Movement. In fact, I thought the Child's Hill Society stood alone. I was so interested in getting the 'divi.' that I walked two miles to the Store every time I wanted a few things. My shilling soon grew into a pound and I began to think I was eating myself into a banking account. I put a few shillings on to my share capital and I felt that I should have a few pounds in time for a rainy day. Alas! my hopes were all, blighted. By the time I had managed to save £12 the Society failed, and I lost every penny with the exception of 1/8 which was my share of what was left. It was a great blow to me at the time, but, remembering the old saying, 'what can't be cured must be endured,' I set to work to endure the loss as cheerfully as I could.

During the time the Society was in existence, an Education Committee was formed and through them a Branch of the Women's Co-operative Guild. Now, in looking back, I can truthfully say that, although I lost £12 in money through the break-up of the Society, I gained far more than £12 worth of knowledge, and my life was brightened to such an extent that everything seemed changed. The Education Committee arranged lectures on all kinds of subjects which I used to attend, and the lectures gave me the knowledge I so badly needed. Then one day my husband brought me two tickets for a tea and social which he asked me to use. I could not very well spare the time, but I did not like to waste the tickets for I knew it was a big sacrifice out of my husband's little bit of pocket money. So I managed to go and take a friend with me. We had a nice tea, some songs and speeches, and then, after a speech by Miss Llewelyn Davies, names were taken to form a branch of the Women's Co-operative Guild. I was asked to join but told them I could not as I was far too busy. I thought a meeting in the middle of the week was quite impossible. I still had to wash and iron for my living. However, the old lady who had been so kind to me at my confinement gave my name in, and explained to me afterwards that she thought it would do me good to go to a meeting once a week and leave my worries behind me for a few hours. She also told me she thought I might be useful in a meeting of this kind. I joined the Guild and found the benefit my neighbour had predicted. It meant a long walk to the meeting and back, something fresh to listen to while there, and something to think about all the week. I was not used to working-women managing their meetings. I had attended Mothers' Meetings, where ladies came and lectured on the domestic affairs in the workers' homes that it was impossible for them to understand. I have boiled over many times at some of the things I have been obliged to listen to, without the chance of asking a question. In the Guild we always had the chance of discussing a subject. The Guild was more to my mind than the Mothers' Meeting, so I gave up the Mothers' Meeting and attended the Guild. ... I had only been a member ten months when I was elected President, and from that time till I came off the National Central Committee in 1922, I was in office of some kind.

When I had been a Guild member about a year, I took up a share in my own name. I had learnt in that time that women should take an active part in the Co-operative Movement and that they should attend quarterly meetings of their Societies. That was the reason I took up a share. I was nominated for a seat on the Management Committee by a very progressive man who thought me a woman with some common sense, but there was such a storm at the idea of a woman a Management Committee that I did not seek election, and the members put my husband on instead.

...

The education I got in the Guildroom made me understand more about the laws of the country. So when I was ready to buy my house I had put the mortgage in my name. This caused a little friction between my husband and myself. He thought that although I had earned and saved the money, the house should certainly be bought in his name. He said it did not look respectful for a woman's name to be put on the deeds when she had a husband alive. I thought different, and so the house is mine.

Sometimes my husband rather resented the teachings of the Guild. The fact that I was determined to assert my right to have the house in my name was a charge against the Guild. The Guild, he said, was asking women think too much of themselves. I did not quite agree with him there, though I did and still do think the Guild has been the means of making its members think more of themselves than ever they did before. The Guild's training altered the whole course of my life. When I look back and think what my life might have been without its training and influence, I shudder. I was living in a house with two other families whose only ideas in life were work and sleep, and, for recreation, a visit each evening to the public-house or a cheap music hall. They tried very hard to induce me to go with them, and possibly, if I had not been connected with the Guild, when my baby died I might have fallen a victim to the drink habit. It is impossible to say how much I owe to the Guild. It gave me education and recreation. The lectures I heard gave me so much food for thought that I seldom felt dull, and

I always had something to talk to my husband about other than the little occurrences of daily life. Then I learnt in the Guild that education was to be the workers' best weapon, and I determined if it were to be at all possible that my son should have as good an education as I could give him. From a shy, nervous woman, the Guild made me a fighter. I was always willing to go on a Deputation if there was a wrong to be righted, or for any good cause, local or national.

. . .

My experience as a midwife was very useful when the Guild had the campaign for the National Care of Maternity. I am always proud of the fact that I was invited to speak on the first deputation (to government) connected with it. This was to get Maternity Benefit included in the Insurance Act.

. . .

In 1917 I spoke on a deputation to Lord Rhondda at the Local Government Board...The deputation put before him a large scheme for the National Care of Maternity...He said he could only give us half an hour, but he listened very patiently for an hour and a half. At the end he said he would put the points before the Cabinet, and said he had no idea there was such a well-organised body of working-women as the Women's Co-operative Guild.

During the last years, events of great interest to me were the international meetings of Cooperative Guildswomen which were now being held. I have been to three of these – at Basle, where I read a paper on the Guild, at Ghent, and at Stockholm, and I have paid my own expenses.

* From Mrs. Layton 'Memories of Seventy Years', in M.L. Davies, ed., *Life As We Have Known It* (London, 1931), 1; 20; 34; 37–41; 47–9; 53–4.

The Schlaraffia *in Hamburg (Germany) was a romantic club founded first in 1874. It was a refuge from everyday concerns, offered sociability, and its own cult of rituals, language, chronology, and social order. Schlaraffia, or the land of cockayne and milk and honey, was a medieval fantasy world with an imagined aristocratic order and its own version of Latin – attractive in its contrast to a modern society of class, industry, and party politics. 'Lulu' served the* Schlaraffen *as a general cry of support or greeting.**

The association was founded as the 'Schlaraffische club' [society of milk and honey] on January 1 1893 by Knight 'Schnedderrengdeng vom Elefantenryssel [elephant trunk]'. He had been knighted by Knight 'Ulrich von Hutten', the ancestral and arch chancellor of the High 'schlaraffische' ancestral empire 'Praga', and founder of the 'Schlaraffia Altonavia' in 1885. After its breakup during the winter of 1887, it continued on hanseatic soil as the 'Urschlaraffenbund'. When the latter club came to an end, Knight 'Schnedderrengdeng of Schlaraffen' found suitable material in the members of the 'Club Sociability of 1889' which then appropriately transformed itself in the above-mentioned 'schlarafische' style.

Since the formation of this club in March 1889, the 'schlaraffische' establishment honoured in genuine 'schlaraffischer' sovereignty, this moment as the time of foundation. After Count 'Ubi der Wasserdychte [water-tight]' – the formerly initiated Chief-'Schlaraffe' of the 'Schlaraffia Hammonia', who subsequently had also been Chief-'Schlaraffe' of the 'Altonavia' and of the 'Urschlaraffenbund' – and a further six knights of the 'Urschlaraffische' association had joined the nine founding members in the same year, the name of the empire was changed to ' "Schlaraffia Hammaburgia" of 1589'. In the 382nd session, the Chief-'Schlaraffe' 'Castor der Beständige [the constant]', who had gone through the same 'schlaraffische' path of life as the Lordship 'Ubi', joined the Empire as well. In the 493rd session on 7 December 1904, when the Empire set itself up to celebrate the 500th session, the chronology already used by the all-embracing 'Schlaraffia' was adopted. Years were thus counted from the establishment of the first 'Schlaraffia', the 'High "Praga" ' on 10 October 1859, as in the year 'Anno Uhui' [A.U.] 45 ... Henceforth, the Empire saw itself as founded on the first of the first month 'A.U.' 34 (thus 1893) ...

Until the 526th S. [s.a.] on the 27th of the 9th month 'A.U.' 46, when 'Knight Rheingold' was elected Chief-'Schlaraffe', the empire was led by three Chief-'Schlaraffen' ... Chief-'Schlaraffen' were the Knights 'Schnedderrengdeng', 'Vasco da Gama', 'Ubi', 'Fettspeck der Habgierige [fat slob the greedy]', 'Blaubart der Verbißene [Bluebeard the dogged]', 'Bumfidel von und zu auf Löwensteyn', and 'Crambambuli der Kitzler [the tickler]'. Personal differences now meant that the office of the 'Oberschlaraffe' was filled with one 'Oberschlaraffen' and two 'Oberschlaraffischen' councillors. ...

Until the 400th session ... frequent 'allschlaraffische' visits were noticeable, but since then visits from the German and Austrian Knighthoods became more prominent. A beautiful friendship with the Knighthood 'Cosy Clan Hammaburg' did already exist since the entry of Knight 'Vasco da Gama' into the Empire, 1893. However, now personal friendships grew more and more into a full Brotherhoods-in-Arms, also with other friendly alliances, which in many cases led to the cordial exchange of letters and frequent personal encounters with their Warriors. On 21 January 1914, in its 835th session, the Empire gave up its isolated position and joined the 'General German Order of Knights', active all over Germany and Austria, under the name: 'Association of the Uhu-Knights of Hammaburg, formerly "Schlaraffia"

Hammaburgia'. While the association already had at its disposal a healthy membership, this now became superfluous because the General German Order commanded one that afforded greater advantage, the Knights now gained at times of necessity access to the rich treasures of the Order.

That this financial support, strengthened through the ethical aims of the association, cannot be praised enough: may the cultivation of chivalry, brotherhood, art and humour, as well as noble friendship between men, make for a stronger and more enduring association after the end of the world war. Then the motto of the association will rightly persist:

'In arte voluptas!'	'Fideliter et constanter!'
Let the Eminent preside in Grace!	The Chancellorship
'Lulu!'	'Meerspatz v. d. Mühlenburg.'

* Bund der Uhuritter auf Hammaburg ... 25 jähriges Bestandesfest [1918], cit. in Herbert Freudenthal, *Vereine in Hamburg: Ein Beitrag zur Geschichte und Volkskunde der Geselligkeit* (Hamburg, 1968), 214–15, translated by Timo Thoms and the editors.

Organic associationalism and the critique of liberalism

Ferdinand Tönnies (1855–1936), founding father of sociology with Max Weber and Georg Simmel. Refused to give up his membership in the Society for Ethical Culture, which promoted social reform and self-improvement, required in exchange for a professional chair. This extract from Gemeinschaft und Gesellschaft *contrasts the large-scale and commercial civil society with small-scale tight community, two systems which he thought in tension throughout history.**

Gesellschaft, an aggregate by convention and law of nature, is to be understood as a multitude of natural and artificial individuals, the wills and spheres of whom are in many relations with and to one another, and remain nevertheless independent of one another and devoid of mutual familiar relationships. This gives us the general description of 'bourgeois society' or 'exchange Gesellschaft,' the nature and movements of which legislative economy attempts to understand; a condition in which, according to the expression of Adam Smith, 'Every man ... becomes in some measure a merchant, ...' Where merchants, companies, or firms or associations deal with one another in international or national markets and exchanges, the nature of the Gesellschaft is erected as in a concave mirror or as in an extract.

The generality of this situation is by no means, as the famous Scotchman imagined, the immediate or even probable result of the innovation that labor is divided and products exchanged. It is more a remote goal with respect to which the development of the Gesellschaft must be understood. To the extent that this goal is realized, the existence of a Gesellschaft in the sense that it is used here is real at a given time. It is something in the process of becoming, something which should be conceived here as personality of the general will or the general reason, and at the same time (as we know) it is fictitious and nominal. It is like an emanation, as if it had emerged from the heads of the persons in whom it rests, who join hands eagerly to exchange across all distances, limits, and scruples, and establish this speculative Utopia as the only country, the only city, in which all fortune seekers and all merchant adventurers have a really common interest. As the fiction of money is represented by metal or paper, it is represented by the entire globe, or by a circumscribed territory.

In the conception of Gesellschaft the original or natural relations of human beings to each other must be excluded. The possibility of a relation in the Gesellschaft assumes no more than a multitude of mere persons who are capable of delivering something and consequently of promising something. Gesellschaft as a totality to which a system of conventional rules applies is limitless; it breaks through its chance and real boundaries constantly. In Gesellschaft every person strives for that which is to his own advantage and affirms the actions of others only in so far as and as long as they can further his interest. Before and outside of convention and also before and outside of each special contract, the relation of all to all may therefore be conceived as potential hostility or latent war. Against this condition all agreements of the will stand out as so many treaties and peace pacts. This conception is the only one which does justice to all facts of business and trade where all rights and duties can be reduced to mere value and definitions of ability to deliver. Every theory of pure private law or law of nature understood as pertaining to the Gesellschaft has to be considered as being based upon this conception. Buyer and seller in their manifold types stand in relation one to the other in such a manner that each one, for as little of his own wealth as possible, desires and attempts to obtain as much of the wealth of others as possible. The real commercial and business people race with each other on many sprinting tracks, as it were, trying each to get the better of the other and to be the first to reach the goal: the sale of their goods and of as large a quantity as possible. Thus they are forced to crowd each other out or to trip each other up.

The loss of one is the profit of the other, and this is the case in every individual exchange, unless owners exchange goods of actually equal value. This constitutes general competition which takes place in so many other spheres, but is nowhere so evident and so much in the consciousness of people as in trade, to which, consequently, the conception is limited in its common use. Competition has been described by many pessimists as an illustration of the war of all against all, which a famous thinker has conceived as the natural state of mankind.

However, even competition carries within it, as do all forms of such war, the possibility of being ended. Even enemies like these – although among these it may be the least likely – recognize that under certain conditions it is to their advantage to agree and to spare each other. They may even unite themselves together for a common purpose (or also – and this is the most likely – against a common enemy). Thus competition is limited and abolished by coalition.

In analogy to this situation, based upon the exchange of material goods, all conventional society life, in the narrower sense of the word, can be understood. Its supreme rule is politeness. It consists of an exchange of words and courtesies in which everyone seems to be present for the good of everyone else and everyone seems to consider everyone else as his equal, whereas in reality everyone is thinking of himself and trying to bring to the fore his importance and advantages in competition with the others. For everything pleasant which someone does for someone else, he expects, even demands, at least an equivalent. He weighs exactly his services, flatteries, presents, and so on, to determine whether they will bring about the desired result. Formless contracts are made continuously, as it were, and constantly many are pushed aside in the race by the few fortunate and powerful ones.

Since all relations in the Gesellschaft are based upon comparison of possible and offered services, it is evident that the relations with visible, material matters have preference, and that mere activities and words form the foundation for such relationships only in an unreal way. In contrast to this, Gemeinschaft as a bond of 'blood' is in the first place a physical relation, therefore expressing itself in deeds and words. Here the common relation to the material objects is of a secondary nature and such object are not exchanged as often as they are used and possessed in common. Furthermore, Gesellschaft, in the sense which we may call moral, is also entirely dependent upon its relations with the state, which has not entered our theory so far because the economic Gesellschaft must be considered prior to it.

. . .

City life and Gesellschaft down the common people to decay and death; in vain they struggle to attain power through their own multitude, and it seems to them that they can use their power only for a revolution if they want to free themselves from their fate. The masses become conscious of this social position through the education in schools and through newspapers. They proceed from class consciousness to class struggle. This class struggle may destroy society and the state which it is its purpose to reform. The entire culture has been transformed into a civilization of state and Gesellschaft, and this transformation means the doom of culture itself if none of its scattered seeds remain alive and again bring forth the essence and idea of Gemeinschaft, thus secretly fostering a new culture amidst the decaying one.

To conclude our theory, two periods stand thus contrasted with each other in the history of the great systems of culture: a period of Gesellschaft follows a period of Gemeinschaft. The Gemeinschaft is characterized by the social will as concord, folkways, mores, and religion; the Gesellschaft by the social will as convention, legislation, and public opinion. The concepts correspond to the types of external social organization, which may be classed as follows

A.   Gemeinschaft

1. Family life = concord. Man participates in this with all his sentiments. Its real controlling agent is the people (*Volk*).
2. Rural village life = folkways and mores. Into this man enters with all his mind and heart. Its real controlling agent is the commonwealth.
3. Town life = religion. In this the human being takes part with his entire conscience. Its real controlling agent is the church.

B. Gesellschaft

1. City life = convention. This is determined by man's intentions. Its real controlling agent is Gesellschaft per se.
2. National life = legislation. This is determined by man's calculations. Its real controlling agent is the state.
3. Cosmopolitan life = public opinion. This is evolved by man's consciousness. Its real controlling agent is the republic of scholars.

With each of these categories a predominant occupation and a dominating tendency in intellectual life are related in the following manner:

(A) 1. Home (or household) economy, based upon liking or preference, viz., the joy and delight of creating and conserving. Understanding develops the norms for such an economy.
   2. Agriculture, based upon habits, i.e., regularly repeated tasks. Co-operation is guided by custom.
   3. Art, based upon memories, i.e., of instruction, of rules followed, and of ideas conceived in one's own mind. Belief in the work and the task unites the artistic wills.
(B) 1. Trade based upon deliberation; namely, attention, comparison, calculation are the basis of all business. Commerce is deliberate action per se. Contracts are the custom and creed of business.
   2. Industry based upon decisions; namely, of intelligent productive use of capital and sale of labor. Regulations rule the factory.
   3. Science, based upon concepts, as is self-evident. Its truths and opinions then pass into literature and the press and thus become part of public opinion.

In the earlier period family life and home (or household) economy strike the keynote; in the later period commerce and city life. If, however, we investigate the period of Gemeinschaft more closely, several epochs can be distinguished. Its whole development tends toward an approach to Gesellschaft in which, on the other hand, the force of Gemeinschaft persists, although with diminishing strength, even in the period of Gesellschaft, and remains the reality of social life.

* From Ferdinand Tönnies, *Fundamental Concepts of Sociology (Gemeinschaft und Gesellschaft)*, translated by Charles P. Loomis (New York: American Book Company, 1940 [1887]), 87–90; 270–2.

Otto von Gierke (1841–1921), leading German jurist, whose erudite work on the historical evolution of Genossenschaft, *or fellowship in which members are*

*voluntarily united, shaped political as well as legal thought. Gierke believed that
the organic ability of the* Genossenschaft *to think and act as one was unique to
Germany. Here he discusses similarities and differences between medieval and
modern associations.**

[1]   Man owes what he is to union with his fellow man. The possibility of
forming associations [*Associationen*], which not only increase the power of
those alive at the time, but also – and most importantly, because the existence
of the association outspans that of the individual personality – unite past
generations with those to come, gave us the possibility of evolution, of history.

As the progress of world history unfolds inexorably, there rises the unending
arch of the noble edifice of those organic associations which, in ever greater
and increasingly broad spheres, lend external form and efficacy to the
coherence of all human existence and to unity in all its varied complexity.
From marriage, the highest of those associations which do not outlast the
life of the individual, come families, extended families [*Geschlechter*], tribes
and nations, local communities [*Gemeinden*], states and confederations in rich
gradations; and there is no conceivable limit to this development, other than
that at some time in the remote future all men unite in a single organised
common life and give visible expression to the fact that they are simply
elements of one great whole.

But this development from apparently insurmountable complexity to
unity presents only one facet of social progress. All the life of the intellect,
all human excellence would atrophy and be lost if the idea of unity were
to triumph alone to the exclusion of all others. The opposing principle
forges its path with equal power and necessity; the idea of the plurality that
persists within every all-embracing unity, the particular within the general,
the principle of the rights and independence of all the lesser unities which
go to make up the greater whole, down to the single individual – the idea
of *freedom.*

[2]   The struggle of these two great principles determines one of the most
powerful motive forces in history. Their reconciliation, in a form suited to
the age, nationality, culture and all other existing circumstances, represents
the good fortune of a people; one-sided dominance of one or other, or
unequal or unsuitable division of their domain, is its misfortune. And as up to
the present all those splendid world empires which neglected freedom for the
sake of unity have collapsed, so no people which was incapable of limiting
the independence of its constituent parts in favour of a higher unity has
been able to withstand the tempests of history.

. . .

Of all the peoples mentioned in history, none has been so deeply or
powerfully gripped by the opposing forces depicted above, none is more

suited by its innermost temperament to the realisation of both principles and therefore to their final reconciliation, than the Germanic people. It seems almost as if this people alone had been called to create states which are at once united and free, as if the Latin peoples only had a share in this in so far as they had received a fraction of Germanic characteristics with the fraction of Germanic blood flowing in their veins, or had borrowed them from institutions created by the Germanic spirit.

Second to none in the march to universality and in their ability to organise states, surpassing most in their love of freedom, the Germanic people have a gift other peoples lack, by means of which they have given the idea of freedom a special substance and the idea of unity a more secure foundation – they have the gift of forming fellowships [*Genossenschaften*]. The people of antiquity recognised, as do the non-Germanic peoples of today, the existence, between the highest generality and the individual, of many gradations of natural and arbitrary associations. But their love of the corporate life, their sense of family, community and nation, their ability and enthusiasm for free association, cannot even remotely be compared with that inexhaustible Germanic spirit of association, which alone is able to guarantee an independent existence to all the lesser conformations within the state, while maintaining sufficient power to create from the still uncommitted energy within the people a vast profusion of lively, active fellowships, inspired not from above but from within, for the most general as well as the most isolated purposes of human existence.

. . .

The victory in principle of the concept of the absolute state and of individualism was determined when the storms of the French Revolution were carried over into Germany, when, following the dissolution of the Empire, territorial dominion was transformed into sovereignty, and the revolutionary legislation completely or partly adopted. From then till now it has been a question of slow progress towards the realisation of both principles in detail, which today is almost complete. The idea of the absolute state has more and more asserted itself in a state unity carried virtually to the point of centralisation, in the formation of modern administrative organisations, and in a levelling-out of local differences in public law, verging on standardisation. On the other hand, the barriers which separated the individual from direct contact with the state, and produced inequality in public Right were increasingly disposed of: privileges and exemptions, the estates' prerogatives, patrimonial powers, differences occasioned by religious creed, trade and business monopolies, and the inequality of public impositions, were increasingly abolished. At the same time, the old associations which fettered the individual in agriculture, trade and status were broken up or robbed of their binding power.

If, in all these areas, modern developments appear to be solely the result of ideas which had for centuries been determining the direction of the sovereign state, and whose realisation is brought nearer, consciously or unconsciously, by each step forward, in our century quite a different principle is at work. It works partly in association with older ideas and partly alongside them. The value of our modern upheavals would in fact be very questionable if they were influenced solely by that power which used its positive creative energy only in favour of unconditional state unity, and whose effect on all other organisms was only to negate and dissolve them; and if their inevitable result was a one-sided culmination in a centralised and mechanistic state and an atomised people. We owe the fact that such is not the case, and never will be, to the reawakened *spirit of association*. By endeavouring to fill all public associations from below with an independent communal life and by building together the particles, into which the nation had threatened to disintegrate, into countless new combinations, organic in structure and containing inherent vigour, this is the real positive principle which shapes the new epoch for the development of the German law and constitution in our century. It, above all others, gives us a firm guarantee that the epoch will not represent the old age of the German people, but rather the full bloom of its manly vigour.

The *modern association movement* is still so much in its early stages that its nature can scarcely be defined and it has no proper history of its own. It ought to be clear, therefore, that it is in essence a new and distinctive phenomenon and that its development will be ever upwards.

The essence of the modern association movement clearly brings it much closer to the medieval union movement than to the privileged corporation system of later days. In most points it is the direct opposite of the latter; while in relation to the medieval system of union, it is but a higher stage of development of the same principle. Thus the modern system of association offers many analogies with the medieval system of union. It too comes from within the people and builds upwards from below. It too is an expression of the awakening national consciousness and the vigour of the people [*Volksbewusstsein* ... *Volkskraft*] with quite free self-help creating forms of the self-determination and self-management they have longed for. As the medieval union was set against the idea of lordship and service, so the modern association sets its face against the idea of a sovereign standing above and beyond the whole. Likewise, it is combated, restricted and prohibited by representatives of the old principle, who cannot however quite succeed in smothering the new idea. Modern association, like union, is rooted in freedom; and it too tries to build ever wider spheres on to narrow ones. The privileged corporation's corporative separateness, exclusivity, rigidity of form and privatisation of public rights is no less alien to it.

In contrast to the pronounced corporate forms of the intervening period, the modern association, like the medieval union, has an air of constant flux – the essential mark of a time of strong growth. Hence it is rich in transitional forms and intermediate structures, in short-lived phenomena which exist only to pave the way for a fuller legal structure, in a wealth of intersections and combinations which it is difficult to systematise. To an even greater extent than in the Middle Ages, countless forms of community [*Gemeinschaft*] emerge from the modern association. These almost fill the gulf between the conceptual opposites of a personal society (or proprietorial community) and a fellowship endowed with an independent legal personality (or living community). Just as, lastly, union had the dual effect of remodelling fellowships based on necessity and recreating fellowships based on will, so that no clear boundary could be drawn here, so too the modern system of association operates in both areas with no clear demarcation.

There are, however, alongside these analogies, fundamental points of difference between the modern phase of the fellowship system and its medieval manifestation. The higher development of public and private life on the one hand, and the more precise definition of legal terminology on the other, along with the multiplication of forms, has brought about a division of the fellowship system into many branches. Although there are links between these, they are much more sharply distinct from each other than were the medieval forms of community. In the first instance, groups with their own legal personality emerge in distinction to mere communities and societies. Among the former, groups comprising states, whose existence is independent of free will, are much more distinct than before from freely formed associations. Of the utmost importance is the fact that public and private law have separated out, so that groups with importance in the public sphere are put together and organised on principles of public law, and private-law corporations on principles of private law. The danger of their being transformed into privileged corporations thereby disappears.

But the most important difference between the modern and the medieval is that, through the continued splitting-up of group life, fellowships are formed more and more for single purposes; so that finally, in contrast to the medieval tendency to extend each group of fellows over the whole person and simply make it into a community [*Gemeinschaft*], the opposite tendency has prevailed: *the purposes of each individual association are precisely defined,* and its organisation adapted and its significance limited accordingly. Even the highest association – the state – has its purposes, and therefore the limits of its scope prescribed by this modern trend.

* From Antony Black, ed., *Community in Historical Perspective: A Translation from Das Deutsche Genossenschaftsrecht (The German Law of Fellowship [1868–1913])*, by Otto von Gierke, translated by Mary Fischer (Cambridge: Cambridge University Press, 1990), 2–4; 118–20.

John Neville Figgis (1866–1919), Anglican writer and a pupil of Maitland, who had introduced Gierke to English readers. Figgis' principal concern was to remove state control over the affairs of various churches. Churches or other associations had no special privileges, but at the same time they should be free to run their own affairs. In this extract he rejects the idea of individualism and state collectivism alike. Far from being separate individuals connected only through the state, he saw a hierarchy of overlapping societies which respected each other's distinctive functions, including clubs, associations, trade unions and the Church.*

Since the corporate society is only a *persona ficta*, with the name given it by the law, but no real inward life, we have on this view but two social entities, the State on the one hand and the individual on the other. The rights or actions of the one are private, those of the other are public. The State may be of any kind of structure, monarchic, aristocratic, or purely collectivist; but in all cases there are recognised by the law, no real social entities, no true powers, except the sovereign on the one hand with irresistible authority, and the mass of individuals on the other. Societies, so far as they exist, are mere collections of individuals who remain unchanged by their membership, and whose unity of action is narrowly circumscribed by the State, and where allowed is allowed on grounds quite arbitrary. Under such a view there can be no possible place for the religious body, in the sense of a Church living a supernatural life, and the claim is quite just that no Church should have any standard of morals different from those of the State.

But is not this woefully to misconceive the actual facts of social life, as they present themselves to our eyes, and to get a wrong notion of the State? Let me give an instance. Throughout the education controversy much has been heard against the iniquity of privately managed schools receiving public money, at least in the form of rates (for the income-tax is not concerned with conscience). Now surely (except in the case of the one-man manager) this is a total misconception. As opposed to State management, perhaps the word private may be admitted, but when it implies, as it ought, purely individual management, a false view is suggested. These social bodies other than the State are not only not private, but in their working they are more akin to the State than they are to the individual. I mean that both of them are cases of a society acting as one, to which the individual members are subject. The relations between the member and his society are more akin to those of a citizen to a State than to anything in the individual. It is very easy to say that universities, colleges, trade unions, inns of court, &c. &c., are purely private, and in one sense it is true; they are not delegates of the State or parts of its machinery; but they are in a very real sense public, *i.e.* they are collective, not individual, in their constitution. The popular use of the word 'Public School' to denote a school under collective management is a far more reasonable and realistic habit, though I suppose that it is not technically justified. The point is that it is the public communal character of all such institutions that is the salient fact; and that we do wrong to adopt a rigid division into public and private, if we mean by the latter any and every institution that is not a delegation from the State. What we actually see in the world is not on the one hand the State, and on the other a mass of unrelated individuals; but a vast complex of gathered unions, in which alone we find individuals, families, clubs, trades unions, colleges, professions, and so forth; and further, that there are exercised functions within these groups which are of the nature of government, including its three aspects, legislative, executive, and judicial; though, of course, only with reference to their own members. So far as the people who actually belong to it are concerned, such a body is every whit as communal in its character as a municipal corporation or a provincial parliament.

Not only, however, is this view false to the true character of the State; it is entirely wrong in its view of the individual citizen. As a matter of fact, personality is a social fact; no individual could ever come to himself except as a member of a society, and the membership of any society does not leave even the adult individual where he was. There is an interpenetration of his life with that of the society, and his personality is constantly being changed by this fellowship. Too often on the part of those who strongly believe in human personality, the necessities of controversy against doctrines which virtually deny it has led to an insistence on the individual to the neglect of the social side. Correction of this error will be found in a very valuable book by Mr. Wilfrid Richmond, *Personality as a Philosophical Principle*. We cannot, however, too often emphasize in regard to politics, that not the individual but the family is the real social unit, and that personality as a fact never grows up except within one or more social unions. That, however, will be met by the claim that this is just what citizenship means; that 'the State is prior' to the individual, and that true personality is to grow up in the great collective union of national life. This seems to me to lie at the root of the difficulty.

When Aristotle uttered his famous dictum, the State meant, as all know, a small body of persons, not more than could be gathered in one place; and although we may hold that the antique State was too all-embracing, at least it was not unreasonable to maintain that the compact City-State of ancient Greece was the social home of all the individuals comprising it, and no more was needed. In the modern world, however, no such assertion is possible. Whatever the State may attempt, she cannot be the mother of all her citizens in the same sense as the City-State of old; and, as a fact, men will grow to maturity and be moulded in their prejudices, their tastes, their capacities, and their moral ideals not merely by the great main stream of national life, but also, and perhaps more deeply, by their own family connections, their local communal life in village or town, their educational society (for it is of the essence of education to be in a society), and countless other collective organisms. It is these that make up the life of the modern world, and to deny them all real existence or power, whether it be in the interests of legal theory or of an abstract economic collectivism, seems to me to be in principle false to the facts, and in practice to be steering straight for the rocks.

...

[I]t would appear a more reasonable maxim to get a theory of law and government not by laying down an abstract doctrine of unity, but by observing the facts of life as it is lived, and trying to set down the actual features of civil society. What do we find as a fact? Not, surely, a sand-heap of individuals, all equal and undifferentiated, unrelated except to the State, but an ascending hierarchy of groups, family, school, town, country, union, Church, &c. &c. All these groups (or many of them) live with a real life; they act towards one another with a unity of will and mind as though they were single persons; they all need to be allowed reasonable freedom, but must be restrained from acts of injustice towards one another or the individual; they are all means by which the individual comes to himself. For in truth the notion of the isolated individuality is the shadow of a dream, and would never have come into being but for the vast social structure which allows a few individuals to make play, as though they were independent, when their whole economic position of freedom is symbolic of a long history and complex social organization. In the real world, the isolated individual does not exist; he begins always as a member of something, and as I said earlier, his personality can develop only in society, and in some way or other he always embodies some social institution. I do not mean to deny the distinctness of individual life, but this distinction can function only inside a society. Membership in a social union means a direction of personality, which inter-penetrates it, and, according to your predilection, you may call either an extension or a narrowing; it is in truth both. You cannot be a member of any society and be the same as though you were not a member; it affects your rights and duties, limits at once and increases your opportunities, and makes you a different being, although in many different degrees, according to the nature of the society and the individual member. You are not merely John Doe or Richard Roe, but as John may probably be a member of the Christian Church by baptism, a Doe by family, an Englishman by race; all three are social institutions, which have grown into you. In addition to this you are a member of a school, an alumnus of a college, a sharer in this club, a president of that, and so forth. All these groups and unions have their effect, and limit and develop your life, make you do, or refrain from doing, what otherwise you would not, and in so far prevent you being a free and untramelled citizen of the State. More than that, they penetrate your imagin-ation and your thought and alter not only what you do but what you want to do. Between all these groups there will be relations, and not merely between the individuals composing them. To prevent injustice between them and to secure their rights, a strong power above them is needed. It is largely to regulate such groups and to ensure that the coercive force of the State exists. It does not create them; nor is it in many matters in direct and immediate contact with the individual. The claim of the Church in matters of education is the claim that she shall be recognised as a group, in which the natural authority over its members extends to the provision of a social atmosphere; and this ought to be admitted, provided the requirements of citizenship in secular culture be provided and controlled.

All this, it will be said, lessens the hold of the State over the individual. But this is needful the moment you reach any large and complex society. In a developed state of civilisation many interests must be allowed social expression, which in one sense are a separating influence. Even a member of a musical club is so far separated from those who are excluded; and he is changed by the fact of this club-life, which enters into him. In the Middle Ages there was an appropriate dress for every calling; under the modern notion we have all been trying to dress alike, and most of us doing it very badly. The old custom survives in clergy and in butcher boys, and we are seeing revivals in the costumes of boy scouts. Instead of an iron uniformity, we need more and more a reasonable distinction of groups, all of which should be honourable. There is a whole philosophy in school colours.

Recent discussions are making men ask once more in matters other than religion, what are the limits of the authority of Parliament. The idolatry of the State is receiving shrewd blows. It is said, however, especially in regard to the Church, that to recognise its rights is dangerous. But if it is a fact, it must be more dangerous not to recognise its real life. The same is true of individuals. However you may proclaim with M. Combes that 'there are no rights but the rights of the State,' you find individuals who habitually act as if they had them; and even when you go on to say that 'there is no authority but the authority of the republic,' you do not in practice prevent all kinds of societies from behaving in a way that implies authority over their members. Nor can you. It is impossible. Society is inherent in human nature, and that means inevitably the growth of a communal life and social ties.

* From John Neville Figgis, *Churches in the Modern State* (London: Longmans, Green, and Co., 1913), 67–73; 87–92.

Carlo Cattaneo (1801–69), Italian publicist and intellectual. Educated in law, he wrote on a variety of subjects ranging from chemistry and geology to social and economic problems of his time. Cattaneo became one of the revolutionary leaders during the Milan Rebellion of 1848. After the reoccupation of Milan by Austria, he settled in Switzerland and remained a staunch opponent of the monarchy. The *selection here sees him insisting that liberalism must embrace federalism if the horrors of nationally homogenizing politics are to be avoided.**

Civil Society and the State

Civil nations hold within themselves various principles, each aspiring to have sway over the state and to model it into an exclusive system. But before the work can be completed, new principles develop in an unforeseen manner, and direct the current of interest and opinion in other directions. ... [The result is that] *the more civil a people, the more numerous are the principles contained in the society*: the militia and the priesthood, property and commerce, the privileged and the plebeian. ... Thus history is the eternal conflict between different principles that tend to absorb and mould civil society. Rarely does a principle become hegemonic, except over a long period of time and with conscious perseverance. ... And those who invoke perpetual peace and a universal republic in all of the realms of the earth, ... do not see into what abyss of inertia and cowardice the whole of human species would plunge, if petrified into a system, without imitations and without contrasts, without fears and without hopes, without history and without that which would be worthy of history.

Principles of civil society seem to us to behave like quantities, whose point of equilibrium radically changes when some is added or subtracted even minimally. We believe as well that a new social order does not presuppose a new series of data. ... We do not believe that the mind becomes the immediate servant of the data that appear before it. ... It is not because of the dissimilarity of data that Pitt and Fox voice their daily and irreconcilable differences of opinion in the British Parliament; it is not because of the divergence of information that the manufacturer is fighting for the free introduction of grain and the farmer is calling for restriction. ... The truth is that men choose to keep in mind those factors that suit their inclinations, and they would like opposite factors not to exist or would have other people not know about them or believe them; and that most readers tend to choose among all the newspapers the one that cultivates and flatters their opinions and interests. For this reason, the mere reading and the mere possession of a book is considered by the French courts as an admission of taking a position, and a predisposition to take that position to its logical conclusion.

It is an illuminating fact that in England, despite the ancient freedom of the press, opinions are much more *limited* and *uniform* than in countries where the restraints on the freedom of the press confine the multitudes to a limited and uniform body of data. From this we see how much predominance the will has over opinion. ...

All legislative reforms may be considered transactions between prevailing interests. Now, the concept of transaction excludes the concept of system; it even involves conflict of systems, *incapable of destroying each other, forced to live with each other*. But these transactions, when expressed in laws, become the structures and the limits to which all daily acts of living together adapt themselves. .... [T]he process of legislation is tortuous as the course of rivers, which is also a transaction between the motion of waters and the inertia of earth. Every civil society holds within itself an inevitable and unalterable reservoir of critical views, which springs from particular ideal systems and their respective *utopias*. ...

The state may be viewed as an enormous transaction between all the demands that the development of society engenders and multiplies every day. Property and commerce, legitimate and available interests, wealth and thrift, the useful and the beautiful, *daily conquer or defend the imposing and general demands a portion of the public space which competition allots them*. And the supreme formula for good government and society is one in which no demand outweighs another in importance and nothing is negated by anything else. ... And all those changes that we have grandiloquently called revolutions are none other than *the disputed admission of another social element*, whose presence cannot be established without pressure and fluctuation of all the existing interests.

...

To many, *uniformity*, a mandarin-like uniformity, is all that counts, which, as we unfortunately see in reality, is neither *agreement* nor *strength!* The most serious thought that they [the creators of Italian unification] have is to apply a new coat of white to an old house. It seems to them a major accomplishment to re-name aldermen and call them priors, to call the head of the commune mayor. ... The only law of the new Italian commune is the law of obedience. The commune is the last appendage, that which trails at the bottom of the prefecture and the deputy prefecture. The municipality is no longer the municipality. The entire system is based on erroneous ideas. In 1814 the mayors [*podesta*] and the councillors nominated by the king did not lift a finger to save the realm. Some of them welcomed the Austrians, ringing the bells in celebration. Such is the solidity of bureaucratic institutions. Those who sow servility usually reap betrayal ... No, the laws of Piedmont, no matter how patched up and embroidered, cannot be, not for ten years, not for a day, the law of the new Italy.

Remedies

Only two states, the American federation and the Swiss federation, have demonstrated, even in these troubled times, the ability to sustain themselves. There the general order does not invade the local order: it doesn't humiliate, discourage, or oppress. It doesn't create resentment. It doesn't impose its will with the machinery of an insensitive force. It isn't extravagant with capital nor does it impoverish the family. Since industry is not worsened, it can nourish the hand it exploits less avariciously and less meanly; and it can also venture advantageously into the furthest of markets. Now it remains to be seen how well other peoples, predestined by traditions and opinions or imperative circumstances to other forms of government, can nonetheless approximate this ideal of brotherly law and high economy. It remains to be seen how much more honest and extensive one can render the practice of freedom, how much more natural and enduring one can render popular consensus, so as to spread interest in the deliberative processes of government and to attract the greatest number of thinkers and interested people to it.

Certainly we do not wish to impose limits and obstacles to the development of good administration [in united Italy]; and we will be very careful not to close a single door to the strong and robust ideas of which the common weal is in so much need. But we would also like to ensure, in keeping with the goal that ministerial responsibility be not just an empty word, that public opinion does not lose sight of the terms of judgment and comparison, and that the country does not lose a guide through the labyrinth of laws and norms of government. To repeat, we would like to see statesmen leaving office to give an account of themselves, and face and meet the public judgment sooner rather than later. ...

It is not enough to inscribe decentralization into law. We have to prepare it to enter into the customs, destroying the worn-out habits inherited from despotic governments whose end has been to imitate France and accumulate the power in few hands and in a few centers. Between a past in which government was everything, could do anything, abused everything, and a future, which may not be that far away, and in which the central government, ridding itself of abusive powers, will be decentered permitting the rise of a self-governing society organized into associations and fortifying itself within the private sphere of initiative, ... the omniscience and the omnipotence of the State will remain a pretense for some, an excuse for others and a bad for everybody.

In Italy, he who does not take local patriotism into account will always sow in the sand. ... The communes are the nation in the most intimate nursery of liberty. ... But the liberty [of free cities] became license for all sorts of temptations, abuses of victory, and imitations of private wars and feudal vengeances. The idea of equality of rights in the disparity of force, the idea of federal constitutional law, was a ray of light reserved to illuminate future generations. Even now [1858] throughout Italy some cities try to dominate others and try to gain some kind of right of primogeniture and hegemony that, if successful, will bring back ancient jealousies and create new sources of problems.

What needs to be done is to better organize our haphazard forces in order to facilitate a shift in favour of our views, as they germinate deep within the bosom of civil society. We need, as much as possible, to show that our views nourish the mental life of Italy.

. . .

[Associations of workers in Genoa have] recently revealed to a heedless generation the way in which the associations of Italian workers in other centuries knew how to create a thriving, free and glorious homeland. That aura of new and brotherly life, that today one feels vibrating throughout the cities of the peninsula and the islands, has been stirred into motion. . . . It is only in this way that we will be sure of the final outcome of our destiny. Only when the workers are thoughtful and willing and at the ready as [the Genoese] are, can they help each other to tear down the hopes of the relentless enemies of our freedom. Armies have never saved Italy.

We are all workers if we make ourselves useful to humanity. And those who promote the influence of the working classes on the legislative body are not fomenting discord but justice and goodwill. . . . What is important, then is not the top of the pyramid but its base. The great work of association started a few months ago (1862). . . . Associations must be ever varied in membership and interests [they must have the advantage of spontaneity and variety]. Only in this way people of all classes will become aware of their respective collective interests. We need to oppose the interests of all to the interests of the few, refashion with the people communal government and submerge [central] hegemony in the sea of civil society [or the nation] . . .

[Workers and their leaders] have not yet realized that federalism is the only unity possible in Italy. Federalism is a plurality of active centers, bound together by the common interest of the promises made to one another and of national identity. . . . Piedmont is the only organized and living power center and stronger than the masses. . . . To restraint and balance it, we must give life to other centers. In building consensus and a truly free and moral unity, we must protect and defend all the autonomous spheres of action that exist in the country.

The liberty of speech, press, association, conscience, movement, etc. constitutes the antecedents of sovereignty. Sovereignty forms an equation with government. If we are not self-governing, we are not sovereign; sovereignty signifies mastery and mastery excludes the master; thus the suppression of privilege, thus the concept of [republican government] . . . He who does his own bidding, he who determines the right of his own ideas and desires is said to be free; liberty is the will in its rational and fullest development; liberty is republic and republic is plurality – that is, federation. Federal principles of organization are the theoretics of liberty, the only possible theory of self government in action. . . . A grand prediction can be advanced: Europe either remains autocratic or becomes the United States of Europe.

* From Carlo Cattaneo, 'Richerche sul progetto di una strada di ferro da Milano a Venezia' in A. Bertolino, ed., *Scritti economici*, Vol. 1 (Florence: Le Monnier, 1956 [1836]), 112–77; 'Considerazioni sulle cose d'Italia nel 1848' in G. Salvemini and E. Sestan, eds,

Scritti storici e geografici (Florence: Le Monnier, 1957 [1850–51]), 125–337; 'Filosofia della rivoluzione' in N. Bobbio, ed., *Scritti filosofici* (Florence: Le Monnier, 1960 [1851]), 272–86; 'Lettera a Lodovico Frapolli, 5 novembre 1851' in R. Caddeo, ed., *Epistolario* (Florence: Le Monnier, 1952 [1851]), 119–25; 'Lettera a Luigi Tentolini, a Massagno, 24 aprile 1852' in R. Caddeo, ed., *Epistolario* (Florence: Le Monnier, 1952 [1852]), 156–8; 'La città considerata come principio ideale delle istorie italiane' in G. Salvemini and E. Sestan, eds, *Scritti storici e geografici*, Vol. 2 (Florence: Le Monnier, 1957 [1858]), 382–437; 'All'Associazione degli operai genovesi' in M. Boneschi, ed., *Scritti politici*, Vol. 3 (Florence: Le Monnier, 1965 [1859]), 377–8; 'Prefazione al volume IX del Politecnico' in M. Boneschi, ed., *Scritti politici*, Vol. 4 (Florence: Le Monnier, 1965 [1860]), 64–82; 'Control l'Ordinamento del Regno: Problemi sull'Europa – Studi sull'Italia' in M. Boneschi, ed., *Scritti politici*, Vol. 4 (Florence: Le Monnier, 1965 [1861]), 209–10; 'Lettera a Adriano Lemmi, a Torino 10 luglio 1862' in R. Caddeo, ed., *Epistolario*, Vol. 4 (Florence: Le Monnier, 1956 [1862]), 61–2; 'Lettera ad Agostino Bertani, a Genova, maggio 1862' in R. Caddeo, ed., *Epistolario*, Vol. 4, 55–7; 'Raccolta di scritti politici e sulla pubblica istruzione' in M. Boneschi, ed., *Scritti politici*, Vol. 3 (Florence: Le Monnier, 1965 [1863]), 129–37; 'Sulla legge comunale e provinciale' in M. Boneschi, ed., *Scritti politici*, Vol. 4 (Florence: Le Monnier, 1965 [1864]), 414–40. We thank Filippo Sabetti for kind assistance.

G.D.H. Cole (1889–1959), socialist theorist and academic, began his career before the First World War as an opponent of Sidney and Beatrice Webb. His distaste for their bureaucratic socialism led him to become the champion of guild socialism, which flourished, largely as an academic movement, in the immediate aftermath of the war. In this selection, he can be seen arguing, with perhaps naïve idealism, for a world based on liberty, trust and variety.*

A Theory of Democracy

I also want to make it clear that Guild Socialism is not a purely industrial theory. It is – certainly so far as I am concerned – rather an accident that Guild Socialism has taken a mainly industrial form. The reason why we are talking mainly about the organisation of industry is that industry is in such a beastly muddle that until you have straightened it out it is no good talking about anything else. That is why our National Guild doctrine appears mainly as a doctrine of industrial organisation. But the theory on which the Guild conception rests is much wider than any purely industrial theory. It rests fundamentally on a particular conception of democracy, essentially different from the conception of democracy which was almost generally accepted in the nineteenth century. Our conception of democracy is this: that it is nonsense to talk of one man representing another, or a number of others; that there is no such thing as representation of one person by another, because in his very nature a man is such a being that he cannot be represented. But that is not a denial of forms of representative government properly understood; it is merely to say that unless representative government conforms to certain canons, it will be misrepresentative government. Our next step is to try lay down the canons to which representative government must conform if it is to be really representative. We say that the only way in which there can be real representation is when the representative represents not another person but some group of purposes which men have in common; that you never ought to try to represent Smith and Jones and Brown by means of Robinson, but that, if Smith, Jones, and Brown have a common interest in some particular thing whether as producers or as football players or in any other capacity, it is quite legitimate for them to choose Robinson to execute for them and on their behalf their common purpose. That is to say, all true representation, if we are right, is not representation of persons, but only representation of common purposes; or, to put it in other words, any real representation is necessarily functional representation.

If that is so, then in social organisation, if it is to be democratic, you must follow this principle of function. If you want to have a democratic Society you can only get it by making Society democratic in all its different parts, in relation to all the various functions which have to be performed in that Society. Therefore you must treat the problem of industry as one problem, and see that you get it organised on democratic lines by itself. You must take the problem of politics and see that you get that organised on democratic lines by itself. You must take all the other problems that arise in Society, and see that in each of its compartments or departments Society is organised on democratic basis. It is only then, by putting together these different democratic organisations which exist for the expression of particular groups of social purposes, that you can build up a really democratic Society. As long as you conceive of Society as finding its expression in some one form of representative institution, you will inevitably go astray and get a misrepresentative instead of a really representative institution, but as soon as you conceive of Society as a whole and try to make all the parts really democratic, you get your best chance and your only chance of making the whole democratic.

We have worked out that theory mainly in relation to one part of social organization – the industrial sphere, and we have concentrated on that sphere because, until you get the industrial organisation straightened out, you do not stand the faintest chance of straightening out anything else. As long as you have the present chaos in industry, as long as men and women live the sort of life they are living in industry to-day, as long as you have the present state of war between the various parties who are supposed to be co-operating in the task of production, it is no good expecting that your Society as a whole will function decently or that you will have any real democracy in any of its parts; because the disorder in the industrial system is fatal to order in any part of the Society. Therefore that on which attention has first to be concentrated is straightening out as far as may be the industrial system, bringing it into harmony with real democratic principles, and then going on to introduce this new sanity into the other parts of Society as well.

...

The Motive of Service

You have, if you object to Guild Socialism, to show a system under which they will be more likely to do that than they will under Guild Socialism. I personally believe that a system under which a man has a reasonable control of the conditions of his own working life, and also, as a citizen, of the conditions of his political life, offers the best guarantee that you can have, because it offers the best opportunity for a man to give free service to the community and at the same time to express himself as a citizen and as a consumer, as well as in his capacity as a producer. But I certainly think you must rely, for securing that the various Guilds will work for the public service, and not for their own advantage, mainly upon enlisting a new motive in industry and on making a real appeal to the motive of public service, given under free conditions. I do not want, and no Guild Socialist wants, the miners or any other group of workers to own the industry in which they are concerned. In the situation which has arisen to-day, we stand with the Collectivists in the demand for national ownership of industry. We believe the industries ought to be taken over and owned by the public. The difference between our theory and other theories that are put forward for the control of industry when nationalised lies simply in our belief that when you nationalise an industry that does not mean that the public has got to administer it, or rather that the public has got to appoint bureaucrats to administer it for them. We believe the right way of running an industry is to hand it over to be worked by the people who know the best possible way of working it efficiently; on the one hand by the technicians who understand how the industry is to be made efficient on its scientific and commercial side, and on the other hand by the manual workers without whose co-operation you cannot get the goods turned out.

The Case for Public Ownership

We want public ownership of industry for this reason, that if any industry produces a surplus – or whatever surplus any industry produces – we desire that surplus to pass not into the pocket of the industry in question, but into the national exchequer, to become a part of the revenue of the whole country. In just the same way we do not desire the prices of commodities produced and of services rendered to be fixed by those who run those services or produce those commodities. We believe that the prices of commodities and services ought to be fixed by the community as a whole, that those are matters not for the body of working producers alone, but for the whole body of the people to determine, because the price of a commodity is something which affects the consumer even more nearly than it affects the producer. What we demand for the workers by hand and brain is not the entire control of the economic process right from production to consumption, but the control of the productive processes and the processes of distribution allied with production. We demand that the workers shall control those parts of the industry which are concerned with the way in which goods are turned out and services rendered, and that they shall organise themselves for the producing of those goods and the rendering of those services, but as soon as the producer comes into contact with the consumer, as soon as the consumer is directly affected, as he is in prices, as he is in the division of the surplus realised in the industry, then we recognise the consumers' right to make his voice heard. More than that, we recognise the right of the consumer to criticise to the full the way in which the productive processes are carried on by the producer, and, in the miners' recommendations to the Coal Commission, which are as good an expression of immediate Guild policy as you will find, that point of view is clearly and explicitly recognised in the proposal for a separate Consumers' Council related to the Mining Guild, and representing the community from the consumers' side. Therefore, we want communal control of industry and democratic control of industry. These are two sides of our programme which cannot be divided; and they are equally essential for the creation of any Guild Socialist Society.

. . .

'Human Nature'

The last thing I want to say is a sentence or so about the problem of 'human nature.' It is impossible to lecture on almost any conceivable subject without being asked whether you believe that human nature has changed, and it is always wise to forestall some of the obvious questions in order to get on to the interesting ones. What, then, is the ordinary man really like? That may seem rather a large question to raise at this hour. Many people would tell you the ordinary man does not want to be free, but only cares to be let alone, to get along with things without being too much interfered with. I do not believe that is true. I believe that the ordinary man might indeed very often say that all he wants is to be let alone. But if you let him alone I do not believe he would do decent work, or would enjoy himself; he would very soon get extremely bored. What the ordinary man really does want is to have an opportunity of expressing himself if he desires to do so, to have many opportunities of expressing himself in different directions, not because he will use those opportunities all the time or universally but because he will be able to use them if he wants to. It is a very nice thing to feel that you have a ticket for this course of lectures, even if you don't come to all the lectures, and it is a very nice feeling that you have a sort of universal pass for human freedom, even if you are not particularly concerned in exercising human freedom in all its forms. I prefer to have a vote even when

I would die sooner than vote for any of the candidates standing, and I believe my feeling is the common feeling.

The Man in the Street

That is, I believe a very important point that many people go wrong about. They say the ordinary man does not want really to control industry, therefore it does not matter whether he has a chance to do so or not. That is a profound mistake. We must organise industry on such a basis that every man does get a chance to control it, not because we believe that every man will take equal advantage of that chance, but because the whole atmosphere of industry will change if that chance is given, and because that will mean that the people who do actually control industry will be controlling it with the consent of the rest, and everybody will feel that he is really co-operating – that he really counts, and that the people who are controlling industry are doing their job under his direction. If we can only get into industry that feeling not merely of consent, but of co-operation, even if it is not the most active co-operation that can be desired, then we shall change to a great extent the spirit in which work is done. I believe the change will go much further, and that if we provide the right conditions, a very much larger proportion of people than now will be active and keen in exercising a real control over industry, although at the same time I believe no less that if you once get industry decently organised it will cease to occupy the disproportionate place that it occupies in men's minds to-day, and instead of being the main thing in our minds it will sink back into being a quite minor and humdrum thing about which we need not bother; and I hope when we have got that feeling it will not be necessary for me to go on lecturing and bothering about industry. Certainly, I shall leave industry to look after itself, and get on with something else. Meanwhile, I suppose I must go on talking for a few years yet.

Trusting People

Finally, the last problem of human nature is whether you are prepared to take the risk of trusting people or not. I remember the old Socialist question always used to be on the lines that you could not trust the people to work under conditions of industrial self-government. The Collectivists never did trust people a bit. I do not know whether they have changed now or not; at any rate a few years ago, even if they did not trust the people, they had some hope of building through bureaucratic Socialism a sort of Society that would work. That hope has gone. There is no hope in bureaucratic Society, no hope that it would work, even if anyone still desired to bring it into existence. Nor is there hope or chance of capitalism lasting much longer. We have to find some new way of facing the problem of industrial organisation. Neither the old consumers' Socialism, nor Capitalism, is capable of turning out the goods. That puts it up to you either to accept what I am saying, or else to find some way by which you can induce men to go on producing, by means other than the means which were employed right through the nineteenth century – the means of hunger and fear. Almost the only reason why people have worked in the past, why people have consented to go on working under such miserable, unjust conditions, has been that they have been frightened, that they have been starved. If that breaks down – and it is everywhere breaking down to-day – then either men won't go on working at all or else they will go on working for some quite different reason.

* From G.D.H. Cole, *Guild Socialism* (London: The Fabian Society, 1920), 6; 12–13; 16–17.

Emile Durkheim (1858–1917), French sociologist and educational theorist, was always obsessed with the problem of social cohesion in modern society. This selection from the preface to the second edition of his great The Division of Labour in Society *(1st edition 1893, 2nd edition 1897) outlines one of his main mechanisms of social reform. The state stood too far away from the individual to allow for moral integration; but the family had become too small a unity to create cohesion in a modern complex world. Hence Durkheim sought to create corporations to replicate the spirit of guilds within the social condition of modernity. These would end class conflict by having employer and worker as part of the same enterprise, and they would serve as transmission belts of cohesion and information from the top to the bottom of society.*

It is this anomic state that is the cause, as we shall show, of the incessantly recurrent conflicts, and the multifarious disorders of which the economic world exhibits so sad a spectacle. For, as nothing restrains the active forces and assigns them limits they are bound to respect, they tend to develop haphazardly, and come into collision with one another, battling and weakening themselves. To be sure, the strongest succeed in completely demolishing the weakest, or in subordinating them. But if the conquered, for a time, must suffer subordination under compulsion, they do not consent to it, and consequently this cannot constitute a stable equilibrium. Truces, arrived at after violence, are never anything but provisional, and satisfy no one. Human passions stop only before a moral power they respect. If all authority of this kind is wanting, the law of the strongest prevails, and latent or active, the state of war is necessarily chronic.

That such anarchy is an unhealthy phenomenon is quite evident, since it runs counter to the aim of society, which is to suppress, or at least to moderate, war among men, subordinating the law of the strongest to a higher law

. . .

Neither political society, in its entirety, nor the State can take over this function; economic life, because it is specialized and grows more specialized every day, escapes their competence and action. An occupational activity can be efficaciously regulated only by a group intimate enough with it to know its functioning, feel all its needs, and able to follow all their variations. The only one that could answer all these conditions is the one formed by all the agents of the same industry, united and organized into a single body. This is what is called the corporation or occupational group.

. . .

[Our discussion] shows us how the corporation has fallen into discredit for about two centuries, and, consequently, what it must become in order to take its place again among our public institutions. We have just seen, indeed, that in the form it had in the Middle Ages it was narrowly bound to the organization of the commune. This solidarity was without inconvenience as long as the trades themselves had a communal character. While, as originally, merchants and workers had only the inhabitants of the city or its immediate environs for customers, which means as long as the market was principally local, the bodies of trades, with their municipal organization, answered all needs. But it was no longer the same once great industry was born. As it had nothing especially urban about it, it could not adapt itself to a system which had not been made for it. First, it does not necessarily have its centre in a city; it can even be established outside all pre-existing rural or urban agglomerations. It looks for that territory where it can best maintain itself and thrive. Thus, its field of action is limited to no determined region; its clientele is recruited everywhere. An institution so entirely wrapped up in the commune as was the old corporation could not then be used to encompass and regulate a form of collective activity which was so completely foreign to the communal life.

And, indeed, as soon as great industry appeared, it was found to be outside the corporative regime, and that was what caused the bodies of trades to do all in their power to prevent industry's progress. Nevertheless, it was certainly not freed of all regulation; in the beginning the State played a role analogous to that which the corporations played for small-scale commerce and urban trades. At the same time as the royal power accorded the manufacturers certain privileges, in return it submitted them to its control. That is indicated in the title of royal manufacturers. But as it is well known how unsuited the State is for this function, this direct control could not fail to become oppressive. It was almost impossible from the time great industry reached a certain degree of development and diversity; that is why classical economists demanded its suppression, and with good cause. But if the corporation, as it then existed, could not be adapted to this new form of industry, and if the State could not replace the old corporative discipline, it does not follow that all discipline would be useless thenceforward. It simply meant that the old corporation had to be transformed to continue to fill its role in the new conditions of economic life. Unfortunately, it had not enough suppleness to be reformed in time; that is why it was discarded. Because it did not know how to assimilate itself to the new life which was evolving, it was divorced from that life, and, in this way, it became what it was upon the eve of the Revolution, a sort of dead substance, a strange body which could maintain itself in the social organism only through inertia. It is then not surprising that a moment came when it was violently expelled. But to destroy it was not a means of giving satisfaction to the needs it had not satisfied. And that is the reason the question still remains with us, and has become still more acute after a century of groping and fruitless experience.

The work of the sociologist is not that of the statesman. We do not have to present in detail what this reform should be. It will be sufficient to indicate the general principles as they appear from the preceding facts.

What the experience of the past proves, above all, is that the framework of the occupational group must always have relations with the framework of economic life. It is because of this lack of relationship that the corporative regime disappeared. Since the market, formerly municipal, has become national and international, the corporations must assume the same extension. Instead of being limited only to the workers of a city, it must enlarge in such a way as to include all the members of the occupation scattered over the territory, for in whatever region they are found, whether they live in the city or the country, they are all solidary, and participate in a common life. Since this common life is, in certain respects, independent of all territorial determinations, the appropriate organ must be created that expresses and regularizes its function. Because of these dimensions, such an organ would necessarily be in direct contact with the central organ of the collective life, for the rather important events which interest a whole category of industrial enterprises in a country necessarily have very general repercussions of which the State cannot fail to take cognizance; hence it intervenes. Thus, it is not without reason that royal power tended instinctively not to allow great industry outside its control when it did appear. It was impossible for it not to be interested in a form of activity which, by its very nature, can always affect all society. But this regulatory action, if it is necessary, must not degenerate into narrow subordination, as happened in the seventeenth and eighteenth centuries. The two related organs must remain distinct and autonomous; each of them has its function, which it alone can take care of. If the function of making general principles of industrial legislation belongs to the governmental assemblies, they are incapable of diversifying them according to the different industries. It is this diversification which constitutes the proper task of the corporation.[1] This unitarian organization for a whole country in no way excludes the formation of secondary organs, comprising workers of the same region, or of the same locality, whose role would be to specialize still more the occupational regulation according to the local or regional necessities. Economic life would thus be regulated and determined without losing any of its diversity.

For that very reason, the corporative regime would be protected against that tendency towards immobility that it has often been charged with in the past, for it is a fault which is rooted in the narrowly communal character of the corporation. As long as it was limited to the city, it was inevitable for it to become a prisoner of tradition as the city itself. As in a group so restricted, the conditions of life are almost invariable, habit exercises a terrific effect upon people, and even innovations are dreaded. The traditionalism of the corporations was thus only an aspect of the communal traditionalism, and had the same qualities. Then, once it was ingrained in the mores, it survived the causes which had produced and originally justified it. That is why, when the material and moral concentration of the country, and great industry which is its consequence, had opened minds to new desires, awakened new needs, introduced into the tastes and fashions a mobility heretofore unknown, the corporation, which was obstinately attached to its old customs, was unable to satisfy these new exigencies. But national corporations, by virtue of their dimension and complexity, would not be exposed to this danger. Too many diverse minds would be in action for stationary uniformity to be established. In a group formed of numerous and varied elements, new combinations are always being produced. There would then be nothing rigid about such an organization, and it would consequently find itself in harmony with the mobile equilibrium of needs and ideas.

Besides, it must not be thought that the entire function of the corporation is to make rules and apply them. To be sure, where a group is formed, a moral discipline is formed too. But the institution of this discipline is only one of the many ways through which collective activity is manifested. A group is not only a moral authority which dominates the life of its members; it is also a source of life *sui generis*. From it comes a warmth which animates its members, making them intensely human, destroying their egotisms. Thus, in the past, the family was the legislator of law and ethics whose severity went to extremes of violence, at the same time that it was the place where one first learned to enjoy the effusions of sentiment. We have also seen how the corporation, in Rome and in the Middle Ages, awakened these same needs and sought to satisfy them. The corporations of the future will have a complexity of attributes still greater, by reason of their increased growth. Around their proper occupational functions others which come from the communes or private societies will be grouping themselves. The functions of assistance are such that, to be well filled, they demand feelings of solidarity between assistants and assisted, a certain intellectual and moral homogeneity such as the same occupation produces. A great many educational institutions (technical schools, adult education, etc.) equally seem to have to find their natural environment in the corporation. It is the same for aesthetic life, for it appears in the nature of things that this noble form of sport and recreation develops side by side with the serious life which it serves to balance and relieve. In fact, there are even now syndicates which are at the same time societies of mutual aid; others found common houses where there are organized courses, concerts, and dramatic presentations. The corporative activity can thus assume the most varied forms.

There is even reason to suppose that the corporation will become the foundation or one of the essential bases of our political organization. We have seen, indeed, that if it first begins by being outside the social system, it tends to fix itself in it in proportion to the development of economic life. It is, therefore, just to say that if progress continues to be made in this direction, it will have to take a more prominent and more predominant place in society. It was formerly the elementary division of communal organization. Now that the commune, heretofore an autonomous organism, has lost its place in the State, as the municipal market did in the national market, is it not fair to suppose that the corporation also will have to experience a corresponding transformation, becoming the elementary division of the State, the fundamental political unity? Society, instead of remaining what it is today, an aggregate of juxtaposed territorial districts, would become a vast system of national corporations. From various quarters it is asked that elective assemblies be formed by occupations, and not by territorial divisions; and certainly, in this way, political assemblies would more exactly express the diversity of social interests and their relations. They would be a more faithful picture of social life in its entirety. But to say that the nation, in becoming aware of itself, must be grouped into occupations, does not this mean that the organized occupation or corporation should be the essential organ of public life?

Thus the great gap in the structure of European societies we elsewhere point to would be filled. It will be seen, indeed, how, as advances are made in history, the organization which has territorial groups as its base (village or city, district, province, etc.) steadily becomes effaced. To be sure, each of us belongs to a commune, or a department, but the bonds attaching us there became daily more fragile and more slack. These geographical divisions are, for the most part, artificial and no longer awaken in us profound sentiments. The provincial spirit has disappeared never to return; the patriotism of the parish has become an archaism that cannot be restored at will. The municipal or departmental affairs affect and agitate us in proportion to their coincidence with our occupational affairs. Our activity is extended quite beyond these groups which are too narrow for it, and, moreover, a good deal of what happens there leaves us indifferent. There is thus produced a spontaneous weakening of the old social structure. Now, it is impossible for this organization to disappear without something replacing it. A society composed of an infinite number of unorganized individuals, that a hypertrophied State is forced to oppress and contain, constitutes a veritable sociological monstrosity. For collective activity is always too complex to be able to be expressed through the single and unique organ of the State. Moreover, the State is too remote from individuals; its relations with them too external and intermittent to penetrate deeply into individual consciences and socialize them within. Where the State is the only environment in which men can live communal lives, they inevitably lose contact, become detached, and thus society disintegrates. A nation can be maintained only if, between the State and the individual, there is intercalated a whole series of secondary groups near enough to the individuals to attract them strongly in their sphere of action and drag them, in this way, into the general torrent of social life. We have just shown how occupational groups are suited to fill this role, and that is their destiny. One thus conceives how important it is, especially in the economic order, for them to emerge from that state of inconsistency and disorganization in which they have remained for a century, since these occupations today absorb the major part of our collective forces.[2]

Perhaps now we shall be better able to explain the conclusions we reached at the end of our book, *Le Suicide*. We were already proposing there a strong corporative organization as a means of remedying the misfortune which the increase in suicides, together with many other symptoms, evinces. Certain critics have found that the remedy was not proportionate to the extent of the evil, but that is because they have undervalued the true nature of the corporation, and the place to which it is destined in social life, as well as the grave anomaly resulting from its disappearance. They have seen only an utilitarian association whose effect would at best bring order to economic interests, whereas it must really be the essential element of our social structure. The absence of all corporative institution creates, then, in the organization of a people like ours, a void whose importance it is difficult to exaggerate. It is a whole system of organs necessary in the normal functioning of the common life which is wanting. Such a constitutive lack is evidently not a local evil, limited to a region of society; it is a malady *totius substantiae*, affecting all the organism. Consequently, the attempt to put an end to it cannot fail to produce the most far reaching consequences. It is the general health of the social body which is here at stake.

That does not mean, however, that the corporation is a sort of panacea for everything. The crisis through which we are passing is not rooted in a single and unique cause. To put an end to it, it is not sufficient to regulate it where necessary. Justice must prevail. ... But if the corporative reform does not dispense with the others, it is the first condition for their efficacy. ... [N]ew difficulties will arise which will remain insoluble without a corporative organization. Up to now, it was the family which, either through collective property or descendence, assured the continuity of economic life, by the possession and exploitation of goods held intact, or, from the time the old familial communism fell away, the nearest relatives received the goods of the deceased. In the case of collective property, neither death nor a new generation changed the relations of things to persons; in the case of descent, the change was made automatically, and the goods, at no time, remained unowned and unused. But if domestic society cannot play this role any longer, there must be another social organ to replace its exercise of this necessary function. For there is only one way of preventing the periodic suspension of any activity: a group, perpetual as the family, must possess goods and exploit them itself, or, at the death of the owner, receive them and send them to some other individual holder to improve them. But as we have shown, the State is poorly equipped to supervise these very specialized economic tasks. There is, then, only the occupational group which can capably look after them. It answers, indeed, two necessary conditions; it is so closely connected with the economic life that it feels its needs, at the same time having a perpetuity at least equal to the family. But to fill this role, it must exist and be mature enough to take care of the new and complex role which devolves upon it.

* From Emile Durkheim, *The Division of Labor in Society*, translated by G. Simpson (New York: The Free Press, 1933 [1893]), 2–3; 5; 22–31.

[1] This specialization could be made only with the aid of elected assemblies charged to represent the corporation. In the present state of industry, these assemblies, in the same way as tribunals charged with applying the occupational regulations, should evidently be comprised of representatives of employees and representatives of employers, as is already the case in the tribunals of skilled trades; and that, in proportions corresponding to the respective importance attributed by opinion to these two factors in production. But if it is necessary that both meet in the directing councils of the corporations, it is no less important that at the base of the corporative organization they form distinct and independent groups, for their interests are too often rival and antagonistic. To be able to go about their ways freely, they must go about their ways separately. The two groups thus constituted would then be able to appoint their representatives to the common assemblies.

[2] We do not mean that the territorial divisions are destined to disappear entirely, but only that they will become of less importance. The old institutions never vanish before the new without leaving any traces of themselves. They persist, not only through sheer force of survival, but because there still persists something of the needs they once answered. The material neighborhood will always constitute a bond between men; consequently, political and social organization with a territorial base will certainly exist. Only, they will not have their present predominance, precisely because this bond has lost its force. Moreover, we have shown above, that even at the base of the corporation, there will always be found geographical divisions. Furthermore, between the diverse corporations of the same locality or region there will necessarily be special relations of solidarity which will, at all times, demand appropriate organization.

4
Under Assault

Vladimir Ilich Lenin (1870–1924), professional revolutionary, founder of the Russian Communist Party (Bolsheviks), and the first leader of the Soviet Union. His political ideas were formed by the revolutionary literature of his time, and especially Marx's Das Kapital. *In his later years, he moved away from some of Marx's ideas and articulated his criticisms in his famous* What Is To Be Done? *(1902) and other works. Here, he sets out the main principles on which the new Russian Soviet Republic was to be based: a free and voluntary union of the propertyless classes where power is vested in the toiling masses and their authorized deputies; an end to all forms of exploitation through a reorganization of society along socialist lines; and a recognition of the right to self-determination of nations.**

The Constituent Assembly resolves:

I.

1. Russia is hereby declared a republic of Soviets of Worker's, Soldiers' and Peasants' Deputies. All power centrally and locally belongs to the Soviets.
2. The Russian Soviet Republic shall be constituted on the principle of a free union of free nations, as a federation of Soviet national republics.

II.

Making it its fundamental aim to abolish all forms of exploitation of man by man, to put a complete end to the division of society into classes, mercilessly to crush the resistance of the exploiters, to establish a socialist organisation of society and to achieve the victory of socialism in all countries, the Constituent Assembly further resolves:

1. Private property in land is thereby abolished. All land, together with all structures, farm property, and other appurtenances of agricultural production, is declared to be the property of the toiling people.

2. The Soviet laws on workers' control and on the Supreme Council of National Economy are hereby confirmed with the object of guaranteeing the power of the toiling people over the exploiters, and as a first step towards the complete transformation of the factories, workshops, mines, railways, and other means of production and transport into the property of the workers' and peasants' state.
3. The passing of all the banks into the possession of the workers' and peasants' state is hereby confirmed as one of the conditions for the emancipation of the toiling masses from the yoke of capitalism.
4. Universal labour service is hereby instituted with the object of abolishing the parasitic sections of society.
5. In order to guarantee sovereign power for the toiling masses, and in order to remove all possibility of the restoration of the power of the exploiters, the arming of the toilers, the creation of a socialist Red Army of workers and peasants and the complete disarming of the propertied classes are hereby decreed.

III.

1. Expressing its firm determination to wrest mankind from the clutch of finance capital and imperialism, which have in this most criminal of wars drenched the world in blood, the Constituent Assembly declares its complete adherence to the policy of the Soviet power of tearing up the secret treaties, organising widespread fraternisation between the workers and peasants of the warring armies, and achieving at all costs and by revolutionary means a democratic peace among the nation, without annexations and indemnities, and on the basis of the self-determination of nations.
2. With the same purpose in view, the Constituent Assembly insists on a complete break with the barbarous policy of bourgeois civilisation, which has built the well-being of the exploiters of a few chosen nations on the enslavement of hundreds of millions of toiling people in Asia, in the colonies in general, and in the small countries.

   The Constituent Assembly welcomes the policy of the Council of People's Commissars, which has proclaimed the complete independence of Finland, commenced the evacuation of troops from Persia and declared freedom of self-determination for Armenia.
3. The Constituent Assembly regards the Soviet law on the cancellation of the loans issued by the governments of the tsar, landlords and bourgeoisie as a first blow to international bank and finance capital, and expresses its conviction that the Soviet government will firmly pursue this path until the international workers' revolt against the yoke of capital has completely triumphed.

IV.

Having been elected on the basis of party lists drawn up prior to the October Revolution, when the people were still not in a position to rise *en masse* against the exploiters, when they still did not realise the full strength of the resistance shown by the latter in defence of their class privileges, and when they had not yet addressed themselves to the practical task of building a socialist society, the Constituent Assembly considers that it would be fundamentally wrong, even from a formal point of view, to set itself up against the Soviet power.

In point of fact, the Constituent Assembly considers that now, when the people are fighting the last fight against the exploiters, there can be no place for exploiters in any of the organs of government. The power must be vested solely and entirely in the toiling masses and their authorised government – the Soviets of Workers', Soldiers' and Peasants' Deputies.

Supporting the Soviet power and the decrees of the Council of People's Commissars, the Constituent Assembly considers that its own duty must be limited to establishing a fundamental basis for the socialist reconstruction of society.

At the same time, with the object of creating a really free and voluntary, and therefore firm and stable, union of the toiling classes of all the nations of Russia, the Constituent Assembly limits its own duty to the establishment of the fundamental principles of a Federation of Soviet Republics of Russia, while leaving it to the workers and peasants of each nation to decide independently at their own sovereign Soviet Congress whether they shall participate in the federal government and in the other federal Soviet institutions, and on what terms.

*From Vladimir Ilich Lenin, 'Draft Declaration of the Rights of the Toiling and Exploited People', in his *Selected Works*, Vol. 6 (London: Lawrence and Wishart, 1936 [1918]), 452–4.

*Carl Schmitt (1888–1985), German jurist. Schmitt criticized liberal democracy during the difficult years of the young Weimar republic. After the Nazi seizure of power in 1933, he became initially a leading supporter of Nazi measures, including the removal of Jews from his profession. From 1937 he further and further retreated from national-socialism into inner emigration and, after the war, was briefly imprisoned and lost his university position. Here the young Schmitt rejects the equation of democracy with a liberal parliamentary system, and instead of accepting diversity and plurality, looks to a general organic will to be represented by an individual leader.**

The situation of parliamentarism is critical today because the development of modern mass democracy has made argumentative public discussion an empty formality. Many norms of contemporary parliamentary law, above all provisions concerning the independence of representatives and the openness of sessions, function as a result like a superfluous decoration, useless and even embarrassing, as though someone had painted the radiator of a modern central heating system with red flames in order to give the appearance of a blazing fire. The parties (which according to the text of the written constitution officially do not exist) do not face each other today discussing opinions, but as social or economic power-groups calculating their mutual interests and opportunities for power, and they actually agree compromises and coalitions on this basis. The masses are won over through a propaganda apparatus whose maximum effect relies on an appeal to immediate interests and passions. Argument in the real sense that is characteristic for genuine discussion ceases. In its place there appears a conscious reckoning of interests and chances for power in the parties' negotiations; in the treatment of the masses, posterlike, insistent suggestion or – as Walter Lippmann says in his very shrewd, although too psychological, American book *Public opinion* – the 'symbol' appears.[1] The literature on the psychology, technique, and critique of public opinion is today very large. One may therefore assume as well known today that it is no longer a question of persuading one's opponent of the truth or justice of an opinion but rather of winning a majority in order to govern with it. What Cavour identified as the great distinction between absolutism and constitutional regimes, that in an absolute regime a minister gives orders, whereas in a constitutional one he persuades all those who should obey, must today be meaningless. Cavour says explicitly: I (as constitutional minister) persuade that I am right, and it is only in this connection that his famous saying is meant: 'The worst chamber is still preferable to the best ante-chamber.' Today parliament itself appears a gigantic antechamber in front of the bureaus or committees of invisible rulers. It is like a satire if one quotes Bentham today: 'In Parliament ideas meet, and contact between ideas gives off sparks and leads to evidence.' Who still remembers the time when Prevost-Paradol saw the value of parliamentarism over the 'personal regime' of Napoleon III in that through the transfer of real power it forced the true holders of power to reveal themselves, so that government, as a result of this, always represents the strongest power in a 'wonderful' coordination of appearance and reality? Who still believes in this kind of openness? And in parliament as its greatest 'platform?'

The arguments of Burke, Bentham, Guizot, and John Stuart Mill are thus antiquated today. The numerous definitions of parliamentarism which one still finds today in Anglo-Saxon and French writings and which are apparently little known in Germany, definitions in which parliamentarism appears as essentially 'government by discussion,' must accordingly also count as moldy.

...

A popular presentation sees parliamentarism in the middle today, threatened from both sides by Bolshevism and Fascism. That is a simple but superficial constellation. The crisis of the parliamentary system and of parliamentary institutions in fact springs from the circumstances of modern mass democracy. These lead first of all to a crisis of democracy itself, because the problem of a substantial equality and homogeneity, which is necessary to democracy, cannot be resolved by the general equality of mankind. It leads further to a crisis of parliamentarism that must certainly be distinguished from the crisis of democracy. Both crises have appeared today at the same time and each one aggravates the other, but they are conceptually and in reality different. As democracy, modern mass democracy attempts to realize an identity of governed and governing, and thus it confronts parliament as an inconceivable and outmoded institution. If democratic identity is taken seriously, then in an emergency, no other constitutional institution can withstand – the sole criterion of the people's will, however it is expressed. Against the will of the people especially an institution based on discussion by independent representatives has no autonomous justification for its existence, even less so because the belief in discussion is not democratic but originally liberal.

...

Bolshevism and Fascism by contrast are, like all dictatorships, certainly antiliberal but not necessarily antidemocratic. In the history of democracy there have been numerous dictatorships, Caesarisms, and other more striking forms that have tried to create homogeneity and to shape the will of the people with methods uncommon in the liberal tradition of the past century. This effort belongs to the undemocratic conception, resulting from a blend of liberal principles in the nineteenth century that a people could only express its will when each citizen voted in deepest secrecy and complete isolation, that is, without leaving the sphere of the private and irresponsible, under 'protective arrangements' and 'unobserved' – as required by *Reich* voting law in Germany. Then every single vote was registered and an arithmetical majority was calculated. Quite elementary truths have thus been lost and are apparently unknown in contemporary political theory. 'The people' is a concept in public law. The people exist only in the sphere of publicity. The unanimous opinion of one hundred million private persons is neither the will of the people nor public opinion. The will of the people can be expressed just as well and perhaps better through acclamation, through something taken for granted, an obvious and unchallenged presence, than through the statistical apparatus that has been constructed with such meticulousness in the last fifty years. The stronger the power of democratic feeling, the more certain is the awareness that democracy is something other than a registration system for secret ballots. Compared to a democracy that is direct, not only in the technical sense but also in a vital sense, parliament appears an artificial machinery, produced by liberal reasoning, while dictatorial and Caesaristic methods not only can produce the acclamation of the people but can also be a direct expression of democratic substance and power.

Even if Bolshevism is suppressed and Fascism held at bay, the crisis of contemporary parliamentarism would not be overcome in the least. For it has not appeared as a result of the appearance of those two opponents; it was there before them and will persist after them. Rather, the crisis springs from the consequences of modern mass democracy and in the final analysis from the contradiction of a liberal individualism burdened by moral pathos and a democratic sentiment governed essentially by political ideals. A century of historical alliance and common struggle against royal absolutism has obscured the awareness of this contradiction. But the crisis unfolds today ever more strikingly, and no cosmopolitan rhetoric can prevent or eliminate it. It is, in its depths, the inescapable contradiction of liberal individualism and democratic homogeneity.

---

* From Carl Schmitt, 'From Preface to the Second Edition (1926): On the Contradiction between Parliamentarism and Democracy', in his *The Crisis of Parliamentary Democracy*, translated by Ellen Kennedy (Cambridge, Mass.: MIT Press, © 1992), 6–7; 15–17, reprinted with permission of the publisher.

[1] Walter Lippmann, *Public Opinion* (London: George Allen & Unwin, 1922). A recently published book – interesting, witty, and important despite all its leaps of thought is Wyndham Lewis, *The Art of Being Ruled* (London: Chatto & Windus, 1922). Lewis explains the transition from the intellectual to the affective and sensual through modern democracy, which initiates a general 'feminization' that suppresses the manly.

Kurt Tucholsky (1890–1935), satirical essayist and journalist. Tucholsky was a leading German pacifist and anti-fascist writer in the inter-war years, working first in Germany, then in Paris and Goteborg. Here he pokes fun at obsessive club members.*

I joined my club when an old pal kept suggesting
that this was something I'd find interesting;
    I was alone and thought it sounded fine.
Now I'm a comrade, colleague, member of the association –
the pin I wear reveals my affiliation
    with that old club of mine.

We have a president and a recorder,
a treasurer who keeps our house in order,
    and so on down the line.
We also have a noisy opposition
but they won't get the slightest recognition
    in that old club of mine.

I've been committee chairman since September,
I won't pull rank on any other member –
    that would be asinine ...
And yet it's good to know, I say it gladly,
that they depend on me and need me badly
    in that old club of mine.

Out there I'm just a slob like any other.
Here I am I, and fellow man, and brother,
    part of a grand design
The by-laws hover high above our meeting.
Time goes so fast, and evening hours are fleeting,
    in that old club of mine.

Here in my club I am alert and witty.
Those on the outside I can only pity –
    it seems they have no spine.
Long wave our flag, we let it bravely flutter.
I do not mind the insults people utter;
    call me a jackass – I have no objection-
    but if you slur my club in this connection,
        watch my collective German pride rise high!
        Hail B.V.D.! Freedom! Phi Beta Pi!
            Here's where I live.
        And here shall be my tomb and shrine:
        In that old club of mine.

* 'Das Mitglied', this translation is based on *Germany? Germany?: a Kurt Tucholsky Reader*, Harry Zohn, ed. (Manchester: Carcanet Press, 1990 [1926]), 173 f., with a few changes by the editors, reprinted with permission.

Antonio Gramsci (1891–1937), Italian Communist leader imprisoned by Mussolini, had a major impact on Western Marxism as the result of the publication of his Prison Notebooks. His most essential contribution was to add to Marxism a concern with cultural hegemony, that is, the character and effects of cultural practices *within civil society. Although he changed the Marxist analysis of the working of power in this way, he should not, however, be seen as moving Marxism toward pluralism.**

The use of the phrase 'in depth' is intentional, because 1917 has been studied – but only either from superficial and banal viewpoints, as when certain social historians study the vagaries of women's fashions, or from a 'rationalistic' viewpoint – in other words, with the conviction that certain phenomena are destroyed as soon as they are 'realistically' explained, as if they were popular superstitions (which anyway are not destroyed either merely by being explained).

The question of the meagre success achieved by new tendencies in the trade-union movement should be related to this series of problems. One attempt to begin a revision of the current tactical methods was perhaps that outlined by L. Dav. Br. [Trotsky] at the fourth meeting, when he made a comparison between the Eastern and Western fronts. The former had fallen at once, but unprecedented struggles had then ensued; in the case of the latter, the struggles would take place 'beforehand'. The question, therefore, was whether civil society resists before or after the attempt to seize power; where the latter takes place, etc. However, the question was outlined only in a brilliant, literary form, without directives of a practical character [1933–34; 1st version 1930–32].

. . .

In Russia the State was everything, civil society was primordial and gelatinous; in the West, there was a proper relation between State and civil society, and when the State trembled a sturdy structure of civil society was at once revealed. The State was only an outer ditch, behind which there stood a powerful system of fortresses and earthworks: more or less numerous from one State to the next, it goes without saying – but this precisely necessitated an accurate reconnaissance of each individual country [1930–1932].

. . .

The separation of powers, together with all the discussion provoked by its realisation and the legal dogmas which its appearance brought into being, is a product of the struggle between civil society and political society in a specific historical period. This period is characterised by a certain unstable equilibrium between the classes, which is a result of the fact that certain categories of intellectuals (in the direct service of the State, especially the civil and military bureaucracy) are still too closely tied to the old dominant classes. In other words, there takes place within the society what Croce calls the 'perpetual conflict between Church and State', in which the Church is taken as representing the totality of civil society (whereas in fact it is only an element of diminishing importance within it), and the State as representing every attempt to crystallise permanently a particular stage of development, a particular situation. In this sense, the Church itself may become State, and the conflict may occur between on the one hand secular (and secularising) civil society, and on the other State/Church (when the Church has become an integral part of the State, of political society monopolised by a specific privileged group, which absorbs the Church in order the better to preserve its monopoly with the support of that zone of 'civil society' which the Church represents) [1931–32].

...

In the (anyway superficial) polemic over the functions of the State (which here means the State as a politico-juridical organisation in the narrow sense), the expression 'the State as *veilleur de nuit*' corresponds to the Italian expression 'the State as policeman' and means a State whose functions are limited to the safeguarding of public order and of respect for the laws. The fact is glossed over that in this form of regime (which anyway has never existed except on paper, as a limiting hypothesis) hegemony over its historical development belongs to private forces, to civil society – which is 'State' too, indeed is the State itself.

It seems that the expression *veilleur de nuit*, which should have a more sarcastic ring than 'the State as policeman', comes from Lassalle. Its opposite should be 'ethical State' or 'interventionist State' in general, but there are differences between the two expressions. The concept of ethical State is of philosophical and intellectual origin (belonging to the intellectuals: Hegel), and in fact could be brought into conjunction with the concept of State – *veilleur de nuit*; for it refers rather to the autonomous, educative and moral activity of the secular State, by contrast with the cosmopolitanism and the interference of the religious-ecclesiastical organisation as a mediaeval residue. The concept of interventionist State is of economic origin, and is connected on the one hand with tendencies supporting protection and economic nationalism, and on the other with the attempt to force a particular State personnel, of landowning and feudal origin, to take on the 'protection' of the working classes against the excesses of capitalism (policy of Bismarck and of Disraeli).

These diverse tendencies may combine in various ways, and in fact have so combined. Naturally liberals ('economists') are for the 'State as *veilleur de nuit*', and would like the historical initiative to be left to civil society and to the various forces which spring up there – with the 'State' as guardian of 'fair play' and of the rules of the game. Intellectuals draw very significant distinctions as to when they are liberals and when they are interventionists (they may be liberals in the economic field and interventionists in the cultural field, etc.). The catholics would like the State to be interventionist one hundred per cent in their favour; failing that, or where they are in a minority, they call for a 'neutral' State, so that it should not support their adversaries [1935; 1st version 1930].

...

We are still on the terrain of the identification of State and government – an identification which is precisely a representation of the economic–corporate form, in other words of the confusion between civil society and political society. For it should be remarked that the general notion of State includes elements which need to be referred back to the notion of civil society (in the sense that one might say that State = political society + civil society, in other words hegemony protected by the armour of coercion). In a doctrine of the State which conceives the latter as tendentially capable of withering away and of being subsumed into regulated society, the argument is a fundamental one. It is possible to imagine the coercive element of the State withering away by degrees, as ever-more conspicuous elements of regulated society (or ethical State or civil society) make their appearance [1930–32].

...

Attitude of each particular social group towards its own State. The analysis would not be accurate if no account were taken of the two forms in which the State presents itself in the language and culture of specific epochs, i.e. as civil society and as political society. The term 'statolatry' is applied to a particular attitude towards the 'government by functionaries' or political society, which in everyday language is the form of State life to which the term of State is applied and which is commonly understood as the entire State. The assertion that the State can be identified with individuals (the individuals of a social group), as an element of active culture (i.e. as a movement to create a new civilisation, a new type of man and of citizen), must serve to determine the will to construct within the husk of political society a complex and well-articulated civil society, in which the individual can govern himself without his self-government thereby entering into conflict with political society – but rather becoming its normal continuation, its organic complement. For some social groups, which before their ascent to autonomous State life have not had a long independent period of cultural and moral development on their own (as was made possible in mediaeval society and under the absolute regimes by the juridical existence of the privileged Estates or orders), a period of statolatry is necessary and indeed opportune. This 'statolatry' is nothing other than the normal form of 'State life', or at least of initiation to autonomous State life and to the creation of a 'civil society' which it was not historically possible to create before the

ascent to independent State life. However, this kind of 'statolatry' must not
be abandoned to itself, must not, especially, become theoretical fanaticism
or be conceived of as 'perpetual'. It must be criticised, precisely in order
to develop and produce new forms of State life, in which the initiative of
individuals and groups will have a 'State' character, even if it is not due to
the 'government of the functionaries' (make State life become 'spontaneous')
[1931–32].

. . .

It is worth considering the extent to which Gentile's 'actualism' corresponds
to the positive phase of the State, whereas Croce provides the opposition to
this. The concept of 'unity in the act' allows Gentile to recognise as 'history'
what is anti-history for Croce. For Gentile history is entirely State history,
while for Croce it is 'ethical-political'. In other words, Croce seeks to maintain
a distinction between civil society and political society, between hegemony
and dictatorship; the great intellectuals exercise hegemony, which presupposes
a certain collaboration, i.e. an active and voluntary (free) consent, i.e. a liberal,
democratic regime. Gentile sees the economic-corporate phase as an ethical
phase within the historical act: hegemony and dictatorship are indistin-
guishable, force and consent are simply equivalent; one cannot distinguish
political society from civil society; only the State, and of course the State-
as-government, exists, etc. [1930–32].

*From Antonio Gramsci, *Selections from the Prison Notebooks of Antonio Gramsci*, translated
and edited by Quintin Hoare and Geoffrey Nowell Smith (New York: International
Publishers, 1987), 235–6; 238; 245; 261–3; 268–9; 271, reprinted with permission.

*Joseph Goebbels (1897–1945), Nazi propaganda minister. Like Hitler and many
Nazis, Goebbels was a failed artist. After his unsuccessful novel, he became a leading
journalist and modern propagandist for the Nazi party. A cynical power-oriented
individual but skilled orator, Goebbels here attacks the 'squabbling' between social
and political groups that comes with democratic politics and pluralism and turns
instead to the organic spirit of the nation and the need for state compulsion.**

We are *nationalists* because we see the *nation* as the only way to bring all the
forces of the nation together to preserve and improve our existence and the
conditions under which we live.

The *nation* is the organic union of a people to protect its life. To be
national is to affirm this union *in word and deed*. To be national has nothing
to do with a form of government or a symbol. It is an affirmation of *things*,
not forms. Forms can change, their *content* remains. If form and content

agree, then he nationalist affirms both. If they conflict, the nationalist fights *for the content and against the form*. One may not put the symbol above the content. If that happens, the battle is on the wrong field and one's strength is lost in formalism. The real *aim of nationalism, the nation*, is lost.

That is how things are today in *Germany*. Nationalism has turned into bourgeois patriotism and its defenders are battling windmills. One says *Germany* and means the monarchy. Another proclaims *freedom* and means *Black–White–Red* [The imperial colours]. Would our situation today be any different if we replaced the republic with a monarchy and flew the black–white–red flag? The *colony* would have different wallpaper, but its nature, its content would stay the same. Indeed, things would be even worse, for *a façade that conceals the facts* dissipates the forces today fighting against slavery.

Bourgeois patriotism is *the privilege of a class*. It is the real reason for its decline. When 30 million are *for* something and 30 million are *against* it, *things balance out and nothing happens*. That is how things are with us. We are the world's Pariah not because we do not have the courage to resist, rather because our entire national energy is *wasted* in eternal and unproductive *squabbling between the right and the left*. Our way only goes downward, and today one can already predict when we will fall into the abyss.

Nationalism is more wide-reaching than *internationalism*. It sees things as they are. *Only he who respects himself can respect others*. If as a *German* nationalist I affirm Germany, how can I hold it against a *French* nationalist who affirms *France*? Only when there affirmations conflict in vital ways will there be a *power-political* struggle. Internationalism cannot undo this reality. Its attempts at proof fail completely. And even when the facts seem to have some validity, *nature, blood, the will to life, and the struggle for existence on this hard earth* prove the falsity of fine theories.

The sin of bourgeois patriotism was to confound a certain economic form with the national. It connected two things that are entirely different. *Forms of the economy*, however firm they may seem, are changeable. *The national is eternal*. If I mix the eternal and the temporal, the eternal will necessarily collapse when the temporal collapses. This was the real cause for the collapse of liberal society. It was rooted *not in the eternal*, but in *the temporal*, and when the temporal declined it took the eternal down with it. Today it is only an excuse for a system that brings growing economic misery. That is the only reason why *international Jewry* organizes the battle of the proletarian forces against both powers, the economy and the nation, and defeat them.

From this understanding, the young nationalism draws its absolute demand. *The faith in the nation* is a matter for everyone, never a group, a class or an economic clique. The eternal must be distinguished from the temporal. Maintaining a rotten economic system has nothing to do with nationalism, which is an affirmation of the Fatherland. I can love Germany and hate capitalism. Not only *can* I, I *must*. Only *the annihilation of a system of exploitation carries with it the core of the rebirth of our people.*

...

The sin of liberal thinking was to overlook *socialism's nation-building strengths*, thereby allowing its energies to go in anti-national directions. The sin of *Marxism* was to degrade *socialism* into a question of *wages and the stomach*, putting it in conflict with the state and its national existence. An understanding of both these facts leads us to a new sense of socialism, which sees *its nature as nationalistic, state-building, liberating and constructive.*

The bourgeois is about to leave the historical stage. In its place will come the *class of productive workers, the working class*, that has been up until today oppressed. It is beginning to fulfill its political mission. It is involved in a hard and bitter struggle for political power as it seeks to become part of the national organism. The battle began in the *economic* realm; it will finish in the *political*. It is not merely a matter of pay, not only a matter of the number of hours worked in a day – though we may never forget that these are essential, perhaps even the most significant part of the socialist platform – but it is much more a matter of incorporating a powerful and responsible class in the state, perhaps even to make it the *dominant* force in the future politics of the Fatherland. The *bourgeois* does not want to recognize the strength of the *working class*. Marxism has forced it into a straightjacket that will ruin it. While the *working class* gradually disintegrates in the *Marxist* front, bleeding itself dry, *the bourgeois and Marxism* have agreed on the *general lines of capitalism*, and see their task now to protect and defend it in various ways, often concealed.

We are *socialists* because we see *the social question as a matter of necessity and justice* for the *very existence of a state for our people*, not a question of cheap pity or insulting sentimentality. The worker has a *claim* to a living standard that corresponds to what he *produces*. We have no intention of *begging* for that right. Incorporating him in the state of organism is not only a critical matter for him, but *for the whole nation*. The question is larger than the eight-hour day. It is a matter of forming a *new state consciousness* that includes every productive citizen. Since the political powers of the day are neither willing nor able to create such a situation, *socialism must be fought for*. It is a *fighting slogan* both inwardly and outwardly. It is aimed domestically at the bourgeois parties and Marxism at the same time, because both are sworn enemies of the workers' state. It is directed abroad at all powers that threaten our national existence and thereby the possibility of the coming *socialist national state*.

Socialism is possible only in a state that is united domestically and free internationally. The bourgeois and Marxism are responsible for failing to reach both goals, domestic unity and international freedom. No matter how national and social these two forces present themselves, they are the sworn enemies of a socialist national state.

...

We do not enter parliament to use *parliamentary methods*. We know that the *fate of the peoples is determined by personalities*, never by parliamentary majorities. The essence of parliamentary democracy is the *majority*, which destroys personal responsibility and *glorifies the masses*. A few dozen rogues and crooks run things behind the scenes. *Aristocracy* depends on *accomplishment*, the rule of the most able, and the subordination of the less capable to the will of the leadership. *Any form of government* – no matter how democratic or aristocratic it may outwardly appear – rests on compulsion. The difference is only whether the compulsion is a blessing or a curse for the community.

What we demand is new, decisive and radical, revolutionary in the truest sense of the word. That has nothing to do with rioting and barricades. It may be that that happens here or there. But it is not an inherent part of the process. *Revolutions are spiritual acts*. They appear first *in people*, then in politics and the economy. New people form new structures. The transformation we want is first of all spiritual; that will necessarily change the way things are.

This revolutionary act is beginning to be visible in us. The result is a new type of person visible to the knowing eye: the *National Socialist*. Consistent with his spiritual attitude, the *National Socialist makes uncompromising demands* in politics. There is no *if and when* for him, only an *either – or*.

*From Joseph Goebbels, 'Those Damned Nazis', in the *German Propaganda Archive*, at www.calvin.edu/cas/gpa. with thanks to Randall Bytwerk. The pamphlet was published in Joseph Goebbels and Mjölnir, *Die verfluchten Hakenkreuzler. Etwas zum Nachdenken* (Munich: Verlag Frz. Eher, 1932).

Victor M. Perez-Diaz (b. 1938), Spanish political scientist, is the author of a number of books concerned with Spain's transition from authoritarian rule. In this passage he explains that the state gained enormous salience within a particular period of European history. It was seen as having the capacity to ensure national unity and economic well-being, and accordingly gained enormous powers and great authority. Civil society could not flourish in such a world.

The state and civil society face each other as two differentiated sets of actors and institutions engaged in a number of reciprocal exchanges. But in order to understand these exchanges we have to take into account the fact that the state confronts civil society in a plural capacity. First, the state has the 'real' status of being both a coercive apparatus and a service provider. But the state also has the 'symbolic' capacity of being a prominent actor in the public sphere.

. . .

It is my belief that the general tendency toward state growth over the last two hundred years or so has been supported by a vision of the state as the bearer of a moral project, which has been called by different names – nationalism, modernization, and social reform, among others. Today we are witnessing a generalized crisis of such a vision (and among its corresponding institutions) in both western and eastern Europe. The theme of the return of civil society is an expression of that crisis.

. . .

Underlying the process of formation of the national states in western countries and the different phases of state and societal protagonism over the last two centuries, there was a cultural process at work. States appeared and then grew, and not merely because those institutions filled an empty space between an international order and a domestic arena, or because a series of fortunate, daring, and ruthless rulers were able to take advantage of the competition between states to playoff against one another the demands of different groups within their own population. They appeared and grew also because (and to the extent that) all the institutional inertia and group strategies were embedded in a political culture, at the heart of which we find an argument that portrayed the state as the bearer of an extraordinary moral project. By contrast, the gradual loss of plausibility of this argument lies at the heart of the present-day change of phase in the relative prominence of state and society, and at the heart of society's increasing resistance to further state growth.

The rise of this notion of a moral project required the cooperation of political elites and cultural elites. While the monarchs and their allies did the actual work of defeating rival contenders, rounding up territories, and developing armies and tax-levying systems and other institutions, an intellectual tradition developed which took a relatively consistent view of the modern state and instilled meaning and moral justification in those practical endeavors. In order to do that, these state intellectuals had to construct a metaphysical fiction, a theory of state sovereignty, and a moral argument.

As a result of the metaphysical fiction, the state acquired an autonomous existence. Although the term *state* was first used with a denotation close to the modern one in the sixteenth century, not until the eighteenth century did it come to refer to a corporate actor, transcending the human beings of which it was composed, including the state's rulers (who began to identify themselves as 'the first servants of the state') and their families or dynasties. This corporate actor was said to have a will, a vision, and a capacity to act on its own.

At the same time, the term took on a sort of aura, inspiring awe and respect. After much indoctrination by secular and religious elites, this aura was gradually accepted, and finally taken for granted, by the population. The invention of the concept of sovereignty played a crucial role in this process, for it allowed the ruler to be more than a suzerain, or bearer of supreme power, in which case he would still have to reckon with others who had an autonomous power source of their own, either a religious or a secular one. Now, by being the bearer of sovereign power, the state could pretend to be the source of all the other powers. Thus, the state would permit these other powers to exist, but only as subordinate to state power and contingent on state recognition, since, at least on principle, the state's powers could not be limited or checked by any other institution.

But since these were extraordinary claims – indeed, they ran against the institutional complexity and political fragmentation of much of the European experience – they had to be grounded in an elaborate moral argument, which was driven home through a prolonged period of indoctrination, institutional work, and the 'shock therapy' of catastrophic wars.

The dramatic religious wars of the sixteenth and seventeenth centuries provided the decisive stimulus, and the initial structure of plausibility, for that moral argument to take hold. Kings grounded their claims to absolute or sovereign power on the need to guarantee domestic peace and to avert civil wars, which they did either by insisting on the religious conformity of their subjects or by allowing only a limited degree of religious toleration. Thinkers of different persuasions, such as Pascal and Hobbes, agreed that civil war, whether because of religious or constitutional considerations, should be considered the worst of all possible evils; that justice or the public good should be defined first and foremost as the kind of social order that would make civil war impossible; and that the public authority should uphold that order, and should count on their subjects' submission to it.

Successive generations of intellectuals expanded this moral argument in different directions. They ended up with three theories which fleshed out the moral tasks of the modern state: those of nationalism, citizenship, and modernization. First, they made the state responsible for the defense of a new principle of collective identity in a world of competing nation-states. Second, they made the state responsible for the creation of a community of citizens and of a public sphere where these citizens would meet their rulers on a nearly equal footing. Third, they made the state responsible for the economic prosperity and the social integration of society – or, to use a term which would come into play in the twentieth century, they made the state responsible for modernizing the country.

Once this work was done, the next step was to convince people not only that the world should be understood as divided into a number of such sovereign states, each one, on principle, second to none, but also that all of world history should be read as a sort of epic drama portraying the process of formation of those states and the challenges by which they test their sovereign claims against one another. An additional dramatic effect was obtained by pointing at the different historical configurations (or combinations of types of economic growth, social integration, and political regimes) of the various nation-states; by asserting that a higher morality was embedded in one configuration as against another; and finally by persuading people of the absolute value they should grant these assertions so as to be ready to fight and die for national interests and national values.

Thus, an all-encompassing 'master fiction' developed, combining a cognitive map (which appealed to the need people had for orienting themselves in a perplexing world) and a dramatic script (which appealed to the people's emotional needs for expressing their altruistic, aggressive, and self-destructive drives). This master fiction became persuasive enough to be taken for granted by several generations of Europeans in the course of the nineteenth and twentieth centuries. As a result of it, people developed feelings of moral obligation, and even of a sacred duty, vis-a-vis the state, and went as far as to justify the sacrifice of their property, their liberty, and their lives for their country. This moral disposition was put to a bitter test in a succession of wars.

Now, in stating that today we are witnessing the decline of the state as the bearer of a moral project, I mean that this master fiction has lost its plausibility. It has become increasingly doubtful that in today's world the state is or should be the bearer of a national identity, the state is or should be the focus of public life, the state is or should be the main actor in a process of modernization and therefore the key to economic growth and social integration.

*From Victor M. Perez-Diaz, *The Return of Civil Society: The Emergence of Democratic Spain* (Cambridge, Massachusetts: Harvard University Press, Copyright © 1993 by the President and Fellows of Harvard College), 58; 61; 66–9, reprinted with permission.

*Michael J. Sandel is professor of government at Harvard University, and a leading communitarian critic of right-based liberalism. Here he argues that procedural liberalism has been unable to stop the erosion of active citizenship and community in the twentieth century.**

The problems in the theory of procedural liberalism show up in the practice it inspires. Over the past half-century, American politics has come to embody the version of liberalism that renounces the formative ambition and insists government should be neutral toward competing conceptions of the good life. Rather than tie liberty to self-government and the virtues that sustain it, the procedural republic seeks a framework of rights, neutral among ends, within which individuals can choose and pursue their own ends.

But the discontent that besets American public life today illustrates the inadequacy of this solution. A politics that brackets morality and religion too completely soon generates its own disenchantment. Where political discourse lacks moral resonance, the yearning for a public life of larger meaning finds undesirable expression. Groups like the Moral Majority seek to clothe the naked public square with narrow, intolerant moralisms. Fundamentalists rush in where liberals fear to tread. The disenchantment also assumes more secular forms. Absent a political agenda that addresses the moral dimension of public questions, attention becomes riveted on the private vices of public officials. Political discourse becomes increasingly preoccupied with the scandalous, the sensational, and the confessional as purveyed by tabloids, talk shows, and eventually the mainstream media as well. It cannot be said that the public philosophy of contemporary liberalism is wholly responsible for these tendencies. But its vision of political discourse is too spare to contain the moral energies of democratic life. It creates a moral void that opens the way for intolerance and other misguided moralisms.

A political agenda lacking substantive moral discourse is one symptom of the public philosophy of the procedural republic. Another is the loss of mastery. The triumph of the voluntarist conception of freedom has coincided with a growing sense of disempowerment. Despite the expansion of rights in recent decades, Americans find to their frustration that they are losing control of the forces that govern their lives. This has partly to do with the insecurity of jobs in the global economy, but it also reflects the self-image by which we live. The liberal self-image and the actual organization of modern social and economic life are sharply at odds. Even as we think and act as freely choosing, independent selves, we confront a world governed by impersonal structures of power that defy our understanding and control. The voluntarist conception of freedom leaves us ill equipped to contend with this condition. Liberated though we may be from the burden of identities we have not chosen, entitled though we may be to the range of rights assured by the welfare state, we find ourselves overwhelmed as we turn to face the world on our own resources.

The inability of the reigning political agenda to address the erosion of self-government and community reflects the impoverished conceptions of citizenship and freedom implicit in our public life. The procedural republic that has unfolded over the past half-century can now be seen as an epic experiment in the claims of liberal as against republican political thought. Our present predicament lends weight to the republican claim that liberty cannot be detached from self-government and the virtues that sustain it, that the formative project cannot be dispensed with after all. The procedural republic, it turns out, cannot secure the liberty it promises because it cannot inspire the moral and civic engagement self-government requires.

If the public philosophy of contemporary liberalism fails to answer democracy's discontent, it remains to ask how a renewed attention to republican themes might better equip us to contend with our condition. How would a political agenda informed by the civic strand of freedom differ from the one that now prevails? Is self-government in the republican sense even possible under modern conditions? If so, what economic and political arrangements would it require, and what qualities of character would be necessary to sustain them?

How American politics might recover its civic voice is not wholly a speculative matter. Although the public philosophy of the procedural republic predominates in our time, it has not extinguished the civic understanding of freedom. Around the edges of our political discourse and practice, hints of the formative project can still be glimpsed. As the reigning political agenda lost energy in the 1980s and 1990s, these residual civic impulses quickened. Americans of various ideological persuasions groped to articulate a politics that reached beyond the terms of the procedural republic and spoke to the anxieties of the time.

These groupings, however partial and inchoate, gesture nonetheless toward the kind of political debate that would accord greater attention to republican themes. These expressions of Americans' persisting civic aspirations have taken two forms; one emphasizes the moral, the other the economic prerequisites of self-government. The first is the attempt, coming largely but not wholly from the right, to revive virtue, character-formation, and moral judgment as considerations in public policy and political discourse. The second involves a range of efforts, coming mostly though not entirely from the left, to contend with economic forces that disempower communities and threaten to erode the social fabric of democratic life.

. . .

Given the limits of cosmopolitan politics, the attempt to save democracy by globalizing citizenship, as Progressives once sought to save democracy by nationalizing citizenship, is unlikely to succeed. The analogy between the globalizing impulse of our time and the nationalizing project of theirs holds to this extent: We cannot hope to govern the global economy without transnational political institutions, and we cannot expect to sustain such institutions without cultivating more expansive civic identities. This is the moment of truth in the cosmopolitan vision. Human rights conventions, global environmental accords, and world bodies governing trade, finance, and economic development are among the undertakings that will depend for public support on inspiring a greater sense of engagement in a shared global destiny.

But the cosmopolitan vision is wrong to suggest that we can restore self-government simply by pushing sovereignty and citizenship upward. The hope for self-government lies not in relocating sovereignty but in dispersing it. The most promising alternative to the sovereign state is not a one-world community based on the solidarity of humankind, but a multiplicity of communities and political bodies – some more, some less extensive than nations – among which sovereignty is diffused. The nation-state need not fade away, only cede its claim as sole repository of sovereign power and primary object of political allegiance. Different forms of political association would govern different spheres of life and engage different aspects of our identities. Only a regime that disperses sovereignty both upward and downward can combine the power required to rival global market forces with the differentiation required of a public life that hopes to inspire the reflective allegiance of its citizens.

In some places, dispersing sovereignty may entail according greater cultural and political autonomy to subnational communities – such as Catalans and Kurds, Scots and Quebecois – even while strengthening and democratizing transnational structures, such as the European Union. Or it may involve modes of devolution and subsidiarity along geographic rather than ethnic and cultural lines.

. . .

The global media and markets that shape our lives beckon us to a world beyond boundaries and belonging. But the civic resources we need to master these forces, or at least to contend with them, are still to be found in the places and stories, memories and meanings, incidents and identities that situate us in the world and give our lives their moral particularity.

The public philosophy by which we live bids us to bracket these attachments, to set them aside for political purposes, to conduct our political debates without reference to them. But a procedural republic that banishes moral and religious argument from political discourse makes for an impoverished civic life. It also fails to answer the aspiration for self-government; its image of citizens as free and independent selves, unencumbered by moral and civic ties they have not chosen, cannot sustain the public spirit that equips us for self-rule.

*From Michael J. Sandel, *Democracy's Discontent: America in Search of a Public Philosophy* (Cambridge, Massachusetts: The Belknap Press of Harvard University Press, Copyright © 1996 by Michael J. Sandel), 322–4; 345; 349–50, reprinted with permission.

5
Revival

Václav Havel (b. 1936), Czech playwright and political dissident. His participation in the liberal reforms of the Prague Spring (1968) and political activities in its aftermath were followed by arrests and four years in prison. After his release from prison Havel continued to take part in politics and became a leading figure in the Civic Forum, pressing for democratic reforms. In 1989 he became Czechoslovakia's first non-communist leader since 1948, and also served as president to the new Czech Republic until 2003. In this selection Havel argues for the need to have an 'independent life of society' – civic attitudes and social self-organization comprising its core. He further points out a new focus in politics, based on the parallel structures coming from ordinary people, as presenting a desirable alternative to the notions of traditional parliamentary democracy in realizing an independent individual and societal existence.*

The point where living within the truth ceases to be a mere negation of living with a lie and becomes articulate in a particular way, is the point at which something is born that might be called the 'independent spiritual, social and political life of society'. This independent life is not separated from the rest of life ('dependent life') by some sharply defined line. Both types frequently coexist in the same people. Nevertheless, its most important focus is marked by a relatively high degree of inner emancipation. It sails upon the vast ocean of the manipulated life like little boats, tossed by the waves but always bobbing back as visible messengers of living within the truth, articulating the suppressed aims of life.

What is this independent life of society? The spectrum of its expressions and activities is naturally very wide. It includes everything from self-education and thinking about the world, through free creative activity and its communication to others, to the most varied free, civic attitudes, including instances of independent social self-organization. In short, it is an area in which living within the truth becomes articulate and materializes in a visible way.

Thus what will later be referred to as 'citizens' initiatives', 'dissident movements' or even 'oppositions', emerge, like the proverbial one-tenth of the iceberg visible above the water, from that area, from the independent life of society.

. . .

At a certain stage in its development, the independent life of society and the 'dissident movements' cannot avoid a certain amount of organization and institutionalization. This is a natural development and unless this independent life of society is somehow radically suppressed and eliminated, the tendency will grow. Along with it, a parallel political life will also necessarily evolve, and to a certain extent it exists already in Czechoslovakia. Various groupings of a more or less political nature will continue to define themselves politically, to act and confront each other.

These parallel structures, it may be said, represent the most articulated expressions so far of 'living within the truth'. One of the most important tasks the 'dissident movements' have set themselves is to support and develop them. Once again, it confirms the fact that all attempts by society to resist the pressure of the system have their essential beginnings in the pre-political area. For what else are parallel structures than an area where a different life can be lived, a life that is in harmony with its own aims and which in turn structures itself in harmony with those aims? What else are those initial attempts at social self-organization than the efforts of a certain part of society to live – as a society – within the truth, to rid itself of the self-sustaining aspects of totalitarianism; and, thus, to extricate itself radically from its involvement in the post-totalitarian system? What else is it but a non-violent attempt by people to negate the system within themselves and to establish their lives on a new basis, that of their own proper identity? And does this tendency not confirm once more the principle of returning the focus to actual individuals? After all, the parallel structures do not grow a priori out of a theoretical vision of systemic changes (there are no political sects involved), but from the aims of life and the authentic needs of real people.

. . .

Historical experience teaches us that any genuinely meaningful point of departure in an individual's life usually has an element of universality about it. In other words, it is not something partial, accessible only to a restricted community, and not transferable to any other. On the contrary, it must be potentially accessible to everyone; it must foreshadow a general solution and, thus, it is not just the expression of an introverted, self-contained responsibility that individuals have to and for themselves alone, but responsibility to and for the *world*. Thus it would be quite wrong to understand the parallel structures and the parallel *polis* as a retreat into a ghetto and as an act of isolation, addressing itself only to the welfare of those who had decided on such a course, and who are indifferent to the rest. It would be wrong, in short, to consider it an essentially group solution that has nothing to do with the general situation.

. . .

In other words, the parallel *polis* points beyond itself and only makes sense as an act of deepening one's responsibility to and for the whole, as a way of discovering the most appropriate *locus* for this responsibility, not as an escape from it.

. . .

It would appear that the traditional parliamentary democracies can offer no fundamental opposition to the automatism of technological civilization and the industrial-consumer society, for they, too, are being dragged helplessly along by it. People are manipulated in ways that are infinitely more subtle and refined than the brutal methods used in the post-totalitarian societies. But this static complex of rigid, conceptually sloppy and politically pragmatic mass political parties run by professional apparatuses and releasing the citizen from all forms of concrete and personal responsibility; and those complex focuses of capital accumulation engaged in secret manipulations and expansion; the omnipresent dictatorship of consumption, production, advertising, commerce, consumer culture.

. . .

[T]o cling to the notion of traditional parliamentary democracy as one's political ideal and to succumb to the illusion that only this 'tried and true' form is capable of guaranteeing human beings enduring dignity and an independent role in society would, in my opinion, be at the very least shortsighted.

I see a renewed focus of politics on real people as something far more profound than merely returning to the everyday mechanisms of Western (or if you like bourgeois) democracy. In 1968 I felt that our problem could be solved by forming an opposition party that would compete publicly for power with the Communist Party. I have long since come to realize, however, that it is just not that simple and that no opposition party in and of itself, just as no new electoral laws in and of themselves, could make society proof against some new form of violence. No 'dry' organizational measures in themselves can provide that guarantee, and we would be hard pressed to find in them that God who alone can save us.

...

These structures should naturally arise from *below* as a consequence of authentic social 'self-organization'; they should derive vital energy from a living dialogue with the genuine needs from which they arise, and when these needs are gone, the structures should also disappear. The principles of their internal organization should be very diverse, with a minimum of external regulation.

* From Václav Havel. 'The Power of the Powerless' [1978] *Living in Truth*, Jan Vladislav ed. (London: Faber, 1987), 85; 102–4; 116–17; 119.

Chris Hann (b. 1953), social anthropologist, undertook fieldwork in villages in Hungary and Poland in the decade before the collapse of communism within the Soviet sphere. Frequent return to his fieldwork sites has convinced him that the shock re-introduction of market principles had led to a decline in living standards, thereby doing much to undermine the possibility of civil society in the region.*

My own views about civil society have been coloured particularly by its use in the context of the transformation of Eastern Europe. Indeed this was the principal terrain on which the popularity of the term became firmly established in the 1980s. I was, and remain, very sceptical of the way 'society' was invoked by some 'dissident' intellectuals and by various commentators outside the region to imply that Eastern European populations were united in their opposition to socialist governments. In this discourse, civil society is a slogan, reified as a collective, homogenised agent, combating a demonic state. For example, Václav Havel argues that his socialist predecessors in power imposed a uniform model of central control upon society. According to Havel,[1] 'It is as easy to do that as it is to smash a piece of antique, inlaid furniture with a single blow from a hammer. But it is infinitely more difficult to restore it all, or to create it directly.'

Later in the same article Havel argues that 'communism brought history, and with it all natural development, to a halt. ... National and cultural differences were kept on ice.' Here again are metaphors that have been widely used since 1989, but can one really accept that East European societies were placed in some kind of deep freeze for forty years? It seems to me that there was in fact continuous movement and great diversity among and within each of the East European countries. In some countries, such as Poland ... the range of social activities was very extensive. There were some important common traits in the 'eastern bloc', but a stark contrast with the allegedly natural and free development of 'civil society' in the west does not take us very far in understanding the changes wrought by socialism. Where

Havel reviles 'the intrinsic tendency of communism to make everything the same', many East Europeans still, in spite of everything, feel that its fundamental motivations were the highly moral ones of increasing entitlements and making people more equal. It has always seemed to me that many citizens, especially in the countryside, were empowered in the socialist period, that is, they became better able to express their social identities, in conditions of relative material prosperity. (No doubt this is less true of Czechoslovakia than of some of its neighbours, while in extreme cases, such as Romania in the 1980s, this generalisation does not apply at all.) This is little understood in western countries because coverage of the region focuses on the high culture produced by intellectual elites, among whom Havel himself is an outstanding figure. However, millions of East Europeans, and not just a few former communist *apparatchiks*, have now shown in elections that they wish to preserve some of the radical changes which took place in their societies under socialism. They do not accept that the new elites have a monopoly of the moral high ground, since there is little evidence in either eastern or western countries that the *laissez-faire* prescriptions of those who equate the rhetoric of 'natural development' with that of 'market economy' can enable the majority of citizens to realise Havel's romantic and Utopian ideals.

Others have argued that the main distinguishing feature of the opposition to communism in Eastern Europe was its *anti-political* character. According to this view, the recent revolutions in Eastern Europe were the first in human history *not* to be concerned with establishing some form of rational Utopia. Hence the new post-communist political associations are not really like political parties at all, since the revolutions have made any kind of rational political order impossible. Instead, these societies are seen as characterised by unfettered egoism and consumerism. Only individuals exist, and they are allegedly devoid of significant human relationships. A superficial inspection of the East European scene lends some support to this analysis. In spite of multiparty elections and the vigorous promotion of market-oriented economic policies, it has not been easy to establish the rich network of associations outside of the state that comprises the essence of the romanticised western model of civil society. Sometimes this can be linked to the withdrawal of state subsidies: for example, movements such as the Young Pioneers have suffered from cuts and repression, though evidence from several countries indicates their continuing popularity among young people.

However, a model of social life as based on depoliticised, atomised individuals, attractive though it has been to some philosophers, is unlikely to be convincing to many anthropologists. The young people who no longer wear the uniforms of Pioneers are forming other relationships and networks, and sometimes they may seek support from appropriate levels of the state. The assumption of an overriding antagonism between the state and society is futile. If these terms can serve at all, the task must be to investigate their complex and continuous interactions. This certainly should not be restricted to the mapping of political opposition to authoritarian regimes. Radical opposition to socialism was restricted to small, politically conscious fragments of populations, and it should also be remembered that many of those who struggled to change communist systems did so from space they managed to find *within* the state (including its large education and research establishments).

The errors in western diagnoses of the social conditions of late socialist societies have recently become very obvious. Levels of disaffection from the new elites are typically as high or higher than before. Havel himself writes of 'the post-communist nightmare.' Some people may feel that with the demise of communism they are better able to assert, their individual rights, notably the right to own property. But for many citizens it is far from clear that their rights have been enhanced in any *substantive* way: the re-emergence of Rotary clubs is little consolation when you no longer have secure employment. ... Civil society is no longer, in the mid-1990s, the emotive slogan that it became for many East European intellectuals in the 1980s.

[T]he concept of civil society is now central to western aid programmes in Eastern Europe, linked intimately to privatisation aid. ... [T]he more elusive the realisation of civil society becomes, the more its virtues seem to be extolled in some quarters and, in the case of Eastern Europe, the more blame is piled on to communists and their predecessors for making it so difficult to replicate the conditions of western civil society in the east. Although the popularity of the term is now fading in Eastern Europe, in many other parts of the world the expansion of democracy is articulated explicitly in terms of civil society. The term has been used in basically similar ways in recent work on Latin America and sub-Saharan Africa. ... Faced with this proliferation, it can no longer suffice simply to dismiss civil society rhetoric as an extension of the cold war and the rhetoric of totalitarianism. Its obvious attractions to large numbers of people throughout the world establish a strong claim on anthropological attention. The appeal is all the more remarkable in that the dominant western model of civil society seems less conducive to social cohesion and successful economic performance than starkly opposed models of social order, such as those of East Asia. Perhaps the biggest puzzle is why so many people in the modern west have faith in this model and preach it to others, when it offers only a partial and misleading guide to the organisation of their own societies.

---

* From Chris Hann, 'Introduction: Political Society and Civil Anthropology', in Chris Hann and Elizabeth Dunn, eds, *Civil Society: Challenging Western Models* (London: Routledge, 1996), 7–10, reprinted with permission.
[1] Václav Havel, 'The Post-Communist Nightmare', *New York Review of Books*, 27 May (1993).

Leszek Kolakowski (b. 1927), Polish philosopher and analyst of Marxism in theory and practice, offers in this selection a powerful account of the difficulties involved in trying to re-establish self-identity in modern social conditions. Such attempts are likely to run into logical contradictions, with the efforts to maintain them likely to lead to considerable political horror.*

Marx ... thus took over the Hegelian distinction of civil society and the state, while denying their permanence and the necessity of their separation. The civil society is a whole mass of conflicting individual and group aspirations, empirical daily life with all its conflicts and struggles, the realm of private desires and private endeavours. To Hegel, its conflicts are rationally moderated, kept in check and synthesized in the superior will of the state, this will being independent of any particular interest. To Marx the state, at least in its present form, far from being a neutral mediator, is the tool of some particular interests disguised as the illusory universal will. Man as citizen and as private person is two different and separated beings, but only the latter, the member of the civil society, is the 'real' concrete being; as a citizen he participates in the abstract community owing its reality to ideological mystification. This mystification was unknown in mediaeval society where class division was directly expressed in the political order, i.e. the segmentation of the civil society was reflected in the political organism. Modern societies, having abrogated the direct political validity of class stratification, split social life into two realms and this division is carried over into each individual existence; it became a contradiction within every human being, torn between his status as a private person and his role as a citizen. Consequently political emancipation – in defiance of Bruno Bauer's philosophy – must not be confused with human emancipation. The former may politically cancel the differences between people in ownership or in religion, i.e. make the differences politically insignificant and thus liberate the state from religious or class distinctions (by, for example, the abolition of ownership qualifications in political activities or of legal privileges for certain denominations). This change, important though it may be, does not abrogate either religious or class division in society and allows them to keep working. It leaves untouched the separation of civil from political society; the former is still a realm of real life, egoistic and isolated for every individual, the latter provides life with collective character but only in an abstract illusory form. The aim of human – as opposed to political – emancipation is to restore to collective life its real character or to restore the collective character to civil society.

. . .

1. There is no reason to believe that the restoration of the perfect unity of the personal and communal life of every individual (i.e. the perfect, internalized

identity of each person with the social totality, lack of tension between his personal aspirations and his various social loyalties) is possible, and, least of all, that it could be secured by institutional means. Marx believed such an identity had been achieved in stagnant primitive communities. However, even if this romantic image is well founded, nothing substantiates the hope that it can be resuscitated in the predictable future: it would presuppose an unprecedented moral revolution running against the whole course of the past history of culture. To believe that a basis for such a unity may be laid down first in coercive form (i.e. the violent destruction of civil society and its replacement by the omnipotence of an oppressive state) and will grow subsequently into an internalized voluntary unity, amounts to believing that people who have been compelled to do something by fear are likely later to do the same thing willingly and cheerfully. From everything we know about human behaviour the opposite is more probable.

2. The social equivalent of this unity of person was thought of as the unity of civil and political society. This in its turn was conceived of as a community in which political power had become unnecessary. Such a community is inconceivable unless one of two conditions is fulfilled. The first: that no conflicts of interest arise between groups or individuals, so that economic management does not need to be associated with political power and public instruments of mediation or moderation are not necessary. Only if all conflicts of human interests were rooted in class division (in the Marxian sense of the word) – which is obviously not the case – could we expect this condition to be satisfied in the future. The second condition: that all decisions in public matters, however insignificant, are taken directly by the community as a whole in a democratic manner. Such a system, if practicable, would not abolish conflicts of interest (and thus would not comply with the requirements of perfect unity) but would be capable of moderating them without creating separate political bodies for this purpose. This ideal was patterned in anarchist thought upon mediaeval Swiss villages and, of course, cannot be attributed to Marx. If not for historical, then for technical reasons it is obviously impracticable in any community larger than a mediaeval Swiss village. Societies based on a universal – and still spreading – interdependence of all elements of the technological and economic structures are bound to produce separate bodies both for economic management and for mediating the conflicting aspirations of different sections, and these bodies will in turn always produce their own particular interests and loyalties.

3. The growth of the economic responsibilities of central powers is an undeniable tendency which may be noticed in different political systems. Not only is the trend towards nationalizing larger and larger segments of production, transport, trade and exchange system inevitably accompanied by the rise of bureaucracy. The same may be said about all tasks which, it is widely acknowledged should rest on the shoulders of central powers: the welfare, health and education systems, the control of wages, prices, investment

and banking, the protection of the natural environment and the exploitation of natural resources and land. It is not impossible, but it is difficult to be consistent when one fulminates at the same time against both the growth of bureaucracy and the uncontrolled wastefulness of the operation of private industry; more often than not, increasing control over private business means increasing bureaucracy. The urgent question is how society can tame its expanding bureaucracy and not how it can dispense with it. Representative democracy presupposes separate bodies with special privileges in deciding on public matters, and thus it cannot secure the ideal of the perfect unity of civil and political society. It may be said in general that representative democracy carries a great number of vices and only one virtue. All its blemishes and dangers are easily found in the Marxist literature. And its only virtue is that nobody as yet has invented anything better.

I believe that socialist thinking which is centred on its traditional topics (how to ensure for the working society more equality, more security, more welfare, more justice, more freedom, more participation in economic decision) cannot at the same time be infatuated with prospects of the perfect unity of social life. The two kinds of preoccupation run against each other. The dream of perfect unity may come true only in the form of a caricature which denies its original intention: as an artificial unity imposed by coercion from above, in that the political body prevents real conflicts and real segmentation of the civil society from expressing themselves. This body is almost mechanically compelled to crush all spontaneous forms of economic, political and cultural life and thus deepens the rift between civil and political society instead of bringing them closer to each other.

If it is asked whether this result was somehow inscribed in the original Marxian thought, the answer is certainly 'no' if 'inscribed' means 'intended'. All evidences are there to show that the primordial intention was the opposite of what grew out of it. But this primordial intention is not, as it were, innocent. It could scarcely be brought to life in a basically different form, not because of contingent historical circumstances but because of its very content.

The dream of a perfectly unified human community is probably as old as human thought about society; romantic nostalgia was only a later incarnation. This dream has been philosophically reinforced by that element in European culture which arose from neoplatonic sources. There is no reason to expect that this dream will ever be eradicated in our culture, since it has strong roots in the awareness of a split which humanity has suffered apparently from the very beginning of its existence after leaving animal innocence. And there is no reason to expect that this dream can ever become true except in the cruel form of despotism; and despotism is a desperate simulation of paradise.

*From Leszek Kolakowski, 'The Myth of Human Self-Identity: Unity of Civil and Political Society in Socialist Thought' [1974], in L. Kolakowski and S. Hampshire eds, *The Socialist Idea* (London: Weindenfeld & Nicolson, 1974), 18–20; 32–5.

Michael Walzer, American political scientist, public intellectual and permanent Fellow of the Institute of Advanced Studies (Princeton), suggests in this passage that civil society be understood as a 'project of projects', that is as nothing less than a capstone for other movements of human liberation. It is less a project on its own right than a determination to link and to perfect, through varied means, the spirit of other enterprises.*

I would rather say that the civil society argument is a corrective to the four ideological accounts of the good life – part denial, part incorporation – rather than a fifth to stand alongside them. It challenges their singularity but it has no singularity of its own. The phrase 'social being' describes men and women who are citizens, producers, consumers, members of the nation, and much else besides – and none of these by nature or because it is the best thing to be. The associational life of civil society is the actual ground where all versions of the good are worked out and tested ... and proved to be partial, incomplete, ultimately unsatisfying. It can't be the case that living on this ground is good in itself; there isn't any other place to live. What is true is that the quality of our political and economic activity and of our national culture is intimately connected to the strength and vitality of our associations.

Ideally, civil society is a setting of settings: all are included, none is preferred. The argument is a liberal version of the four answers, accepting them all, insisting that each leave room for the others, therefore not finally accepting any of them. Liberalism appears here as an anti-ideology, and this is an attractive position in the contemporary world. ... [T]his position too, so genial and benign, has its problems.

...

Here, then, is the paradox of the civil society argument. Citizenship is one of many roles that members play, but the state itself is unlike all the other associations. It both frames civil society and occupies space within it. It fixes the boundary conditions and the basic rules of all associational activity (including political activity). It compels association members to think about a common good, beyond their own conception of the good life. Even the failed impact upon the Solidarity union: it determined that Solidarity was a Polish union, focused on economic arrangements and labor policy within the borders of Poland. A democratic state, which is continuous with the other associations, has at the same time a greater say about their quality and vitality. It serves, or it doesn't serve, the needs of the associational networks as these are worked out by men and women who are simultaneously members and citizens. I shall give only a few obvious examples, drawn from American experience.

Families with working parents need state help in the form of publicly funded day care and effective public schools. National minorities need help in organizing and sustaining their own educational programs. Worker-owned companies and consumer cooperatives need state loans or loan guarantees; so do (even more often) capitalist entrepreneurs and firms. Philanthropy and mutual aid, churches and private universities, depend upon tax exemptions. Labor unions need legal recognition and guarantees against 'unfair labor practices', and professional associations need state support for their licensing procedures. And across the entire range of association, individual men and women need to be protected against the power of officials, employers, experts, party bosses, factory foremen, directors, priests, parents, patrons; and small and weak groups need to be protected against large and powerful ones. For civil society, left to itself, generates radically unequal power relationships, which only state power can challenge.

Civil society also challenges state power, most importantly when associations have resources or supporters abroad: world religions, pan-national movements, the new environmental groups, multinational corporations. We are likely to feel differently about these challenges, especially after we recognize the real but relative importance of the state. Multinational corporations, for example, need to be constrained, much like states with imperial ambitions; and the best constraint probably lies in collective security, that is, in alliances with other states that give economic regulation some international effect. The same mechanism may turn out to be useful to the new environmental groups. In the first case, the state pressures the corporation; in the second it responds to environmentalist pressure. The two cases suggest, again, that civil society requires political agency. And the state is an indispensable agent – even if the associational networks also, always, resist the organizing impulses of state bureaucrats.

Only a democratic state can create a democratic civil society; only a democratic civil society can sustain a democratic state. The civility that makes democratic politics possible can only be learned in the associational networks; the roughly equal and widely dispersed capabilities that sustain the networks have to be fostered by the democratic state. Confronted with an overbearing state, citizens, who are also members, will struggle to make room for autonomous associations and market relationships (and also for local governments and decentralized bureaucracies). But the state can never be what it appears to be in liberal theory, a mere framework for civil society. It is also the instrument of the struggle, used to give a particular shape to the common life. Hence citizenship has a certain practical preeminence among all our actual and possible memberships. That's not to say that we must be citizens all the time, finding in politics, as Rousseau urged, the greater part of our happiness. Most of us will be happier elsewhere, involved only sometimes in affairs of state. But we must leave the state open to our sometime involvement.

Nor need we be involved all the time in our associations. A democratic civil society is one controlled by its members, not through a single process of self-determination but through a large number of different and uncoordinated processes. These needn't all be democratic, for we are likely to be members of many associations, and we, will want some of them to be managed in our interests, but also in our absence. Civil society is sufficiently democratic when in at least some of its parts we are able to recognize ourselves as authoritative and responsible participants. States are tested by their capacity to sustain this kind of participation – which is very different from the heroic intensity of Rousseauian citizenship. And civil society is tested by its capacity to produce citizens whose interests, at least sometimes, reach farther than themselves and their comrades, who look after the political community that fosters and protects the associational networks.

I mean to defend a perspective that might be called, awkwardly, 'critical associationalism.' I want to join, but I am somewhat uneasy with, the civil society argument. It can't be said that nothing is lost when we give up the singlemindedness of democratic citizenship or socialist cooperation or individual autonomy or national identity. There was a kind of heroism in those projects – a concentration of energy, a clear sense of direction, an unblinking recognition of friends and enemies. To make one of these one's own was a serious commitment. The defense of civil society doesn't seem quite comparable. Associational engagement is conceivably as important a project as any of the others, but its greatest virtue lies in its inclusiveness, and inclusiveness does not make for heroism. 'Join the associations of your choice' is not a slogan to rally political militants. And yet that is what civil society requires: men and women actively engaged – in state, economy, and nation, and also in churches, neighborhoods, and families, and in many other settings too. To reach this goal is not as easy as it sounds; many people, perhaps most people live very loosely within the networks, and a growing number of people seem to be radically disengaged – passive clients of the state, market dropouts, resentful and posturing nationalists. And the civil society project doesn't confront an energizing hostility, as all the others do; its protagonists are more likely to meet sullen indifference, fear, despair, apathy, and withdrawal.

. . .

The civil society project can only be described in terms of all the other projects, against their singularity. Hence my account in these pages, which suggests the need (1) to decentralize the state so that there are more opportunities for citizens to take responsibility for (some of) its activities; (2) to socialize the economy so that there is a greater diversity of market agents, communal as well as private; and (3) to pluralize and domesticate nationalism, on the religious model, so that there are different ways to realize and sustain historical identities.

None of this can be accomplished without using political power to redistribute resources and to underwrite and subsidize the most desirable associational activities. But political power alone cannot accomplish any of it. The kinds of 'action' discussed by theorists of the state need to be supplemented (not, however, replaced) by something radically different: more like union organizing than political mobilization, more like teaching in a school than arguing in the assembly, more like volunteering in a hospital than joining a political party, more like working in an ethnic alliance or a feminist support group than canvassing in an election.

...

Most men and women have been trapped in one or another subordinate relationship, where the 'civility' they learned was deferential rather than independent and active. That is why democratic citizenship, socialist production, free enterprise, and nationalism were all liberating projects. But none of them has yet produced a general, coherent, or sustainable liberation. ... The projects have to be revatilized and brought together, and the place to do that is in civil society, the setting of settings, where each can find the partial fulfillment that is all it deserves.

Civil society itself is sustained by groups much smaller than the demos or the working class or the mass of consumers or the nation. All these are necessarily fragmented and localized as they are incorporated. They become part of the world of family, friends, comrades, and colleagues, where people are connected to one another and made responsible for one another. ... Civil society is a project of projects; it requires many organizing strategies and new forms of state action. It requires a new sensitivity for what is local, specific, contingent – and, above all, a new recognition (to paraphrase a famous sentence) that the good life is in the details.

* From Michael Walzer, ed., *Toward a Global Civil Society* (Berghahn Books: Oxford and New York, 1995), pp. 16–27; Walzer's article first appeared in *Dissent*, spring 1991, reprinted with permission.

The Madres de Plaza de Mayo *or Mothers of the Disappeared protested against the military regime in Argentina (1976–83), a period when thousands of people disappeared without a trace. The interviews here were taken by Jo Fisher in 1985 and 1987 and reveal the symbolic and emotional workings of solidarity in this informal social movement.**

Dora de Bazze: Our first problem was how we were going to organize meetings if we didn't know each other. There were so many police and security men everywhere that you never knew who was standing next to you. It was very dangerous. So we carried different things so we could identify each other. For example one would hold a twig in her hand, one might carry a small purse instead of a handbag, one would pin a leaf to her lapel, anything to let us know this was a Mother. We used to go to the square and sit on the benches with our knitting or stroll about, whispering messages to each other and trying to discuss what else we could do.

Sometimes we met in churches. Most of us were very religious. At that time I was a believer too, so we went to the churches to pray together, 'Our Father. ...' and at the same time we would be passing round tiny pieces of folded paper, like when you're in school, cheating in a test. Then we hid them in the hems of our skirts in case we were searched later. Only the smallest churches, a long way out, lost in the middle of nowhere, would let us in. The rest closed their doors when they found out we were Mothers.

We tried to produce leaflets as well – we had to do it secretly because it was illegal of course – and little stickers saying the Mothers will be in such and such a place on such and such a day and *'¿Dónde están nuestros hijos desaparecidos?'* [Where are our disappeared children?] or *'Los militares se han llevado nuestros hijos'* [The military have taken our children]. We went out at night to stick them on the buses and underground trains. And we wrote messages on peso notes so that as many people as possible would see them. This was the only way we could let people know that our children had been taken, and what the military government was doing, because when you told them they always said, 'They must have done something.' There was nothing in the newspapers; if a journalist reported us, he disappeared; the television and radio were completely under military control, so people weren't conscious. In the beginning we had no support at all. ...

Aída de Suárez: The headscarves grew out of an idea of our dear Azucena. It was at the time when thousands of people walked to Lujan on the annual pilgrimage to pay homage to the Virgin. We decided to join the march in 1977 because many of us were religious and also because we thought it would be a chance for us to talk to each other and organize things. But as some of the Mothers were elderly and wouldn't be able to walk, and we would all be coming from different places, we thought, how will we be able to identify each other amongst all those people, because many thousands go, and how can we make other people notice us? Azucena's idea was to wear as a head scarf one of our children's nappies, because every mother keeps something like this, which belonged to your child as a baby. It was very easy to spot the headscarves in the crowds and people came up to us and asked us who we were. We'd managed to attract attention so we decided to use the scarves at other meetings and then every time we went to Plaza de Mayo together. We all made proper white scarves and we embroidered on the names of our children. Afterwards we put on them *'Aparición con Vida'* [literally 'Reappearance with life'] because we were no longer searching for just one child but for all the disappeared.

We used to go to the military regiments together to look for other women like us. The only way we could communicate was by word of mouth and we had to find a way to find other women, not just in Buenos Aires but women from all over the country. The press was silent. The only one which ever wrote anything about us was the English one, the [*Buenos Aires*] *Herald*. I went to ask for information at the *Herald*'s offices many times. It was very dangerous for journalists to show any interest in us.

. . .

Hebe de Bonafini: To me the Mothers are women who have broken with many aspects of this system we live in. First, because we went to the Streets to confront the dictatorship, because we were capable of doing things that men couldn't do. We've broken with the system because we aren't a political party and yet we still have political influence. We continue in the same way as before. I think this is what's difficult to understand. We are listened to much more than if we had become a political party. I think that without being a political party we have a political line, not party political, but we have a political line which is resolute. Without wanting to be deputies or senators, we are the opposition to the government, the opposition this country doesn't have.

We're always invited to speak at conferences, to open meetings. We are supported by a lot of people in the world. We have lots of groups of young people who come here to help us with our campaigns. The groups in solidarity with the *Madres de Plaza de Mayo* are growing inside and outside the country and they have to support whatever we are doing, things that sometimes seem crazy, like covering Government House with headscarves to show we are a barrier against injustice and the military '*no pasarán*'.[1] It's a very different way of fighting but it's a way which has influenced women in Uruguay, Chile, Colombia, El Salvador and in all the countries where there are *desaparecidos*. I believe that every country should find its own form of struggle to suit its situation. We have built our own defences and antibodies to defend ourselves against our enemies.

I think we are an organization fighting for life and freedom. The fight for life isn't just about words. The words 'peace', 'freedom', 'human rights' are so over-used that they've become dead words. We have learnt that in reality, life and peace and freedom are rarely defended in this world. We try to share with people what we have learnt over these ten years, what the streets and the struggle have taught us, which is to defend life, even with our own lives if necessary.

I don't think the Mothers are feminists, but we point away forward for the liberation of women. We support the struggle of women against this *machista* world and sometimes this means we have to fight against men. But we also have to work together with men to change this society. We aren't feminists because I think feminism, when it's taken too far, is the same as, *machismo.* So yes, we want to say that we agree that women should have the same place as men, not above or below, but equal, and we have pointed a very clear way forward to this. I think we have also raised some new possibilities for women, the most important of which is the possibility of the socialization of motherhood. This is something very new.

The woman I was before gave me the preparation, the maternal feelings and the tenderness to be the woman I am today, because in spite of the fact that I'm a very tough person, some people say like a 'warm rock', we never separate our feelings, our tenderness, the human part, from the politics. I believe this is very important. It's there the 'two women' come together: this 'warm rock' that they say I am today and the tenderness of having been a mother and of having been brought up in a small working-class community, which I believe is a beautiful thing which few people can experience now.

I've always had to continue with the housework, to wash, iron, cook, clean. I'm not a rich person. Now I live alone with my daughter and we continue doing these things. I believe the most difficult thing is to continue being the person you've always been and to keep your feet on the ground. I cook here for everyone. For me cooking for twenty is the same as cooking for one, and we like to eat together because this is also a part of our struggle and our militancy. I want to continue being the person I've always been. Sometimes I'm criticized for wearing a housecoat and slippers in public but I'm not going to change. Of course my life is different. I still receive threats, I'm still followed. That's always in the background, but the other thing is much more powerful, what you have to do for those who are not here.

We're going to continue in the same way because we still haven't got justice. They've tried to convert us into the mothers of dead children and put an end to the problem of the *desaparecidos.* We will never accept they are dead until those responsible are punished. If we accepted that, we would be accepting that murderers and torturers can live freely in Argentina. They can't negotiate with the blood of our children. The *Madres de Plaza de Mayo* are never going to permit that.

---

*From Jo Fisher, *Mothers of the Disappeared* (Boston: South End Press, 1989), 53–4; 157–8.

[1] To mark the tenth anniversary of the Mothers' first meeting in Plaza de Mayo white headscarved signed by supporters from all over the world were hung around the square. *'No pasarán'* (They will not pass) is the slogan used by Nicaraguan supporters of the Sandinista gouvernment.

Gerhard Ruden, East German dissident. A construction engineer by training, he became drawn into political activities through the Protestant church. This excerpt gives an account of the political education and opposition of an average citizen in socialist East Germany.*

My political activities started within the realm of the church. I am a Protestant Christian. Since about 1979 our pastor began to talk about problems concerning the environment, and I quickly became very interested in that particular topic. We started with little things, riding a bike instead of taking the car, or collecting household garbage. But we also debated the more global aspects of these problems.

The other important problem, of course, had to do with the accelerating arms race. We organized meetings, seminars, and things of that kind in the Sankt Michaels parish.

. . .

Our first activities were not very spectacular. Initially, we merely tried to enter some kind of communication process with the official state organs, such as representatives of the district council, of the city council, or of the factories. We actually managed to initiate dialogue with representatives of one plant that was particularly interesting to us: the Energie Kombinat, the plant that was mainly involved in building the nuclear reactor near Magdeburg. We basically attempted to convince them that nuclear energy was too dangerous to pursue. Of course, this was perhaps a bit naive on our part, but we thought it was worth a try. . . .

The next thing we organized was a seminar on human rights issues [in 1988], which was a pretty spectacular event at the time. We mainly discussed criminal justice procedures in the GDR. Actually, we wanted to write an alternative criminal law, but we ran out of energy and time. The revolution, you see, sort of got in our way [laughing]. . . .

. . .

How many people were active in your group?

Actually, not all that many, about 12 who regularly showed up. But out of those 12, only four or so were really active, organizing events, writing petitions, and such. . . . It just required a lot of courage. Like when we wrote a letter to Honecker – to sign something like that took some guts. The fear among the population in the GDR was so strong, and so pervasive, that people sometimes asked me in utter astonishment, 'How can you dare to do that?' . . .

In one letter we wrote to Honecker we accused him of always saying the same thing in his annual New Year addresses, of always making the same promises without ever doing anything to live up to them. Not surprisingly, we routinely got replies from some of his cronies that said absolutely nothing – replies that inadvertently supported our underlying point, of course. . . .

The last large event that took place before the revolution had to do with the local elections in May of 1989.

Grass-roots activists in virtually every city in the GDR had organized something on the occasion of this election. How did that happen? Was there some sort of nationwide plan, or at least some communication throughout the country?

No, unfortunately we did not manage to pull that off. It was certainly what many of us had hoped for. I think at the next election we would have succeeded in coordinating our efforts nationwide, in finding a GDR-wide strategy of how best to push the state to its limits. . . . A long time before the elections, in the fall of 1988, we had already written letters to the party district leadership concerning the next elections. Actually, it was a letter of demands. At that time we had already stopped requesting things politely. After all, if one did that, nothing ever happened anyway.

I remember that throughout 1988 we had an ongoing discussion about how best to write letters to the authorities, how best to obtain a positive result without getting creamed. Should we continue to write these rather submissive 'shake hands' letters, or should we be a little more forceful? We reached the conclusion that we had offered our cooperation long enough; now it was time to make demands, to demand those basic civil rights that one should actually be able to take for granted anyway.

So in the fall of 1988 we stated very clearly 'we demand closeable voting booths; we demand that the party of a given candidate is written right next to the name of the candidate; we demand that the name of this candidate has to be marked,' that is, active voting rather than the usual passive voting [where one only crossed out the names of the candidates one did not want to be elected].

After that, we were invited to the district leadership. We were greeted by the secretary of the district leader. . . . He approached us in a very rough, 'class-struggle' kind of fashion. Obviously, he wanted to impress us, to influence us, to force us to reconsider our position. He came straight out saying, 'The primary goal is to maintain the power of the working class. You can say about that whatever you want,' he told us, 'but the question of power has been resolved in the GDR by the working class and its representative, the Socialist Unity Party.' It's incredible how they talked to you.

In any case, shortly before we were about to leave again, I casually remarked to him, 'You know, I am not as uptight as you seem to be about this question of who holds power. The SED has held power for forty years now. Might it not be time to give someone else a chance?' Wow, talk about uptight, his reaction was more than just uptight. They began to exert all sorts of pressure, not only on me, but also on the firm where I was currently employed, and, of course, on the church. For instance, they told members of my parish that 'the person who runs the peace group in your parish, Mr. Ruden, plays a very subversive role in this group. He tries to exploit it for his goal of undermining the power of the working class.'

After that, they scheduled another meeting, not only with me, but also with my employer and the church leadership, with the obvious purpose of reprimanding me severely and, ultimately, silencing me. They talked down to us, or rather yelled down to us, just like the security police. To their utter dismay, however, most of the others they had summoned supported me, and thus there was not much they could do to me after all.

. . .

But, however much our activity upset the party, there is also no question that all these grass-roots groups caused quite a few stomachaches for the church hierarchy over the years. Nevertheless, during this local election they, too, realized that they should support us, that there were extremely good and competent people in their ranks who had drafted these election complaints, and who had organized all the protests as a result of the blatant election fraud we had revealed. Somehow the church had to realize that we had gotten more done than they had, despite the fact that they had all those experts, lawyers, and such, and we were just self-organized small groups with no funds, little support – little of anything, in fact. We were the ones who put our fingers right on all those blatant injustices, who came right out and dared to call a spade a spade.

You see, the state and party people did not stop at violating their own laws. The way they had prepared the elections was not right, the way the actual election process took place was full of violations, and on top of that they had obstructed our rightful attempts to oversee the election process. They actually kicked us out of most of the polling places. ...

So, they had undermined themselves to such an extent that they could not, logically, prevail in a conversation with us, no matter how they tried to cloak it in the language of class struggle. They were bankrupt.

* From Dirk Philipsen, *We Were the People: Voices from East Germany's Revolutionary Autumn of 1989* (Durham: Duke University Press, © 1993), 167; 169–71, reprinted with permission of Duke University Press.

*Pierre Rosanvallon was born in 1948. Initially an adviser to the French trade union CFDT in the 1970s, he became Director of France's l'École des Hautes Etudes en Sciences Sociales. A leading social and political thinker, he here focuses on the decline of social visibility in Western welfare states, a critique that shifted attention to alternative more civil-society based systems of assistance.**

The welfare state is a way of reintroducing an economic element into the sphere of the social by correcting and compensating for the effects of the market. The crisis afflicting this state derives principally from the way economic considerations were asserted, rather than from the economic principles *per se*. The machinery for engendering mutual support has become abstract, formal and diffuse. The development of bureaucratic practices and the growing burden of social regulation are fed by this abstraction and in turn reinforce it; hence the relative drop in their efficacy. As a means of reconciling social and economic factors, the welfare-state principle ends up operating in an excessively remote fashion. Increasingly, it towers above society; the gap it has created between the individual and the social sphere is now too great.

How can it be remedied? There is no other course possible but to bring society close to itself. There must be an effort to fill out society, to increase its density by creating more and more intermediate locations fulfilling social functions, and by encouraging individual involvement in networks of direct mutual support. The welfare state derives essentially from an inadequate reading of social geography. It disregards its patterns of closeness or remoteness, dissemination or agglomeration. However, mechanisms of distribution and the supply of collective services are affected by the spatial structures of the social sphere. The situation of individuals cannot be understood independently of their location in social space. Poverty, for instance, cannot be defined entirely in terms of income. The degree of people's isolation and their location (town or country) can exacerbate the effects of low income. An individual who receives a minimum state pension but has a kitchen garden and enjoys close family and neighbourhood ties has a different standard of living from someone living cut off in a sixth-floor city flat.

What is meant by 'filling out' society? At the outset, it is necessary to clear away a fundamental misconception. This concerns the utopia of 'community': the formation of small groups in which individuals would constitute a sort of extended family on a virtually self-sufficient basis. What is striking about this utopia is that it conceives the alternative to the society of market relations, individualism and desocialization in the nostalgic terms of a return to the community form.

The methodological distinction between the organic community and the individualistic society, considered as sociological ideal-types, is here transformed into a value judgement. The problem becomes that of rediscovering the 'good' community, as opposed to the 'bad' society. Logically associated with this value judgement is a veritable historical mythology concerning the evolution of family structures. From Bonald to Le Play, traditionalist 'sociology' sought to construct an imaginary object: the extended patriarchal family as a vast grouping of solidarity among the generations. Not until the research by Philippe Ariès did we discover that 'the often described theoretical evolution of the extended family into the nuclear family has no basis in reality.' It is therefore impossible to *return* to a form of extended family. Although, broadly speaking, the accession of the individual has been the central characteristic of modernity, this does not mean it can be condemned as negative and made to serve as the basis for overhasty historical reconstructions. The transition from *Gemeinschaft* to *Gesellschaft* did not entail the transformation of generous mutual support into widespread egoism.

On the contrary, Gesellschaft evolved precisely because it seemed a formidable instrument of emancipation. The city always meant both the marketplace and a domain of freedom. It encouraged greater freedom by extending the bounds of the possible: deterritorializing individuals by making them independent of the land to which they had been previously assigned, thereby saving them from the repetitive and stifling circle of a circumscribed universe. Throughout the nineteenth century, the emancipatory nature of the town was asserted again and again. This phenomenon still applies. It would be an illusion to think that it is now finished. On the contrary, there is evidence everywhere that the demand for independence that typifies our culture is still a vital factor. Women's growing involvement in employment is a sign of this. Their entry into the labour market is the precondition for greater independence, despite the implicit exploitation. We are only just detecting the first signs of a new revolution: children's desire for independence from their parents. There is even a movement in Sweden that demands the right of children to 'divorce' their parents (financial independence being asserted as a right)!

The failure of the various communitarian experiments in the 1960s and 1970s is linked to the extraordinary power of this aspiration for autonomy and independence. It cannot be ignored when defining an alternative to the welfare state. The goal of closer relations within society cannot be achieved by means of nostalgic and backward-looking scenarios. It is pointless to dream of a renewed 'hearth and home' as a counterbalance to market-based socialization. How otherwise are we to reconcile the emergence of new non-state forms of mutual support with the desire for autonomy?

It is important to stress that there can be no *theoretical* response to this question. It is not necessary to define a sociological ideal-type that would be neither community nor society: to imagine a social 'model' between holism and individualism, as Louis Dumont puts it. The formulation of a social policy is not something to be confused with the definition of a sociological concept. The 'sociohistorical' is never a pure expression of an ideal-type; it is always a complex and tangled reality which the sociologist seeks to unravel. In any event, the welfare state would have failed long ago if society were in fact as it is represented ideal-typically: merely a collection of individuals, forever fragmented in a radical way. The only reason our society functions is because it actually contradicts – albeit partially and to a limited degree – the individualist schema through which it is represented. For instance a number of sociologists, such as Agnès Pitrou, have demonstrated the existence of underground networks of family solidarity, whose economic importance would seem to be much greater than is often supposed. The growth of underground economy within the present crisis is also partly an expression of this capacity of the social fabric to engender within itself ways of resisting external shocks. While these various hidden 'shock absorbers' – all too rarely taken into account by economists or sociologists – no longer suffice, it is essential to recognize their existence, because without them the state intervention requirement would have been still greater. The alternative to the welfare state consists in appreciating their role and encouraging their extension.

It is precisely all these various forms of transversal socialism – from formal associations to informal co-operative initiatives for supplying service – that can help make mutual support once more the affair of society. The growth of such 'sociability' depends on the immediate term on increased free time. Lack of free time and social rigidity, in fact, go hand in hand. The less free time individuals enjoy, the greater are the demands they make on the state and the more they dependent on the market. The can involve themselves in mutual support initiatives, extend their neighbourhood ties and establish various kinds of *ad hoc* solidarity only if they have the time to do so. From this perspective, reducing working hours is not just an economic argument for cutting unemployment; it is also a condition of learning new forms of life. Such promotion of closer ties within society should not, however, be viewed in the narrow sense of setting up stable, closed microcommunities. What is rather required is a multiplicity of temporary or limited associations – a type of multisocialization, whose pluralism of forms of sociability is by no means a constraint upon liberty, but instead an extension of each individual's freedom.

. . .

If the social sphere were to become more visible and capable of recognizing itself this would encourage the establishment of more genuine relations of mutual assistance, even if the procedures governing them would be more conflict-prone. Today an opposite trend prevails, in which the entire machinery of social contributions is becoming increasingly invisible. The welfare state is operating within a fog, so to speak. Few wage-earners have any idea how much is deducted from their pay in real terms (the notion of gross wages meaning nothing either to the enterprise or to the employee). Value added tax, which accounts for about half of the revenues collected, is a 'painless' tax whose size is not appreciated by the consumer; only personal income tax allows those concerned to see clearly how much they are paying. It is no longer possible for individuals to discern the connection between individual deductions and the social uses to which they are put. The result is a universal lack of responsibility.

The only way for the welfare state to become better accepted is to make its machinery operate explicitly for everyone. Obviously there are risks involved in such greater truthfulness. It calls for recognition of the realities normal macrosociological concepts usually suppress or ignore: side benefits, the extreme heterogeneity of the wage system, and disparities in taxation. Greater visibility has its price. It can engender tensions and conflicts. The difficulties inherent in face-to-face encounters between individuals and groups are illustrated in publicizing salaries, wages or taxation contributions.

A totally visible society, in which everyone would live under the gaze of everyone else, would be intolerable. Girard (in *La Violence et le sacré*) has shown clearly how societies have a need to produce mechanisms for limiting the explosive effects produced by radically confrontational situations. But we run no risk of that at the present time – far from it, in fact. After all, what is more natural than the sort of tension created by living together, a tension of which class struggle is only one manifestation? Surely that is the function of democracy: to provide scope for the expression and treatment of this difficulty, of which the existence of opposing political parties is the sign? Conflict and society are inseparable terms. The acceptance of conflict lies at the heart of the process of the self-production of the social. Far from denying or ignoring conflict under the guise of an improbable 'consensus', the democratic ideal makes such conflict productive and constructive. In this sense, social visibility and the growth of democracy go hand in hand.

*From Pierre Rosanvallon, 'The Decline of Social Visibility', in John Keane, ed., *Civil Society and the State: New European Perspectives* (London: Verso, 1988), 206–9; 211–12, reprinted with permission.

*Jürgen Habermas (born 1929), a leading German public thinker and proponent of the critical tradition of the Frankfurt School. Habermas is best known for developing a discourse ethics. Here he presents a view on the practice of communication in civil society and its relationship to political society.**

This sphere of civil society has been rediscovered today, in wholly new historical constellations. The expression 'civil society' has in the meantime taken on a meaning different from that of the 'bourgeois society' of the liberal tradition, which Hegel conceptualized as a 'system of needs,' that is, as a market system involving social labor and commodity exchange. What is meant by 'civil society' today, in contrast to its usage in the Marxist tradition, no longer includes the economy as constituted by private law and steered through markets in labor, capital, and commodities. Rather, its institutional core comprises those nongovernmental and noneconomic connections and voluntary associations that anchor the communication structures of the public sphere in the society component of the lifeworld. Civil society is composed of those more or less spontaneously emergent associations, organizations, and movements that, attuned to how societal problems resonate in the private life spheres, distill and transmit such reactions in amplified form to the public sphere. The core of civil society comprises a network of associations that institutionalizes problem-solving discourses on questions of general interest inside the framework of organized public spheres. These 'discursive designs' have an egalitarian, open form of organization that mirrors essential features of the kind of communication around which they crystallize and to which they lend continuity and permanence.

Such associations certainly do not represent the most conspicuous element of a public sphere dominated by mass media and large agencies, observed by market and opinion research, and inundated by the public relations work, propaganda, and advertising of political parties and groups. All the same, they do form the organizational substratum of the general public of citizens. More or less emerging from the private sphere, this public is made of citizens who seek acceptable interpretations for their social interests and experiences and who want to have an influence on institutionalized opinion- and will-formation.

. . .

The political system which must remain sensitive to the influence of public opinion, is intertwined with the public sphere and civil society through the activity of political parties and general elections. This intermeshing is guaranteed by the right of parties to 'collaborate' in the political will-formation of the people, as well as by the citizens' active and passive voting rights and other participatory rights. Finally, the network of associations can assert its autonomy and preserve its spontaneity only insofar as it can draw support from a mature pluralism of forms of life, subcultures, and worldviews. The constitutional protection of 'privacy' promotes the integrity of private life spheres: rights of personality, freedom of belief and of conscience, freedom of movement, the privacy of letters, mail, and telecommunications, the inviolability of one's residence, and the protection of families circumscribe an untouchable zone of personal integrity and independent judgment.

The tight connection between an autonomous civil society and an integral private sphere stands out even more clearly when contrasted with totalitarian societies of bureaucratic socialism. Here a panoptic state not only directly controls the bureaucratically desiccated public sphere, it also undermines the private basis of this public sphere.

. . .

Basic constitutional guarantees alone, of course, cannot preserve the public sphere and civil society from deformations. The communication structures of the public sphere must rather be kept intact by an energetic civil society. That the political public sphere must in a certain sense reproduce and stabilize itself from its own resources is shown by the odd *self-referential character of the practice of communication in civil society*. Those actors who are the carriers of the public sphere put forward 'texts' that always reveal the same subtext, which refers to the critical function of the public sphere in general. Whatever the manifest content of their public utterances, the performative meaning of such public discourse at the same time actualizes the function of an undistorted political public sphere as such. Thus, the institutions and legal guarantees of free and open opinion-formation rest on the unsteady ground of the political communication of actors who, in making use of them, at the same time interpret, defend, and radicalize their normative content. Actors who know they are involved in the *common* enterprise of reconstituting and maintaining structures of the public sphere as they contest opinions and strive for influence differ from actors who merely use forums that already exist. More specifically, actors who support the public sphere are distinguished by the *dual orientation* of their political engagement: with their programs, they directly influence the political system, but at the same time they are also reflexively concerned with revitalizing and enlarging civil society and the public sphere as well as with confirming their own identities and capacities to act.

. . .

In fact, the *interplay* of a public sphere based in civil society with the opinion – and will-formation institutionalized in parliamentary bodies and courts offers a good starting point for translating the concept of deliberative politics into sociological terms. However, we must not look on civil society as a focal point where the lines of societal self-organization as a whole would converge.

. . .

The self-limitation of civil society should not be understood as incapacitation. The knowledge required for political supervision or steering, a knowledge that in complex societies represents a resource as scarce as it is desirable, can certainly become the source of a new systems paternalism. But because the administration does not, for the most part, itself produce the relevant knowledge but draws it from the knowledge system or other intermediaries, it does not enjoy a natural monopoly on such knowledge. In spite of asymmetrical access to expertise and limited problem-solving capacities, civil society also has the opportunity of mobilizing counterknowledge and drawing on the pertinent forms of expertise to make *its own* translations. Even though the public consists of laypersons and communicates with ordinary language, this does not necessarily imply an inability to differentiate the essential questions and reasons for decisions. This can serve as a pretext for a technocratic incapacitation of the public sphere only as long as the political initiatives of civil society fail to provide sufficient expert knowledge along with appropriate and, if necessary, multi-level translations in regard to the managerial aspects of public issues.

The concepts of the political public sphere and civil society introduced above are not mere normative postulates but have empirical relevance. However, additional assumptions must be introduced if we are to use these concepts to translate the discourse-theoretic reading of radical democracy into sociological terms and reformulate it in an empirically falsifiable manner. I would like to defend the claim that *under certain circumstances* civil society can acquire influence in the public sphere, have an effect on the parliamentary complex (and the courts) through its own public opinions, and compel the political system to switch over to the official circulation of power. Naturally, the sociology of mass communication conveys a skeptical impression of the power-ridden, mass-media-dominated public spheres of Western democracies. Social movements, citizen initiatives and forums, political and other associations, in short, the groupings of civil society, are indeed sensitive to problems, but the signals they send out and the impulses they give are generally too weak to initiate learning processes or redirect decision making in the political system in the short run.

. . .

The political system is vulnerable on both sides to disturbances that can reduce the *effectiveness* of its achievements and the *legitimacy* of its decisions, respectively. The regulatory competence of the political system fails if the implemented legal programs remain ineffective or if regulatory activity gives rise to disintegrating effects in the action systems that require regulation. Failure also occurs if the instruments deployed overtax the legal medium itself and strain the normative composition of the political system. As steering problems become more complex, irrelevance, misguided regulations, and self-destruction can accumulate to the point where a 'regulatory trilemma' results. On the other side, the political system fails as a guardian of social integration if its decisions, even though effective, can no longer be traced back to legitimate law, The constitutionally regulated circulation of power is nullified if the administrative system becomes independent of communicatively generated power, if the social power of functional systems and large organizations (including the mass media) is converted into illegitimate power, or if the lifeworld resources for spontaneous public communication no longer suffice to guarantee an uncoerced articulation of social interests.

The independence of illegitimate power, together with the weakness of civil society and the public sphere, can deteriorate into a 'legitimation dilemma,' which in certain circumstances can combine with the steering trilemma and develop into a vicious circle. Then the political system is pulled into the whirlpool of legitimation deficits and steering deficits that reinforce one another.

* From Jürgen Habermas, *Between Facts and Norms: Contributions to a Discourse Theory of Law and Democracy*, translated by William Regh (Cambridge: Polity Press, 1996; orig. German edn. 1992), 366–71; 385–6, reprinted with permission.

6
Contemporary Debates

Communitarian controversies

Robert Putnam (born 1941) is Professor of Public Policy at Harvard University.
Here, he seeks to find the reason behind the steady decline in civic engagement in
the United States since the 1960s, and focuses on television as being the 'culprit'.*

I have been wrestling with a difficult mystery...concern[ing] the strange
disappearance of social capital and civic engagement in America. By 'social
capital' I mean features of social life – networks, norms, and trust – that enable
participants to act together more effectively to pursue shared objectives.... I
use the term 'civic engagement' to refer to people's connections with the
life of their communities, not only with politics.

...

Beginning with those born in the last third of the nineteenth century
and continuing to the generation of their great-grandchildren, born in the
last third of the twentieth century, we find relatively high and unevenly
rising levels of civic engagement and social trust. Then rather abruptly we
encounter signs of reduced community involvement, starting with men
and women born in the early 1930s. Remarkably, this downward trend in
joining, trusting, voting, and newspaper reading continues almost uninter-
ruptedly for nearly 40 years. The trajectories for the various different indicators
of civic engagement are strikingly parallel: Each shows a high, sometimes
rising plateau for people born and raised during the first third of the
century; each shows a turning point in the cohorts around 1930; and each
then shows a more or less constant decline down to the cohorts born
during the 1960s.

...

[T]he most parsimonious interpretation of the age-related differences in civic engagement is that they represent a powerful reduction in civic engagement among Americans who came of age in the decades after World War II, as well as some modest additional disengagement that affected all cohorts during the 1980s. These patterns hint that being raised after World War II was a quite different experience from being raised before that watershed. It is as though the postwar generations were exposed to some mysterious X-ray that permanently and increasingly rendered them less likely to connect with the community. Whatever that force might have been, it – rather than anything that happened during the 1970s and 1980s – accounts for most of the civic disengagement that lies at the core of our mystery.

But if this reinterpretation of our puzzle is correct, why did it take so long for the effects of that mysterious X-ray to become manifest? If the underlying causes of civic disengagement can be traced to the 1940s and 1950s, why did the effects become conspicuous in PTA meetings and Masonic lodges, in the volunteer lists of the Red Cross and the Boy Scouts, and in polling stations and church pews and bowling alleys across the land only during the 1960s, 1970s, and 1980s?

The visible effects of this generational disengagement were delayed by two important factors. First, the postwar boom in college enrollments raised levels of civic engagement, offsetting the generational trends. As Warren E. Miller and J. Merrill Shanks observe in their as yet unpublished book *The American Voter Reconsidered* [*The New American Voter*, 1996], the postwar expansion of educational opportunities 'forestalled a cataclysmic drop' in voting turnout, and it had a similar delaying effect on civic disengagement more generally.

Second, the full effects of generational developments generally appear several decades after their onset, because it takes that long for a given generation to become numerically dominant in the adult population. Only after the mid-1960s did significant numbers of the 'post-civic generation' reach adulthood, supplanting older, more civic cohorts. The long civic generation born between 1910 and 1940 reached its zenith in 1960, when it comprised 62 percent of those who chose between John Kennedy and Richard Nixon. By the time that Bill Clinton was elected president in 1992, that cohort's share in the electorate had been cut precisely in half. Conversely, over the last two decades (from 1974 to 1994) boomers and X-ers (that is, Americans born after 1946) have grown as a fraction of the adult population from 24 percent to 60 percent.

In short, the very decades that have seen a national deterioration in social capital are the same decades during which the numerical dominance of a trusting and civic generation has been replaced by the dominion of 'post-civic' cohorts. Moreover, although the long civic generation has enjoyed unprecedented life expectancy, allowing its members to contribute more than their share to American social capital in recent decades, they are now passing from the scene. Even the youngest members of that generation will reach retirement age within the next few years. Thus, a generational analysis leads almost inevitably to the conclusion that the national slump in trust and engagement is likely to continue, regardless of whether the more modest 'period effect' depression of the 1980s continues.

Our Prime Suspect

To say that civic disengagement in contemporary America is in large measure generational merely reformulates our central puzzle. We now know that much of the cause of our lonely bowling probably dates to the 1940s and 1950s, rather than to the 1960s and 1970s. What could have been the mysterious anticivic 'X-ray' that affected Americans who came of age after World War II and whose effects progressively deepened at least into the 1970s?

Our new formulation of the puzzle opens the possibility that the zeitgeist of national unity, patriotism, and shared sacrifice that culminated in 1945 might have reinforced civic-mindedness. On the other hand, it is hard to assign any consistent role to the Cold War and the Bomb, since the anticivic trend appears to have deepened steadily from the 1940s to the 1970s, in no obvious harmony with the rhythms of world affairs. Nor is it easy to construct an interpretation of the data on generational differences in which the cultural vicissitudes of the sixties could play a significant role. Neither can economic adversity or affluence easily be tied to the generational decline in civic engagement, since the slump seems to have affected in equal measure those who came of age in the placid fifties, the booming sixties, and the busted seventies.

I have discovered only one prominent suspect against whom circumstantial evidence can be mounted, and in this case, it turns out, some directly incriminating evidence has also turned up. ...

The culprit is television.

First, the timing fits. The long civic generation was the last cohort of Americans to grow up without television, for television flashed into American society like lightning in the 1950s. In 1950 barely 10 percent of American homes had television sets, but by 1959, 90 percent did, probably the fastest diffusion of a major technological innovation ever recorded. The reverberations from this lightning bolt continued for decades, as viewing hours grew by 17–20 percent during the 1960s and by an additional 7–8 percent during the 1970s. In the early years, TV watching was concentrated among the less educated sectors of the population, but during the 1970s the viewing time of the more educated sectors of the population began to converge upward. Television viewing increases with age, particularly upon retirement, but each generation since the introduction of television has begun its life cycle at a higher starting point. By 1995 viewing per TV household was more than 50 percent higher than it had been in the 1950s.

Most studies estimate that the average American now watches roughly four hours per day (excluding periods in which television is merely playing in the background). Even a more conservative estimate of three hours means that television absorbs 40 percent of the average American's free time; an increase of about one-third since 1965. Moreover, multiple sets have proliferated: By the late 1980s three-quarters of all U.S. homes had more than one set, and these numbers too are rising steadily, allowing ever more private viewing. Robinson and Godbey are surely right to conclude that 'television is the 800-pound gorilla of leisure time.' This massive change in the way Americans spend their days and nights occurred precisely during the years of generational civic disengagement.

Evidence of a link between the arrival of television and the erosion of social connections is, however, not merely circumstantial. The links between civic engagement and television viewing can be instructively compared with the links between civic engagement and newspaper reading. The basic contrast is straightforward: Newspaper reading is associated with high social capital, TV viewing with low social capital.

Controlling for education, income, age, race, place of residence, work status, and gender, TV viewing is strongly and negatively related to social trust and group membership, whereas the same correlations with newspaper reading are positive. Within every educational category, heavy readers are avid joiners, whereas heavy viewers are more likely to be loners. In fact, more detailed analysis suggests that heavy TV watching is one important reason *why* less educated people are less engaged in the life of their communities. Controlling for differential TV exposure significantly reduces the correlation between education and engagement.

Viewing and reading are themselves uncorrelated – some people do lots of both, some do little of either – but 'pure readers' (that is, people who watch less TV than average and read more newspapers than average) belong to 76 percent more civic organizations than 'pure viewers' (controlling for education, as always). Precisely the same pattern applies to other indicators of civic engagement, including social trust and voting turnout. 'Pure readers,' for example, are 55 percent more trusting than 'pure viewers.'

In other words, each hour spent viewing television is associated with less social trust and less group membership, while each hour reading a newspaper is associated with more. An increase in television viewing of the magnitude that the U.S. has experienced in the last four decades might directly account for as much as one-quarter to one-half of the total drop in social capital, even without taking into account, for example, the indirect effects of television viewing on newspaper readership or the cumulative effects of lifetime viewing hours. Newspaper circulation (per household) has dropped by more than half since its peak in 1947. To be sure, it is not clear which way the tie between newspaper reading and civic involvement works, since disengagement might itself dampen one's interest in community news. But the two trends are clearly linked.

* From Robert Putnam, 'The Strange Disappearance of Civic America', *American Prospect*, 25 (Mar/Apr. 1996), 34–48, reprinted with permission.

Michael Schudson teaches sociology at the University of California, San Diego. He writes extensively on the history of news and the public sphere in the United States. In this excerpt he presents us with a critique of Putnam's argument on the decline of civic-mindedness.*

The concept of politics has broadened enormously in 30 years. Not only is the personal political (the politics of male–female relations, the politics of smoking and not smoking), but the professional or occupational is also political. A woman physician or accountant can feel that she is doing politics – providing a role model and fighting for recognition of women's equality with men – every time she goes to work. The same is true for African American bank executives or gay and lesbian military officers.

The decline of the civic in its conventional forms, then, does not demonstrate the decline of civic-mindedness. The 'political' does not necessarily depend on social connectedness: Those membership dues to the NRA [National Rifle Association] are political. Nor does it even depend on organized groups at all: Wearing a 'Thank you for not smoking' button is political. The political may be intense and transient: Think of the thousands of people who have joined class action suits against producers of silicone breast implants or Dalkon shields or asbestos insulation.

Let us assume, for argument's sake, that there has been a decrease in civic involvement. Still, the rhetoric of decline in American life should send up a red flag. For the socially concerned intellectual, this is as much off-the-rack rhetoric as its mirror opposite, the rhetoric of progress, is for the ebullient technocrat. Any notion of 'decline' has to take for granted some often arbitrary baseline. Putnam's baseline is the 1940s and 1950s when the 'long civic generation' – people born between 1910 and 1940 – came into their own. But this generation shared the powerful and unusual experience of four years of national military mobilization on behalf of what nearly everyone came to accept as a good cause. If Putnam had selected, say, the 1920s as a baseline, would he have given us a similar picture of decline?

Unlikely. Intellectuals of the 1920s wrung their hands about the fate of democracy, the decline of voter turnout, the 'eclipse of the public,' as John Dewey put it or 'the phantom public' in Walter Lippmann's terms. They had plenty of evidence, particularly in the record of voter turnout, so low in

1920 and 1924 (49 percent each year) that even our contemporary nadir of 1988 (50.3 percent) does not quite match it. Putnam himself reports that people born from 1910 to 1940 appear more civic than those born before as well as those born after. There is every reason to ask why this group was so civic rather than why later groups are not.

The most obvious answer is that this group fought in or came of age during World War II. This is also a group that voted overwhelmingly for Franklin D. Roosevelt and observed his leadership in office over a long period. Presidents exercise a form of moral leadership that sets a norm or standard about what kind of a life people should lead. A critic has complained that Ronald Reagan made all Americans a little more stupid in the 1980s – and I don't think this is a frivolous jibe. Reagan taught us that even the president can make a philosophy of the principle, 'My mind's made up, don't confuse me with the facts.' He taught us that millions will pay deference to someone who regularly and earnestly confuses films with lived experience.

The 'long civic generation' had the advantages of a 'good war' and a good president. Later generations had no wars or ones about which there was less massive mobilization and much less consensus – Korea and, more divisively, Vietnam. They had presidents of dubious moral leadership – notably Nixon, whom people judged even in the glow of his latter-day 'rehabilitation' as the worst moral leader of all post-World War II presidents. So if there has been civic engagement in the past decades, it may be not a decline but a return to normalcy.

If the rhetoric of decline raises one red flag, television as an explanation raises another. Some of the most widely heralded 'media effects' have by now been thoroughly discredited. The yellow press had little or nothing to do with getting us into the Spanish–American War. Television news had little or nothing to do with turning Americans against the Vietnam War. Ronald Reagan's mastery of the media did not make him an unusually popular president in his first term (in fact, for his first 30 months in office he was unusually unpopular).

Indeed, the TV explanation doesn't fit Putnam's data very well. Putnam defines the long civic generation as the cohort born from 1910 to 1940, but then he also shows that the downturn in civic involvement began 'rather abruptly' among people 'born in the early 1930s.' In other words, civic decline began with people too young to have served in World War II but too old to have seen TV growing up. If we take 1954 as a turning-point year – the first year when more than half of American households had TV sets – Americans born from 1930 to 1936 were in most cases already out of the home and the people born the next four years were already in high school by the time TV is likely to have become a significant part of their lives. Of course, TV may have influenced this group later, in the 1950s and early 1960s when they were in their twenties and thirties. But this was a time when Americans watched many fewer hours of television, averaging five hours a day rather than the current seven, and the relatively benign TV fare of that era was not likely to induce fearfulness of the outside world.

All of my speculations here and, most of Putnam's assume that one person has about the same capacity for civic engagement as the next. But what if some people have decidedly more civic energy than others as a function of, say, personality? And what if these civic spark plugs have been increasingly recruited into situations where they are less civically engaged?

Putnam accords this kind of explanation some attention in asking whether women who had been most involved in civic activities were those most likely to take paying jobs, 'thus lowering the average level of civic engagement among the remaining homemakers and raising the average among women in the workplace.' Putnam says he 'can find little evidence' to support this hypothesis, but it sounds plausible.

A similar hypothesis makes sense in other domains. Since World War II, higher education has mushroomed. Of people born from 1911 to 1920, 13.5 percent earned college or graduate degrees; of those born during the next decade, 18.8 percent; but of people born from 1931 to 1950, the figure grew to between 26 and 27 percent. A small but increasing number of these college students have been recruited away from their home communities to elite private colleges; some public universities also began after World War II to draw from a national pool of talent. Even colleges with local constituencies increasingly have recruited faculty nationally, and the faculty have shaped student ambitions toward national law, medical, and business schools and corporate traineeships. If students drawn to these programs are among the people likeliest in the past to have been civic spark plugs, we have an alternative explanation for civic decline. Could there be a decline? Better to conceive the changes we find as a new environment of civic and political activity with altered institutional openings for engagement. Television is a part of the ecology, but in complex ways. It is a significant part of people's use of their waking hours, but it may be less a substitute for civic engagement than a new and perhaps insidious form of it. TV has been more politicized since the late 1960s than ever before. In 1968, *60 Minutes* began as the first money-making entertainment news program, spawning a dozen imitators. *All in the Family* in 1971 became the first prime-time sitcom to routinely take on controversial topics, from homosexuality to race to women's rights. *Donahue* was first syndicated in 1979, *Oprah* followed in 1984, and after then, the deluge.

If TV does nonetheless discourage civic engagement, what aspect of TV is at work? Is it the most 'serious,' civic-minded, and responsible part – the news? The latest blast at the news media, James Fallows's *Breaking the News*, picks up a familiar theme that the efforts of both print and broadcast journalists since the 1960s to get beneath the surface of events has led to a journalistic presumption that no politician can be trusted and that the story behind the story will be invariably sordid.

All of this talk needs to be tempered with the reminder that, amidst the many disappointments of politics between 1965 and 1995, this has been an era of unprecedented advances in women's rights, gay and lesbian liberation, African American opportunity, and financial security for the elderly. It has witnessed the first consumers' movement since the 1930s, the first environmental movement since the turn of the century, and public health movements of great range and achievement, especially in antismoking. It has also been a moment of grass-roots activism on the right as well as on the left, with the pro-life movement and the broad-gauge political involvement both locally and nationally of the Christian right. Most of this activity was generated outside of political parties and state institutions. Most of this activity was built on substantial 'grassroots' organizing. It is not easy to square all of this with an account of declining civic virtue.

*From Michael Schudson, 'What If Civic Life Didn't Die?', in *American Prospect*, 25 (Mar/Apr. 1996), 17–20, reprinted with permission.

*Theda Skocpol is Professor of Government and Sociology and the Director of the Center for American Political Studies at Harvard University. Her more recent works have dealt with US politics in a historical and comparative perspective. Here, she challenges the notion that civil society exists outside the realm of politics and government. Instead, she demonstrates their historical interconnectedness, while also arguing for the need to revitalize political democracy in order to salvage civic vigour.**

[W]hy didn't new locally rooted federations emerge to replace those that started to fade in the 1960s? To some degree they did, for example in the environmental movement. Yet new federations did not grow enough to carry on the organizational tradition of the PTA, the Elks, and the American Legion. Why not brings me to my last argument – about the Tocqueville romanticism that not only undergirds right-wing versions of the civil society debate, but also influences aspects of Putnam's research. Of course Putnam does not share Gingrich's hostility to the welfare state. Yet he often speaks of social capital as something that arises or declines in a realm apart from politics and government.

A romantic construction of Tocqueville supposes that voluntary groups spring up de novo from below, created by individuals in small geographic areas who spontaneously decide to associate to get things done 'outside of' government and politics. Supposedly this is what Alex de Tocqueville saw in early national America. But local spontaneity wasn't all that was going on back then. True, once local villages and towns passed a threshold of 200 to 400 families apiece, voluntary associations tended to emerge, especially if there were locally resident business people and professionals. But research on America in the early 1800s shows that religious and political factors also stimulated the growth of voluntary groups. In a country with no official church and competing religious denominations, the Second Great Awakening spread ideas about personal initiative and moral duty to the community. In addition, the American Revolution, and the subsequent organization of competitive national and state elections under the Constitution of 1789, triggered the founding of newspapers and the formation of local and trans-local voluntary associations much faster and more extensively than just nascent town formation can explain. The openness of the U.S. Congress and state legislatures to organized petition drives, the remarkable spread of public schooling, and the establishment of U.S. post offices in every little hamlet were also vital enabling factors, grounded in the very institutional core of the early U.S. state. (As a nobleman critical of the centralized bureaucratic state of contemporary post-revolutionary France, Tocqueville naturally riveted on the absence of a bureaucratic state in early America. He briefly acknowledged but did not emphasize the effects of early American govern-ment on the associations of civic society.)

In the latter part of the nineteenth century came another great wave of U.S. voluntary group formation – this time prominently featuring three-tiered federations of associations at the local, state, and national level. Again, political events and processes were critical, along with industrialization, urbanization, and immigration. The Civil War and its aftermath encouraged ties between central and local elites and groups. Between the mid-1870s and the mid-1890s the intense electoral competition of locally rooted, nation-spanning political parties encouraged the parallel formation of voluntary federations, and gave them electoral or legislative leverage if they wanted it – as groups such as the Grand Army of the Republic, the Grange, and the Women's Christian Temperance Union most decidedly did.

Twentieth-century voluntary federations were often built from the top down, deliberately structured to imitate and influence the three tiers of U.S. government, and encouraged by parts of the federal government itself. Thus the American Legion was launched from the top by World War I military officers and later nurtured by the Veterans Administration. And the American Farm Bureau Federation was encouraged by the U.S. Department of Agriculture. The PTA itself, now romanticized as a purely local voluntary group, did not originally bubble up from below. It was founded in 1897 as the National Congress of Mothers (and renamed the PTA in 1924). The original Congress of Mothers was knit together from above by elite women. It started out as the brainchild of a new mother married to a prominent lawyer in Washington, DC. She decided to launch a women's organization resembling the U.S. Congress and paralleling the levels of U.S. government, so that 'mother thought' could be carried into all spheres of American life. Once the Congress of Mothers began to take shape, as prominent women wrote to their counterparts in states and localities, it immediately turned to influencing local, state, and national governments to work in partnership with it for the good of all mothers and children. From its very inception, the Congress of Mothers/PTA was actively involved in public policymaking and the construction of a distinctively American version of the welfare state.

Although U.S. history contradicts the premises of Tocqueville romanticism, this vision has insinuated itself into current scholarship about U.S. civil society. Political patterns and developments (such as levels of trust in government, and rates of electoral participation or attendance at public meetings) are treated simply as 'dependent variables.' The assumption is that local voluntarism is fundamental, the primary cause of all that is healthy in democratic politics and effective governance, in contrast to the dreaded 'bureaucratic state.' But just as Marxists are wrong to assume that the economy is the primal 'substructure' while government and politics are merely 'superstructure,' so Tocqueville romanticists are wrong to assume that spontaneous social association is primary while government and politics are derivative. On the contrary, U.S. civic associations were encouraged by the American Revolution, the Civil War, the New Deal, and World Wars I and II; and until recently they were fostered by the institutional patterns of U.S. federalism, legislatures, competitive elections, and locally rooted political parties.

Civil Decline Reconsidered

From the 1960s onward the mechanics of U.S. elections changed sharply. Efforts to mobilize voters through locally rooted organizations gave way to television advertising, polling and focus groups, and orchestration by consultants paid huge sums with money raised from big donors and mass mailings. Around the same time, the number of lobbying groups exploded in Washington, DC. Both business groups and 'public interest' groups proliferated. Advocacy groups have clashed politically, yet their structures have become remarkably similar.

By now, almost all are led by resident professional staffs, and funded more by outside donors or commercial side ventures than from membership dues. If today's advocacy groups connect at all to society at large, they do so through mailings of magazines, newsletters, and appeals for donations to millions of individuals. The American Association of Retired Persons (AARP), founded in 1958, now has around 35 million members fifty years of age and older. But only 5 to 10 percent of AARP members participate in local affiliates, and new members join after getting a letter in the mail, not an invitation to a local club meeting. The AARP is not like the locally rooted federations that once dominated the ranks of nationwide U.S. voluntary associations.

Just as younger adults were turning away from traditional voluntary associations, America's ways of doing electoral politics and legislative advocacy were sharply transformed. Television was certainly a major factor, as were computerized modes of data analysis and direct-mail targeting.

Complementary changes happened in the media, and in ways of doing policy business in the federal bureaucracy and Congress. Interlocking transformations added up to a new set of constraints and opportunities for voluntary groups. No longer do the great local-state-national federations, rooted in face-to-face meetings in localities, have a comparative advantage in mediating between individuals and politicians, between localities and Washington, DC. Professional and business elites increasingly bypass such federations. One exception, on the right, is the Christian Coalition, which since the late 1980s has successfully melded top-down and bottom-up styles of political mobilization.

Throughout much of U.S. history, electoral democracy and congressionally centered governance nurtured and rewarded voluntary associations and locality-spanning voluntary federations. But since the 1960s, the mechanics of U.S. politics have been captured by manipulators of money and data. Among elites new kinds of connections are alive and well. Privileged Americans remain active in think tanks, advocacy groups, and trade and professional associations, jetting back and forth between manicured neighborhoods and exotic retreats. Everyone else has been left to work at two or three poorly paid jobs per family, coming home exhausted to watch TV and answer phone calls from pollsters and telemarketers.

How ironic it would be if, after pulling out of locally rooted associations, the very business and professional elites who blazed the path toward local civic disengagement were now to turn around and successfully argue that the less privileged Americans they left behind are the ones who must repair the nation's social connectedness, by pulling themselves together from below without much help from government or their privileged fellow citizens. This, I fear, is what is happening as the discussion about 'returning to Tocqueville' rages across elite America.

Progressives who care about democratic values should pause before joining this new 'consensus.' They should not hastily conclude that the answers to most of America's problems lie in civil society understood apart from, or in opposition to, government and politics. The true history of civic associationalism in America gives the lie to notions propagated by today's government bashers and government avoiders.

Organized civil society in the United States has never flourished apart from active government and inclusive democratic politics. Civic vitality has also depended on vibrant ties across classes and localities. If we want to repair civil society, we must first and foremost revitalize political democracy. The sway of money in politics will have to be curtailed, and privileged Americans will have to join their fellow citizens in broad civic endeavors. Re-establishing local voluntary groups alone will not suffice.

* From Theda Skocpol, 'Unravelling from Above', in *American Prospect*, 25 (Mar/Apr. 1996), 20–5, reprinted with permission.

Robert Putnam here looks back at history and how technological changes, just as they do today, led to the depletion of social capital in nineteenth-century America. The solution to this depletion came from institutional changes. To counter the decline of civic life today, he proposes the reconstruction of civic organizations as well as a more active involvement on the part of academics in the United States.*

Over the course of the last generation, a variety of technological, economic and social changes have rendered obsolete a stock of American social capital. Because of two-career families, sprawl, television and other factors, Americans are no longer as eager to find time for the PTA, or the Elks club, or the Optimists, There are measurable bad effects for the United States that flow from this social capital deficit.

Now, return to a hundred years ago. At the end of the nineteenth century in the United States, the stock of social capital in America was in a similarly depleted state. America had just been through 30–40 years of dramatic technological, economic and social change that had rendered obsolete institutions and informal patterns of social engagement. Urbanization, industrialization and immigration meant that people no longer had the tight communities of friends that were present back on the farm, and they no longer had the institutions they had enjoyed back in the village in Poland or in Iowa.

At the end of the nineteenth century, America suffered from all of the same symptoms of the social capital deficit that the nation has experienced over the past couple of decades. These include high crime rates, decay in the cities, concern about political corruption, poorly functioning schools, and a widening gap between the rich and everyone else. Then as now, the erosion of social capital happened for the same reason: technological change rendered obsolete the ways Americans had previously connected.

Then, amazingly, Americans fixed the problem. In a very short period of time, at the end of the nineteenth century, most of today's most important civic institutions were invented: the Boy Scouts, the American Red Cross, the League of Women Voters, the National Association for the Advancement of Colored People (NAACP), the Knights of Columbus, the Sons of Norway, the Sons of Italy, the Urban League, the Kiwanis club, the YWCA, the 4-H club, the Rotary club, the Community Chest and most trade unions. It is actually hard to name a major civic institution in American life today that was not invented at the end of the nineteenth century or the beginning of the twentieth century.

In that period, as now, it was very tempting to say, 'Life was much better back in the old days'. At the end of the nineteenth century, 'the old days' meant 'on the farm,' when everyone knew each other. Similarly, it might be tempting today to say, 'Life was much nicer back in the 1950s. Would all women please report to the kitchen? And turn off the television on the way'. Of course, America should no more return to the days of gender segregation than it should return to a pre-industrial agricultural economy. Instead, Americans today must do what their forebears did a century ago: create new institutions to fit new times. Americans need to reinvent the Boy Scouts or the League of Women Voters or the Sons of Italy.

Here, there is a close connection between British history and American history. Many of the organizations that were 'invented' in the United States at the end of the nineteenth century actually were imported from England, where they had been invented in the mid-Victorian era, probably in response to very similar social problems. Such organizations include the Boy Scouts and the Salvation Army. These patterns suggest that there may be periods in many countries, not just the United States, in which there are bursts of civic reconstruction. Now, the challenge to Americans as a people is to put in a hard ten or twenty years figuring how to reconnect in an era of new demographic, economic and cultural realities. It is not an option to say, 'It doesn't matter if we connect with other people'. There are measurable reasons why connecting does matter.

It remains to be seen what those new ideas and strategies will be. Some might seem a little crazy. One can only imagine the response in some quarters when civic leaders said creating an organization called the Boy Scouts would be a solution to the street-urchin problem – that if urchins get shorts, beanies and badges, this would be a substitute for friends on the farm. In hindsight, we can see which inventions of that period were successful; but it is harder to see the ones that were unsuccessful. Today as then, there will be a lot of false starts. Quite interestingly, the late-nineteenth century was a period almost unique in American intellectual history in the sense that there was a very close connection, and a lot of direct exchanges, between academics and practitioners. Some American academics are now trying to create a similar situation in which scholars no longer spend all their time writing for obscure journals read only by other scholars, but rather spend more time learning from practitioners who are addressing vital public issues. In short, addressing the social capital deficit in contemporary society is far from a hopeless task, but it will require that social scientists descend from our ivory tower.

* From Robert Putnam, 'Civic Disengagement', *Government and Opposition* 36 (Spring 2001), 154–6, reprinted with permission.

*David Blunkett, leading New Labour politician in Britain and, since 2001, Home Secretary. Raised in the industrial northern town of Sheffield and long active in local government, he here discusses a project for renewing democracy at the community level, combining ideas of active citizenship with thoughts on the need for order and shared values.**

Most politicians have been schooled in forms of dialogue which are 'one-to-one' or 'one-to-many'. Network technology means that there is now an opportunity for conversation which is 'many-to-many'. Its use has been harnessed most by the new protest groups, but we should reclaim it for mainstream politics. The benefits to our civic culture and the quality of public decision-making could be significant.

If this is to have a positive impact, we must avoid such conversation descending into a cacophony of mutual incomprehension. The proliferation of communication channels can also undermine and fragment the 'public space' in which political issues are debated. Experiments in creating 'virtual communities' have often found that technology contributes to social capital and civic collaboration in situations where it reinforces existing relationships, such as in neighbourhoods. But, where these networks and relationships are weak, new technology can increase social isolation and fragmentation.

A revitalisation of our public political culture through such media is a precondition of the renewal of democratic participation, but it is not sufficient. Building on my earlier arguments, I believe we can sketch out an agenda for this renewal with nine key elements.

First, we need a wider spread of asset ownership, so that more people have a direct stake in society and its democratic governance. The evidence suggests that this will improve civic awareness and political commitment.

Second, we should improve political literacy, social and moral responsibility and community involvement amongst the adult population through citizenship education, including for new entrants to the UK, and wider community learning opportunities related to the demands of ordinary life. Democracy has to be learned and practiced. It is difficult to trust or influence political change without any real understanding of the workings of political systems. Citizens need skills of negotiation, persuasion, open-mindedness and self-organisation to engage with complex issues. Indeed, the ability to communicate effectively is now critical, for those entering the country for the first time, as well as those who have been failed by the school system in the past.

Third, we should extend opportunities for deliberative democracy through neighborhood meetings, resident consultations, citizens' juries, 'town hall' debates and other forums. We must learn the lessons of community capacity-building. Consultation with local communities for regeneration programmes is now the norm. While this is a huge advance on old practices, it is just a start. We need to develop wider opportunities for local and neighborhood deliberation. Without them, the new Local Strategic Partnerships could become local magistracies.

Fourth, we should consider making registration to vote compulsory. In New Zealand, turnout was 79 per cent before compulsory registration. It rose to 90 per cent afterwards. Compulsory registration is preferable both to automatic registration, which requires no individual effort, and compulsory voting, which compels the citizen to undertake a political act which should result from individual volition. At present, individuals are not under a duty to register to vote – only to return a correctly filled-out registration form once one is received from the local authority. Those least likely to vote have the lowest rates of voter registration.

Incentives to vote should also be explored – not simply those which make it easier to vote, but those which link voting to wider social participation. These might include automatic entry into prize or lottery draws or the automatic provision of a discount card for local theatre, leisure and other facilities.

Fifth, we should expand mutual and community associations in which people come together to discuss and debate social and political issues, building new networks of engagement, what Robert Putnam calls 'bridging' social capital. Social consensus and mutual respect are forged through these overlapping networks of participation and common interest. They are what give real meaning to the idea of a 'public sphere' which goes beyond the big public institutions and the media. In this context, we should examine the role of the workplace in civic life, through promoting employee volunteering and after-work civic discussion in office spaces.

Sixth, we must ensure better representation of women and ethnic minorities in democratic decision-making at all levels, from local authorities to the Assemblies and Parliaments of the UK, so that people see their society properly reflected in its democratic institutions. The same is true for non-elected bodies and quangos.

Seventh, we must seek to expand volunteering, particularly among those who don't usually volunteer – the young, ethnic minorities and the socially excluded. Volunteering builds up the commitment and skills upon which formal democracy depends. Volunteering programmes should build on the successes of new initiatives, such as Millennium Volunteers, Timebank and the CitizensConnection website. With links to school curricula and qualifications, young people would have direct incentives to participate. Government also has a responsibility. The Prime Minister has asked Permanent Secretaries to promote volunteering in the civil service. Almost every form of public service delivery could benefit from systematic voluntary involvement. This is not about replacing the basic responsibilities of the state, but about building networks of informal mutual support around hospitals, museums, social service providers and schools. Millennium Volunteers has shown how these forms of civic and voluntary engagement rely on a particular kind of enabling infrastructure.

Eighth, we should find ways to renew democratic engagement. This is partly about building on successful experiments, such as the Scottish Right of Petition and electronic voting for local elections and easier postal voting. It is also about continuing to reform both the Commons and the Lords, something to which the Leaders of both Houses are clearly committed. As noted previously, honesty about the precise power and role of Parliament and the executive is important. This is not to denigrate the position of

Parliament, but to recognise the reality of contemporary global power structures, both social and economic, which are not subservient to traditional political institutions. Yet it is questionable whether Parliament ever enjoyed such supremacy. We deluded ourselves by believing that the world changed because Parliament decided and the civil service acted. Such self-delusion contributed to disengagement from and cynicism towards politics. Recognition of the possibilities and limitations of Parliament both as a platform and a facilitator for others to act is an essential prerequisite. We must stop believing that politicians 'do' everything and recognise that effective and smart politicians can enable others to do things for themselves that would otherwise not be possible.

Finally, we need to bridge the gap between the aspirations of citizens and the capacity of governments to act on them. This is important to renew confidence in public services. It is primarily an institutional challenge: in some circumstances we can make the State deliver more effectively, by being more focused, more responsive and more transparent. Active government can make a difference, as we showed through the [British] New Deal and the literacy hour. But in the longer term, people's ability to fulfil their aspirations will depend on a much wider range of organisations and associations, and on whether their social attachments and identities can be reflected in ways of organising which help to get things done.

It will take more than leaner government and greater customer focus to achieve this. In our second term of government, we need, therefore, to redouble our efforts to stimulate a wide ecology of organisations in civil society. Such organisations cover a very broad spectrum. Their common characteristic should be in linking individual voluntary and social commitments with organisational capacity to articulate the interests of particular social groups, providing for social need, developing a forum for debate, educating and informing. How can such organizations – be they libraries, parks, media organisations or credit unions – become social resources, where they don't just provide a service or information source, but also reinforce wider norms of public engagement, mutual commitment and common interest?

. . .

Power in contemporary society goes far beyond the checks and balances of formal democracy described in the textbooks of traditional liberal political theory. When the institutions of representative democracy were designed, the 'separation of powers' was seen as the best way to limit absolute power and encourage accountability. But power is now both more widely dispersed and more concentrated in specific parts of society, in ways that render much of this traditional theory obsolete. The legitimacy and effectiveness of the great institutions of the State are being questioned by citizens and threatened from these new centres of power.

Although the formal pillars of democratic power remain, they must relate to the other important economic and social interests at local, national or European level: corporations, trade unions and pressure groups; NGOs and local communities within civil society; and the traditional and new media, which exert considerable control over the political culture. Sometimes, governments can forge political alliances with different interests in a common cause. The campaigns that led to the overthrow of apartheid in South Africa or the Jubilee 2000 campaign to cancel Third World debt are both good examples. They demonstrate that partnerships between the state and civil society can strategically mobilise power from very different sources when it is concentrated towards a common goal.

However, the consequence of this analysis is that the models of power in which many contemporary debates are framed are simply inadequate. They set up politicians and the political process in direct opposition to currents of thought and action in wider civil society. Yet political power is not simply about obtaining popular legitimacy and then exercising it. It is also about giving political legitimacy and support to people to participate and engage in change themselves. Governments can facilitate political and pressure group activity, empowering people as consumers or citizens to take action on issues of concern to them. But people must be ready to exercise power, in transparent and responsible ways, for themselves. This is also true for companies, particularly those large corporations whose influence has grown enormously, whose contribution to social well-being through corporate social responsibility can be considerable.

More widely, the reform of the State itself is a precondition for the development of genuine, active partnerships with civil society. We have to build institutions capable of functioning effectively in the new environment, using power in its new forms, working with the grain of the new identities. We have to take seriously the new forms of identity which are emerging as societies continue to change and channel institutional reform in new directions.

. . .

The checks and balances that are necessary in any democratic system, and the drive for reform and modernisation, bring us back to the fundamental issues of how to achieve progressive change while retaining confidence in the political process, and maintaining the order and security crucial to any civilised society. If people's sense of dissatisfaction is not given proper expression through politics, it turns to anger. This can erupt into disruption and violence. Some legitimate protests can now be hijacked by nihilistic violence which has turned against all authority. Political violence has furthered many causes in history and has not been entirely banished from the politics of many parliamentary democracies. So the renewal of a democracy is a precondition of its survival. People will turn to anti-democratic practices if democracy does not allow the articulation of wider pressures and demands. Likewise, democracy relies on social order – where this breaks down, those who reject democracy flourish.

It is the job of government and of public institutions to help maintain the rules which ensure order. But they cannot do it simply by imposing themselves; they depend on a culture of active reciprocity which is essential to civilised societies. Such a culture cannot be sustained where most people become frightened to go out, are interested only in themselves and their own families and rely solely on private consumption for satisfaction and fulfilment in life. It relies on wider social well-being.

This presents a basic challenge for politics. If we want to extend and enrich freedom, we have to develop new and positive forms of social cohesion and stability. Since social order cannot be equated with the authoritarian or bureaucratic power of the state, we must therefore extend freedom in tandem with responsibility. To do this we need an active civil society and strong civic culture with new and effective forms of partnership.

* From David Blunkett, *Politics and Progress: Renewing Democracy and Civil Society* (London: Politico's Publishing, 2001), 137–41; 161–2; 165–6.

Nancy L. Rosenblum (b. 1947), political theorist in the Department of Government at Harvard University, is the author of a series of books dealing with questions of civil society, most notably Membership and Morals *(Princeton: Princeton University Press, 1998). In this selection she suggests that associational life is far from attractive if it is compelled – thereby making us aware that entry into and exit from social groups is necessary for a society to be genuinely civil.**

What bounds on an association's freedom to elect members are defensible? In an early case involving the Benevolent and Protective Order of Elks, a district court ruled that a black applicant's 'interest in joining the private club of his choice surely does not constitute a basic right of citizenship.' This decision frames the issue correctly; legally compelled association is justified when exclusion denotes second-class citizenship. Other familiar reasons for compelled association such as avoiding harm to personal dignity and securing self-respect are, in contrast, indefensible. When these strands of justification are unraveled, the grounds for government interference with association freedom – to ban women from all-male eating clubs, non-Jewish women from Hadassah, or men from women's business groups, and vice versa – turn out to be severely limited, even if the membership policy is pejorative, or taken as such. The reasons for freedom of association are another subject, though I propose several contrarian points briefly at the end.

I suggest that affiliation with voluntary associations in which we are wanted and willing members is a key source of self-respect; that discrimination may be safely contained in these groups; and that because associations often owe their origin to a dynamic of affiliation and exclusion, resentment and self-affirmation, liberal democracy is consistent with and even requires the incongruence between voluntary groups and public norms that always accompanies freedom of association.

. . .

Those who see a seamless web of public and private life and a unity of moral disposition deny that people have the capacity or inclination to discriminate discriminatingly. Beyond that, they argue that when government fails to interfere with membership restrictions and to protect against 'second-class membership,' it 'morally legitimizes and potentially encourages a practice both courts and legislatures have decried as one of the most significant evils in modern society.' On this view, government has an obligation to mandate moral education, affirming the equal worth of excluded individuals, redressing dignity harms broadly understood, and enforcing acceptable democratic behavior in almost every arena except for the most intimate (small businesses are exempt from antidiscrimination law on the presumption that they are family affairs).[1] Government has many avenues for public communication and the promotion of approved conduct and messages, of course, not only in its authoritative capacity as educator but also in its activities as employer, owner, grantor, and patron. But this extravagant case for the obligation to educate demands more than seizing official occasions for proclamations and exhibitions of liberal democratic practices, and more than prohibiting 'state action' in which government is insinuated into private conduct. Advocates of congruence are stern didacts, and would use the law to compel voluntary associations to promote approved messages and to prohibit disfavored ones. They are willing to 'press club members into service to send society a message of inclusion and equality.' They reject the liberal fundamental 'that private individuals may not be used as the involuntary instruments of a state lesson.'

. . .

The standard thesis on voluntary association in America sees the process as determinedly practical, stressing cooperation in socially useful tasks. In contrast to aristocratic orders, Tocqueville explained, the 'independent and feeble' citizens of a democratic nation must 'learn voluntarily to help one another.' Collective action is a practical imperative, and he remarked on 'the extreme skill with which the inhabitants. ... succeed in proposing a common object to the exertions of a great many men, and in getting them voluntarily to pursue it.' The heyday of association in America was the rush into clubs in the mid-nineteenth century: 'The churches, clubs, lodges, temperance and reading societies of natives and immigrants encouraged social ties that made the formation of death benefit, accident, and unemployment pools possible.' This is the 'civic culture' social scientists look to for the social capital that overcomes free riding and the tragedy of the commons. It is similar to pragmatists' enthusiasm for 'communities of inquiry and practice' that generate their own internal discipline and organization to encourage the perfection of a craft, skill, or science, product, technique, or performance. The Jaycees put themselves in this company when they warn that compelled association would have a 'chilling effect' on their charitable works and civic activities.

This standard, sanguine view of association suffers from a naive liberal expectancy. It has always had its acid detractors. Washington's Farewell Address condemned 'all combinations and associations, under whatever plausible character, with the real design to direct, control, counteract, or awe the regular deliberation and action of the constituted authorities,' and accusations of faction, real or imagined, are leveled at every imaginable group. Civic republicans follow Rousseau in devising schemes to eliminate 'Hobbesian' self-preferring groups and the social hierarchies that get their foothold in private circles; clubs, lodges, parishes, and gangs 'were not media which could nourish effective and inclusive community growth. [A] city of such private associations was a city of closed social cells.' There are innumerable 'lapsarian theories of groups' as combinations of individuals corrupted by self-love. And romantic individualists see all joining as a pitiful lack of self-reliance. The usefulness of groups escaped Thoreau entirely; the best neighborliness is 'minding your own business,' he thought, and the true reformer is 'one perfect institution in himself.' 'At the name of a society all my repulsions play,' Emerson confessed. 'Men club together on the principle: "I have failed, and you have failed, but perhaps together we shall not fail."' In liberal democracy, romantic aloofness is as insufferable as exclusive groups; it too is perceived as aristocratic self-distancing, and generally despised. Nonetheless, romantic individualism points up the dark underside of gregariousness: dependence, craving for the good opinion of others, hypocrisy, and the desire of those excluded to join together and inflict the same on others. These are not just incidental accompaniments of voluntary association; they are among its sources.

The permanent dynamic of affiliation and exclusion is linked not only to the social and cultural pluralism of an open liberal democracy but also to the fact that our conceptions of social status are unstable. It is reported that 'private social clubs with discriminatory membership policies are fast becoming extinct' (the average age of membership is sixty-two). The reasons doubtless have less to do with legal challenges than with changing ideas about social precedence. Freemasons, Shriners, Elk, and Moose are endangered species when groups of middle-aged white men are eyed with suspicion, and when prospective members find secret handshakes and the Moose's cape and tah (hat spelled backwards) laughable. The St. Andrews Society recently contemplated admitting women to their 237-year-old club dedicated to upholding Scottish traditions and Scottish charity. They debated whether the association could survive without women members or whether St. Andrews did enough for women already by allowing them to attend the annual banquet (seated at segregated tables in the balcony) and the Tartan Ball (where they could sit at tables with men). It is fair to suppose that potential younger members were not so much outraged by the group's discriminatory practices as put off by the fact that St. Andrews could not possibly satisfy contemporary desires for social status, and its affairs did not appear to be fun.

The contemporary 'politics of recognition' bears a family resemblance to the dynamics of affiliation and exclusion, particularly insofar as theorists emphasize the variability of cultural group membership, symbolic boundaries, and 'ethnic options.' But at least among academic theorists and as regards cultural (not racial) groups, the terms of discussion are often idealized. 'Identity,' 'recognition,' the emergence of self-understanding from 'dialogue' with 'significant others' are maddeningly benign. We have lost Hawthorne's cold eye on the snobbery and malice of associations, whether they have power and privileges or not. Association and exclusion, the creation of boundaries that others regard as discriminatory and anti-democratic go on everywhere, except perhaps at the very bottom. Yet it is considered disrespectful to say that people who have been subject to discrimination want the solace and revenge of compensatory, exclusive, and sometimes hostile associations of their own. The dynamic of exclusion is a virtual taboo, or is attributed entirely to vulnerability and the contingent need for self-protection. The motivational root of members' expressions of affiliation with cultural groups is supposed to be the 'epistemological comforts of home,' not access to jobs and positions, social status, or sheer resentment. Only rarely do we observe that language emphasizing identity and values 'has often provided the excuse – as well as the emotional fuel' for action aimed at getting a share, fair or not, of social and economic goods, and not only at the top. Sociologists may be wrong in describing the revival of ethnic groups in the United States as a self-conscious racist response to the civil rights movement and to celebrations of racial and ethnic identity by nonwhite groups, but they are right to be skeptical that these associations advance mutual understanding.

To the extent that the public culture and institutions of liberal democracy are strong, and sentiments of exclusiveness cannot result in withholding legal rights and publicly available goods, the dynamic of exclusion will take the form of avid voluntary association. The dynamic is eminently democratic. Indeed, as gains in first-class citizenship by previously marginal groups and real security for public standing increase, we can expect to see the number and intensity of these associations grow too. The genuinely antiliberal, anti-democratic claim that 'we' are the 'real citizens' and others permanently second class because their inferiority is a matter of inherited or unalterable attributes will never disappear, but voluntary associations can contain even this discrimination, as the 'safety-valve' thesis suggests.[2] What Rawls's picture of 'noncomparing groups' gets wrong, then, is that the morally useful world of multiple associations and multiple hierarchies is one of comparing groups. Without this dynamic, which operates more freely in a liberal democracy than anywhere else, there would be many fewer sources of the 'primary good' of self-respect – and less containment of irrepressible exclusiveness.

Coda: Democracy and Disassociation

The moral imperative of compelled association misses the mark. The critical dilemma for liberal democracy in the United States today is not exclusion from restricted membership groups but isolation. Genuine anomie is evidenced less by declining membership in traditional associations (others are burgeoning) than by the way ghettoization, chronic unemployment ('unemployment means having nothing to do – which means having nothing to do with the rest of us'),[3] and characterological impediments to sociability (among them aggressiveness and depression) put the whole range of associational life beyond reach. In the case of anomic individuals condemned to a 'culture of segregation,' both public standing and self-respect may well depend almost entirely on being drawn into voluntary associations. But these are the very people who lack resources for organizing groups and occasions for being recruited into existing ones. A newspaper report on the decline of the Loyal Order of Moose Lodge in Roxbury, Massachusetts, described the lodge's plan to give up its capes and to attract young men by launching a drum and bugle corps. The difficulty seemed immense even to the hopeful Moose: 'If, they're already into drugs, it'll be hard to get them into the drum and bugle corps.' We know very little about how to get socially isolated individuals to become joiners, still less about how to keep them. Accounts of recruitment by gangs and hate groups indicate that young men are not attracted to them because these groups reflect their own racist ideas and ambitions but simply because they are solicited. They have nothing better to do and nowhere else to go. Given this scenario, it is no surprise that the life span of membership in racist groups is short and that members cycle away, often into persistent disassociation and personal chaos.

Recruiting the disassociated or supporting the creation of associations of their own requires intensive effort 'on the ground.' It is unlikely that the energy and flux of voluntary association can be directed from above; associations implanted from outside have a high failure rate. Recognizing that indigenous local efforts are the most successful, government programs have sought to fill the associational void by exploiting every potential group as a basis for positive social organizing. One proposal cast street gangs as sources of social capital, if only they could be diverted from apprenticeship for crime and self-destruction. We can sympathize with Nathan Glazer, sceptical but stumped: 'In the absence of the natural forms of informal social organization, what alternatives do we have?' The terrible, palpable self-exclusion of anomie may be intractable. But if it is not, the process of association that is capable of generating stable membership and self-respect in anomic outsiders will replicate the dynamic not only of affiliation but also of exclusion, of 'comparing groups.' It is another reason – not sanguine to be sure, but familiarly democratic – to minimize legally compelled association and the logic of congruence on which it rests.

* From Nancy L. Rosenblum, 'Compelled Association: Public Standing, Self-Respect, and the Dynamic of Exclusion', in Amy Gutmann, ed., *Freedom of Association* (Princeton, N.J.: Princeton University Press, 1998), 75–6; 89–90; 100–3, reprinted by permission of Princeton University Press.

[1] The partial exceptions are religious associations and certain political groups protected by the First Amendment.

[2] Hannah Arendt made a similar argument in 'Reflections on Little Rock,' though she drew the boundary line in the wrong place, exempting schools and places of public accommodation. If discrimination is permitted in the social sphere and confined there, it is less likely to erupt and to color politics (she condones civil rights activity on behalf of voting rights) or personal life (the 'most outrageous' violation of human rights is antimiscegenation laws criminalizing mixed marriage). 'Discrimination is as indispensable a social right is a political right.' 'Reflections on Little Rock', *Dissent*, 6 (Winter 1959), 60–1; 66; 45–56.

[3] Robert Kennedy, cited in Michael Sandel, *Democracy's Discontent: America in Search of a Public Philosophy* (Cambridge: Harvard University Press, 1996), 302.

*Joshua Cohen and Joel Rogers are, respectively, Goldberg Professor of the Humanities at the Massachusetts Institute of Technology, and Professor of Law, political science, and sociology at the University of Wisconsin, Madison. Here they present a project for reinvigorating democracy by strengthening groups and associations.**

Prominent among the problems of democratic theory and practice are the 'mischiefs of faction' produced in mass democracies by 'secondary associations' – the wide range of nonfamilial organizations intermediate between individuals or firms and the institutions of the state and formal electoral system. Such associations play a central role in the politics of modern democratic societies. They help to set the political agenda, to determine choices from that agenda, to implement (or to thwart the implementation of) those choices and to shape the beliefs, preferences, self-understandings and habits of thought and action that individuals bring to more encompassing political arenas. Stated abstractly, the problem of faction consists in the potential of secondary associations to deploy their powers in ways that undermine the conditions of well-ordered democracy.

. . .

Emphasizing both qualitative variations among groups and the 'artifactual' aspect of associations, we suggest that the range of cures for the mischiefs of faction is commonly understood too narrowly. The potential cures are not limited to the options of imposing stringent constitutional limits on the affirmative state, accommodating groups while seeking to ensure equality in the 'pluralist bazaar', or constructing cloistered deliberative arenas alongside that bazaar. In addition to these strategies, and in many respects preferable to them, is the cure of using public powers to encourage less factionalizing forms of secondary association – engaging in an artful democratic politics of secondary association. More positively stated, the same deliberate politics of association can harness group contributions to democratic order. By altering the terms, conditions and public status of groups, we believe, it can improve economic performance and government efficiency and advance egalitarian-democratic norms of popular sovereignty, political equality, distributive equity and civic consciousness (discussed later in this essay). This deliberate politics of associations and the view of contemporary democratic govern-ance that embraces it as essential to such governance we call 'associative democracy'.

. . .

Associative democracy draws on an egalitarian ideal of social association. The core of that ideal is that the members of a society ought to be treated as equals in fixing the basic terms of social cooperation – including the ways that authoritative collective decisions are made, the ways that resources are produced and distributed, and the ways that social life more broadly is organized. The substantive commitments of the ideal include concerns about fair conditions for citizen participation in politics and robust public debate, an equitable distribution of resources and the protection of individual choice. Lying at the core of social democratic practice in Northern Europe, this conception figures centrally in the most compelling arguments for the affirmative welfare state, including arguments made within such quintes-sentially liberal orders as the United States.

. . .

[W]e assume that there is broad commitment to the abstract ideal of a democratic society – a society of equals that is governed both by its members and for them. In particular, citizens are understood to be equals in respect of certain basic capacities, including the capacity to evaluate the reasonableness of the rules of association and to govern their conduct in the light of those evaluations and the capacity to formulate and to pursue their aspirations against the background of those rules. Reflecting this abstract democratic ideal and giving it substance are six more specific conditions: popular sovereignty, political equality, distributive equity, civic consciousness, good economic performance and state competence.

These six conditions plainly have different relations to the abstract ideal of democracy. Popular sovereignty and political equality (the popular control or 'by the people' aspect of democracy) are fundamental procedural implications of that ideal. Distributive equity, by contrast, interprets the notion of the general welfare (the responsiveness, or 'for the people' aspect of democracy) in light of the fundamental idea of citizens as equals. Civic consciousness, by which we minimally mean an understanding of and willingness to act to uphold conditions that embody the abstract ideal, contributes to the stability of arrangements satisfying that ideal. And adequate economic performance and state competence are among the conditions required to provide for the general welfare and to sustain confidence in democratic order. For present purposes, however, the precise nature of these connections matters less than the fact that these conditions represent widely shared standards of performance for a modern, democratic society and that they enjoy natural connections to the abstract conception of democratic order. If the problem of faction, then, consists in the threat that secondary associations can present to democratic order, that problem can reasonably be specified by reference to threats to these more particular conditions of democracy.

. . .

The core idea of associative democracy is to curb faction through a deliberate politics of association while netting such group contribution to egalitarian-democratic governance. It seeks neither to abolish affirmative governance nor to insulate the state from society nor simply to open a bazaar of bargaining among more equally endowed groups. Instead, it proposes to act directly on the associative environment of public action in ways that make associations less factionalizing and more supportive of the range of egalitarian-democratic norms.

The tools of this reform project would be the conventional tools of public policy (taxes, subsidies, legal sanctions), as applied through the familiar decision-making procedures of formal government (legislatures and administrative bodies, as overseen by the courts). In general terms, the aims of the project are given by the norms of democratic governance. More specifically, this means action in three sorts of area. Where manifest inequalities in political representation exist, associative democracy recommends promoting the organized representation of presently excluded interests. Where group participation undermines popular sovereignty or democratic deliberation, it recommends encouraging the organized to be more other-regarding in their actions. And, where associations have greater competence than public authorities for achieving efficient and equitable outcomes, or where their participation could improve the effectiveness of government programs, it recommends encouraging a more direct and formal governance role for groups.

This last point about governance may be the most immediate. In many areas of economic and social concern – from the environment and occupational safety and health to vocational training and consumer protection – egalitarian aims are badly served by the state-market dichotomy, which still dominates mainstream debate about how those aims should be pursued. Often, the right answer to the question 'Should the state take care of the problem, or should it be left to the market?' is a double negative.

This seems so in three ideal-typical classes of regulatory problems. In the first, non-market public standards on behavior are needed, which government has the competence to set, but the objects of regulation are so diverse or unstable that it is not possible for the government to specify just how those standards should be met at particular regulated sites. Much environmental regulation presents problems of this sort. In the second, public standard-setting is needed, which government has the competence to do, but the objects of regulation are sufficiently numerous or dispersed to preclude serious government monitoring of compliance. Consider the problems of occupational safety and health enforcement. In the third, uniform public standards are needed, but it lies beyond the competence of either markers or governments to specify and secure them, as doing either requires the simultaneous coordination of private actors and their enlistment in specifying the behavior sought. Here, consider the difficulties of getting private firms to agree on standards for vocational training and to increase their own training efforts.

Where these sorts of problems are encountered, associative governance can provide a welcome alternative or complement to public regulatory efforts because of the distinctive capacity of associations to gather local information, monitor behavior and promote cooperation among private actors. In such cases, the associative strategy recommends attending to the possibility of enlisting them explicitly in the performance of public tasks.

Basically, then, associative democracy departs from the observations that groups inevitably play a fundamental role in the politics of mass democracies, that the threat of faction is real and that groups could make a substantial contribution to democratic order. It observes further that the 'right' sorts of association do not arise naturally. It then proposes to supplement nature with artifice: through politics, to secure an associative environment more conducive to democratic aims.

...

[T]he idea of associative democracy may seem of little relevance to the United States. More than any other economically advanced mass democracy, the United States has a strongly anti-collectivist political culture, a weak state and a civil society dominated by (relatively disorganized) business interests. The potential for artifice granted, this context poses obvious problems for the associative strategy. At best, it might be thought, the absence of any initial favoring conditions make the strategy irrelevant. There is simply not enough to get started down the path of democratic associative reform. At worst, it might be feared, pursuit of the strategy under these conditions would be a political nightmare. Giving new licence to a congeries of group privilege and particularism would exacerbate inequalities and further corrupt and enfeeble the state.

Such concerns have considerable force and deserve a fuller answer than we can provide here. Briefly, however, while we acknowledge the anti-collectivism of much of US political culture, we also see considerable experimentation now going on with associative solutions to policy problems in such areas as regional health and welfare service delivery, local economic development, education and training, and environmental regulation, among many others.

There is, for example, a tradition of delivering many welfare and social services through secondary associations – community organizations, churches, volunteer agencies, and the like. While such organizations often have substantial autonomy in designing the appropriate service mix for the communities they are asked to serve, they are also increasingly inextricably dependent on government fees for such services for their own survival. Much 'public' input in local economic development is decided, for good or ill, in 'community development corporations' heavily subsidized government grants representing different admixtures of independent neighborhood associations and business firms. In education, parent-teacher associations are commonly vested with substantial powers in determining the budget and curriculum of elementary and secondary public schools, and those schools increasingly look to local business interests for support in setting standards on student performance. In training, the largest single training program in the United States, the Job Training Partnership Act (JTPA), is almost wholly administered through 'private industry councils' dominated, by statute, by local business interests. In environmental regulation, from the deliberate promotion of bargaining among industry and environmental groups as a prelude to standard-setting at the federal level to the promotion of bargaining between business and community organizations over the appropriate implementation of environmental standards in local neighborhoods and regions, policy is rife with secondary associations exercising de facto public powers.

Some of these efforts display the great strengths of associative governance; others display its many dangers. Our point here is simply that such governance in fact goes on widely, even in this liberal culture, and its incidence provides a natural basis for more deliberate, and democratic, associative strategies.

Moreover, while we acknowledge the weakness of the US state, we think that at least some sorts of associative reforms can make it stronger. Particularly given a weak state, it is important that group empowerment proceed in a way that is reliably positive-sum with state power. But this merely requires judgment in the choice of associative strategies. It does not generally bar their pursuit. And while we acknowledge, finally, the overwhelming business dominance of the US polity, we think this again simply constrains choice in the groups that are advantaged through the associative strategy. If business is too powerful, then associative resources should be provided to labor or other non-business dominated groups; the current imbalance is not an argument for abandoning the general idea.

*From Joshua Cohen and Joel Rogers, 'Secondary Associations and Democratic Governance', in Joshua Cohen and Joel Rogers, eds, *Associations and Democracy: The Real Utopias Project*, Vol. 1 (London: Verso, 1995), 7; 9; 34–5; 44–6; 77–9, reprinted with permission.

Beyond Europe

David Strand is professor of political science at Dickinson College and an expert on Chinese politics. Here he discusses the ambiguity between state and civil society and the relative limits of a critical public sphere in twentieth century China.*

[In the early twentieth century] urban Chinese were actually well positioned to voice their views on public issues and act in concert. At the same time, the state was anxious to control and manage citizen participation, a goal even self-conscious and self-interested groups did not normally oppose in principle.

An example of the continuing power of this combination of dependency and autonomy is the rise of 'professional associations' (*fatuan*) in the late Qing and early Republican period. First formed in 1903 these chambers of commerce, bankers' associations, and lawyers' associations were organized both in recognition of the existing activism of local elites and of the need to guarantee their loyalty. These *fatuan* became the most powerful non-governmental bodies in many cities and towns; they received seals and authorizing documents, from the government and were subject to regulation by the Ministry of Agriculture and Commerce. As Keith Schoppa has pointed out, in this program of 'politicization by government edict ... official rule (*guanzhi*) had co-opted elite proponents of self-rule (*zizhi*).' Local elites including 'gentry' degree-holders as well as merchants had been harping on the need for greater local autonomy for some time. Now these elites, long accustomed to managing their own communities, found themselves given a new legal status as members of formal associations by a state anxious to gain new power over local affairs.

From their inception and through the Republican period, the *fatuan* took on a double role as an extension of state power and as a medium for crystallizing social interests. This occurred despite government attempts to make associations such as chambers of commerce, dependent on official power and to restrict their activities to the narrow legal mandate to 'maintain the stability of the market.' Governments also tried to prevent additional groups from claiming *fatuan* status. The Beijing Student Federation had a long-running disagreement with the police in the 1920's over whether it was a *fatuan* and therefore entitled to hold meetings and discuss matters of concern to students.

For its part, an organization like a chamber of commerce sought to act independently as a representative of the merchant community (*shangmin* or *shangjie*) and city people (*shimin*) as a whole. Embattled chamber leaders defended 'group autonomy' (*tuanti zidong*) against attempts by officials and warlords to encroach on merchant prerogatives. Chambers of commerce also performed official functions. This provision of public goods and services was sometimes done in cooperation with official agencies like the police, sometimes in cooperation with other private individuals and groups, and sometimes alone. *Fatuan* leaders often had ties to government officials and higher-level political factions. They were formally dependent on the state for their authority, but their political base was firmly grounded in the social group or groups they represented. Modern Chinese citizens are the recipients of this mixed legacy of dependence and autonomy. They remain vulnerable to state ideology and control and yet have attempted (with varying degrees of success) to protect themselves from state power through myriad social ties and connections.

Despite its constraints and limitations, locally based politics in the late Qing and early Republican periods appears to have shared some of the critical dynamism found in late 18th-century and 19th-century European cities such as Paris and London, where salons and coffeehouses produced a steady stream of independent commentary about politics. Jürgen Habermas has written extensively about the development of this new European social basis to politics, arguing that it marked the emergence of a 'public sphere' (*Öffentlichkeit*). In the 1920's, a similar public sphere was developing in Beijing. Although the Chinese capital lacked London's coffeehouses, it had intellectual salons as well as locality inns (*huiquan*) with their locality clubs (*tong-xianghui*), merchant and craft guilds, bathhouses, restaurants, teahouses, brothels, public parks, pavilions and temples which functioned as mini-convention centers for guilds and political groups. These social organizations and spaces hosted and housed a lively associational and public life.

But how far to extend the comparison? The existence of a European public sphere assumed a clear distinction between state and society and between public and private realms. Private individuals, newly empowered by capitalism and a sense of social autonomy, were able to wrest control of the public sphere away from princely authority. In Habermas's terms, 'publicity' – the traditional commitment to advertisement of rank and status – was displaced by 'rational-critical debate' – a modern commitment to advancing a point of view or interest – buttressed by the private control of public institutions like newspapers. Along these lines, Rowe points to evidence of a less dramatic, but nevertheless detectable, division between the public and the private in late imperial China. The 'traditional dichotomy between private (*si*) and public (*gong*) came to be muted by a growing belief that private interest, if sufficiently enlightened, could simultaneously serve the interests of society.' Hankou merchants lived by this principle, the notion that one can 'consider righteous conduct as profitable (*yiyi weili*)'. Of course this is not the same as saying profits themselves are righteous or that private points of view or interests have a privileged claim on public discourse. But it is moving in that direction.

Private interests and an autonomous sense of self, both of which supported entry into the public sphere, were in turn rooted in the group on the basis of premodern Chinese civil society. Guildsmen from Huizhou or students from Shandong naturally tended to club together. A Western progression from individual interest to group affiliation to public voice could be easily rearranged in the Chinese case to begin with the group and progress individual action on behalf of self, group or larger cause. During the May Fourth era, the most powerful claims made in and through the public sphere were corporate rather than individual or strictly private, These corporate bodies included old organizations like guilds and locality clubs and new ones like labor unions and student federations. Thus, they were committed to both the realm of 'feudal' publicity and to the realm of rational–critical debate. Following established civic traditions these organizations not only provided a cloak of legitimacy for private interests, they also appropriated, when possible government functions.

In the Republican period, they commonly assumed a quasi-governmental role. For example, chambers of commerce, student and labor unions and any other group with territory and interests to defend maintained their own militia, pickets, bodyguards, and thugs. While the inability of the Republican state to monopolize the means of violence was a signal failure and sign of 'war-lordism,' it can be argued that the devolution of government functions to private groups in this and other areas (like the provision of welfare services) was also a sign of strength and resilience on the part of society.

This kind of social autonomy had direct political consequences. In 1919, shortly before the May 4th Incident representatives of journalists, merchants, members of parliament, and students organized a Beijing 'Foreign Affairs Association' (*waijiao xiehui*) in order to lobby the government on the Shandong issue. This was an illegal organization despite the fact that it represented officially chartered associations like the chamber of commerce. Nonetheless, the social status of the notables involved and the legal standing of the organizations it represented gave the body quasi-legal standing. Accordingly, the government finally agreed to receive its representatives.

After May 4, the Foreign Affairs Association was active in organizing further protests and in cooperating with student demonstrators. It called for a rally in Beijing's Central Park on May 7, the fourth anniversary of Japan's hated 'Twenty-One Demands,' which represented another infringement on Chinese sovereignty. Thousands of residents converged on Changan Avenue and the park entrance at the appointed hour only to be blocked by 2,000 police, cavalry, and soldiers. The leaders then tried to hold the meeting outside Tiananmen, but soldiers prevented them from doing so. Demonstration leaders finally retired to guild halls located in the Outer City.

During the 1920's, police and soldiers often attempted to keep city people from using public spaces for political purposes. For example, they would cordon off the space outside Tiananmen (which at that time was not a 'square' in a formal sense but a walled-in area dotted with trees), run fire drills there, hire entertainers to distract people's attention, or, even, as part of a long-term strategy, plant more trees to displace demonstrators. But as a general rule, the authorities refrained from attacking the corporate bodies themselves (short of placing them under a kind of 'house arrest' by surrounding, say, a college campus). A tradition of corporate self-regulation gave citizens a base from which to voice their demands. Even though citizens could not depend on their constitutional rights being enforced, belonging to an established group provided a modicum of protection. In this fashion, a modern, public politics was built upon the network of affiliations associated with China's premodern civil society.

Why did the state show such restraint toward such groups? Although warlord regimes of the time were weak, repression was one thing itinerant generals and their troops could do pretty well (to echo a comment made about China's government today). Certainly, limits on the intrusion of the state into the public realm were not the result of constitutionalism or liberal values. Part of the answer may lie in the impressive foundation for social communication alluded to above: the huge number of places to meet and the long list of organizations capable of being put to political use. ... But the most important reason has to do with the dual function of public bodies and the double meaning of 'public' in the modern Chinese tradition. As Mary Rankin has shown in her recent study of Zhejiang in the post-Taiping period, when local elites carved out a bigger role for themselves as managers of local society, they made themselves indispensable to their communities and to officialdom. At the same time, they began to take a lively interest in broader public affairs. Local degree-holders attacked corrupt and arrogant officials, calling them 'bandits,' and deplored the apparent willingness of the government to appease the foreign powers. In the 1920's, chamber of commerce leaders and others joined with students and intellectuals in voicing these same complaints as well as others associated with the rise of the new affliction of warlordism.

Governments, at least in the short run, could easily dismiss criticism. It was not so easy for them to dispense with the order, and the social services related to order, that local elites and the organizations they headed traditionally provided in Chinese society. No doubt, government ministers or warlords disliked hearing the bitter complaints that came out of local chambers of commerce on issues ranging from foreign policy to money supply. But governing a city, or sojourning in a city as a government body, without a cooperative chamber of commerce or bankers' association, was not an attractive alternative. Without the cooperation of these quasi-governmental bodies, a powerholder would have been forced to do more than collect taxes, or take the taxes the chamber of commerce collected for him. Lacking the constitutional rights associated with a free society, local elites and the constituents they represented relied on a strong claim to social indispensability to defend and advance their views and interests.

Having suggested the extent of the public sphere's influence during this period, and its peculiar corporate nature and quasi-governmental status, I would like to look at some of its other, special characteristics, which determined its limits and fragility as well as its power. First, despite the relative autonomy of *fatuan* and other corporate bodies, chamber of commerce leaders could be arrested on trumped up charges like embezzlement of corporate funds, and newspaper editors could be shot for attacking a warlord in print. Both the Nationalists and Communists were as illiberal as warlord strongmen in this regard. The politically festive air of Republican cities could easily give way to carnage. Just as the May Fourth Movement prefigured the 1989 pro-democracy movement, the unprovoked attack by the bodyguards of warlord politician Duan Qirui that killed 50 peaceful protesters and wounded 200 more in Beijing on March 18, 1926, to mention just one example, provides a precedent for the bloodletting of June 4, 1989. Such limits on the use of coercion by governments and parties as existed were more often the result of political stalemate – a rough sort of pluralism by default – than of acceptance of constitutional rules of the game.

One of the results of this vulnerability was the prevalence of 'soft' organizations, the best examples of which were the peace preservation associations (*zhian weichi hui*). These associations governed Beijing and other cities in times of military emergency, when one government had fled and the next had yet to arrive. They were made up of local notables like ex-premiers, bankers, or chamber of commerce presidents. If warlords attacked them, they simply packed up and went home, first taking out an advertisement in the newspaper saying the situation was impossible. These soft bodies functioned a bit like the collapsible barriers and dividers built on superhighways to limit damage to everyone involved in a crash. Similarly, if the chamber of commerce itself came under pressure, members could abandon it for a guild or locality club, or retreat further to shop or compound. Individuals who were prominent or notorious enough fled to the foreign controlled Legation Quarter or took a train to Tianjin, the nearest port city. When the pressure eased, the abandoned organizations could be redeployed and reinflated with individuals of suitable status and position. 'Civil society' did not draw a line in the dirt and dare the state, or some state-like entity, to step over it. That would have been foolhardy. It might also have been one of the few ways of giving real substance to the ideas of self-government that were all the rage in the 1920's.

Another factor that limited the critical power of the public sphere related, ironically, to the tremendous success of the May 30th Movement of 1925 in mobilizing city people to participate in mass politics. This movement, like the May Fourth Movement, was triggered by an imperialist outrage (in this case the killing of Chinese civilians by foreign-led police in Shanghai). But while it followed the May Fourth pattern of student-led protests, the May 30th Movement was able to draw far broader participation by city people. The biggest rally of the movement in Beijing took place on June 10, 1925, when a hundred thousand people gathered outside Tiananmen and rallied around a central stage occupied by Nationalist and Communist politicians (allied at the time in a united front). More than 150 groups participated, including the chamber of commerce, guilds, clubs of radical intellectuals, student unions, and worker organizations. Most carried banners showing their affiliation. Participants such as merchants, teachers, workers, students, and journalists were further divided into various 'circles' (*jie*) placed at the corners of the square.

The May 30th Movement displayed a kind of 'spontaneous regimentation' in which participants appeared with workmates and schoolmates in impressive order. Indeed, the assemblies outside Tiananmen were a visual representation of much of organized urban society. Although individuals were encouraged to attend, most people came with their group. In addition to offering protection, group affiliation provided the kind of vertical connections to bosses and patrons and horizontal ties to colleagues and comrades necessary for the rapid mobilization of crowds. Craftsmen arrived under the leadership of their labor bosses, and merchants and shop clerks came under the auspices of hierarchically organized guilds.

The ideals of equality and inclusiveness conveyed by the 'Citizens Assembly' banner that dominated the center of the demonstration were thus offset by the elitist and exclusive nature of many of the participating groups. The demonstrations outside Tiananmen and the marches that wound their way around the city had more than a little in common with medieval European processions, which by their corporate character, not only presented a show of unity but also pointed up the deep divisions among groups and classes.

...

The halting reemergence of a civil society suggests the potential for independent authority over politics. Whereas the unit-based nature of urban society once contained spontaneous participation in politics, these Leninist social and economic arrangements now lend structure to mass protests. The state itself is so huge and stratified that sections of it threaten to fall off like pieces of poorly laminated plywood. Earlier in the century, social groups themselves developed a quasi-governmental identity; groups participating in movements brought corporate order (and sometimes competition) to the scene outside Tiananmen. Society could attack the state by creating, or threatening to create, its own police forces, tax-collecting agencies, schools, charities, and welfare programs. Now, elements of the state, broadly conceived to include state-controlled institutions like universities, newspapers, and factories, have developed an independent social identity. They can attack the state by creating a Chinese version of the East European strategy of 'social self-defense.' In the past, this ambiguity between state and society redounded to the advantage of the regime in its quest for political and social control. But now, the state's increasing difficulty in controlling itself can trigger the sudden enlargement of society, as we witnessed last year. As was indicated by the defecting journalists from the official media, workers in state enterprises, researchers, and office personnel in 1989, the state, or portions of it, could form the social basis of protest against the regime itself.

The 1989 movement erupted without extensive organization or an organized leadership and followed a cultural logic of protest that fed on a popular sense of a disturbed moral atmosphere. For this reason, the evils of corruption ultimately were a more salient issue for many participants and sympathizers than democracy. But then democracy has often initially gained ground as an 'oppositional ideal. ... a polemical notion whose function is to oppose, not to propose. The utterance of "democracy" is a way of saying no to inequality, injustice, and coercion.'

This negative message fitted perfectly with the traditional tone of the movement. The manner in which a cultural motif could be used as a surrogate for organization was a remarkable development. As suggested above, this cultural production had a social basis. What has troubled symphatizers, as well as some participants, is the apparent dominance of form over substance. But even in the 1920s, the critical-rational element in public debate always had a strong component of publicity, both in the sense of modern propaganda and in the sense of representation of status (students as heirs of the literati tradition or water carriers as a semi-hereditary occupational group). Faced with a regime that refuses to 'listen' and is committed to undermining, when it can, social communication and voluntary association, the democracy movement's culturally derived attack made perfect sense.

*From David Strand, 'Protest in Beijing: Civil Society and Public Sphere in China', *Problems of Communism*, 39 (May–June 1990), 4–7; 18–19, reprinted with permission.

Jeffrey N. Wasserstrom and Liu Xinyong, respectively, have been teaching history at Indiana University and social science at Syracuse University. Here they discuss the specific factors of state, party and hierarchical organizations that, they argue, limit the meaningfulness of Western notions of civil society and public sphere in the Chinese context.

[T]he variable content and form of civil societies and public spheres has received too little attention. Thus one finds comparative discussions of Eastern Europe and China in the late 1980s that contrast the strength of civil society in the former with its weakness in the latter, without looking closely at qualitative differences between the traditions of, say, Polish clerics and Chinese entrepreneurs (two groups associated with the carving out of public spheres for autonomous action in their respective lands). This culturally and historically flattened approach to civil society, and the assumptions associated with it concerning the inevitable connection between capitalism and democratization, is important not only because of its influence on Western China specialists but also because of its impact on Chinese dissidents themselves. A speech given in the early 1990s by Wan Runnan, who is both president of the Stone Corporation and a leader of Minzhen (Federation for a Democratic China), illustrates this point. Speaking at Berkeley's China Forum, Wan's topic was the 'development of the private sector in China and its relationship with the establishment of a civil society.' He began by noting that 'civil society was totally wiped out' during the 'first years of totalitarian rule by the Chinese communists,' then proceeded to make the following statement:

> Now as we all know, democracy is to a large degree based upon the exist-
> ence of a very exuberant civil society, *gongmin shehui*. I recently talked with
> Yu Yingshi at Princeton University and he delved into this lack of civil
> society in China, which in his opinion is the major difference between
> Chinese and Western society.

If Wan used this statement as a starting point for exploration and went on to provide evidence to support his assumptions, we would not single it out for criticism. Unfortunately, as has happened too often in the discourse on 1989, the statement was left to stand on its own as though it was axiomatic. Wan felt no need to defend the assumption that the more vibrant the civil society and market economy of a given land, the more democratic its political institutions would be. This assumption is troubling for several reasons and open to question on a variety of grounds. Nevertheless what is of the greatest concern here is that this assumption infers that civil society can be under-stood in quantitative terms – that an equation can be formulated and solved without reference to qualitative issues, such as the institutions, traditions, and symbols that make a particular society tick.

The problem with this idea is that ... the Chinese and European cases are qualitatively as well as quantatively different with regard to civil society institutions.

...

The years immediately preceding the protest movement of 1989 were undeniably, like those that preceded the struggles of 1919 and 1925, ones in which a wide variety of student associations were formed. It is likewise undeniable that the months leading up to the June 4 massacre were ones in which members of other urban groups were engaged in a flurry of organiza-tional activity ... These facts are certainly worth mentioning, and the search for 'sprouts of civil society' in these two eras is by no means a pointless one, since newly formed *shetuan* clearly played key roles in shaping the mass movements of 1919, 1925, and 1989. The problem with simply stating these things and then moving on is that to do so obscures key differences between the civil society organizing of the warlord and Dengist eras. ... One of the most significant of these differences has to do with class boundaries. The campus organizations formed in the 1980s tended to be based on a single class. Exceptions to this were groups whose members included both people active in private enterprises like the Stone Corporation and people affiliated with universities. But the 'multiclass' nature of some of these groups was ambiguous at best; since many of the entrepreneurs involved were also *zhishifenzi* in the broader sense of the Chinese term. ... [C]ampus groups seldom established connections between intellectuals and workers.

The situation was very different in the warlord era. Some of the pre-May Fourth equivalents of the democracy salons of the 1980s were popular lecture corps whose main reason for being was to bring students into contact with workers and peasants. Many of the leaders of the May Thirtieth movement, meanwhile, came to their participation in protest mass actions via campus associations that had been involved in helping workers set up laborers' clubs and unions. It is also worth noting that campus *tonxianghui* often had close ties to citywide native-place leagues (*huiguan*), which established networks between members of all social classes from a given place of origin.

...

A related feature of the discourse on civil society and 1989 that troubles us has to do with the hegemonic power of rituals and cultural norms associated with the state. Although there is no reason for those who take Rousseau, Gramsci, or Habermas seriously to do so, many of those who have applied their concepts to China assume that groups operating autonomously from the state apparatus will be relatively unaffected by official social and cultural orthodoxies, especially if such groups think of themselves as espousing ideologies that are counterhegemonic. By this line of reasoning, since salons and autonomous student unions were civil society institutions whose members were committed to democratic ideals different from those of the CCP, we can assume that they would have little in common with official organizations in terms of structure and function. Our own reading of events such as the May Fourth movement leads us to think that this assumption greatly underestimates the power of hegemonic patterns of behavior have to structure social and cultural life, even in the midst of movements for radical change.

...

Ironically ... the mass movement that developed in 1919 was organized along quite 'traditional' lines. The boycotting of Japanese goods was enforced in large part by *shirentuan* (groups of ten), which bore more than a passing resemblance to the smallest collectivity in that most 'Confucian' and bureaucratized of social control structures, the *baojia* mutual responsibility system. Student *shirentuan*, like those organized by other protesters, had designated leaders, as well as other officers with special responsibilities, and (in theory at least) were incorporated into larger groups of one hundred (ten *shirentuan*) and one thousand (one hundred *shirentuan*) run by still more elaborate bureaucracies.

The *shirentuan* were not, moreover, the only Republican era protest groups that resembled state organs, for the dissident unions formed by educated youths had many features (security forces, propaganda bureaus, carefully spelled out hierarchies) reminiscent of the official associations (Western treaty-port as well as Chinese) to which the student activists had been exposed. ... [I]n the process of (consciously or unconsciously) imitating official organizations, protest groups often internalize some of the less appealing features of the orders they oppose.

[T]he distribution of power between men and women within protest leagues was far from equal ... One other sign of the persistence of traditional role casting, despite New Culture movement calls for an end to Confucian subordination of women, is that (as far as we have been able to tell) the most important assignment given to the women's branch of the local student union in Shanghai in 1919 was to sew special caps for protesters to don at rallies.

Writings on 1989 have made it clear that the protest leagues that spearheaded this 'New May Fourth movement' were plagued by some of the same problems as the organizations of the party-state they challenged. Most non-CCP works on 1989 highlight positive features of the protest movement, praising the students for their commitment to non-violence and their interest in new ideas. These same works also point out that the political decision-making process carried out in the open spaces of Tiananmen Square was much more inclusive and egalitarian than that practiced in the Great Hall of the People. As valid as these points are, however, even sympathetic observers and analysts have noted that the political community and the alternative government created in the square also had their dark sides. Foreign eye-witnesses have accused specific student leaders of behaving too much like the CCP officials whose actions the youths condemned, charging the youths with everything from mishandling funds to using security guards to keep themselves aloof from ordinary members of their constituency, to creating their own personality cults. Documents such as the June Second Hunger Strike Proclamation show, moreover, that even at the height of the movement, some dissidents were concerned that the protesters were falling into familiar traps of enforced orthodoxies of opinion, bureaucratization, and the like. The failure of the protesters to form effective multiclass organizations, while perhaps partly attributable to the single-class nature of so many pre-movement civil society associations ... must also be seen as due in part to student internalization of hegemonic ideas relating to social status hierarchies. Similarly, in 1989 as in 1919, radical iconoclasts fell into traditional patterns regarding issues of gender and power.

* From Jeffrey N. Wasserstrom and Liu Xinyong, 'Student Associations and Mass Movements', in Deborah S. Davis, Richard Kraus, Barry Naughton and Elizabeth J. Perry, eds, *Urban Spaces in Contemporary China: The Potential for Autonomy and Community in Post-Mao China* (Cambridge: Cambridge University Press, 1995), 375–82, reprinted with the permission of Cambridge University Press.

Nancy N. Chen teaches anthropology at the University of California, Santa Cruz. Here she looks at the popular breathing practices of qigong *to argue for the spatial and informal dimensions of social practices contributing to civil society.**

In the years following initiation of the post-Mao reforms, the popularity of *qigong* practice (traditional breathing and health exercises) and healing in the People's Republic of China (PRC) grew to such immense proportions that many referred to the phenomenon as *qigong re* (*qigong* fever). Heated discussions, vivid testimonies, and folklore about the miraculous powers of *qigong* spontaneously developed on buses, at work units (*danwei*), even on university campuses. The popularity of *qigong* was fueled by martial arts films and pulp novels, as well as by official bodies of medical science and research institutes. Chinese government estimates in 1990 placed the number of practitioners at 5 percent of the total population (about 60 million persons); more recent estimates raise the number to nearly 200 million.

...

An exploration of the consciousness of ordinary Chinese urbanites is germane to the debate over civil society. While categories of *gong* (public) and *si* (private) lend understanding to how the political and the personal are bounded in Chinese culture, it is important to note not only how these experiences are mutually constructed in the process of urbanization but also how individuals perceive or create such spheres. ... In the present reform period, when the Chinese socialist state is experimenting with free markets and private entrepreneurs, studies of the development of public–private spheres in capitalism suggest useful conceptual tools for viewing emergent relationships among the contemporary Chinese state, civil society, and everyday life. The meaning of *gong* implies public and state ownership. However, institutions, work-units, and official associations are not the only public organizations found in contemporary China. In recent years nonstate associations have expanded possibilities of public life to include the streets, common areas, and even open debates. Although the public sphere and civil society are useful constructs with which to understand city life, practices within these realm should also be examined.

. . .

Although there are innumerable forms and schools of *qigong*, there are three basic forms of practice – as martial art, as meditation practice, and as healing ritual. The first type of *qigong* as martial art is often referred to as 'hard *qigong*' (*ying qigong*). Masters of this form carry out incredible feats such as breaking rocks with the force of *qi* in their hands or moving opponents ten feet away by concentrating their powers of *qi*. The second type, *qigong* practice as meditation, is found more commonly in the early morning in the park, where individuals stand in prescribed stances or sit in lotus position under trees. These practitioners believe that trees have special powers of *qi* that can revive the force of *qi* in their own bodies. Many individuals can be seen hugging trees, rubbing their bodies around the trunk of trees, dancing in circles around trees, or sitting quietly before a tree. The third type, *qigong* practice as healing ritual, poses the greatest threat to the state not only because of the immensely popular following that has grown since the early 1980s but also because of its growing resemblance to a spiritualist cult or millenarian movement. . . .

The formation of *qigong* associations can be viewed in a continuum from officially sanctioned bureaucratic organizations to popular revitalistic movements headed by charismatic leaders. While the basis of their organization depends partly upon the practice being promoted (exercise, meditation, or healing), it is primarily economic and political interests that determine the type of alliances that develop. The four main categories of *qigong* associations are: (1) official bodies that are formed by the state and administered by bureaucrats; (2) legitimate and public groups that have attained official recognition but retain some autonomy in membership and practice; (3) popular, informal groups that are autonomous and exist in a 'gray zone' of activities not necessarily sanctioned by the state; and (4) underground associations that are officially condemned or denounced as dealing in 'false' or 'superstitious' practices.

. . .

This phenomenological transformation is often described as a blissful state of placing one's body in harmony with its surroundings and natural forces. Practitioners are told to relax (*fang song*) and through a litany of points along the body to relate the *qi* in their body to the *qi* in the atmosphere.

Getting in touch with one's body through these traditional points of energy links the body to a universe outside the immediate urban surroundings of the Chinese state. These experiences illustrate what Kleinman terms the 'somato-moral world' where 'hidden transcripts' of identity and meaning are forged. The self is rewritten as a personal being apart from, or disembodied from, the state. The linkages of the mind–body to a different source of power, that of a cosmological order, transgress familiar boundaries of the state. As a devoted practitioner once explained, 'This city is laid out in the image of Buddha. This (park) location corresponds to the sacred *dan tian* [center of *qi* energy]. If you practice here, you will find yourself to be different than when in any other place.' The individual enjoys a topography of the self where layers of meaning and images of power are personally inscribed, carrying imagination to new states of consciousness.

The transformations of self, mind, and body in *qigong* entail a revision of one's understanding and relationship with the natural world. The individual body is not the only entity transformed by this experience. Where once associations such as work-units, schools, or neighborhood committees were the primary form of urban interaction, *qigong* networks create a new community of individuals from diverse backgrounds. Networks based on *guanxi* or familial relationships remain vital to everyday life but *qigong* associations encompass a new sense of urban humanism. As a middle-aged male worker commented with a broad smile, 'I strive to do good in my everyday life. That's how *qigong* has changed me.' Independent voluntary communities buttressed by such a broad base of alliances and meanings contain immense potential. Charismatic leaders and the popular image of *qigong* founded on media and healing narratives have created a sense of autonomous identity that is well entrenched in urban spaces and city life.

The unsettling nature of this process helps explain the state's response. The recent position of the Chinese socialist bureaucracy relative to *qigong* associations and masters indicates great concern over the revitalistic and political potential of such formations. Although *qigong* continues to be promoted by the state as a unique Chinese tradition, the social networks led by charismatic leaders present a latent danger. Popular *qigong* associations resonate with a long tradition of peasant uprisings and heterodox movements, such as the Boxers, who once practiced *qi* exercises to promote their visions of a utopian society. Regulation and intervention by the Chinese socialist state blames society, an ironic turn of events since people take up *qigong* because of disenchantment with official ideology and policy. The state's presence is inserted into everyday life through surveillance of public arenas such as the parks. Categories of 'official' versus 'false' *qigong* are created to permit practitioners of 'superstitious' activities to be taken into custody for questioning. Those who continue to practice in parks do so under red banners and white certificates of legitimately recognized schools of *qigong*. Witch hunts of masters are carried out in the name of fighting corruption.

And boundaries of normality are reestablished through creating a medical disorder called *qigong* deviation.

Rather than think of civil society as 'subaltern' or independent associations in opposition to the state, one should regard it as a more ambiguous relationship. Altered states refer not only to states of consciousness that shape certain experiences in *qigong*, but also to a refiguration of the state through *qigong* practice. Many party members and bureaucrats themselves have either received *qigong* healing treatment, or have been devoted practitioners. One such person remarked in 1990, 'There were only two things I believed in last year – the party and *qigong*. Now I just believe in *qigong*.' While the Chinese socialist state tries to recapture control of center stage through surveillance, public censure, and imprisonment, the dimensions of time and space – two realms of power where *qigong* experience is mediated – remain contested.

* From Deborah S. Davis, Richard Kraus, Barry Naughton, and Elizabeth J. Perry, eds, *Urban Spaces in Contemporary China: The Potential for Autonomy and Community in Post-Mao China* (Cambridge: Cambridge University Press, 1995), 347; 348–9; 353–4; 358–60.

*Ernest Gellner (1925–95), was a modern polymath of Czech Jewish background, who offered nothing less than a philosophy of history for our times. One of his central claims was that Islam was unlikely to secularize in the modern world, and that its insistence of Puritanism and discipline was likely to make it an enemy of civil society.**

The central doctrines of Islam contain an emphatic and severe monotheism, the view that the Message received by the Prophet is so to speak terminal, and that it contains both faith and morals – or, in other words, it is both doctrine and law, and that no genuine further augmentation is to be countenanced. The points of doctrine and points of law are not separated, and Muslim learned scholars are best described as theologians/jurists.

. . .

The fact that, in this way, legislation is pre-empted by the deity has profound implications for Muslim life. ... So, once the idea of a final and divine law came to be accepted, a law which in principle was to receive no further divine additions, and not to allow any human ones, the (human) executive became in the very nature of things distinct from the (divine, but communally mediated) legislative arm of government. Law could be extended at best by analogy and interpretation. Society was thus endowed with both a fundamental and concrete law, each in its way entrenched, and usable by its members as a yardstick of legitimate government. Entrenched constitutional law was, as it were, waiting and ever-ready for all polities. A socially and politically transcendent standard of rectitude was ever accessible, beyond the reach of manipulation by political authority, and available for condemning the *de facto* authority if it sinned against it. It only needed for that standard to possess an earthly ally, endowed with armed might, for the sinning authority – if it was held to be sinful – to be in trouble. The political history of Islam does display the periodic emergence of such a daunting alliance of transcendent rectitude and earthly might.

. . .

Islam, having in the past been an eternal or cyclical reformation, ever reforming the morals of the faithful, but never doing so for good, turned in the course of the past hundred years into a definitive and, as far as one can judge, irreversible reformation. There has been an enormous shift in the balance *from* Folk Islam *to* High Islam. The social bases of Folk Islam have been in large part eroded, whilst those of High Islam were greatly strengthened. Urbanization, political centralization, incorporation in a wider market, labour migration, have all impelled populations in the direction of the formally (theologically) more 'correct' Islam.

Identification with Reformed Islam has played a role very similar to that played by nationalism elsewhere. In Muslim countries it is indeed difficult to distinguish the two movements. The average believer can hardly continue to identify with his local tribe or shrine. The tribe has fallen apart, the shrine is abandoned. By modern standards, both are suspect, a good piece of folklore for tourists, but a little beneath the dignity of an urbanized citizen of a modern state. The city-dweller does not display himself in public at the shrine festival, and still less does he allow his wife, daughter or sister to do so. He does not settle his disputes by calling his cousins to defend or to testify at a shrine, he knows the feud is proscribed and will be suppressed by the police; he knows he can better protect himself by using whatever pull he may have in the official and informal political networks.

Islam provides a national identity, notably in the context of the struggle with colonialism – the modern Muslim 'nation' is often simply the sum-total of Muslims on a given territory. Reformist Islam confers a genuine shared identity on what would otherwise be a mere summation of the under-privileged. It also provides a kind of ratification of the social ascension of many contemporary Muslims, from rustic status to becoming better-informed town-dwellers, or at least town-oriented persons.

. . .

To continue the argument: in Islam, we see a pre-industrial faith, a founded, doctrinal, world religion in the proper sense, which, at any rate for the time being, totally and effectively defies the secularization thesis. So far, there is no indication that it will succumb to secularization in the future either, though of course it is always dangerous to indulge in prophecy. The reasons which have made this achievement possible seem to be the following: all 'under-developed' countries tend to face a certain dilemma. ... The dilemma such countries face is: should we emulate those whom we wish to equal in power (thereby spurning our own tradition), or should we, on the contrary, affirm the values of our own tradition, even at the price of material weakness? This issue was most poignantly recorded in Russian literature of the nineteenth century in the form of the debate between Westernization and Populism/ Slavophilism.

It is painful to spurn one's own tradition, but it is also painful to remain weak. Few under-developed countries have escaped this dilemma, and they have handled it in diverse ways. But what is interesting, and crucial for our argument, is that Islam is ideally placed to escape it.

. . .

[T]here cannot be much doubt about the present situation in the ideological sphere. In the West, we have become habituated to a certain picture, according to which puritan zeal had accompanied the early stages of the emergence of a modem economy, but in which its culmination was eventually marked by a very wide-spread religious lukewarmness and secularization. The sober thrifty work-oriented spirit, which helps amass wealth, is then undermined by the seductions brought along by that which it has achieved. The virtue inculcated by puritanism leads to a prosperity which subverts that virtue itself, as John Wesley had noted with regret.

In the world of Islam, we encounter quite a different situation. Though long endowed with a commercial bourgeoisie and significant urbanization, this civilization failed to engender industrialism; but once industrialism and its various accompaniments had been thrust upon it, and it had experienced not only the resulting disturbance but also some of its benefits, it turned, not at all to secularization, but rather to a vehement affirmation of the puritan version of its own tradition. Perhaps this virtue has not yet been rewarded by a really generalized affluence, but there is little to indicate that a widespread affluence would erode religious commitment. Even the unearned oil-fall wealth has not had this effect.

Things may yet change in the future. But on the evidence available so far, the world of Islam demonstrates that it is possible to run a modern, or at any rate modernizing, economy, reasonably permeated by the appropriate technological, educational, organization principles, *and* combine it with a strong, pervasive, powerfully internalized Muslim conviction and identification.

A puritan and scripturalist world religion does not seem necessarily doomed to erosion by modern conditions. It may on the contrary be favoured by them.

* From Ernest Gellner, *Postmodernism, Reason and Religion* (London: Routledge, 1992), 6–8; 15–16; 18–19; 21–2, reprinted with the permission of the publisher.

*Ashutosh Varshney, (b. 1957), a political scientist at Michigan University, is the author of important books on Indian politics and society. In this passage he takes issue with the view that only modern associations which allow easy entry and exit should be endorsed as civil. This view too easily fails to appreciate the pluralist and progressive character of much associational life within traditional societies.**

According to the conventional notions prevalent in the social sciences, 'civil society' refers to the space in a given society that (a) exists between the family level and the state level, (b) makes interconnections between individuals or families possible, and (c) is independent of the state. Many, though not all, of the existing definitions also suggest two more requirements: that the civic space be organized in *associations* that attend to the cultural, social, economic, and political needs of the citizens and that the associations be modern and voluntaristic, *not ascriptive*. Going by the first requirement, trade unions would be part of civil society, but informal neighborhood associations would not. And following the second requirement, philately clubs and parent-teacher associations would be civic but not an association of Jews in defense of Israel or a black church.

Should we agree with the latter two requirements? Can nonassociational space also be called civic or part of civil society? Must associations, to form part of civil society, be of a 'modern' kind – voluntaristic and cross-cutting rather than ascriptive and based on ethnic affiliations? These questions are not simply theoretical. In many societies, group-based but informal activities – sports, entertainment, festivals – are often part of the space between the state and family life. And the same is true of ethnic associations, whether they are black churches in the United States, right-wing Jewish groups in Israel, or an exclusively Hindu group such as the Vishva Hindu Parishad (VHP), existing both in India and in the Indian diaspora all over the world. All of these groups would meet the first definition of civil society, but none would meet the second. Are they part of civil society or not? Why should informal but group-based activity of citizens be excluded from civil society? Why should ethnic or religious associations not be included?

...

Normative conceptualizations are ... not confined to political philosophy. A normative tenor marks scholarship on civil society as a whole. Consider Ernest Gellner, whose writings on the subject have been plentiful as well as influential. 'Modularity,' argues Gellner, 'makes civil society,' whereas 'segmentalism' defines a traditional society.[1] By 'modularity' Gellner means the ability to rise beyond traditional or ascriptive occupations and associations. Given a multipurpose, secular, and modern education, and given the objective availability of plentiful as well as changing professional opportunities in post-traditional times, modern man can move from one occupation to another, one place to another, one association to another. In contrast, birth assigned occupation and place to traditional man. A carpenter in traditional society, whether he liked it or not, would be a carpenter, and all his kinsmen would be carpenters. He would also not generally be involved in an association; and if he were, it would most likely be an ascriptive guild of carpenters. In such a 'segmental' or traditional society, freedom of will with respect to associations, occupations, or places of living would neither be available nor encouraged, and an ethnic division of labor would exist. An agrarian society, argued Gellner, might be able to avoid the tyranny of the state for, in view of the decentralized nature of the production structure, the low level of communication technology, and the relatively self-sufficient character of each segment, the power of the state would not be able to reach all segments of a traditional society. But that does not mean that such a society would be 'civil,' for instead of a 'tyranny of the state' it would experience a 'tyranny of cousins': 'It thrusts on to the individual an ascribed identity, which then may or may not be fulfilled, whereas a modern conception of freedom includes the requirement that identities be chosen rather than ascribed.' Civil society, concludes Gellner, is not only modern but also based on strictly voluntary, not ethnic or religious, associations between the family and the state.

Both empirically and conceptually, there is an odd modernist bias in the formulations above. Tradition is considered intolerant and incorrigible beyond redemption. And modernity is assumed to promise and deliver such a great deal that much that may be valuable and highly flexible in tradition, including pluralism, is simply defined out of consideration, and much that may be subversive of free will and 'civility' in capitalist, if not socialist, modernity is also, by definition, ruled out of court. Even if choral societies in twelfth-century northern Italy were making it possible for people to connect, their inclusion in civil society *before the rise of modern capitalism*, according to this perspective, is unwarranted.

Each of the major claims in the modernist conception of civil society can be empirically challenged. First, the argument that ethnic or religious associations are ascriptive is only partially correct. A remarkably large number of studies, both in the West and in the developing world, show that ethnic and religious associations combine ascription and choice. Not all Christians have to be members of a church in a given town; not all blacks in a neighborhood are members of a black church; not all members of a caste or linguistic group have to participate in a caste or linguistic association. Moreover, it has also been widely documented that ethnic associations can perform many 'modern' functions, such as participating in democratic politics, setting up funds to encourage members of the group to enter newer professions, and facilitating migration of kinsmen into newer places for modern occupations and modern education.

Many ethnic associations are undoubtedly bigoted with respect to outgroups as well as tyrannical to their own cousins, but that does not exhaust the range of ethnic organizations or the variety of ethnic activities. In many societies in which ethnic groups are arranged hierarchically and some ethnic groups have historically faced prejudice, the ethnic associations of such groups are known to have been among the most effective organizations to fight for ethnic equality in the workplace, politics, and schools. A large number of Jewish associations in the United States, 'lower-caste' organizations in India, Moroccan and Algerian groups in France, and black organizations in contemporary South Africa have performed such roles with considerable distinction, if not always with great success. Similarly, many churches and religious organizations – for example, in Poland and Latin America – are known to have fought the state for democracy and freedom. The forms of association may have been traditional, but the goals pursued were highly modern.

Taking pride in one's ethnic group and working for the group does not, ipso facto, make one 'uncivil.' It matters what the aim of such ascription-based group activity is. That is not a theoretical but an empirical question. Paradoxically for Gellner, modularity for their group is what many ethnic associations may seek, realizing how important it has become to leave traditional callings and move to modern occupations. Moreover, the ethnic form of association may also be based on a highly modern consideration: low transaction costs. It is less difficult to get people together on grounds of similarity than difference, and once such association is formed, perfectly modern goals may be pursued: making organized but nonviolent demands on the political system, teaming up with organizations of different groups to make a 'rainbow coalition' in politics, providing support for entrepreneurship in their community.

In short, the idea that ethnicity or religion is equal to traditionalism and therefore can't perform the functions of civic organizations – allowing people to come together, making public discussion of issues possible, challenging the caprice or misrule of state authorities, promoting modern business activities – has too many exceptions to be considered empirically admissible. Whatever one may think of ethnic associations in general, at least the ethnic associations that meet the functional or purposive criteria specified by normative arguments should be considered part of civil society.

If what is crucial to the notion of civil society is that families and individuals connect with others beyond their homes and talk about matters of public relevance without the interference or sponsorship of the state, then it seems far too rigid to insist that this takes place only in 'modern' associations. Empirically speaking, whether such engagement takes place in associations or in the traditional sites of social get-togethers depends on the degree of urbanization and economic development, as well as on the nature of the political system. Cities tend to have formal associations, but villages make do with informal sites and meetings. Further, political systems may specify which groups have access to formal civic spaces and may form organizations and which ones may not. Nineteenth-century Europe provided the propertied classes access to a whole range of political and institutional instruments of interest articulation; trade unions for workers, however, were slower to arrive.

. . .

To conclude, at least in the social and cultural settings that are different from Europe and North America, if not more generally, the purposes of activity rather than the forms of organization should be the critical test of civic life. Tradition is not necessarily equal to a tyranny of cousins, and capitalist modernity, does not always make civic interaction possible. At best, such dualities are ideal types or are based on normatively preferred visions. Empirically speaking, tradition can often permit challenging the cousins if existing norms of reciprocity and ethics are violated. Similarly, even capitalist modernity may be highly unsocial and atomizing if people in inner-city America stay at home and watch MTV instead of forming neighborhood watch groups or attending to the abandoned children's homes.[2] Informal group activities as well as ascriptive associations should be considered part of civil society so long as they connect individuals, build trust, encourage reciprocity, and facilitate exchange of views on matters of public concern – economic, political, cultural, and social. While doing all of this, they may well be connected with interethnic violence, though intraethnic peace may be maintained. But that is to be established empirically. Theoretically, one should not assume that ethnic associations promote tyranny of cousins or interethnic violence.

* From Ashutosh Varshney, *Ethnic Conflict and Civic Life: Hindus and Muslims in India* (New Haven: Yale University Press, © 2002), 39–44; 46, reprinted with the permission of Yale University Press.

[1] Ernest Gellner, 'The Importance of Being Modular', in John A. Hall ed., *Civil Society: Theory, History, Comparison* (Cambridge: Blackwell, 1995). This article is a good summary of a large number of Gellner's works on civil society, written in the reflective and the activist modes. Many of these writings, including some polemical essays, have been put together in Gellner, *Conditions of Liberty: Civil Society and Its Rivals* (New York: Penguin, 1994).

[2] For discussion of the ways in which civic activity in the United States has declined, see Robert Putnam, 'The Strange Disappearance of Civic America', *American Prospect* (Winter 1996); 'Bowling Alone', *Journal of Democracy* (January 1995); and Putnam, *Bowling Alone* (New York: Simon and Schuster, 2000). *See pp. 227–31 in this reader.*

Augustus Richard Norton (b. 1946), a political scientist at Boston University, had a significant impact on the understanding of civil society within Muslim societies as the result of his important two volume collection on Civil Society in the Middle East *(1995). In this section, he expresses measured optimism because of the growth of associational life. Still, the future of civil society depends upon the transformation of authoritarian rule within the region.**

The symbol of democracy is the contested election and the secret ballot. This is altogether understandable, since the right to cast a meaningful ballot free of coercion is a metaphor for a participant political system. But, democracy does not reside in elections. If democracy – as it is known in the West – has a home, it is in civil society, where a melange of associations, clubs, guilds, syndicates, federations, unions, parties and groups come together to provide a buffer between state and citizen. Although the concept of civil society is resistant to analytical precision, the functioning of civil society is literally and plainly at the heart of participant political systems.

In fact, the icon of the global trend of democratization is civil society. In the face of repression in Latin America, Eastern and Southern Europe, civil society is sometimes credited with thwarting authoritarian designs and challenging arbitrary rule. Nonetheless, civil society did not topple regimes, as much as the regimes crumbled from internal corruption and hollow claims for legitimacy. Civil society was more the beneficiary than the wrecking ball. Moreover, civil society is often idealized as an unmitigated good thing. Like any social phenomenon, civil society can, and, often, does have, a negative side. Self-interest, prejudice and hatred cohabit with altruism, fairness and compassion, and the unrestrained free play of civil society is a chilling thought, not a warm and fuzzy one.

Civil society speaks in a myriad of voices. The vanguard of civil society has been human rights activists, religiously-inspired protest movements, artists, writers and professional groups of lawyers, doctors or engineers who insist on governmental accountability and thereby expose the excesses and the weaknesses of authoritarian rulers. There is no denying the awe-inspiring courage that must be summoned to speak out, to demonstrate, to stand one's ground in circumstances where the policing apparatus is both ubiquitous and untethered by legal restrictions, where the sovereignty of the individual is a gift rather than a right.

Civil society is also grounded in a free economic market and the quest of the bourgeoisie for political differentiation from the state. As Simon Bromley notes, the rallying cry of the bourgeoisie has been liberalism not democracy, but the formation of a civil society is enabling for democracy.

> [A] liberal civil society provides both the structural underpinning of representative democracy and the terrain on which an organized working class can develop. Historically, the latter have proved to be not capitalism's 'grave-diggers' but its democratizers.

The fostering of civil society is a crucial step toward realizing a freer Middle East. One is hard pressed to design a participant political system which could survive very long in the absence of a vibrant civil society. In short, the existence of civil society is central to democracy.

However, civil society enthusiasts often contain their excitement when it comes to the Muslim world, and especially the Middle East. There, civil society is said to be deficient, corrupt, aggressive, hostile, infiltrated, co-opted, insignificant, or absent, depending on which observer one prefers to cite. For instance, in widely read essay, Ernest Gellner notes that Muslim societies 'are suffused with faith, indeed they suffer from a plethora of it, but they manifest at most a feeble yearning for civil society.'

One way, an important way, of assessing the quality of political life in the Middle East is to inquire into the status of civil society there, to plumb their 'yearning' for civil society. As Saad Eddin Ibrahim notes, there has been impressive growth in associations since the mid-1960s to the late 1980s. During this period the numbers grew from 20,000 to 70,000. Of course, only a minority are active and effective. Ibrahim cites a recent study in Egypt showing that 40% of registered associations are actually viable. Among the interesting blossomings of civil society is the emergence of political parties, including 46 in Algeria, 43 in Yemen, 23 in Jordan, 19 in Morocco, 13 in Egypt, 11 in Tunisia, and 6 in Mauritania. But, far more important are the professional syndicates (*niqabat*) which have sometimes given shape to politics. In Sudan, the professional associations effectively overthrew the government in both 1964 and 1985. Significantly, the present Islamist-cum-military government of Sudan rushed to regulate and stifle syndicates, apparently to preclude a reprise. In Egypt, Morocco and Tunisia, the syndicates have often been potent players, not least because of their linkage to international counterparts that enable them to enlist moral protection from abroad.

If, as we assume here, a vital and autonomous civil society is a necessary condition of democracy (though not a sufficient one), what does the present status of Middle East civil society portend? More fundamentally, does civil society exist in the Middle East?[1] Many observers are doubtful that civil society, particularly in the Arab world, is sufficiently diverse or mature to lend durability to open, participant systems. Moreover, a number of respected scholars have expressed skepticism that vibrant, autonomous civil societies will soon emerge in the Arab countries, considering the statist economies that stifle free association and the intolerance of populist Islamist movements. In the Middle East, and particularly in the Arab states, democracy has been bestowed rather than won, and, as the Algerian example illustrates, the gift may be revoked.

. . .

Raymond Hinnebusch argues that economic liberalization in Syria is intended to broaden the regime's political base and to lift disabling economic controls stemming from Syria's failed statist experiment. Though the process is moving forward at a restrained pace, Hinnebusch notes that one result may be a more active civil society but not democracy. Syria's traditional merchants, until recently, were politically muffled and over-regulated. The merchants are benefiting from the economic reforms and are regaining influence in the process. In short, Hinnebusch is pointing to an increasing scope for civil society in Syria. These developments may have significant consequences for the stability of Syria when the inevitable moment of succession arrives. As Hinnebusch notes, it is unlikely that the reemergent civil society will give rise to pressures for democracy. The Syrian regime has grounded its legitimacy in the peasantry and the working class, and the promotion of democracy would, Hinnebusch surmises, enliven anti-capitalist populist forces. Although analysts prone to essentialist arguments posit a post-Hafiz al-Asad struggle along sectarian lines, Hinnebusch's argument points to a different logic of competition. The strata of the society that has benefited from Syria's state dominated economy will be at odds with the revived merchant class.

. . .

One deft appreciation of civil society has stressed the historical specificity of the concept, while expressing doubt that the idea of civil society can travel much beyond western Europe and the United States, but this conclusion smacks of a familiar problem: a confusion of the ideal-typical . . . with the real world. Certainly, the reality of civil society in the West, often contrasts sharply with ideal-typical civil society. Recent examples from eastern and central Europe, as well as from some quarters of the developing world, counsel that a categorical rejection of the idea of civil society in the Middle East is unwarranted, not least because the idea of civil society is fast becoming part of the indigenous intellectual and policy dialogues.

The existence of a civil society implies a shared sense of identity, by means of, at least, tacit agreement over the rough boundaries of the political unit. In a word, citizenship, with associated rights and responsibilities, is part and parcel of the concept. Citizenship underpins civil society. To be a part of the whole is a precondition for the whole to be the sum of its parts. Otherwise, society has no coherence, it is just a vessel filled with shards and fragments. Thus, the individual in civil society is granted rights by the state, but, in return, acquires duties to the state. All governments, but particularly autocracies, tend to trivialize citizenship, emphasizing displays of citizen support and patriotic ceremonies, while paying only lip service to the rights of citizenship. Where the state, through its depredations and failures has lost the loyalty of its citizens, citizenship is an early casualty. As legitimacy crumbles civil society threatens to fragment as well. It is meaningless to speak of civil society in the absence of the state.

Civil society is more than an admixture of various forms of association, it also refers to a quality, civility, without which the milieu consists of feuding factions, cliques, and cabals. Civility implies tolerance, the willingness of individuals to accept disparate political views and social attitudes; to accept the profoundly important idea that there is no right answer. I would like to emphasize that it is as relevant to look for civility within associations as it is to observe it between them. Ironically, groups which espouse democracy and other commendable values often do not exemplify these values internally.

Thus, a robust civil society is more than letterhead stationery, membership lists, public charters and manifestoes. Civil society is also a cast of mind, a willingness to live and let live. The antithesis of civility was grimly revealed by a gunman arrested in the June 1992 killing of Farag Fouda, the Egyptian secularist and critic of Muslim fundamentalism: 'We had to kill him, because he attacked our beliefs.'

Unfortunately, civility is a quality which is missing in large parts of the Middle East. As Mustapha Kamil al-Sayyid observes in his cogent article, even in Egypt, widely revered for an active associational life, civil society is undermined by a deficit in political toleration and constricted by arbitrary government regulation. The absence of civility counsels skepticism about the short-term prospects for democracy in the region; however, if the art of association, as de Tocqueville called it, can be learned, then the promotion of civil society is no less than the creation of the underpinnings of democracy.

When groups and movements do emerge they often come in the form of human rights and women's movements. Both assert fundamental moral claims, namely the dignity of the person and the equality of the individual. Since the claims of such groups are truly basic ones, they are not easily assailed, at least explicitly, by the authorities of the state. Accordingly, they may enjoy more freedom of action than political opposition forces, or those groups which wish to affect the allocation of economic resources. These groups may also be less susceptible to co-optation, since their demands may not easily be assuaged by privilege, position or cash.

Though elements of civil society are likely to stand in opposition to the government, government must play the essential role of referee, rule-maker and regulator of civil society. Civil society, it needs to be emphasized, is no substitute for government. All too often, there is a tendency to commend civil society as a panacea, but the evidence is compelling that the state has a key role to play.

> Democratization is neither the outright enemy nor the unconditional friend of state power. It requires the state to govern civil society neither too much nor too little, while a more democratic order cannot be built through state power, it cannot be built *without* state power.

...

Government remains crucial to the project of political reform in the Middle East, and political reform is vital to insure stability; not stability in any static sense, since it is obvious that the problems that plague governments – inefficacy, faltering legitimacy, and corruption – cannot be wished away. Instead, projects of reform must instill a dynamic stability and that means civil society must have room to breathe.

Given the integral central connection between civil society and democracy, the long-term prospects for successful democratization in Lebanon, Egypt and Iran may be better than is commonly assumed. Moreover, while the Palestinians lack a state, there are, as Muhammad Muslih notes, the stirrings of a vibrant civil society. Whatever political entity finally emerges on the West Bank and in Gaza, there is a sound basis for attributing to the Palestinians a high potential for developing a participant political system. Elsewhere the prospects are more problematic, if not bleaker. In Iraq, civil society has been systematically decimated. Although in the Kurdish region associational life, if not civil society, has been rejuvenated, it is hard to imagine a durable participant system taking root in the entire country any time soon.

* From Augustus Richard Norton, 'Introduction', in his ed., *Civil Society in the Middle East*, Vol. 1 (Leiden: E.J. Brill, 1995), 7–14, reprinted with permission.
[1] The absence of a civil society to counter-balance despotic power was taken to be a marker of Oriental society by Karl Wittfogel in *Oriental Despotism* (New Haven, CT: Yale University Press, 1957), and it is this lacuna that lies at the heart of the Orientalist analysis.

John L. and Jean Comaroff are, respectively, professors of anthropology, and of law and social sciences at the University of Chicago, and experts on African culture

and politics. Here they discuss the specific colonial and post-colonial workings of
*civil society in Africa.**

Received wisdom has it that the concern with civil society in Africa, which became audible in the mid-1980s, followed upon the revival of the Idea in Europe – albeit in response to different local conditions. This might be true of scholarly discourses; also of public spheres that opened up with, or were the transformed by, the end of the cold war. Many of the issues at stake, however, have long been part of the legacy of colonialism here. ... Nineteenth-century 'humanitarian' imperialists ... often framed their mission to Africans in a language of civility that implied universal human rights, norms of citizenship, and legal protections. Some of them, like the radical Reverend John Philip, superintendent of the London Missionary Society in South Africa, spoke openly in favor of 'civil liberties' for colonized peoples; so, too, did the Reverend John Mackenzie, who saw in 'native' customs and modes of governance all the elements of a 'rude' civil society. These 'liberties' were, for the most part, preached rather than practiced, promised but not delivered. As a result, nationalist resistance to overrule was, from the first, formulated in the argot of rights denied and wrongs perpetrated. And it produced a plethora of political organizations, social movements, and voluntary associations.

...

Insofar as civil society in Africa is widely taken to depend on 'the triumph of bourgeois-liberal capitalism,' its future is *not* generally perceived to be a mere matter of materialities, of economic interests alone. For Young, something more elevated is at issue: 'the embrace of the world historical spirit' that invests civic projects with 'immanent purpose.' For the less high-minded, the key to civility resides in mundanities; in things like 'waiting in line for one's turn.' Either way, these formulations are grounded, implicitly or explicitly, in a singular understanding of '*the* world historical spirit.' There is no room here for more than one such spirit, one telos. As Hardt says, Euro-American prescriptions for the establishment of civil order elsewhere – whether their provenance be the academy or the state department – turn on an imagined re-creation of the stages of Western civilization, focusing on one in particular: the consolidation of eighteenth and nineteenth-century capitalist society, with its characteristic social and cultural arrangements, its rights-bearing subjects, its refined manners.

Thus it is that Western-oriented intellectuals, lawyers, entrepreneurs, academics, teachers, and sometimes Christian (never Muslim) leaders are typically seen from outside as the vanguards of civil society in formation. It is they who are thought most likely to commit themselves to the development of an active public sphere, along with its requisite media and voluntary organizations; to create the sites and associations through which bourgeoisies might pursue their interests untrammeled by parochial loyalties, identity politics, or intrusive governments; to equate those interests with the good of society at large, even of 'humankind.' It is they, moreover, who are portrayed as having the potential to complete a process that began in the nationalist movements prior to independence; movements that shared similar liberal aspirations, but whose urbane, European-educated cadres were crushed by absolutist post-colonial regimes as they suppressed political debate, put paid to unfettered enterprise, and all but dissolved the difference between the private and public sectors. As those regimes have run up against history, as they have been assailed by the forces of neoliberal reform and democratization, this new generation of elites has found itself with a nascent opportunity to build civil order afresh, to push for open electoral politics and a free market, to realize the aborted promise of decolonization. And to usher in the African Renaissance of which we spoke earlier. Or so the story goes.

Conceptualized thus, it is hard to see how the narrative of civil society in Africa could be anything more than a replay of Euro-capitalist modernity, of its social and moral forms, its conventional ways and mean(ing)s, its economies of desire, selfhood, and subjectivity. Admittedly, some scholars have pushed the limits of this narrative by acknowledging the need to appreciate local 'rules of the game': the need to observe, as Bayart does, that liberal democratic forms have been variously domesticated across the continent, laying a basis for the 'plural invention of modernity.' But few go on to identify what African hybrids, *Africanized* modes of civil society, might actually look like. Or how they might resonate with ideals of sociality and political accountability that differ from those found in the West. Note the plural here too. The West, after all, was never One.

. . .

[T]he notion of 'one-dimensional' societies is as chimerical outside Africa as within. At least, in the late twentieth century. Popular coalitions, as Bayart acknowledges, are triumphs over impossibility, complex bridges across diverse orders of difference. As such, they are liable to begin as working compromises, but, if they succeed, the chances, anywhere, are that they will proclaim themselves as new orthodoxies. In the world of practical politics, moreover, all reforms, wherever they take root, carry within them new inequalities, at times less and at times more marked than ones they replaced; that, too, is not an African monopoly. Like other continents, Africa has produced its fair share of reformist movements; as elsewhere, they have not always had the capacity to prevail over dominant state structures; as elsewhere, their means and ends have not always matched the narrow criteria of 'civility' laid down in Western ideal-types, in linear narratives of progress, in the conventional categories of Eurocentric political culture.

Perhaps it is this last clause that underlies the continuing uneasiness of normal social science with 'uncool' forms of African association; forms dubbed partisan, parochial, fundamentalist. Perhaps this is what sustains the tendency to undervalue the role of kin-based and ethnic organizations in forming publics and political pressure groups. ... Perhaps this also explains the reluctance to recognize the capacity of 'tradition' to foster new modes of governance. ... Neglected, by the same token, is the salience of religious groups in forging new normative orders of universal scope. ... All these things converge in a single conclusion: that, in Europe and North America, there is thoroughgoing prejudice against the 'universalizing ambitions' of cultures deemed marginal to the 'modern script.' As a consequence, observes Chatterjee, 'the provincialism of the European experience' becomes the 'universal history of progress.'

...

Few have considered the sorts of public sphere presumed by specifically *African* relations of production and exchange, codes of conduct, or styles of social intercourse; by *African* markets, credit associations, informal economies, collective ritual, modes of aesthetic expression, discourses of magic and reason.

Throughout Africa it gave birth, under the midwifery of the imperial state, to a world of difference, discrimination, and doubling: a world in which national, rights- bearing citizenship and primordial, ethnicized subjection – modernist inventions both – were made to exist side by side; a world composed of 'civilized' colonists governed by European constitutionalism and 'native tribes' ruled by so-called customary law. The divisions on which this world was erected – divisions typically represented in stark, manichean binarisms of black and white – might have been transgressed, compromised, hybridized. But, both in the honor and in the breach, they conduced, for colonized peoples, to a deeply conflicted experience of (the promise of) civil society, European-style. And their consequences have endured across the continent in the age of the postcolony, pitting the 'cold' language of individual legal rights and protections against the 'hot' rhetoric of ethnic entitlements.

This African story underscores a more general point: that, even when we set aside its incoherence, the Western conception of civil society, as a *practical* ideology, is riddled with contradictions. Not least in the West. Where it purports to be inclusive and all-embracing, it is founded on exclusion and divisiveness; where it promises equality, it engenders inequity. For the apparently open categories of liberal theory at its core – the nation-state, the individual, civil rights, contract, 'the' law, private property, democracy – all presume the separation of citizens from subjects, nationals from immigrants, the propertied from the unpropertied, the franchised from the disenfranchised, the law-abiding from the criminal, the responsible from the irresponsible, the civic from the domestic; distinctions that belie the ambiguities of everyday life and rule out as many from effective participation in the public sphere as are embraced by it. Indeed, some critics have argued that civil being is largely the prerogative of metropolitan white adult males. Even more fundamental, perhaps, is another contradiction: that the autonomy of civil society from the state, the very autonomy on which the Idea is predicated, is entirely chimerical. It, too, rests on a series of idealized separations, starting with that of political authority from private property. But this separation is, de facto, unsustainable; 'made opaque,' says Samir Amin, 'by the generalization of economic relationships,' which cut across all the coordinates of the social landscape. As the triumph of global capitalism renders various dialects of liberalism the undisputed vernacular of both the world of politics and the world of business, we are reminded of Foucault's insistence that power dissolves the boundaries between public and private, state and society. And makes any notion of a discrete civil society, normatively and narrowly conceived, a cheerful illusion.

. . .

If the impact on African realities of the Idea of civil society is to be fully grasped – recuperated, that is, from a mere play on ideological tropes – its terms must be read against the specificities of local histories; above all, once more, against the uncivil histories of colonial subjection.

. . .

[I]f African civic experiments – like those building on ties through kin or king, for instance – tend to be judged as personalistic and premodern, Islamic ideals of community and citizenship evoke yet stronger reactions. They are often seen as sinister inversions of modernity: as irrational, imperialist, fundamentalist.

. . .

Civility has many habitations, increasingly being indexed, here as elsewhere, through the language of consumption. In all this it might be argued that movements like Izala, by promoting open debate over reigning social and moral orthodoxies, conduce directly to the emergence of civil society in the world of which they are a part. But, like the movements that seek to define it, this form of civil society is frequently a field of argument, 'neither homogenous nor wholly emancipatory.' At once democratic and despotic.

*From John L. and Jean Comaroff, 'Introduction', in their eds, *Civil Society and the Political Imagination in Africa: Critical Perspectives* (Chicago: The University of Chicago Press, ©1999), 16; 19–24; 27–9, reprinted with permission.

*Partha Chatterjee is Professor of Political Science at the Centre for Studies in Social Sciences, Calcutta, India, and Professor of Anthropology at Columbia University, USA. A founding father of the subaltern studies group, he debates civil society here as a universalisation of imperial yet parochial Western European capitalist modernity, and contrasts it with a narrative of community.**

Looking at the relatively untheorized idea of 'the nation' in Western social philosophy, one notices an inelegant braiding of an idea of community with the concept of capital. This is not an archaic idea buried in the recesses of history, nor is it part of a marginal subculture, nor can it be dismissed as a premodern remnant that an absentminded Enlightenment has somehow forgotten to erase. It is very much a part of the here-and-now of modernity, and yet it is an idea that remains impoverished and limited to the singular form of the nation-state because it is denied a legitimate life in the world of the modern knowledges of human society. This denial, in turn, is related to the fact that by its very nature, the idea of the community marks a limit to the realm of disciplinary power. My hypothesis, then, is that an investigation into the idea of the nation, by uncovering a necessary contradiction between capital and community, is likely to lead us to a fundamental critique of modernity from within itself.

But beyond the intellectual history of Europe, our inquiry into the colonial and postcolonial histories of other parts of the world is more likely to enable us to make this critique. The contradictions between the two narratives of capital and community can be seen quite clearly in the histories of anticolonial nationalist movements. The forms of the modern state were imported into these countries through the agency of colonial rule. The institutions of civil society, in the forms in which they had arisen in Europe, also made their appearance in the colonies precisely to create a public domain for the legitimation of colonial rule. This process was, however, fundamentally limited by the fact that the colonial state could confer only subjecthood on the colonized; it could not grant them citizenship. The crucial break in the history of anticolonial nationalism comes when the colonized refuse to accept membership of this civil society of subjects. They construct their national identities within a different narrative, that of the community. They do not have the option of doing this within the domain of bourgeois civil-social institutions. They create, consequently, a very different domain – a cultural domain – marked by the distinctions of the material and the spiritual, the outer and the inner. This inner domain of culture is declared the sovereign territory of the nation, where the colonial state is not allowed entry, even as the outer domain remains surrendered to the colonial power. The rhetoric here (Gandhi is a particularly good example) is of love, kinship, austerity, sacrifice. The rhetoric is in fact antimodernist, antiindividualist, even anticapitalist. The attempt is, if I may stay with Gandhi for a while, to find, against the grand narrative of history itself, the cultural resources to negotiate the terms through which people, living in different, contextually defined, communities, can coexist peacefully, productively, and creatively within large political units.

The irony is, of course, that this other narrative is again violently interrupted once the postcolonial national state attempts to resume its journey along the trajectory of world-historical development. The modern state, embedded as it is within the universal narrative of capital, cannot recognize within its jurisdiction any form of community except the single, determinate, demographically enumerable form of the nation. It must therefore subjugate, if necessary by the use of state violence, all such aspirations of community identity. These other aspirations, in turn, can give to themselves a historically valid justification only by claiming an alternative nationhood with rights to an alternative state.

One can see how a conception of the state-society relation, born within the parochial history of Western Europe but made universal by the global sway of capital, dogs the contemporary history of the world. I do not think that the invocation of the state/civil society opposition in the struggle against socialist-bureaucratic regimes in Eastern Europe or in the former Soviet republics or, for that matter, in China, will produce anything other than strategies seeking to replicate the history of Western Europe. The result has been demonstrated a hundred times. The provincialism of the European experience will be taken as the universal history of progress; by comparison, the history of the rest of the world will appear as the history of lack, of inadequacy – an inferior history. Appeals will be made all over again to philosophies produced in Britain, France, and Germany. The fact that these doctrines were produced in complete ignorance of the histories of other parts of the world will not matter: they will be found useful and enlightening. It would indeed be a supreme irony of history if socialist industrialization gets written into the narrative of capital as the phase when socialist-bureaucratic regimes had to step in to undertake 'primitive accumulation' and clear the way for the journey of capital to be resumed along its 'normal' course.

In the meantime, the struggle between community and capital, irreconcilable within this grand narrative, will continue. The forms of the modern state will be forced into the grid of determinate national identities. This will mean a substantialization of cultural differences, necessarily excluding as 'minorities' those who would not conform to the chosen marks of nationality. The struggle between 'good' and 'bad' nationalism will be played out all over again.

What, then, are the true categories of universal history? State and civil society? public and private? social regulation and individual rights? – all made significant within the grand narrative of capital as the history of freedom, modernity and progress? Or the narrative of community – untheorized, relegated to the primordial zone of the natural, denied any subjectivity that is not domesticated to the requirements of the modern state, and yet persistent in its invocation of the rhetoric of love and kinship against the homogenizing sway of the normalized individual?

* From Partha Chatterjee, *The Nation and Its Fragments: Colonial and Postcolonial Histories* (Princeton, NJ: Princeton University Press, 1993), 237–9, reprinted by permission of Princeton University Press.

Global Civil Society

*John Keane was founding director of the Centre for the Study of Democracy at the University of Westminster (London), and has been Karl Deutsch Professor at the Wissenschaftszentrum Berlin. A leading force in the renaissance of civil society in the 1980s, he here discusses the role of transnational capital in global civil society.**

[G]lobal civil society refers to the contemporary thickening and stretching of networks of socio-economic institutions across borders to all four corners of the earth, such that the peaceful or 'civil' effects of these non-governmental networks are felt everywhere, here and there, far and wide, to and from local areas, through wider regions to the planetary level itself.

Global civil society is a vast, interconnected, and multi-layered social space that comprises many hundreds of thousands of self-directing or non-governmental institutions and ways of life. It can be likened – to draw for a moment upon ecological similes – to a dynamic biosphere. This complex biosphere looks and feels expansive and polyarchic, full of horizontal push and pull, vertical conflict, and compromise, precisely because it comprises a bewildering variety of interacting habitats and species: organisations, civic and business initiatives, coalitions, social movements, linguistic communities, and cultural identities. All of them have at least one thing in common: across vast geographic distances and despite barriers of time, they deliberately organise themselves and conduct their cross-border social activities, business, and politics outside the boundaries of governmental structures, with a minimum of violence and a maximum of respect for the principle of civilised power-sharing among different ways of life.

. . .

The terms 'world civil society' and 'international society' still have their champions, but from the standpoint of the new concept of global civil society their 'governmentality' or state-centredness are today deeply problematic. Neither the classical term *societas civilis* nor the state-centric concept of 'international society' is capable of grasping the latter-day emergence of a non-governmental sphere that is called 'global civil society'. These words, 'global civil society', may well sound old-fashioned, but today they have an entirely new meaning and political significance. This is why the quest to map and measure the contours of global civil society is essential for clarifying both its possible conceptual meanings, its empirical scope and complexity, and its political potential.

The principle is clear – theories without observations are bland, observations without theories are blind – but the task is difficult. Some sketchy data are available thanks to the path-breaking contributions of bodies like the Union of International Associations, the Index on Civil Society project supported by CIVICUS (World Alliance for Citizen Participation), the Ford Foundation-funded comparative study of civil society in 22 countries, and this Global Civil Society Yearbook. These efforts confirm the widespread impression that, during the past century, the world has witnessed a tectonic – two hundred-fold-increase in the number and variety of civil society organisations operating at the planetary level. Today, in addition to many hundreds of thousands of small, medium, and large firms doing business across borders, there are some 40,000 non-governmental, not-for-profit organisations operating at the global level; these international non-governmental organisations (INGOs) currently disburse more money than the United Nations (excluding the World Bank and the International Monetary Fund); while more than two-thirds of the European Union's relief aid is currently channelled through them.

. . .

Dynamism is a chronic feature of global civil society: not the dynamism of the restless sea – a naturalistic simile suggested by Victor Perez-Diaz – but a form of self-reflexive dynamism marked by innovation, conflict, compromise, consensus, as well as rising awareness of the contingencies and dilemmas of global civil society itself.

. . .

[T]hose who speak of global civil society should not lose sight of its elusive, *idealtypisch* quality. The concept of global civil society has what Wittgenstein called 'blurred edges'. It is an ill-fitting term clumsily in search of an intelligent object that is always subject on the run, striding unevenly in many different directions.

Sustained and deeper reflection on the subject, and a willingness to puncture old thinking habits, are definitely warranted. An example is the need to question the current tendency to speak of civil societies as 'national' phe-nomena and thus, to suppose that global civil society and domestic civil societies are binary opposites. In fact, so-called domestic civil societies and the emerging global civil society are normally linked together in complex, cross-border patterns of looped and relooped circuitry.

. . .

What drives this globalisation of civil society? Its activist champions and their intellectual supporters sometimes pinpoint the power of autonomous moral choice. Treading in Gramsci's footsteps, usually without knowing it, they define global civil society as the space of social interaction 'located *between* the family, the state and the market and operating *beyond* the confines of national societies, polities, and economies'. That leads them to speak, rather romantically, of global civil society as a realm of actual or potential freedom, as a 'third sector' opposed to the impersonal power of government and the greedy profiteering of the market (households typically disappear from the analysis at this point). 'Civil society participates along-side – not replaces – state and market institutions', write Naidoo and Tandon. Global civil society 'is the network of autonomous associations that rights-bearing and responsibility-laden citizens voluntarily create to address common problems, advance shared interests and promote collective aspirations'. Such purist images reduce actually existing global civil society to campaign strategies harnessed to the normative ideal of citizens' autonomy at the global level. That in turn creates the unfortunate impression that global civil society is a (potentially) unified subject, a 'third force', something like a world proletariat in civvies, the universal object-subject that can snap its chains and translate the idea of a 'World Alliance for Citizen Participation' into reality, therewith righting the world's wrongs.

Although many things can be said for and against these conceptions, it is worth noting here that their Gramscian bias, which draws a thick line between (bad) business backed by government and (good) voluntary associ-ations, leads them to understate the over-determined character of global civil society. ... [O]ne-sided emphasis on the free civic choices of men and women has the effect of obscuring other planetary forces that currently constrain and enable their actions.

Turbo-capitalism is undoubtedly among the principal energisers of global civil society. To understand why this is so, and what the term 'turbo-capitalism' means, a brief comparison needs to be made with the system of Keynesian welfare state capitalism that predominated in the West after World War II. For some three decades, market capitalist economies like the United States, Sweden, Japan, the Federal Republic of Germany, and Britain moved in the direction of government-controlled capitalism. In terms of the production of goods and services, firms, plants, and whole industries were very much national phenomena; facilitated by international trade of raw materials and foodstuffs, production was primarily organised within territorially-bound national economies or parts of them. Markets were embedded in webs of government. In the era of turbo-capitalism, by contrast, markets tend to become disembedded. Turbo-capitalism is a species of private enterprise driven by the desire for emancipation from taxation restrictions, trade union intransigence, government interference, and all other external restrictions upon the free movement of capital in search of profit. Turbo-capitalism has strongly deregulatory effects, and on a global scale. The transnational operations of some 300 pace-setting firms in industries such as banking, accountancy, automobiles, airlines, communications, and armaments – their combined assets make up roughly a quarter of the world's productive assets – no longer function as production and delivery operations for national headquarters. Bursting the bounds of time and space, language and custom, they instead function as complex global flows or integrated networks of staff, money, information, raw materials, components, and products.

. . .

If the institutions of global civil society are not merely the products of civic initiative and market forces, then is there a third force at work in nurturing and shaping it? It can be argued that global civil society is also the by-product of state or inter-state action, or inaction. Examples are easy to find. Most obvious is the set of political institutions and agreements that play a vital role in fostering the growth of turbo-capitalism, for instance the 'Final Act' of the Uruguay Round of trade negotiations, a 1994 agreement that had the backing of 145 states and that led to the establishment of the World Trade Organisation and to the extension of the principle of freer trade into such areas as copyrights, patents, and services. Meanwhile, in fields like telecommunications and air, land and sea traffic, political bodies such as the International Postal Union, most of them resting formally on agreements to which states are signatories, exercise formidable regulatory powers that enable many parts of global civil society to keep moving at a quickening pace.

Government agencies, much more than corporate philanthropy, also currently play a major, positive-sum role in protecting, funding, and nurturing non-profit organisations in every part of the earth where there is a lively civil society. Included in this category are civil organisations that operate on the margins of the governmental institutions that license them in the first place. Examples include the International Committee of the Red Cross which, although non-governmental, is mandated under the Geneva Convention and is linked to states through the organisation of the International Federation of Red Cross and Red Crescent Societies.

. . .

These well-known examples illustrate the less familiar rule that global civil society should not be thought of as the natural enemy of political institutions. The vast mosaic of groups, organisations, and initiatives that comprise global civil society are variously related to governmental structures at the local, national, regional, and supranational levels. Some sectors of social activity, the so-called anti-government organisations (AGOs), are openly hostile to the funding and regulatory powers of state institutions. Other sectors, for instance those in which the acronym NGO rather means 'next government official', are openly collaborative, either serving as willing contractors for governments or aiming at dissolving themselves into governmental structures.

...

Global civil society is certainly rich in freedoms beyond borders, for example, to invest and to accumulate money and wealth; to travel and to reunite with others; to build infrastructures by recovering memories, protecting the vulnerable, and generating new wealth and income; to denounce and to reduce violence and uncivil war; and, generally, to press the principle that social and political power beyond borders should be subject to greater public accountability. Such freedoms are currently unfolding in a hell-for-leather, Wild West fashion, and are also very unevenly distributed. The freedoms of global civil society are exclusionary and fail to produce equalities; in other words, global civil society is not really global. It is not a *universal* society.

...

Understood normatively as a transnational system of social networks of non-violent polyarchy, global civil society is a wish that has not yet been granted to the world.

...

[C]omplexity alone does not release global civil society from the laws of hubris. It is not only that the plural freedoms of global civil society are severely threatened by a political underworld of secretive, unelected, publicly unaccountable institutions, symbolised by bodies like the IMF and the WTO. The problem of hubris is internal to global civil society as well: just like the domestic civil societies that form its habitats, global civil society produces concentrations of arrogant power that threaten its own openness and pluralism.

...

Global public spheres make it clearer that 'global civil society', like its more local counterparts, has no 'collective voice', that it alone does nothing, that only its constituent individuals, group initiatives, organisations, and networks act and interact. Global publics consequently heighten the sense that global civil society is an unfinished, permanently threatened project. They shake up its dogmas and inject it with energy. They enable citizens of the world to shake off bad habits of parochialism, to see that talk of global civil society is not simply Western bourgeois ideology, even to appreciate that the task of painting a much clearer picture of the rules of conduct and dowries of global civil society, a picture that is absent from most of the current literature on globalisation, is today an urgent ethical imperative.

...

Exactly because of their propensity to monitor the exercise of power from a variety of sites within and outside civil society, global public spheres – when they function properly – can help to ensure that nobody monopolises power at the local and world levels. By exposing corrupt or risky dealings and naming them as such; by wrong-footing decisions-makers and forcing their hands; by requiring them to rethink or reverse their decisions, global public spheres help remedy the problem – strongly evident in the volatile field of global financial markets, which turn over US\$1.3 trillion a day, 100 times the volume of world trade – that nobody seems to be in charge. And in uneven contests between decision-makers and decision-takers – as the developing controversies within bodies like the International Olympic Committee show – global public spheres can help prevent the powerful from 'owning' power privately. Global publics imply greater parity. They suggest that there are alternatives. They inch our little blue and white planet towards greater openness and humility, potentially to the point where power, whenever and wherever it is exercised across borders, is made to feel more 'biodegradable', a bit more responsive to those whose lives it shapes and reshapes, secures or wrecks.

*From John Keane, 'Global Civil Society?', in H. Anheier, M. Glasius, and M. Kaldor (eds), *Global Civil Society Yearbook 2001* (Oxford: Oxford University Press, 2001), 23–4; 26–9; 35–6; 38–9; 41; 43–4. Reprinted with permission.

Dianne Otto teaches in the areas of human rights, international law and criminal law at the University of Melbourne. In this extract she suggests, after noting the rise in international non-governmental associational life, that democratic life might change – in a postliberal manner which would allow international non-governmental actors to have direct influence on policy processes.

1.   The Emergence of International Civil Society

The UN Charter is a statement of 'we, the peoples of the United Nations.' Yet the system it set in place is a system of states rather than of peoples. A growing number of commentators are drawing attention to the many undemocratic features of the UN that circumvent the capacity of peoples, as individuals or nonstate groupings, to participate in international legal processes. This structure institutionalizes the longstanding antipathy of states towards the idea of NGOs and individuals assuming an autonomous role in international affairs.

Despite the Charter's vision of an ancillary role for nongovernmental entities, confined to ECOSOC [Economic and Social Council] responsibilities, there is no doubt that nongovernmental players have had a major effect on global affairs. International organizations and movements have been very influential in shaping the discourse within which international decision-making and action occurs. Concern for the environment, for women's equality, and for disarmament would not have achieved international expression without the backdrop of social and political understandings promoted by NGOs. This civil activity has supported a 'quiet revolution' in the UN system. As mentioned earlier, it has enabled nongovernmental input to enrich the soft law processes of the General Assembly, to contribute informally to areas within the responsibility of the Security Council, and to influence international legislative processes, particularly in the area of human rights. Gus Speth goes so far as to claim that '[a]ll really basic and fundamental changes have been people-led, bottom-up movements' and sees the UNCED [UN Conference on Environment and Development] process as the most recent confirmation of this view.

The tenacious activity of NGOs in the international sphere, despite rigid institutional barriers, reflects the power that people have as citizens. This power expresses an identification or viewpoint, autonomous from governments and markets, which can operate as a 'third system' either within institutional arrangements or as an alternative to them. Marc Nerfin describes this third system as functioning benignly, helping the people to assert their own power and making efforts to listen to those who are never or rarely heard, rather than seeking governmental or economic power. But this is a little short-sighted. It is inevitable that the power of the nongovernmental sector will at least mitigate the exercise of economic and formal political power, and it may eventually provide an alternative that entirely transforms the current arrangements. This is, of course, what many states fear.

There is no single narrative that describes the significance of this third voice in international relations. Broadly, it is based on identification as transnational citizens. In the postliberal view, this identity is multilayered, multinational, and highly participatory. It manifests the force of a common interest that is something more than the aggregate of separate national, interests and vastly more fluid and empowering than the homogenizing hegemonic liberal idea of the universal citizen.

The strength of the emergent transnational social movements indicates that it may be possible to build a socially just global society on diverse and multinational identities. The new social movements are seen by many as heralding an extensive reorganization of international life that simultaneously affirms both local and transnational emancipatory identities. Yet others point out that transnational social movements are limited by their failure to become a coordinated force and are continually fending off cooption by the established structures of power.

There is no doubt that increasing activity in international civil society has catapulted the issue of democracy in the global polity squarely onto the international agenda. The question is whether the UN, with its state-centric world view, can rise to the challenge of reorienting its focus to be inclusive of peoples as well as states. Further, if the UN achieves this first step, the next question is whether this will lead towards a withering away of the system of states. The answer is not clear, but fear of it should not thwart open discussion and debate. States may be an important defense against the emergence of a monotonic, vertical, and hierarchical international government or, alternatively, they may act to impede the development of a more horizontal participatory democratic structure.

As a global community, we need to explore what international democracy might mean. Elements of the third system of international civil society are becoming increasingly insistent that the quiet revolution of their emergence as international actors is as yet unfinished. In the following sections, I outline how liberal and postliberal perspectives imagine transnational cosmopolitan democracy before going on to link this discussion to the ECOSOC review.

2. Liberal Alternatives

Classical liberalism, supplemented by realism, characterizes the current Westphalian model of international relations. The liberal ideas of consent, liberty, and equality are applied to states and operate alongside the realist imperative that ultimately there will be acquiescence to *de facto* power differences between states. The UN Charter reflects all of these components: the consent of states determines the content of international law; the liberty of states is protected by the principle of nonintervention in domestic jurisdictions; sovereign equality is recognized by membership of the UN and GA [General Assembly]; and the balance of world power is acknowledged by the membership, powers and voting rules of the UN's most powerful body, the Security Council.

The UN Charter's failure to outline a significant international role for the NGO community is a consequence of its liberal-realist pact. This scheme constructs the primary identification of individuals as associated with their membership in a national polity. It operates to minimize the opportunity for identification across territorial boundaries which, in turn, creates the optimum civil environment for the pursuit of power politics in relations between states. In this view, human rights violations are matters for the state concerned except where states have agreed to international supervision by way of a treaty or convention or where norms of *jus cogens* are violated.

. . .

3. Postliberal Alternatives

Many transnational social movements define their goals as transformative of the present international order. These visions are based on critiques that question the ability of liberalism to actualize its rhetoric of equality, neutrality, openness, freedom, and rights. They are also concerned with the rigidity of liberal rationality and the privileging of certain perspectives over others by the dualisms implicit in liberal thought.

A significant contribution of postliberal paradigms is their insistence that human identities are multidimensional and fluid. While the importance of national and autonomous individual identities is emphasized in liberal thought, the new social movements stress that identity is considerably more complex. The importance of relational allegiances and commonalities are obvious additional factors. This has been argued for many years by Third World theorists and is implicit in the idea of transnational human solidarity associated with the new social movements. Contributing to these new perspectives are feminists, who highlight the importance of the ethic of care that comes with the recognition of relational connections, and environmentalists, who expand the relational polity to include the rights of future generations.

The multiplicitous foci of the new social movements are in themselves indicative of the enormous potential for human identification – indigeneity, race, culture, spirituality, class, gender, sexuality, and ideology, to name a few. This suggests that identity can be simultaneously local and transnational. While identity is clearly situational, located in a person's specific history and social context, a postliberal view proposes that this can enrich, rather than thwart, a transnational identification that makes experience of the local an important aspect of the global paradigm.

Allied to the idea of multilayered identity is the postliberal emphasis on participatory democracy, in contradistinction to the reliance of republican liberalism on electoral formality and the highly artificial notion of consent through the ballot box. The new social movements are keen to 'scramble' the distinction between national and international polities that characterizes liberal thought. Clearly, national governmental decision-making can have effects that extend beyond territorial boundaries, and it is apt to ask who constitutes the relevant community to whom they should be accountable.

A postliberal conception of cosmopolitan democracy draws on an emancipatory democratic tradition that Chantal Mouffe describes as 'composite, heterogeneous, open, and ultimately indeterminate.' In David Held's view, this would go well beyond the steps of, first, living up to the UN Charter and, second, extending it to include, for example, compulsory jurisdiction to resolve international disputes, including human rights violations, and enabling the GA to generate international law. Held's central concern is that mechanisms be established which can hold states and other international actors directly accountable to the peoples of civil society. In his view, this would include the formation of regional and international democratic assemblies and crossnational referenda, complemented by the deepening and strengthening of local participatory democratic processes. The core emphasis is on open debate and promoting egalitarian values that embrace participation and diversity.

The postliberal perspective, which decenters states and stresses the importance of local participation in the international community, is allied with a postmodern understanding of power. Power is conceptualized as dispersed throughout the global polity rather than, as constructed by liberal theory, centralized in the state and the economy. In the postmodern understanding, the relations of domination and subordination at the micro, local levels of society make possible the global systems of inequalities in power. Consequently, changes in the distribution of power locally will impact upon the macro level of power relations.

The emergence of the new social movements can itself be understood as 'resistance,' which in the postmodern view is one of the products of power. Michele [sic] Foucault describes how the micromechanisms of power at the local level produce local criticisms which, if organized politically, develop into strategies to resist the mechanisms of power. Such an understanding of power leads to a distrust of entities which seek to concentrate power, like the state and perhaps the UN. Alternatively, political formations which promote decentralization, decisionmaking at the local level, and redistributive justice are supported.

In the postliberal view, international civil society consists of a diversity of individuals, institutions, and informal peoples' networks and coalitions. It is a vast, shifting web of interconnections and alliances involving multidimensional human identities. People, rather than governments, are seen as the progressive agents of social history.

The question of the role of NGOs in the international community raises a critical tension within postliberal thought which is perhaps one way of distinguishing between liberal and postliberal Grotians. On the one hand, liberal protagonists are keen to devise alternative institutional arrangements that will change the current system. Leslie Thiele's proposal for international and regional democratic assemblies is one example. On the other hand, postliberals share a basic distrust of institutional structures because of their tendency to homogenize, control, and conservatize participants. Richard Falk's suggestion that the new social movements might be best advised to carve out less compromising spaces at the margins of institutional systems is informed by this latter view. Another approach is Marc Nerfin's suggestion that networking, which operates horizontally and cooperatively, may be an alternative to hierarchical institutional structures.

For present purposes, liberal and postliberal Grotians would generally promote an expansive and emancipatory role for NGOs in the UN. Emphasis would be placed on mechanisms which are inclusive of a diversity of formal and informal NGO formations, which encourage the building of global perspectives from local participation, and which foster open debate and criticism. The assessment of an NGO's 'international standing' would be related to the transnational nature of its concerns and alliances rather than its geographical spread. A high priority would be given to the development of global civil information systems and networks by ensuring that information technology is widely accessible.

* From Dianne Otto, 'NonGovernmental Organizations in the United Nations System: The Emerging Role of International Civil Society', *Human Rights Quarterly*, 18 (1996), 127–30; 133–6, reprinted with permission of Johns Hopkins University Press. All rights reserved by Johns Hopkins University Press.

Miguel Darcy de Oliveira and Rajesh Tandon, are members of Civicus, a pressure groups that considers the extension of human rights as the foundation of contemporary civil society. In this selection they point to such events as The Cairo Population and Development Conference, the Beijing Women's Conference and the Vienna Human Rights Conference as indicators of the increasing power of international civil society.

The bitter experience that many NGOs and civil associations had of fighting authoritarian regimes led some to equate state authority with repression. Times have changed, however, and democratically elected governments have a legitimacy that cannot be overlooked. The collapse of governments can only lead either to chaos and anarchy, as in some African countries where central authority has practically ceased to exist, or to a radically laissez-faire economy, where the unchecked prevalence of market values would transform every social good into a commodity.

. . .

The pressure from civil society and the regulatory authority of the state are both indispensable to promote social justice and balance the power of private monopolies. But it is equally important to acknowledge that, in the same way that they often aggravate poverty and inequality, market mechanisms are also capable of injecting vitality and dynamism in society by taking risks and promoting innovation.

For this to happen, however, it is essential that global economic mechanisms do not overwhelm and stifle the dynamics of local and regional development. The global market accounts for one relevant dimension of economic activity. It cannot, however, subordinate to its logic the infinite diversity of people's strategies for generating wealth and well-being. There are as many markets in the world as the circuits linking producers and consumers. Some are rigidly structured; others are informal and barely visible. Here again, a dynamic balance and complementarity must be explored between the formal and informal sectors as well as between the local, national, regional and global levels of economic activity.

...

Global market mechanisms and structures of world governance can only be democratized through concerted global citizen action. This is the lesson that popular movements have learned in their long struggles to democratize government, the market, and society within each country. The challenge to planetary citizenship is, therefore, to expand to the global arena the struggle for democracy and human development that has so far been carried out basically at the national level.

...

Women have taken the lead in this process. For two decades now they have been pursuing, with energy and consistency, an action agenda of their own targeted at the elimination of gender-based discrimination. Similarly, the actions of Amnesty International in the defense of political prisoners and of Medecins Sans Frontieres in favor of civilian victims of armed conflicts have broken new ground in terms of affirming the right of the world citizen community to overcome claims of national state sovereignty when human lives and people's essential rights are at risk.

An innovative experience in terms of coalition-building comes from the Asia-Pacific region with PP2l, the People's Plan for the 21st Century. Cutting across different categories of sectors within civil society, PP2l has attempted over the past five years to gather citizens, women, indigenous peoples, workers, human rights groups, and social activists in an alliance to propose an alternative development paradigm.

On another level, the global networking and advocacy efforts of NGOs to influence the agenda and outcome of major U.N. global conferences have produced some landmark events. The most comprehensive and best planned of these processes was developed in preparation for and during Rio's Global Forum and Earth Summit in June 1992. It is fair to say that citizens at those events not only educated the public about the issues at stake but also and, for the first time, really asserted their right of sharing responsibility with states for the governance of the planet. Similar mobilization drives were carried out for the Vienna Human Rights Conference and the Cairo Population and Development Conference, and are being implemented in 1995 for the World Summit on Social Development in Copenhagen and the Beijing Women's Conference.

The process of building such global networks is also occurring in relation to the institutions of the market. Besides lobbying and calling for transparency and accountability from multilateral development banks, including the World Bank and the International Monetary Fund, strong associations of consumer groups are also acting at the global level. The International Organisation of Consumers' Unions, for example, has contributed significantly to ensuring greater public accountability of market enterprises.

. . .

Expressing this new global spirit in deeds is one of the foremost challenges to citizens and civil society institutions. Private action for the public good has been lost in the shrill of public for public good or private for private good. Citizens' actions for public good are conceptually and qualitatively different from private, profit-oriented initiatives. Likewise, the government is not the sole repository of all wisdom, concern, and capacity to act for the common good.

Citizen initiatives aimed at addressing public issues and problems are no longer to be considered residual actions. They are now in the center, not the periphery. The actors of civil society are not following the prescriptions of the state or of the market, but creating their own initiatives. In this sense, the nonprofit sector can be said to be not the third, but the primary sector of society.

. . .

Threatened by processes that seem beyond their understanding and capacity to influence, suffering from the alienation produced by global cultural homogenization, many react defensively by going back to ethnocentrism and parochialism. A renewal of the sense of concern and solidarity among citizens could be a powerful alternative to both social fragmentation and the aggressive affirmation of ethnic or religious identities.

This sense of common belonging, however, cannot be sustained by ignoring differences in cultures, religions, languages, or ethnicity. Cutting across traditional boundaries of caste, class, religion, and nation-state, the notion of global citizen action, rooted in a common set of values, implies the acknowledgment and acceptance of diversity as one of the most distinctive characteristics of humankind.

Articulating morality is another emerging challenge for global civil society. In the transition to postmodernism, the traditional value system has almost crumbled. A new ethical and moral code has not yet been universally established. In many parts of the world, the dominance of the state and governmental bureaucracy has promoted a culture of dependence, apathy, secrecy and corruption. The recent dominance of market enterprise has also resulted in individual self-centeredness, profit-over-people orientation, and widespread alienation.

The reassertion of the primacy of civil society calls for the articulation of a set of universal human values. The current crisis of morality is being countered by inspired and value-based citizens' actions worldwide. The source of inspiration for human response to the needs and suffering of individuals and groups is essentially spiritual throughout the world. Spontaneous and committed citizen initiatives are premised on love, compassion, concern for others. These values and inspirations provide meaning and substance to people.

In a world where material acquisitions and consumptions are becoming the dominant ethos, there is an urgent need to bring spirituality to the core of human endeavor. This will constitute the fountainhead of a universal moral code based on our common humanity. The values of diversity, of tolerance and pluralism, of peace and justice, of solidarity and responsibility to unknown others and to future generations need to be proposed and practiced as the anchor for universal humanity and global citizen action.

...

The many institutions that compose the third sector follow very diverse organizational patterns. Some are connected to well-established hierarchical structures; others are extremely zealous of their autonomy. Some cherish egalitarian legal structures; others follow charismatic leaders. Some deal with specific questions; others have a broad, cross-sectoral agenda. Some have grown through decades of institutional building; others have recently been formed in response to emergent needs. Some are large membership organizations; others are flexible action-oriented small groups.

Any attempt to amalgamate all this diversity under a single umbrella organization runs the risk of giving rise to hollow structures. Nor is there any point trying to bring together this immense variety of citizen groups and initiatives in order for all to pursue a common global course of action. Revolutionary parties, in the past, invested themselves with the task of organizing the whole people around a cohesive political project. History has delivered stinging blows to such arrogant grand designs.

* From Miguel Darcy de Oliveira and Rajesh Tandon, in their eds, *Citizens: Strengthening Global Civil Society* (Washington: Civicus: World Alliance for Citizen Participation, 1994), 6–12.

Further Reading

In addition to literature selected in this volume, readers may wish to turn to the following titles for additional discussion and further information on civil society.

Anheier, Helmut, Marlies Glasius and Mary Kaldor (eds). *Global Civil Society 2001* (Oxford, 2001) – and subsequent yearbooks.

Colas, Dominique. *Civil Society and Fanaticism: Conjoined Histories*, trans. by Amy Jacobs (Stanford, Calif., 1997).

Gellner, Ernest. *Conditions of Liberty: Civil Society and its Rivals* (London, 1994).

Glasius, Marlies, Mary Kaldor, David Lewis and Hakan Seckinelgin (eds). *Exploring Civil Society: Political and Cultural Contexts* (London, 2004).

Hall, John A. (ed.). *Civil Society: Theory, History, Comparison* (Cambridge, 1995).

Hoffman, Stefan-Ludwig. *Geselligkeit und Demokratie* (Göttingen, 2003).

Kaviraj, Sudipta and Sunil Kilnani (eds). *Civil Society: History and Possibilities* (Cambridge, 2001).

Keane, John (ed.). *Civil Society and the State: New European Perspectives* (London, 1988).

Keane, John. *Global Civil Society?* (Cambridge, 2003).

Morris, R.J. 'Clubs, societies and associations.' In F.M.L. Thompson, ed. *The Cambridge Social History of Britain, 1750–1950*, III, (Cambridge, 1990).

Putnam, Robert D. *Bowling Alone: The Collapse and Revival of American Community* (New York, 2000).

Riedel, Manfred. 'Gesellschaft, Bürgerliche.' In Otto Brunner, Werner Conze, and Reinhart Koselleck, eds *Geschichtliche Grundbegriffe* (Stuttgart, 1972).

Seligman, Adam B. *The Idea of Civil Society* (New York, 1992).

Taylor, Charles. 'Invoking Civil Society', in Charles Taylor, *Philosophical Arguments* (Cambridge, Mass., 1995).

Trentmann, Frank (ed.). *Paradoxes of Civil Society* (Oxford and New York, 2nd Edn, 2003).

Index